THE ARCHITECTURE OF
SCOTTISH GOVERNMENT

THE ARCHITECTURE OF SCOTTISH GOVERNMENT

FROM KINGSHIP TO PARLIAMENTARY DEMOCRACY

Miles Glendinning

with contributions from Aonghus MacKechnie, Richard Oram and an appendix by Athol Murray

DUNDEE UNIVERSITY PRESS

First published in Great Britain in 2004
Dundee University Press
Tower Building
University of Dundee
Dundee
DD1 4HN

www.dundee.ac.uk/dup

ISBN: 1-84586-000-4

The Publishers gratefully acknowledge the support of the
Scotland Inheritance Fund in the publication of this volume

Set in Garamond

Design and typeset by Mark Blackadder

Printed and bound by The Cromwell Press,
Trowbridge, Wiltshire UK

CONTENTS

ACKNOWLEDGEMENTS

This book was made possible through the contributions of a number of institutions and individuals. Within the Royal Commission on the Ancient and Historical Monuments of Scotland (RCAHMS), the Photographic, Graphic and Finance Departments played a key supporting role, and several Commissioners and senior management staff read and commented on text; Geoffrey Stell was largely responsible for the co-ordination of Chapter 1, and Simon Green and Diane Watters organised the surveys of the buildings on the Holyrood parliament site and other relevant locations. Within the Scottish Executive, we were helped by John Gibbons and Margaret Millar, and (in relation to Chapter 4) Maurice Wilson; within the Scottish Parliament Project Team, we were helped by Barbara Doig, Martin Mustard, Eric Kinsey and John Paterson. Architects and architectural firms who assisted us with information and illustrations on the parliament projects covered in Chapter 5 included Peter Ahrends; Benson & Forsyth; Glass Murray; Keppie Design; Page & Park; Reiach & Hall; RMJM; Ole Wiig; Michael Wilford & Partners. Stefan Muthesius kindly allowed us a preview of his article on nineteenth century parliaments (see Bibliography). Other individuals and institutions to whom we are indebted for assistance include the following: Anstruther Defence Establishment Preservation Trust (ADEPT); Rebecca Bailey; Gordon Barclay; Ian Campbell; Nicola Carr; Paul Cathcart; Helen Clark; Pat Dennison; A.A.M. Duncan; John & Marie Duncan; Alec Finlay; Janet Foggie; Julian Goodare; Iain Gray; Grant Horsley; Sandra Hunter; Helen Jones; Derek Kendall; John Lowrey; Alan Macdonald; James Mitchell; David Page; Charles Prosser; Ted Ruddock; Scottish Catholic Archive (Christine Johnston); Anne and Grant Simpson; James Simpson; Fiona Sinclair; Chris Smout; Margaret Stewart; Sandy Stoddart; Ben Tindall; Peter Wilson; Sue Wilson.

AUTHOR AND CONTRIBUTORS

MILES GLENDINNING
(editor and co-author)
Head of the RCAHMS Threatened Buildings and Topographical Surveys. He has co-authored and edited numerous books on architecture and the city, including *Tower Block* (1994), *A History of Scottish Architecture* (1996), *Rebuilding Scotland* (1997), *Clone City* and *Home Builders* (both 1999).

AONGHUS MACKECHNIE
(co-author)
Principal Inspector of Historic Buildings with Historic Scotland. He was editor and co-author of *David Hamilton, Architect* (1993), and co-author of *Minerva's Flame; The Great Houses of James Smith of Whitehill* (1995).

RICHARD D. ORAM
(co-author)
Senior Lecturer in Scottish Medieval History, Stirling University. Publications include *Scottish Prehistory* (1997) and *Scotland's Kings and Queens: Royalty and the Realm* (1997).

ATHOL L. MURRAY
(appendix)
Keeper of the Records of Scotland (Scottish Record Office), 1985–1990. Former Vice-President of the Society of Antiquaries of Scotland. He has written extensively on the Scottish exchequer: publications include the introduction to *Accounts of the Treasurer of Scotland* (1978).

ILLUSTRATIONS

CHAPTER 3

CHAPTER 4

INTRODUCTION

The Legacy of Antiquity

Miles Glendinning

The new Scottish parliament building, whose commissioning and construction initially stimulated the writing of this book, is a specialised complex dedicated to a national legislature of representative democracy, and expressed architecturally as a striking 'image'. As such, it forms part of an internationally accepted building tradition, established for at least two centuries; a tradition which seems to us today so self-explanatory that it can be taken for granted. There may be vigorous debate about the detailed architectural design, working procedures, or constructional troubles of Scotland's new parliament, but the general building type appears to us universal, even timeless.

From a longer historical perspective, however, the picture looks quite different. Present-day Western representative democracy, and its architectural settings, are the results of specific historical and social processes within Europe and North America, which have spanned many centuries. Dominant among those conditions has been an eagerness for constant, radical change – a 'modernity' which spread beyond the circumscribed horizons of feudal and religious society until it ultimately aspired to dominate the whole world, whether through imperialist capitalism or mass collectivism. In the course of those processes of change, personalised monarchical concepts of sovereignty were replaced by a wide variety of ideals of representative government of people in the mass. The concept of the national legislature housed in a purpose-built monumental building, which emerged in the nineteenth century, was one of the most prominent outcomes of these changes. In itself, the monumental parliament or council building was hardly a direct expression of 'democracy' as such: in many ways, with its integrated supporting offices and services, it was a community in its own right, dedicated to serving itself. Nor would it have been feasible without the complementary contribution of the bureaucratic apparatus of government, and the vast proliferation of other local or specialist institutions with a political and administrative role. The story of modern government is a story of tension between forces of emancipation and change, and forces of domination and stability; and architecture, with its enduring character and requirement for large financial investment, has always been torn between the two. Parliament and government buildings have faced a constant dilemma: should they reflect the ruling power as it is, or promote an ideal of how it could be?

Scotland, situated in a maritime archipelago on the Atlantic edge of Europe, stands at the geographical centre of the age of modernity. The country has often been an active participant in that great adventure, especially in the era of industrial revolution and British imperial power from the late eighteenth century to 1914. The nation's early parliamentary experiences, prior to the incorporating union with England in 1707, provided an important foundation for the later dramatic advances of modernisation – as did other elements of representative government and administration which continued and flourished, in the fields of religion, law and municipal life.

This book traces the way in which the variegated and changeable Scottish concepts of sovereignty, government and democracy from the Middle Ages onwards have been reflected in an equal variety of built forms, ranging from the great halls of medieval monarchy to the assembly halls of nineteenth-century Presbyterianism and the office complexes of twentieth-century state power. And, with an eye to Scotland's outward-looking, Western world-outlook, it looks sideways as well as backwards, setting those developments in their wider international context Scottish ideas of sovereignty, over these centuries, have had a double focus: on the one hand, 'geo-political' concerns with external affiliation, and on the other, internal concerns with social cohesion and organisation. The architecture of sovereignty in Scotland has been concerned not just with 'external relations' but also with a myriad of competing 'sovereignties' *within* the nation. The new national legislature building, and its predecessor of the seventeenth-century, are the two most prominent landmarks in our story: Aonghus MacKechnie's chapter on the seventeenth century Parliament House (Chapter 2) is by far the largest in the book. But it is a mark of the multi-faceted character of Scottish society in the medieval and modern eras that those landmark buildings, far from standing on their own, recede into a crowded townscape of governmental architecture. Arguably the most important elements in this townscape, during the past three centuries, have been the buildings of local government – the buildings which housed and celebrated the burgeoning powers of municipal and civic authority. In this area this book provides a general overview account, designed to complement the in-depth RCAHMS study of the civic buildings of the pre-Reform Act era, *Tolbooths and Town-Houses* (1996).

Before beginning our history of Scottish governmental architecture proper, we first need to address a fundamental issue stemming from this book's historical and international perspective: the fact that the story of constitutional government, and its reflection in architecture, goes back far further than the history of Scotland as a polity or as a nation. It was only from the Middle Ages that formal structures of national government, and buildings to house them, began to spring up in this country. But by then, the Western tradition of political organisation had already accumulated nearly two millennia of history and development, from the sixth or even the seventh century BC onwards. Such a long tradition was not unique in global terms. Most of its force was concentrated in the classical age of Greece and Rome, in which the former invented, and the latter consolidated, a vast range of concepts and institutions. That era was followed by over a millennium of disunity and conflict, and it was only in the nineteenth century that European power decisively outstripped that, for instance, of China. But what was unique about the Western tradition, for good or bad, was its restless dynamism and its competitive, conflict-based framework for the development of ideas.

THE *RES PUBLICA* AND ITS ARCHITECTURE

It was in classical Greece, and above all in Athens during the fifth century BC, that the Western tradition of constitutional government and sovereignty first emerged. By the following century, Aristotle's

Politics could list well-defined categories of government, each in its ideal and debased forms: monarchy/tyranny, aristocracy/oligarchy, democracy/mob rule. None of these corresponded to the specific organisational patterns of modern politics. This was, after all, a small-scale, unspecialised and face-to-face society, with menial work carried out by slaves, and no separation of religious and secular. As a result, there was no Greek conception of the 'state' as an autonomous entity, no ancient bureaucracy.[1] The architectural consequences were that while the design of the legislative meeting-halls themselves was intensively pursued, anticipating some of the most important patterns of the modern world, the ancillary administrative building types that are so important today were then almost unknown.

The overall organisational trend in the politics of the myriad of Greek city-states, from the sixth century onwards, was a clear move from monarchy and aristocracy towards democracy, led by Athens, where, by the mid-fifth century, the entire male citizen body could meet and vote directly on political issues, as well as provide large jury panels to control the public and private lawcourts. To ensure that the principle of direct democracy was unrestricted by entrenched elites, all the officials who advised the citizen assembly (*ekklesia*) were selected by lot. These included the 500-strong *boule* (council), who prepared the business of the assembly, and the *prytaneion*, a presidential committee made up of one-tenth of the council members. By the fourth century, the general principle of popular sovereignty and the mechanism of a democratic assembly, working in tandem with a council and magistrates, had spread widely across the Greek world. Although later, in response to the curbing of the general autonomy of the Greek city-states under Macedonian and Roman hegemony, the balance of power shifted back towards the more oligarchic and monarchical elements within these constitutions, the ideals of popular sovereignty, and of the constitution as a balance of political forces, had been established for good.

What were the architectural responses to these remarkable developments? In general, the largest, most democratic types of gatherings were accommodated in open-air settings, while the smaller and more elitist bodies were housed in enclosed buildings. In the planning of spaces of assembly, we will see throughout this book a tension of internal direction, between assemblies dominated by the presiding officials and those dominated by the people. Greek democratic assembly spaces were extreme examples of the latter. The simplest meeting place for a citizen assembly was in the central public and commercial space of any Greek city-state, the *agora*. When it came to the construction of purpose-designed accommodation, citizen *ekklesiai* showed a striking overlap with theatres; the most prominent example was the amphitheatre, with seats for 6,000, excavated for the fifth-century Athenian *ekklesia* on the hill of the Pnyx.

For councils and magistrates, smaller purpose-built halls and offices were constructed, initially with a strong affinity to linear-planned temples, with benches facing each other, but gradually moving towards more compact centralised layouts similar to the *ekklesia* type; the late fifth-century *bouleuterion* in Athens, for example, was broad and rectangular with four columns supporting the roof, and a semi-circular layout of benches around the central space. In smaller communities, the same pattern might be extended to the popular assembly. The *ekklesiasterion* at Priene, built probably around 200 BC to accommodate the entire citizen population of 600–700, features a U-plan tiered auditorium of stone benches with a gallery behind and an altar in the centre. A multi-columned rectangular hall, the Tesilion, capable of seating 6,000, was built in 371 BC at Megalopolis for the council of the Arcadian League; its columns radiated outwards from a central speaking position. The few officials needed to support the work of such assemblies could be readily accommodated in small buildings, such as the circular Athenian tholos, or in the colonnaded stoas which adjoined many agoras: there was no such thing as an ancient 'office building'[2]

The seven centuries of Roman power consolidated the range of constitutional ideas mapped out by the Greeks, by tying them to an authoritative and enduring system of government legitimacy. Rome, too, was a face-to-face society, in contrast to the social classes and bureaucracies of the modern world: it was no coincidence that the same word, *litterae*, was used for public administration and literature. Roman political history was divided into the oligarchy-dominated Republic and the monarchical Principate (or Empire), the division between the two being the assumption of power by the first emperor, Augustus, over the years 31–27 BC. What both phases had in common was a determination to preserve the *res publica* – the forms of constitutional government through public office and legal procedure – from

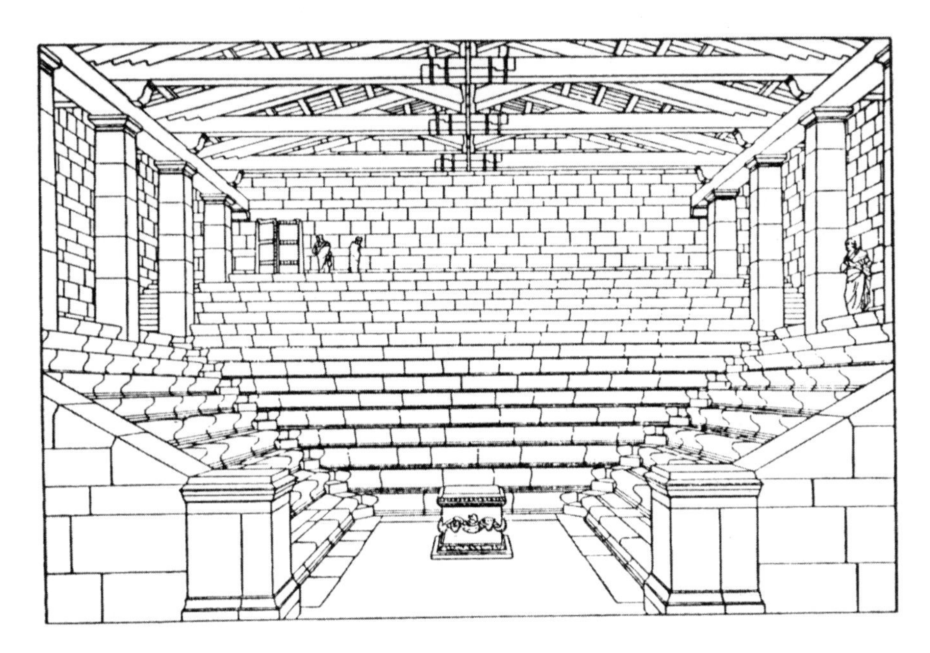

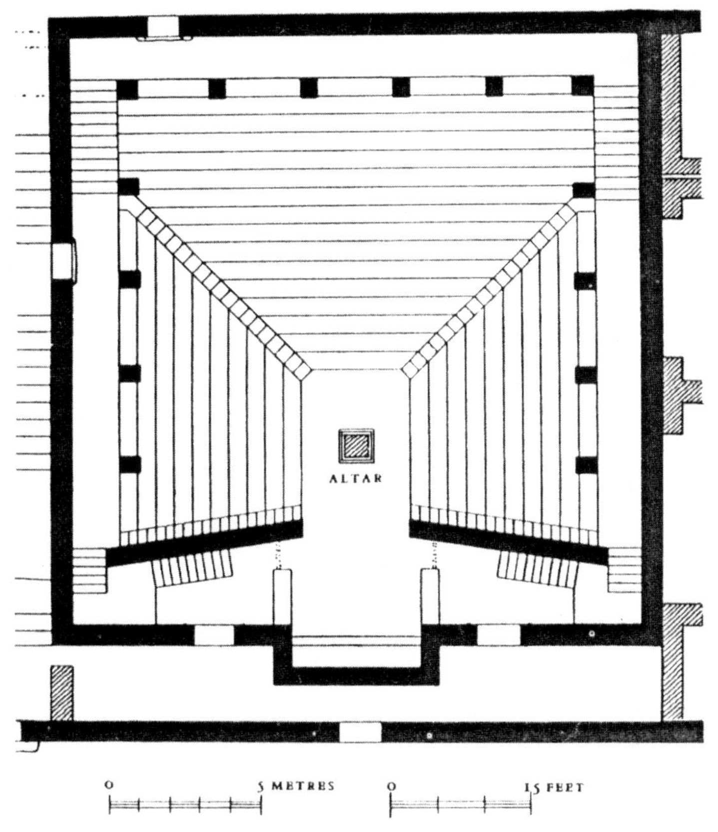
ALTAR
0
5 METRES
0
15 FEET

the arbitrary rule associated with the word *regnum*, or the rule of kings. The Roman constitution was always one of extreme complexity. Under the Republic, popular sovereignty rested on a number of overlapping assemblies, but these could not initiate legislation themselves; laws were presented mainly by the senior magistrates, the consuls and praetors, who enjoyed great executive authority. But this power was regulated by the overriding moral and religious force of the advice of the Senate, a 300-strong state council made up of former magistrates. In the opinion of the Greek historian Polybius, this system amounted to a highly flexible 'mixed' constitution combining the best elements of democracy, oligarchy and monarchy.[3] Its central principles were a balance between conflicting forces, and the delegation and regulation of power: ideas that were to be of enduring influence up to the present day. But during the first century BC, it became increasingly unstable, and the last of a succession of authoritarian popular leaders, Octavianus (Augustus), replaced it with a quasi-monarchy, the Principate, constructed ingeniously out of constitutional elements, so as to preserve the appearance of the *res publica*.

The architecture of Roman politics reflected the balance of forces within the *res publica*. Public buildings and the open-air fora had the same multi-purpose, face-to-face character as in Greece, but a new type of public, judicial and commercial meeting-hall with nave and aisles, the basilica, was developed from the early second century BC. The building forms devoted to legislature carried on the Greek division between open assemblies and enclosed councils, but the former, being much less powerful (especially under the Principate), were held in diffuse open-air spaces, with fenced-in voting enclosures, canvas roofing, and a permanent tribune for orators.[4] Councils were usually accommodated either in temples or in rectangular temple-like buildings, with one porticoed frontage, solid side walls and a strongly linear plan. The purpose-built home of the Senate, by the Roman Forum, was called the *curia* – a name which also applied to council-houses of priestly colleges. The present building, the *curia Iulia*, begun in the early first century BC, is a tall, rectangular block, laid out internally around a central axis, with rows of benches along either side wall, facing each other. Seating was by rank, with senior senators at the front, and the president's tribune at the far end.

These patterns were endorsed at the beginning of the Principate by the architectural writer Vitruvius – not just in relation to Rome

0.1. Priene, *Ekklesiasterion*, *c.*200 BC, restored interior and plan.

itself, but also for other towns across the empire, in which he recommended that a municipal senate-house should be built alongside a treasury and prison on one side of the forum. But the latter was usually far eclipsed in grandeur by the main temple and the basilica, where much of the real public business was transacted, and the rule of law enforced. These groups of buildings demonstrated the way in which the *res publica*, if local roots as well as central prestige were fostered, could be given stability across a vast and diverse territory. There was no question of 'direct democracy' on the Athenian pattern; but a large number of people had a real stake in delegated and representative power.

THE TWO POWERS: THE RISE OF THE CHRISTIAN EMPIRE

By the sixth century AD, the entire structure of Roman governmental order had collapsed, and the Roman Empire had split into two halves, a Greek-speaking east and a Latin-speaking west. But the substance of Roman power had been replaced by something even more powerful and influential on the modern world – by 'Rome' as an idea.[5] The adaptability of classical civilisation had already shown itself in the development of the Roman *res publica* and the principate out of the Greek concepts of democracy, aristocracy and monarchy. Now a far more radical process of change was under way, as these ideas were adapted to the needs of two new epochs in European civilisation. The first, lasting more than a millennium, was the rise and ascendancy of monotheistic Christianity. The second was the era which corresponds to the time-scale of this book – the rise of the secular nation-state, from the late medieval period onwards. From then on, following the end of antiquity, we increasingly witness the emergence of concepts and developments with direct bearing on the later experience in Scotland: the tension between church and state, the conflict between absolute monarchy and attempts to revive *res-publica* constitutionalism, the clashes between central power and local pride.

The rise of Christianity in Europe coincided with a steady shift towards more authoritarian systems of government. During the late Roman empire, the emperors had become absolute monarchs supported, especially in the eastern provinces, by a rigid caste system.

OPPOSITE TOP.
0.2. Forum Romanum, present-day view showing the first century BC *curia* (Senate-house) on right and Capitoline Hill in background.

OPPOSITE BELOW.
0.3. Pompeii, ruins of first century AD municipal council-chamber, showing remains of members' seats facing each other on the side walls.

These developments deeply affected the development of Christianity, and were in turn shaped by its own monotheistic characteristics, which had turned religion into a driving, proselytising force with its own systems of values and claim to universal applicability. New Testament Christianity, with its stress on human community, was a diverse and, potentially, highly 'democratic' organisation; the Greek word for 'church' was *ekklesia*. But such ideas were soon far outweighed by hierarchical structures reflecting the growing authoritarian tendencies in secular society. These took two main forms.

The first was that of a dependence on temporal power, a tendency which began in the fourth century, with the patronage of the church by Roman emperors from Constantine onwards. The other responded to the growing fragmentation of secular kingdoms in Western Europe, by envisaging the church as an 'empire' in its own right. The key element in this movement was the gradual emergence of the Bishop of Rome – the Pope – as the undisputed head of the western church, and the conversion of Rome from an imperial capital to a 'city of God'. The pope's authority, however, was that of a *princeps* rather than a *rex*, ruling in collaboration with a range of magistrates and council-like bodies. Pope Gelasius I (492–6) enunciated the theory of the 'two powers', that spiritual power is not only separate but superior to temporal power. From the twelfth century, papal power and prestige reached its climax, with a vast structure of legalistic hierarchy and bureaucracy supporting the new, trans-European empire of 'Christendom'.[6]

From the fourteenth century, that balance would alter, as the church became enfeebled by conflict and decay, and the power of the individual nations, including Scotland, began to grow: the story which begins in the next chapter.

From that point, right up until the twentieth century, the 'two kingdoms' would be locked in conflict, from one end of Europe to the other. The potential of this nascent system of nation-states for governmental innovation was first aired in microcosm in the constitutional experiments of the wealthy Italian city-states of the late Middle Ages, whose fierce local pride, or *campanilismo*, led them to revive and adapt the diverse Greek formulas for the modern world. In the eleventh and twelfth centuries, numerous towns developed autonomous assemblies and executive consuls, supported by a proliferation of committees and administrators.

These lively and variegated communities stood halfway between the scale of cities and small nations, but their instability led to a revival of authoritarian rule from the twelfth century.[7]

Architecturally, the Christian era's trend towards more authoritarian power structures was reflected in a diminution of the scope for specialised or purpose-built political and administrative buildings. Right up to the Renaissance, as the next chapter will show in the case of Scotland, governmental and judicial activities tended to take place within buildings of general secular or religious power, such as the palace of king or bishop, or if a space for a larger assembly was needed, in a church or a square, or just an open space. And assemblies were arranged in a highly directional manner, with subjects facing a king. The Roman world's linear-planned basilica pattern was adapted for religious use, and became the basic layout of churches and cathedrals, while within secular architecture the great hall became the dominant place of covered assembly, either within castellated houses or palaces or within urban collective institutions such as guild-halls. Outside, the urban meeting space of the agora/forum survived little altered as the arcaded Italian piazza or the north European market-place.

The Italian city-states, with their wealth and community pride, were the first to begin to modify this pattern, by beginning programmes of social and public building linked to specialised building types. Public administration was housed in a special type of freestanding public palazzo, influenced by the great town halls of Northern Europe, with a ground-floor arcade and a great council hall above. By the mid-fourteenth century, non-governmental and proto-capitalistic functions were beginning to be hived off from the civic palazzi, for example into separate market buildings. And the exponential growth of paper-based bureaucracy in the republics began to create a demand for purpose-built office space. In Florence, for instance, limited office accommodation was provided in the Palazzo Vecchio of 1299–1314, followed in 1560–80 by Giorgio Vasari's much larger 'Palazzo degli Uffizi' (offices); the two 140m-long repetitively-expressed parallel wings, entered from a U-shaped continuous corridor, housed thirteen different bodies, including guilds, commissioners, and conservators. As the force of the Renaissance grew, projects for ideal cities incorporated these specialised civic buildings as elements within a regular and stately antique-classical vision. In Venice, a grandiose forum complex was developed around St Mark's

Square from the thirteenth century onwards, to accommodate the various representative councils and administrative bodies of the republican oligarchy, the Doges having become symbolic figureheads. These included halls for the Senate, the Council of Ten, and the Great Council (an aristocratic assembly of between 300 and 1,600 members); there was also a state library, mint, prison, granary, and clock tower, as well as the Basilica of St Mark. The Doge's Palace was internally rebuilt in classical style after a 1574 fire, and the square was externally unified by arcading throughout.[8]

THE LEGACY

The central governmental legacy of the classical and Christian traditions was an assumption that absolute sovereignty or permanent authority was impossible. There was always a question mark, always a possibility of a challenge from a competing idea. For most of the Middle Ages, that possibility remained very much in the background. But as the Italian republics showed, growth in wealth, population and social diversity could begin to unlock its potential force. The eventual result in Northern European countries such as Scotland, far from any return to classical Athenian democracy or Roman elite rule, was a new and modern conception of 'representative' democracy – national *and* civic – which was made up of autonomous legislative communities supported by equally autonomous bureaucracies. In other modern European countries, there were also new forms of tyranny, bolstered by institutions of mass assembly and solidarity. For all of these changes, antiquity and early Christanity remained a legitimising framework, and a source of ever-mutating names of concepts and institutions. For example, when a new supreme civil law court was first set up in Scotland in the early sixteenth century, it seemed only natural that its members should be styled 'Senators of the College of Justice'.

For the architecture of governmental assembly, the antique and medieval legacy was more direct, combining elements of the meeting-place patterns of antiquity – namely, the *ekklesia* amphitheatre and the introverted council-chamber – with the great hall of Northern Europe. The main contribution of the centuries covered by this book was to flesh out these types with a range of specialised ancillary and

0.4. Palazzo degli Uffizi, Florence (Giorgio Vasari, 1560–80): the first large scale 'government office building'.

administrative buildings. In architecture, symbols and images were as important as specific building types. And the most enduring and powerful image of all, in Scotland just as elsewhere in Europe, was that of the 'city on a hill' as an emblem of authority and sovereignty, whether in the sense of imperial, Capitoline secular power or in that of a city of God, a Jerusalem-like place of reverence and pilgrimage.

NOTES

1. Aristotle, *Politics*, 1300b, 4–5.
2. R. Sennett, *Flesh and Stone*, New York, 1994; A.W. Lawrence, *Greek Architecture*, London, 1983 edition, 332–59.
3. Polybius, 6.11.11.
4. Livy, XXVII.36.
5. Gregory the Great, *Homily on Ezekiel*, II.6.22.
6. R. P. McBrien (general editor), *The Harper-Collins Encyclopedia of Catholicism*, New York, 1995, 243 ff; H. Kung, *Structures of the Church*, New York, 1964.
7. McBrien, *Encyclopedia of Catholicism*, 1091; D. Waley, *The Italian City-Republics*, London, 1969.
8. H. Honour, *Companion Guide to Venice*, London, 1965.

CHAPTER ONE

Community of the Realm: The Middle Ages

Richard D. Oram

ANTECEDENTS

In this chapter, we begin by dealing with places in Scotland which lacked the formal, regularised architectural characteristics of the governmental and assembly settings of Mediterranean antiquity, and which have today mostly vanished. Yet here too, since the earliest times, the exercise of power produced a specialist architecture of power, however unfamiliar its forms may seem to us.

In Scotland, as in other prehistoric societies throughout Europe, rulers and chieftains underscored their authority through the buildings in which they based themselves. Hillforts, for example, provided a striking visual declaration of the might of the tribes and their rulers, while the building of brochs proclaimed the aspirations of potentates on a more local level. In both, however, it was the fortification which gave physical weight to the notional authority of their occupants. Over time, a greater sophistication emerged in their planning, with a hierarchical use of the internal space – where inner 'lordly' citadels were divided from outer enclosures which housed the lesser members of the community and the industrial complexes – serving to lend greater psychological impact to the projection of lordship.[1] Such sites functioned as more than simply fortresses, acquiring a symbolism in the records of the time as centres of power and seats of administration and economic wealth.[2] Within them, kings and rulers constructed formal settings for the projection of their might through ceremonial occasions and, most importantly, feasting.

There is little excavated evidence for these buildings, but glimpses of what comprised such a kingly site can be seen fossilised in early writings. St Columba's biographer, Abbot Adomnan of Iona, for example, although he himself may never have visited the Pictish royal centre near Inverness, gives some ideas of what he, writing in the 690s, expected Columba to have seen there in the 560s. He describes it as a strongly fortified site which contained both a 'royal hall', used for formal feasting, and a separate king's 'house'. Perhaps significantly, however, Columba's meeting with the Pictish king took place in the open air.[3]

As in Rome, open-air assemblies played a vital part in the ceremonial and practice of early Scottish kingship. One function of such occasions was the public proclamation of law. The making and issuing of laws are amongst the oldest attributes of medieval kingship, and reports of their enactment in Scotland are as ancient as the kingdom itself. The promulgation of a new law code would have been a stage-managed, ceremonial affair at one of the traditional seats of kingly power. In *c.*860, for example, Domnall mac Ailpin (Donald I, 858–62), introduced the laws of the Scots to what had formerly been Pictland in a highly symbolic ceremony at Forteviot, the ancient centre of the kings of Fortriu.[4] The choice of site was surely not coincidental, for the landscape around Forteviot possessed a ritual significance stretching back into the Neolithic period, and had evidently been developed as a major royal centre under the last two generations of the powerful and sophisticated Pictish monarchy of the early ninth century.[5] Here was a seat of power already nearly four millennia old by the time that Domnall proclaimed his law code.

In the absence of more detailed archaeological examination, it is difficult to discuss centres of early Scottish kingly and lordly power other than in generalisations, but it is arguable that in the later eighth and earlier ninth centuries kingship, particularly within Pictland, was undergoing rapid evolution. From the reign of Oengus I mac Fergus (729–61), a politically sophisticated clergy had aligned itself with politically ambitious rulers, with the church promoting the concept of a 'national' monarchy in place of the somewhat shadowy regional kingdoms. By the early 800s, influences from late Roman Imperial and Carolingian traditions of authority were permeating Picto-Scottish society. This can be seen most clearly in the emergence of a dynastic succession to the kingship.

There can be no doubt of the centrality of the church to the spread of these ideas: a stable and secure monarchy in the European tradition provided the best environment within which the ecclesiastical hierarchy could develop and extend its influence. In return for royal protection and the identification of kings with the work of the church, the church gave the divine 'seal of approval' to rulers and sanctioned their exercise of kingly power. This is revealed in the reigns of Constantine mac Fergus and Oengus II mac Fergus, where major new ecclesiastical centres were founded at Dunkeld and St.Andrews by monarchs who were assuming the attributes of continental kingship.[6]

Continental, and also Anglo-Saxon, influences were not restricted to abstract concepts such as the nature of kingship or to the exercise of kingly power, but had a broader impact on the physical manifestations of authority, most obviously in the architecture of power. With the exception of a magnificent sculptured archway from a now lost ninth-century church, the buildings of the palace complex at Forteviot have vanished, possibly swept away by river erosion. Analogy with other near-contemporary sites elsewhere in Britain and Europe, however, allows a rough idea of the physical layout of Forteviot to be obtained. Its main component would have been a ceremonial hall, a descendant of the absorption into barbarian cultures of the Roman basilican tradition, as was the case at Yeavering in Northumberland and the great Carolingian palace-complex at Ingelheim in Germany, which would have served as 'a great visual theatre for the display of royal power'.[7] Excavated examples of such halls, as at Doon Hill near Dunbar, or where identified through aerial photography, as at Sprouston in Roxburghshire, lie further down the social scale but give a fair impression of the physical layout of such complexes.[8] At Sprouston, a substantial aisled hall with separate, smaller annexes at the opposed gable ends lay at the heart of one phase of the developed complex. Such halls form a distinctive element within Germanic lordly society, but drew their inspiration ultimately from the Roman forms.[9] Within Picto-Scottish territory, no such hall has been identified with certainty, but the cropmark site of Monboddo near Laurencekirk in the Mearns, detected through aerial photography, would seem to indicate their existence.[10] Built of timber, these structures have left no upstanding remains, but some impression of the interior of an aisled hall of this kind, albeit in stylised form, can be obtained from the sculpted hog-back gravestone in the churchyard at Luss in Dunbartonshire.[11]

Central though the hall may have been to the exercise of certain attributes of early kingship, it is also clear from Forteviot that the major Neolithic ritual monuments in the landscape around it must have played a significant and active rôle in its functioning. It has been suggested that the earthworks of the henges were still upstanding and that while 'there can be no question of direct continuity of function ... the social elites may have deliberately used or associated themselves with these monuments of the past in order to both promote and legitimise their own interests'.[12] Such association between the monuments of remote prehistory and the vocabulary of power in early medieval Celtic society has been little explored in Scotland, but it is a clearly recognised commonplace in relation to Irish kingship, with key royal centres such as Tara and Knowth sited in the midst of Neolithic and Bronze Age ritual complexes.[13] It is a pattern of 'historical landscape' which is recognisable throughout the Middle Ages, where for example Robert Bruce sought to strengthen his royal legitimacy through direct association with the Canmore past, and down to the present, with attempts at the political exploitation of traditional symbols and historic architectural settings of nationhood.

Used as we are to the location of our courts of law and seats of government in splendid and architecturally symbolic buildings, we have failed in the past to give due recognition to the continued importance throughout the Middle Ages, as in classical antiquity, of open-air settings for these most vital of public functions.
Although halls were important stages for displays of kingly power before assemblies of nobles and churchmen, they were not unique. This can be seen more clearly at the main rival to Forteviot as the seat of kingly power in early historic Scotland: Scone.

Scone has a recorded history extending back to the early eighth century, but the site was largely developed as the inauguration place of Scottish kings from the time of Cinaed mac Ailpin (Kenneth I, 843–58).[14] Here the ceremonial focus evidently lay out of doors on the low mound now known as the Moot Hill, but earlier referred to as the Hill of Faith or Hill of Credulity.[15] This hill possessed a more general significance as a place of assembly and law-giving, it being here in *c.*906, for example, that Constantin mac Aeda (Constantine II, 900–43) and Bishop Cellach of St Andrews confirmed the application

1.1. Reconstruction plan of Scone Abbey and its environs. (RCAHMS DC 25143)

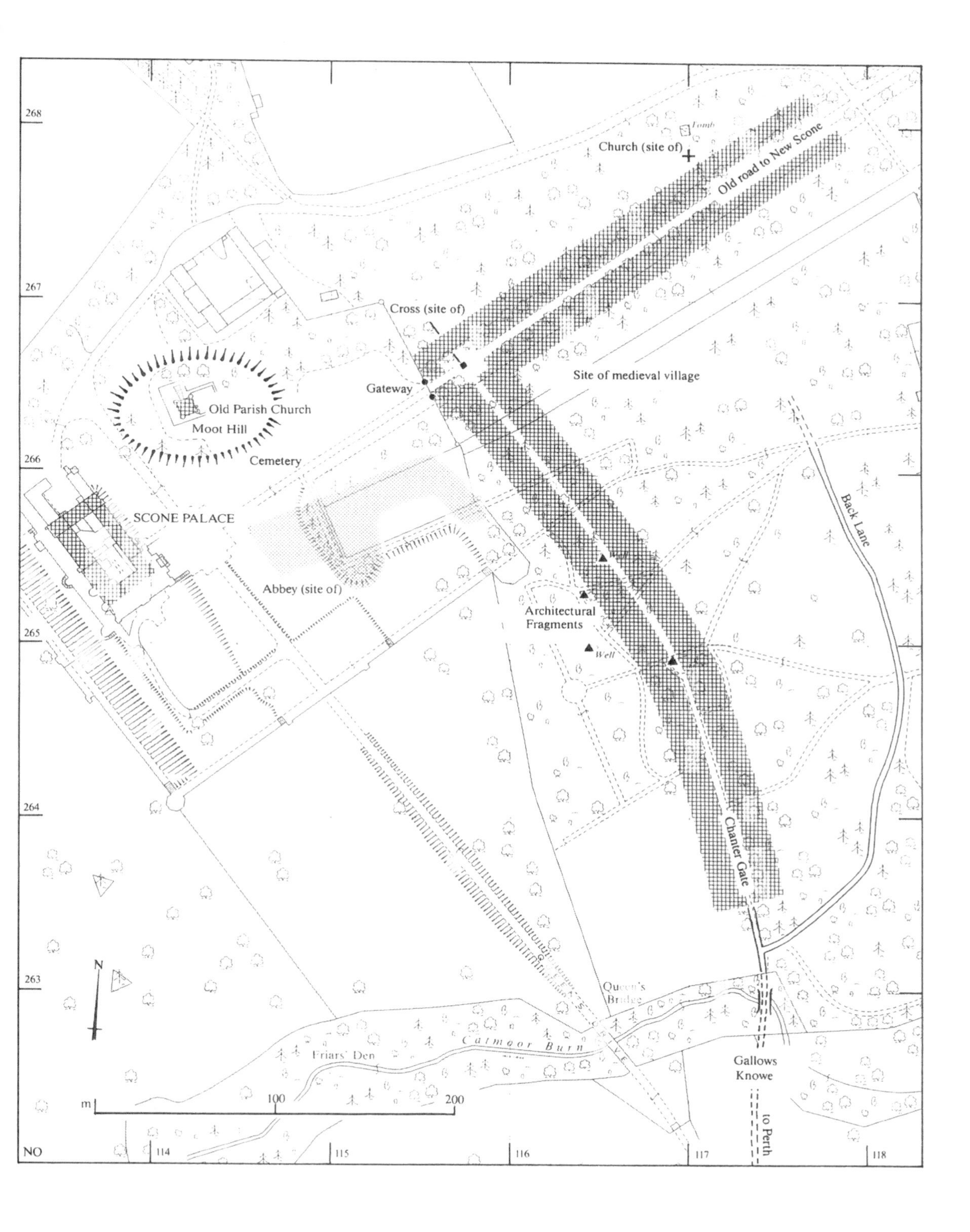

268
267
266
265
264
263
Church (site of)
Tomb
Old road to New Scone
Cross (site of)
Gateway
Site of medieval village
Old Parish Church
Moot Hill
Cemetery
SCONE PALACE
Abbey (site of)
Architectural Fragments
Well
Back Lane
Chanter Gate
Queen's Bridge
Catmoor Burn
Friars' Den
Gallows Knowe
to Perth
N
m
100
200
NO
114
115
116
117
118

of the laws of the Scots to 'the laws and disciplines of the faith, and the rights in churches and gospels', thereby setting their seal on the takeover of Pictish society.[16] Writing of early eleventh-century events in the late fourteenth century, John of Fordun described the 'Moot Hill of the royal seat of Scone' as a place 'where the kings, sitting in their royal robes on the throne, are wont to give out judgements, laws and statutes, to their subjects'.[17] To Fordun, moreover, Scone was 'the chief seat of government' of both Pictish and Scottish kings.[18] It preserved a major ceremonial significance as late as the coronation of King Robert II in March 1371, when, after the crowning and anointment ceremony in the abbey, the following day '... the King seated in the royal seat upon the hill of Scone as is customary, there gathered and compeared in his presence the prelates, earls, barons and nobles ... who all made their homage' to him.[19]

Scone's importance as a seat of power, if only as the location of the king-making ritual, extended over six centuries until its abandonment as the site of royal inaugurations in the fifteenth century, while Forteviot lost its royal significance earlier in the twelfth century.[20] The royalty of these sites, however, has obscured their original significance as the *loci* for assemblies. Indeed, it seems that this associated royalty overwhelmed and subsumed all other functions, with the result that when that royal rôle was withdrawn, both sites lost all significance as judicial or legislative centres. Elsewhere, however, glimpses can be had of the survival of ancient places of assembly into the later Middle Ages. In the 1380s, for example, the Neolithic standing stones at Easter Kingussie functioned as the setting for the head court of the lordship of Badenoch, itself the thirteenth-century political successor of a more ancient unit.[21]

BUILDING CONSENT: THE TWELFTH CENTURY

The traditions of early kingship remained strong in Scotland down to the eleventh century, when growing Anglo-Saxon influences began to remodel the exercise and function of authority. The settings of power, however, appear to have changed little from the ninth century, with monarchs still based on the major royal sites which had evolved under the Picto-Scottish monarchy. Indeed, there had evidently been little change in the architectural vocabulary of lordship, although there had been developments in the technical nomenclature. Lightly fortified complexes centred upon a hall appear to have remained the dominant tradition for all senior ranks in the hierarchy of power from the king through the mormaers – quasi-regal rulers of provinces – to the thanes.[22] The pace of change, however, accelerated sharply from the late 1060s onwards, following the marriage of Malcolm III (Maelcoluin MacDonnchada, 1058–93) to the Anglo-Saxon princess, Margaret. With Margaret and her family came a small but significant group of English émigrés, whose influence in the royal household resulted in the introduction of Anglo-Saxon social and cultural forms, quite disproportionate to their numbers or political weight. Although interrupted in the period 1093–7 by the violent cultural backlash which followed Malcolm's death, the imported traditions had become embedded in the king's family. Once restored to authority in Scotland with the backing of the English crown, the Canmore dynasty identified themselves even more closely with the governmental traditions of the southern kingdom.

Consultation by kings with the great lay and ecclesiastical figures of their realm grew through the twelfth century. Although there was no formal vehicle for this process of consultation, there was growing recognition of the responsibility of kings to seek counsel and advice from their magnates on weighty matters of state.

Following European, and more particularly English, practice, with which the kings of Scots were personally familiar from the early 1100s, the root of this lay in the *curia regis*, the king's court, made up normally of the major office-holders, such as the chancellor and chamberlain, and the core of professional clerks and knights of the king's household.[23] This court had a variety of functions, including judicial responsibilities, the auditing of royal finances, and a straight advisory rôle. It can be seen working in the last capacity in 1198 when the king's *curiales* – courtiers – in court at Forfar advised him on the selection of a suitable candidate for the abbacy of Scone.[24] It evidently, too, fulfilled an important advisory rôle in cases involving inheritance and property disputes, as in 1213, when the court at Edinburgh was the venue for the settlement of a dispute over the earldom of Menteith.[25]

It is quite wrong to think of the *curia regis* as an institution meeting with the formality of tradition with which we are still familiar through modern law courts. Arrangements were much more *ad hoc*, the evidence from England suggesting that the king might simply take counsel from the men standing around him, while the example of Louis IX of France sitting under the oak tree at Vincennes, with his courtiers seated around him on the grass, and decreeing that anyone, regardless of rank, could approach him for justice, stresses the potential informality of medieval royalty.[26] This ease of personal access to the king in an appeal for royal justice was also demonstrated on occasion in early medieval Scottish kingship. In his obituary of King David I (1124–53), Abbot Ailred of Rievaulx described how 'when ready to go a-hunting, his foot was placed in the stirrup and he wished to mount his horse, yet at the voice of a poor man requesting that an audience be given him he drew back his foot, left his horse and returned to the hall . . . and kindly and patiently heard the case for which he had been appealed to'. And that 'he was accustomed to sit at the entrance of the royal hall, and diligently to hear the cases of poor men and old women, who on certain days were called to him singly, in whatever district he came to . . .'[27] Although such setpieces of direct access may have been occasional and staged, and although the dispensing of justice was a different matter from the taking of counsel by the king himself, such accounts should warn us against picturing any formally organised assembly gathering in a specialised meeting-place. Nor need the chambers in which they gathered have been particularly large, for there is no evidence for specialist furnishings being required until the later Middle Ages. Indeed, it is quite likely that on many occasions most of the participants – other than the king – would have remained standing, further reducing the requirement for space. Certain business required wider consultation, when this inner core of the court was expanded by the summoning of members of the senior nobility and clergy. This can be seen in Malcolm IV's 1160 Christmas court at Perth, which was swollen by the attendance of six bishops, seven abbots, three priors, two archdeacons, a dean, five earls and four barons.[28] The dominance of clergy on that occasion was a result of those who had attended the consecration of the bishop of St Andrews joining the king for the Christmas festivities. Councils which discussed primarily secular business were, in turn, dominated by the magnates.[29]

In common with other European states of this period, there was no fixed location for meetings of the *curia regis* or larger councils. The largely informal nature of the body meant that its core could accompany the king as he travelled around the kingdom. Courts were held practically wherever there was a royal residence, evidently within the king's castles where there was presumably both a suitable hall-like venue and adequate accommodation for an enlarged household. Naturally, the key royal strongholds or particularly favoured residences, such as the castles of Edinburgh or Stirling, occur throughout the twelfth and thirteenth centuries most frequently as meeting-places of the *curia regis*. The scale of some of the venues, however, warns us against picturing such occasions as grand affairs. It has recently been argued that the site of Forfar Castle, one of the favourite residences of Scotland's kings, where courts and councils met throughout the twelfth and thirteenth centuries, is now 'enclosed within the back garden of an average town house'.[30] The personal nature and essential informality of royal government at this date must not be forgotten. Business was conducted wherever the king happened to be, as is evident from the number of charters issued throughout the Middle Ages from royal hunting-lodges.[31] This parallels the situation in England, where royal hunting-lodges, such as Woodstock in Bedfordshire and Clarendon in Wiltshire, the latter close to the twelfth-century centre of English government in Winchester, accommodated key assemblies in the reign of Henry II.[32] At Clarendon the nucleus of the palace complex was an arcaded great hall, aisled like the nave of a church, which served as the meeting-place of Henry's councils. There were halls of this form at most of the major English royal residences – for example, Winchester and Westminster – and it is probable that the architecture of the chief Scottish royal sites, certainly from the reign of David I, who had started his career in the household of his brother-in-law, Henry I of England, was modelled closely on English practices. Unfortunately, the wars which ravaged Scotland from 1296 onwards saw the destruction of most of these traditional royal foci. Only some shapeless masonry fragments atop a scarped earthwork remain of the early castle at Clunie between Dunkeld and Blairgowrie, which was developed as a royal hunting-lodge from the reign of David I, who issued a charter there,[33] but especially by his grandson, William.[34] Of Kincardine near Fettercairn, foundations and low walling survive at the castle site developed originally by William in the late twelfth century, but probably rebuilt in stone by his son, Alexander II, whose major residential development at Kinclaven on the Tay above Perth likewise survives in a fragmentary state. Elsewhere, subsequent phases of rebuilding have obliterated or obscured any remaining traces of the twelfth- and thirteenth-century layouts.

In the period 1174–89, the choice of some locations was dictated by the loss of the more traditional settings following William the Lion's surrender to Henry II in the Treaty of Falaise, which obliged him to hand over the castles of Berwick, Edinburgh, Jedburgh, Roxburgh and Stirling, if required to do so by his overlord. Jedburgh and Stirling were never occupied by an English garrison, but Henry chose to exercise his right over the remaining three: Edinburgh was held until 1186, and Berwick and Roxburgh were not returned to William until 1189. In place of Edinburgh, William made greater use of residences at Haddington and Linlithgow, the former being the scene in March 1181 of a major assembly.[35] At neither does any trace of the early royal residence survive.

A few assemblies in this period were both larger in scale and of longer duration, on account of the importance of the business under discussion. In 1182, for example, an unlocated three-day assembly discussed the vexed issue of the disputed election of a new bishop of St Andrews.[36] The two most important assemblies of the period, however, in 1188 and 1189–90, congregated in places which had no clearly royal associations and which lacked obvious buildings in which such gatherings could meet. The first was at Birgham, a minor settlement on the Tweed between Kelso and Coldstream which enjoyed some status in the twelfth and thirteenth centuries as a meeting-place on the Border, made famous by the two parliaments there in March and July 1290 which agreed the marriage of the Maid of Norway to Edward, Prince of Wales.[37] There was neither castle nor parish church at this place, nor any surviving evidence for some alternative substantial structure, such as a teind barn. This suggests that 'the king of Scots himself with almost all the bishops and earls and barons of his land, and with an endless multitude of his vassals' might have met in the open air, foreshadowing Louis IX of France's *al fresco* councils; or there may have been tented accommodation, which could have facilitated committee-like discussions in smaller sub-groups. The second of these assemblies took place at Musselburgh in late 1189 or early 1190 to discuss the raising of a tax to pay the 10,000 merks promised to Richard I of England for his cancellation of the Treaty of Falaise.[38] Musselburgh does not appear to have been a royal burgh in the twelfth century and by the early fourteenth century was a burgh under the abbot of Dunfermline, which implies again that there was no obvious focus in the form of a royal castle at which this assembly could gather. The parish church may have provided a suitable venue, but there is still the problem of why such a minor location should have been the meeting-place for so important an assembly when the royal centre of Edinburgh lay so close. Late fourteenth- and fifteenth-century accounts locate this meeting in Holyrood Abbey, an altogether more likely venue for a gathering of the prelates and magnates of the realm, but the assembly of a second council at Musselburgh in 1201 indicates that the twelfth-century evidence cannot be discounted.[39]

THE THIRTEENTH CENTURY

The last decade of the long reign of William the Lion saw a burst of activity, concerned primarily with the deteriorating relationship between the Scots and John, king of England. On 24 May 1209 a great council at Stirling, evidently in the castle there, discussed negotiations then in progress with John.[40] In September that year, the great council assembled at Perth, possibly in the parish kirk of St John, to discuss the levying of an aid to pay the 15,000 merks promised by the Scots under the terms of the Treaty of Norham which had arisen from the earlier negotiations.[41] The assembly, however, was literally a washout, for the rivers 'Tay and Almond flowed right through the greater part of the town . . . called Perth . . . king William, his noble son Alexander and his brother the earl of Huntingdon left the same town in a very small boat and looked for dry land, accompanied by a very few of the magnates who happened to be there at that time. Some others among the nobility of Scotland who had likewise been in the same town only just escaped, saving themselves as best they could in small boats or upper rooms'.[42] The Perth council was, understandably, abandoned, and in October/November 1209 reassembled at Stirling, where the arrangements for the aid were finalised.

In the reigns of Alexander II (1214–49) and Alexander III (1249–86) the first records occur of gatherings styled (in Latin) *colloquium*.[43] The word means literally 'a talking together' – the same as the French *parlement*. Indeed, in England during this same period the two terms were used interchangeably in official records. In

Scotland, however, the Latin term prevailed until the reign of John Balliol (1292–6), a consequence, it has been suggested, of the limited use of French among the ruling élite of the kingdom.[44] It is unclear what exactly differentiated a *colloquium* from one of the earlier great councils, for they appear to have been concerned primarily with the same general business of policy, diplomacy and justice. In contemporary England, parliaments were regularly summoned to give assent to the growing financial demands of the crown, which led by the end of the thirteenth century to an enlargement in membership. Taxation was rare in thirteenth-century Scotland and does not appear to have borne heavily on the business of *colloquia* or parliaments until the fourteenth century, particularly after 1326 when parliamentary assent was given to an annual tax for the support of the king for life. This expansion of the financial aspect of parliamentary business then resulted in a broadening of membership, with burgess representatives being summoned infrequently down to 1357 and then on a regular basis thereafter.[45] Only eight meetings described as *colloquia* can be identified for the whole of this period, the first in 1235, supplemented by a handful of meetings of an enlarged royal council called together to discuss urgent business which demanded a speedier response than would be possible if a parliament had to be summoned and assembled. There were probably other, unrecorded assemblies, for example in 1236–7 in the course of the negotiations which led to the 1237 Treaty of York. In 1242, moreover, there were three assemblies to which the name *colloquium* is not applied, but which had clear parliamentary characteristics. The first, in July at Perth, began as an ecclesiastical council attended by all the bishops and senior clerics, but as its business was concerned mainly with the activities of secular magnates who were 'harassing them over teinds and the privileges of the church', the presence of the king, earls and barons of the kingdom had been requested.[46] It is probable that this assembly gathered in St John's Kirk, or the burgh's new Dominican convent (house of friars), which had been founded *c.*1231. The council met in the midst of the growing crisis which followed the suspicious death of Patrick of Atholl at Haddington: the earls took the opportunity to demand royal action against the supposed perpetrators of the act. Under pressure from his nobility, Alexander assigned a date for an assembly at Forfar 'for mature deliberation and discussion of the evidence'.[47] No final decision was made on that occasion, the king instead continuing the assembly to Edinburgh on 26 November, when a formal sentence made with 'the judgement and advice' of the nobility was delivered.[48] Here, the formal advisory and judicial roles of the royal council are unequivocally demonstrated.

Throughout the thirteenth century, councils and *colloquia* appear primarily in these roles rather than as legislative bodies. While there was also a legislative function in its activities, as well as a consensual role where raising of finance was involved, it is as a court that such an assembly emerges most clearly in contemporary records. This should warn us against looking to England as the chief source of influence in the development of the Scottish parliamentary tradition, as the institution which was evolving in thirteenth-century Scotland is in many ways closer to the French model of the *Parlement* of Paris. There, a role as a primarily judicial venue began to predominate under Philip II (1180–1223), but it was the reign of Louis IX (1226–70) that saw the *Parlement* emerge as 'the French royal court of appeal', with its judicial function eventually displacing its earlier advisory and legislative capacity.[49]

It is also perhaps no coincidence that the more regular summoning of *colloquia* gains pace in the reign of Alexander II. This may be an accident of survival in the documentary record, but it does bear close correspondence to the development of the organs of church government in Scotland after 1215, in particular to the emergence of the provincial council of the church.[50] This should come as no real surprise, especially considering the ecclesiastical influence within the royal court, where, for example, the chancellorship was controlled from 1231 to 1247 by William de Bondington, bishop of Glasgow from 1233. Bondington and David de Bernham, bishop of St Andrews, formerly Alexander II's chamberlain, moreover, were intimately familiar with the growing conciliar tradition within the continental church, which had sprung from Innocent III's Fourth Lateran Council of 1215: both set out to attend a council at Rome in 1241 and in 1245 de Bernham attended the First Council of Lyons, an assembly in which much of the business was devoted to discussion of technical matters of law and procedure, and where the financial demands of Innocent IV's papacy were brought under debate.[51] The council was not simply or purely an ecclesiastical forum, its business having a profound impact upon secular affairs and the kings of Europe intervening actively in its debates. Scotland's uniquely close relationship with the papacy in this period, therefore, may have encouraged the quite rapid percolation of ideas concerning the form and function of conciliar government. De Bernham, certainly, was a regular holder of councils within his own diocese, using these assemblies to reform, discipline and organise its administration. The experience of these senior clerics with the precedents of ecclesiastical councils, therefore, may have had a profound influence upon the evolving parliamentary tradition in Scotland, not least in the siting of assemblies. The Lateran Councils, for example, gathered in the great late Roman basilica of St John Lateran in Rome, a building which physically embodied the close identification of imperial power with ecclesiastical authority, while subsequent councils – for example, Lyons (1245 and 1275) or Vienne (1311) – assembled in the archiepiscopal cathedrals of the cities in which they were held. In general this period, as noted in the Introduction, saw the secular power of the Church at its height, across Europe.

Including the ecclesiastical council at Perth, all the recorded Scottish *colloquia* which can be given a precise location within this period occurred at what had emerged as the chief centres of royal government in the later twelfth and earlier thirteenth centuries. What were already the main royal castles, Edinburgh (in which the royal archive and treasury were located)[52] and Stirling, appear to have dominated as the chief meeting-places, but the still highly peripatetic nature of kingship meant that some of the more outlying and smaller royal castles, such as Forfar, served for meetings of councils.[53] Although we have no firm evidence, it can be assumed that it was in the great halls of these castles that the *colloquia* met, while the king's chamber may have sufficed for meetings of his council. In one way, this parallels the situation in thirteenth-century England, where, although London and Westminster were already acquiring their domination of parliamentary life, there was also no fixed venue for assemblies. There, however, the twelfth-century precedent of holding councils in the major royal castles and palaces had been effectively abandoned – with the obvious exception of Westminster – probably as a consequence of the rapid expansion in the scale of parliaments after 1216. By the middle of the thirteenth century, ecclesiastical venues had won favour. In 1259, for example, parliament met in the New Temple at London, where presumably the hall-like qualities of the Temple church or the accommodation provided in the associated buildings marked it out as a suitable setting, while in 1263 it met within St Paul's Cathedral.[54] At Bury St Edmunds in 1267, it was the monastic refectory of the great Benedictine abbey which was pressed into service.[55] There, clearly, it was less the royalty of the venue than the demands of accommodation which determined the location of meetings.

From the following century there is continental evidence for the regular use of monastic refectories as the meeting places of representative assemblies. In the kingdom of Naples and Sicily, for example, Robert of Anjou commenced work in 1310 on the convent of Santa Chiara, which was consecrated in 1340 and became both the burial place of the Angevin kings of Naples and the venue for meetings of the royal council within the refectory. These met there regularly until 1442, when that role was assumed by the refectory of the monastery of San Lorenzo Maggiore, founded in 1265 by King Charles I; the Neapolitan parliament met there until the Napoleonic conquest of southern Italy in 1806. Although there was space in abundance in Charles I's great fortress residence of Castel Nuovo, a conscious decision was taken to make use instead of a monastery with close connections with the ruling dynasty; the shift to San Lorenzo Maggiore was a direct consequence of the capture of Naples by Alfonso of Aragon in 1442 and represented a deliberate break with Angevin tradition.

At Bruges, the refectory of the Carmelite convent was used as the formal assembly-place of various national merchant groups, particularly the German Hanse and Catalan merchants, but possibly also the Scots, until the construction of the Oosterlingenhuis as a specialist venue in 1478. Clearly, the conventional modern image of the monastic precinct as a closed area, free from external secular influences, is quite wide of the medieval reality. Even the heart of the cloister was accessible to, and used by, lay people as the venue for the gathering of merchant guilds, local or national legislative assemblies and secular local tribunals. In Scotland, there is only scanty thirteenth-century evidence for such use of religious buildings as venues for secular assemblies. The fragmentary nature of the written record, however, may conceal a more regular function of such buildings for lay gatherings. There is, for example, an isolated and undated reference to the meeting of a legal tribunal at Holyrood Abbey in Alexander II's reign. This was a lay judicial assembly, where various of the *iudices* of Galloway and of Scotia (the region north of the Forth-Clyde isthmus) gathered in the chapter house of Holyrood to give judgement on Gilleasbuig Mahohegan or Macihacain for his rebellion against the crown.[56] This was purely secular business and touched directly on the king's person and, while members of the Gaelic professional legal class issued the judgement, it is unlikely that they were operating outwith the context of the royal court. Why the judges gathered in the chapter house of the abbey rather than in the castle or some other secular venue within the adjacent burgh can only be guessed at, but it is possible that the judgement formed an item of business of a larger and otherwise unrecorded royal assembly, perhaps connected with the suppression of the Galloway rebellion in 1235 and the partition of the lordship inheritance there between the heiresses of the last native lord. Laconic though this one reference is, it does indicate that the cloister of at least one major Scottish monastery was accessible to, and used by, lay assemblies in the thirteenth century, and suggests that Scotland was in line with contemporary European practice.

The royal great halls also played a key role as venues for assemblies. Today's popular imagination, aided by Sir Walter Scott and Hollywood, sees the great hall as primarily a feasting chamber but, although lavish entertainment was a significant attribute of kingship in the Middle Ages, this function was subsidiary to its primary role as a chamber of state, where the king – in direct continuity of early medieval practice – would hold court both literally and figuratively. Again, we should not picture these chambers as being fitted up with formal fixed furnishings in the later Westminster tradition; perhaps only the high table at the dais end of the hall had any permanency. After all, most early medieval Scottish parliaments lasted for less than a week. Certainly, later medieval exchequer accounts reveal that the major royal halls at Edinburgh, Linlithgow and Stirling were provided with removeable trestle tables and benches. There appears, too, to have been a removeable 'bar', a barrier which separated the formal assembly within the hall from a small area near to the door into which non-members of the council could be admitted if called upon to give evidence or expert legal opinion. We should, thus, probably picture such assemblies as a cluster of nobles and clergy gathered round the king, some seated on benches, others standing, with minor figures, such as the clerks who recorded the proceedings, seated on the floor.[57] The general arrangement was similar to the smaller assemblies of Greek antiquity, but, crucially, the direction of sovereignty was reversed; in Greece the presiding individuals were the servants, rather than the rulers, of the assembly. Comparisons between Scottish governmental institutions and those of antiquity would later begin to assume importance under the Stewarts, with the growing tendency to appeal to classical symbolism of imperial power. But in the twelfth and thirteenth centuries it was, above all, as multi-function ceremonial spaces that the royal halls should be seen, as the settings for ceremonial feasting, investitures, councils and parliaments. None of these early halls has survived in any recognisable form in Scotland, but some impression of their scale and sophistication can be gauged from the restored mid-thirteenth-century hall of the kings of Norway at Bergen, or, closer to home, in the much-altered English royal castle at Dublin, developed from the time of King John (1199–1216) as the seat of English government in the island and where Henry III ordered the construction of a great hall some 37m long.[58]

In Scotland, the nearest parallels are the halls of the greater magnates, best represented in the remains of the earl of Mar's hall at Kildrummy in Aberdeenshire.[59] Like royalty, the earls required a formal ceremonial setting in which to display their power and authority. For them, too, the great hall was more than just a glorified dining-hall in which the extended comital household could assemble *en masse* for meals, for it served as the assembly-place of their law courts and meeting-place of their councils. Indeed, possession of such a hall was evidently viewed as a requirement of their status and remained so into the fifteenth century. The elevation in 1372 of John Dunbar to the earldom of Moray, for example, was followed by the provision of a magnificent new hall at his chief castle of Darnaway. Archibald, 3rd earl of Douglas, and Archibald, 4th earl of Douglas, displayed their status in the halls built at Threave and Bothwell respectively. Even as late as the 1460s, possession of a major ceremonial hall was viewed as an attribute of magnatial power, as was perhaps reflected in the building of a splendid new hall range at Dean Castle by Robert, Lord Boyd, who controlled both the person of the king and, as a consequence, the government of Scotland, in the period 1466–9.[60]

In 1248, parliament met on 1 August in the royal castle at

Stirling.[61] For the first time, we can glimpse the assembly in action, with subsidiary business being transacted away from the formal meetings. On this occasion, a property dispute was settled by arbiters in the *colloquium* proper, which probably met in the great hall of the castle, with the settlement being finalised in the presence of the two parties involved and 'many others' in the king's chamber. At Edinburgh, however, it was not solely the castle which accommodated parliament. In January 1285, the *colloquium* had assembled in the church of Holyrood, perhaps because a larger attendance than could be accommodated comfortably within the castle had been summoned to discuss the pressing issue of the royal succession following the death of Alexander III's heir apparent in January 1284 and the question of the king's remarriage.[62]

The ten years which followed the death of Alexander III in 1286 saw a flurry of conciliar activity which preserved an image of continuity. In this period, the Augustinian abbey at Scone, the inauguration place of Scottish kings, first emerged as a meeting-place for *colloquia* and councils. There had been assemblies here in 1214 and 1249 for the inauguration of kings Alexander II and Alexander III, which, although not strictly *colloquia*, were used by the assembled political community to discuss pressing affairs. This was the case in 1249, where the assembly witnessed the opening moves in the prolonged conflict between Alan Durward, Walter Comyn and their supporters for control of the government of the child-king, Alexander III.[63] A regular or formal role for Scone as a place of assembly, however, did not emerge until the 1280s. Council met there in February 1284, one month after the death of Alexander III's son, and settled the succession on the king's grand-daughter, Margaret of Norway.[64] The implicit 'royalty' of the location may have influenced the decision to summon parliament here on 2 April 1286, two weeks after the king's death, to discuss the succession and formalise arrangements for government in the absence of a monarch.[65] That status, too, may have lain behind the decision of John Balliol, who had been inaugurated king there on 30 November 1292, to summon his first parliament at Scone in February 1293. Underlying this, however, may have been the continuing strong influence of ecclesiastical conciliar precedent, most recently displayed in the Second Council of Lyons of 1274, and reinforced after 1286 by the powerful rôle of the episcopate in the government of the kingless kingdom.

1.2. Darnaway Castle, 1965 view of Great Hall. (RCAHMS MO/214)

Balliol's four-year reign was characterised by administrative continuity from the reign of Alexander III, and by maintenance of the steady expansion of the instruments of royal government – in the form of sheriffdoms – into the western periphery of the kingdom. There were, however, some significant changes, for the most part a consequence of his importing of several key officials from his English-based household. Clerks who had served both his mother, Dervorguilla, and himself in the administration of their extensive properties, were introduced into Scottish royal government. Amongst the most important of the these was Master Thomas of Hunsingore, one of the Balliols' prominent legal servants, who was to be appointed chancellor by his now royal master. The influence of such men was pervasive and long-lasting, especially in the introduction of new terminology in the records of government. One of the most visible changes was the substitution of the Franco-English term 'parliament' for the Latin *colloquium*, a change which became permanent in the struggles of the early fourteenth century.[66]

WAR AND RECOVERY, 1296–1357

The central place held by the major royal castles as the usual venues for parliaments and councils throughout the thirteenth century ended abruptly with the eruption of war with England in 1296. Over the following two decades, most of these sites were first garrisoned by the English or their Scottish adherents, then suffered destruction on their capture by the resurgent Scots under the leadership of Robert Bruce. Throughout Scottish history, relations with England have been one of the main constraining factors on the buildings of government and national assembly; but whereas in later years, and certainly after 1660, that influence was played out by peaceful means, in this period the main constraint was one of warfare and open hostility. Edinburgh provides a useful illustration of the fate of the main royal castles at this time. Garrisoned by Edward I in 1296, it was only retaken by the Scots and slighted in March 1314, and still lay in ruins in July 1336 when the English king, Edward III, ordered its refortification. It remained an English garrison post until 1341, when it was again taken by the Scots, but, although they did not raze it on this occasion, its location in one of the most war-ravaged zones of the kingdom precluded it from reclaiming its place at the heart of royal government until after the conclusion of the war in 1357.

This elimination of the traditional assembly-places in the years after 1296 forced the Scots to press into service what appear at first sight to be some unusual venues in their efforts to maintain a functioning 'national government' in the face of continued English occupation. What becomes immediately apparent is the predominantly ecclesiastical nature of the buildings utilised – parish churches, convents and major monasteries – no doubt a consequence of the particular demands for space raised by such assemblies: it was the hall-like – basilican – qualities of such buildings which suited them to the needs of parliaments. The spiritual nature of such buildings, however, and our post-Reformation perceptions of the separation of church and state, should not obscure the fact that medieval churches fulfilled a broad range of secular roles, including as venues for the settlement of legal contracts. Parish churches, for example, may have served regularly as the meeting-places of sheriff courts after the destruction of many of the old royal castles in the main burghs, as in the case of St Mary's at Hawick in 1342.[67] Presumably, such worldly meetings took place in the nave, away from the spiritual focus in the sanctuary. As discussed above, churches, too, functioned as private meeting-places, the most infamous incidence of this being the confrontation between Robert Bruce and John Comyn in the church of the Greyfriars at Dumfries, which began in the cloister and reached its bloody climax in the chancel before the high altar.[68] Even in the later fifteenth century, churches continued to function as places of secular, political assembly, as occurred at Lauder in 1482 when the disaffected nobility plotted their overthrow of James III's unpopular governmental clique.[69] The regular use of such buildings for parliamentary assemblies, therefore, represented only a development of an already well-established rôle as venues for solemn but otherwise non-religious business.

In most cases there appears to have been a conscious effort to maintain a royal association, either through the holding of the parliament or council in one of the royal burghs free from enemy control, or through meeting at a monastery or church with strong royal or national/patriotic associations, for example Scone or St Andrews. What started as a contingency measure, however, gained the force of tradition in the six decades of intermittent war and partial conquest which extended down to 1357, and ecclesiastical locations remained the most favoured venues for meetings of parliaments or councils until the assassination of James I at Blackfriars in Perth in 1437. Although the use of churches can be written off as an *ad hoc* arrangement which filled the void created by the destruction of the traditional venues, it can also be seen as a direct consequence of the key position held in Scottish government after 1296 by the senior clergy, most notably bishops Wishart, Lamberton and Moray, and the regular traffic with the papacy which formed the centrepiece of Scottish diplomatic initiatives on the continent. Guided by churchmen operating with the papal courts, firstly at Rome and subsequently at Avignon, firmly in mind, and with the experience of both the provincial councils of the Scottish church and the reforming councils of the church in general behind them, clerical precedent may have prevailed.

The trend was established in August 1299 when the gathering of the leading figures in the national cause was used as an opportunity for the holding of a council. In the course of a major raid against English garrison-posts south of the Forth, the Scots held a council at Peebles, the only royal burgh in the region at that time free from enemy occupation.[70] Where in the burgh this meeting was held is unknown, the old royal castle there vanishes from the documentary record earlier in the thirteenth century, but it is probable that either the parish church or the buildings of the Trinitarian friars' convent – the so-called Cross Kirk – outwith the town was the venue.

The growing confidence of the Scots saw a parliament being held in May 1300 at Rutherglen.[71] The selection of this minor western royal burgh as the meeting-place for parliament appears odd, but its strategic location at the head of the Clydesdale routes into the Borders suggests that it, like Peebles, was chosen with a view to following up the assembly with a raid against English garrisons in the south. Here, however, the early royal castle had survived in a functional state and was to become the base for an English garrison after 1304.[72] If the 1300 parliament did not meet there, the most likely alternative is the parish church of St Mary, of which only a fragment of the medieval building remains, but nineteenth-century descriptions of which suggest was over 31.5m long with a broad, aisled nave which could amply accommodate the assembly.[73]

A parliament at Scone in February 1302, at the peak of Scottish successes in the struggle with Edward I and symbolising confidence in the imminent return of King John from his enforced exile, was the last meeting of an independent Scottish parliament until 1309, but in March 1304 Edward I convened a meeting at St Andrews to ratify the surrender terms agreed with the Comyns.[74] It was at St Andrews, too, that Robert I held his first parliament in March 1309, in which a large body of the magnates and chief clergy of the kingdom declared their loyalty to the king, and where the clergy backed a defiant declaration of right in the name of Scottish sovereignty and of Robert Bruce's rights to the throne.[75] Attendance at this highly significant parliament was impressive: seven bishops or their representatives, the abbots and priors of the major monasteries, three earls, representatives of five earldoms whose heirs were minors in ward, representatives of the communities of three more earldoms, seventeen lords, together with 'the barons of all Argyll and the Hebrides' and 'the inhabitants of the whole realm of Scotland acknowledging allegiance to Robert king of Scotland'.[76] Where in St Andrews so large an assembly could meet at this time is open to question. The bishop's castle is a possibility, but a meeting either in the cathedral church or in the buildings of the adjacent Augustinian priory would seem more likely. In the latter, the formal meeting-room of the canons – the chapter-house – was enlarged in the late 1310s, but in 1309 it would have been too cramped to accommodate such a prestigious assembly, even if they were all standing.[77] Instead, the large halls of the prior's house, monastic refectory or guest-house may have been used.

The strongly ecclesiastical character of most of the assembly places for parliaments and councils was maintained for the remainder of Robert I's reign. Councils were held at Arbroath Abbey in 1315 and Newbattle Abbey in March 1320, on which latter occasion the Declaration of Arbroath was probably planned, but it was the major monasteries of Cambuskenneth, Holyrood and Scone which predominated. Cambuskenneth, where parliament assembled in November 1314, was evidently utilised on account of its proximity to Stirling, where the castle had been razed following its surrender to the Scots after Bannockburn. The situation in respect of Holyrood and Edinburgh Castle, which had been destroyed following its recapture in March 1314, is identical. For Scone, however, although proximity to the old royal centre at Perth may have been important, there appears to have been a greater symbolism in the choice of site – the inaugu-

ration church of the kings of Scots – and the abbey emerged in the period down to 1373 as the most regular meeting-place for parliaments and councils. The parallel with Westminster, where the traditional meeting-place of English parliaments and the coronation site of English kings in the Benedictine abbey were contiguous, is quite striking. However, considering the intene hostility between the two kingdoms after 1296, it is perhaps unlikely that Robert saw Westminster as a direct model for emulation.

There may be some significance in the fact that these three abbeys, together with St Andrews, were Augustinian communities, members of an order noted for their hospitality. The parliaments of 1314 and 1326 at Cambuskenneth, of 1317, 1318, 1320, 1323 and 1325 at Scone, and of 1316, 1321 and 1328 at Edinburgh – which were probably all held in Holyrood – were all of particular importance and were well attended. These Augustinian abbeys, presumably, were well-placed to provide suitable accommodation for the large numbers attending these assemblies, although their hospitality must have been strained to the limit. This was evidently the case at Scone in 1390, where major damage was inflicted on the abbey's property by those attending the coronation and first parliament of Robert III.[78]

Suitable living quarters for the chief figures at these meetings were probably provided within the monastic complexes. The king, certainly, can be assumed to have taken over the abbots' lodgings, which would have been the most comfortable available within the abbeys. Where, however, the actual parliaments met within the precincts is less certain. In England, Henry III rebuilt the chapter-house of Westminster Abbey as a splendid octagonal chamber on a grander scale than would have been required by the monks, with the apparent intention that it should serve as a council chamber for meetings of parliament, and it functioned through the later Middle Ages as the usual meeting-place of the Commons. Nothing remains of the abbey buildings at Scone to give any impression of the architectural sophistication of the complex or the scale of the structures in which the parliaments may have met, save for a few sculptural fragments.[79] The records of Robert II's first parliament of March 1371, however, speak of business being conducted there in the king's 'privy chamber in his privy council and afterwards in public in his parliament chamber'.[80] These are unlikely to have been specialist chambers reserved exclusively for such occasions, but would rather

1.3. Aerial view of Cambuskenneth Abbey, site of the 1314 and 1326 parliaments. (RCAHMS A64963)

have been parts of the abbey complex taken over for the king's use. Little of Cambuskenneth, other than its thirteenth-century detached bell-tower, has survived above the lowest masonry courses, but these show that the chapter-house never expanded beyond its early thirteenth-century form of a vaulted room some 21 feet (6.7m) square. The most likely venue here, if not the nave of the abbey church, would have been the refectory, which occupied the south range of the cloister. This was a large chamber, approximately 6m by 20m in dimensions, and could have accommodated such a major assembly as the 1314 parliament.[81] At Holyrood, the substantial monastic refectory in the south cloister range, which survived into the later sixteenth century following conversion into a great hall for the adjoining royal palace, raises the probability that it was the domestic complex, as at Bury St Edmunds, which housed parliaments.[82] There are also fragmentary traces of a large late thirteenth-century octagonal chapter-house nearly 40 feet (12.2m) in diameter with a stone vault carried on a central column, which could have accommodated the meetings of Robert I's parliaments, here following the lines of Henry III's Westminster.[83] Some impression of the appearance of this sophisticated chamber can be obtained from the surviving example of this type in Scotland at Elgin Cathedral.[84] The scale of some of the assemblies, however, suggests that often it may have been in the abbey churches that the formal sessions were held, the architectural splendour of the setting lending additional dignity to what were meetings of national importance.

The meeting-places of the remaining recorded parliaments and assemblies of Robert I's reign, at Inchture in 1312 and Ayr in 1312 and 1315, were dictated by the realities of the moment. In early 1312 the Scots had been besieging Dundee, the last significant English garrison beyond Perth, and, probably in late February, its garrison seems to have negotiated an agreed surrender by a fixed date unless relieved. The parliament of early April 1312 at Inchture, therefore, appears to have been arranged to coincide with the handing over of the burgh. It is perhaps significant in this context that one of the main pieces of business discussed there concerned the military demands of the crown upon the burghs.[85] While Inchture itself lies some 7.5 miles (12km) west of Dundee, the bishop of St Andrews' hall there may have been the only suitably large building remaining in the vicinity of the burgh. Inchture was an ancient property of the bishops and the location of one of their more important country residences.[86] No structural remains survive, but the cropmark traces of what may have been the medieval manorial complex have been detected near the present village.

The Ayr parliament of 1312 and assembly of 1315 were both summoned in connection with military campaigns. In the second half of 1312, in addition to a major raid into northern England, King Robert and his brother, Edward, campaigned in south-western Scotland.[87] Ayr, close to the Bruce heartland in Carrick, probably served as a base of operations in this offensive. Its castle had fallen to the Scots and been dismantled shortly after its last appearance in English records in December 1309.[88] It is likely, therefore, that the 1312 parliament, like that of April 1315 which settled the issue of the royal succession and agreed to Edward Bruce's planned invasion of Ireland, met in the parish church of St John in the burgh.[89] Of this large thirteenth-century church only the western tower survived incorporation into and the subsequent demolition of the Cromwellian citadel, but the remains indicate the existence of an aisled nave in which the parliament could have been accommodated.

The largely ecclesiastical character of the meeting-places for parliaments and councils was maintained for the remainder of the fourteenth century. The abbey at Scone preserved the dominant position it had established under Robert I and was, indeed, to secure a place as the nearest equivalent in Scotland to Westminster in England. After the parliament and coronation here in November 1331 of the child-king, David II, the invasion of the kingdom in 1332 by Edward Balliol and the re-opening in 1333 of both civil war and war with England brought an end to the regular holding of parliaments until 1357, when David was freed from English captivity.[90] As in the first phase of the Wars of Independence, such assemblies as were held down to 1357 were naturally located in those parts of the kingdom which had been recovered from English domination.

The last council or parliament before the re-opening of the wars of Scottish independence assembled at Perth on 2 August 1332, its business to select a new guardian to replace Thomas Randolph, earl of Moray, who had died on 20 July. Its nominee, Donald, earl of Mar, survived only nine days in office, dying with the cream of the Scottish army in the slaughter at Dupplin. The victor of Dupplin, Edward Balliol, held only two parliaments before his grip on Scotland was

broken and he became dependent on English support. The first, held immediately after his coronation at Scone on 24 September 1332, was sparsely attended, with only the prelates and nobility of the areas closest to his base in Perth, which had submitted to him following his victory, present to augment the ranks of the so-called Disinherited Lords, the heirs of men forfeited by Robert Bruce, who had accompanied him to Scotland.[91] His second parliament, at Holyrood in February 1334, was just as poorly attended.[92]

After the crushing defeats of Dupplin in 1332 and Halidon Hill in 1333, it was not until April 1335, when the tide of the war was again running in their favour, that the supporters of David II held a parliament. With Scone effectively controlled by the English garrison of Perth, and with most other major centres still in Balliol's hands, this was held at Dairsie in Fife,[93] a venue decided by the presence of the Scottish leadership at the siege of nearby Cupar, to which they returned in December 1335 following the battle of Culblean.[94] As with Inchture in 1312, it was probably the existence at Dairsie of one of the country residences of the bishops of St.Andrews, the remains of which may be incorporated in the largely late sixteenth-century castle on the site, or the adjacent parish church, which determined its choice as venue.

The Dairsie parliament was followed in spring 1336 by a larger assembly of the magnates at Dunfermline, which elected Sir Andrew de Moray as Guardian.[95] At that date, Dunfermline was one of the few

OPPOSITE TOP.
1.4. Scone Palace, view of entrance facade, 1775 (drawn by A Rutherford). (RCAHMS B10588)

OPPOSITE BELOW.
1.5. Undated drawing of Blackfriars Monastery, Perth. (S Cowan, The *Ancient Capital of Scotland*, London, 1904, 100)

LEFT.
1.6. St Mary's Chapel, off High Street, Perth (the site of the old 'Parliament Hall'); undated drawing. The key to the picture includes the following: (1) window of the old 'Parliament Hall'; (3) windows of the room where the Lords of the Articles sat. (S Cowan, The *Ancient Capital of Scotland*, London, 1904, volume 1, 80)

major abbeys in the kingdom outwith the regional domination of a local English garrison. Not only did it hold strong royal associations as a place of burial, but it also possessed a magnificent complex of recently completed monastic buildings, including a substantial guest range and spacious refectory hall which could have comfortably accommodated such a meeting.[96] The next recorded parliament assembled on 24 October 1339 at Perth which, until its surrender on 17 August, had been the last English stronghold north of the Forth and had served for a while as the centre of Edward Balliol's government of Scotland.[97] The defences of the town had been levelled after its surrender and the countryside around was reportedly so devastated by the activities of both the besieging Scots and the English garrison that supplies could scarcely be found. Indeed, one burgess is said to have resorted to cannibalism.[98] Amidst such devastation, Scone was clearly in no position to host a parliamentary assembly and had, presumably, been thoroughly ransacked. Perth can have been in little better condition, but it was the nearest major royal centre then in Scottish hands to the war zone south of the Forth, and the parliament which assembled here formalised plans for the continuation of the offensive with the siege of Stirling.[99]

Parliament and council remained without fixed venues over the next few years as the Scots consolidated their grip on the lands south of the Forth. Dundee was the venue for meetings in 1340 and 1347 and Aberdeen in 1342. At both, the royal castles had never been reconstructed following their destruction in the earlier wars, but Dundee's large Franciscan convent – Greyfriars – had established a role in the early fourteenth century as meeting-place for church councils and may have fulfilled a similar role for parliament.[100] A similar function may have been performed by the Dominican friary at Aberdeen, which occupied a fairly central position in the burgh in the area known as the Green, although the episcopal palace, adjacent to the cathedral in Old Aberdeen, is a strong contender as an alternative location.[101] By the end of the period, however, it was Scone which had re-established its dominant position as the principal meeting-place of parliaments, with both a council and a full parliament assembling there in 1352. After a lull of nearly 22 largely war-scarred years, for much of which time the abbey had lain in the principal war zone, the release in October 1357 of David II from captivity in England saw Scone restored to the position which it had held under Robert I.

RESTORING TRADITION, 1357–1437

David II's summoning of his first parliament after his release from 11 years of enforced exile was highly symbolic, marking the return of kingly authority to a land in which 'good peace' and government was regarded as having failed in the intervening years.[102] It was presumably no arbitrary decision which led him to hold his council at Scone, the site which his father had all but established as the usual meeting-place for such assemblies. During the mid-fourteenth century, the growing French cultural influence over Scotland was largely responsible for the adoption of the 'three estates' model of parliament; the Scots still to some extent also looked to the English parliamentary model as an exemplar, despite its bicameral arrangement. For the remainder of David's reign, Scone maintained its dominant position, with five out of the eight parliaments summoned between 1364 and 1370 held at the abbey. The remaining three parliaments, however, were held at Perth, presaging the emergence of the burgh in this rôle in the early fifteenth century. For the first of these meetings, in January 1364, parliament assembled in the burgh's Dominican convent, the possible venue for earlier gatherings in 1339 and 1357, and probably used again in the parliaments of 1369 and 1370.[103] The convent was one of the largest and wealthiest Dominican communities in Scotland, and its extensive complex of buildings – including the evidently purpose-built king's house or palace[104] – on the northern edge of the burgh overlooking the North Inch, came to serve as a frequent and favoured residence of the early Stewart kings down to the assassination there in 1437 of James I.[105]

The death of David II did not see an easy transfer of power to his nephew and heir presumptive, Robert the Steward. Soon after the king's death, 'the three estates of the realm met in the royal town of Linlithgow', where some dispute took place over the succession.[106] This meeting lacked both royal authority to assemble and the kingly figure as its focus, but the unexpected death of the king necessitated less formal arrangements. There was, moreover, the precedent of such deliberation in the crisis years after 1286. Where in Linlithgow such a body gathered is open to question. There was a royal residence here under the early Stewarts, destroyed by fire in 1424.[107] This may have served as a meeting-place, but it is perhaps more likely that old St Michael's Church, also destroyed in the fire of 1424, provided the most convenient venue.

The emergency circumstances of 1371–2 were followed by what appeared at first to be continuity of practice, with Scone serving as the venue for the new king, Robert II's, first two parliaments, in March 1372 following his coronation and again in March 1373. After 1373, however, as the new Stewart régime bedded itself into the structure of power within the kingdom, the practice of annual or near-annual parliaments which had been introduced by David was abandoned. Few parliaments were summoned between 1373 and 1389 – that at Scone in October 1378 is the only one recorded – with great councils or councils general (a meeting of the Three Estates, but with smaller membership and less formal procedures, and lacking parliament's judicial rôle) instead serving as the primary forum for discussion and criticism of government policies.[108] Even with these, however, there are no records of meetings until September 1384 when the council gathered in Glasgow.[109] Council-meetings were more regular thereafter, serving as the means of legitimising the *coups* through which first Robert II's eldest son John, earl of Carrick – the future Robert III – and then his second son, Robert, earl of Fife, later duke of Albany, seized executive power from their father. The location of these councils, moreover, demonstrated a decisive shift in the *locus* of political power in Scotland, all of them being held south of the Forth, primarily in Edinburgh.[110] It was in a council at Holyrood Abbey in November 1384 that Carrick secured his position as guardian of the kingdom,[111] while a council held at Edinburgh in December 1388 stripped him of that office and handed it instead to Fife.[112]

For most of the following 30 years, the earl of Fife controlled or dominated the government of Scotland. That control was marked by a shift once again in the main centres of government away from the country south of the Forth, which was the sphere of influence of the earl of Douglas, to Fife's own heartland of power in Stirling and Perthshire. The parliament of March 1389, summoned originally to Scone, was continued in April at Holyrood, the last occasion for ten years that such a gathering met outwith Fife's political power-base.[113] Apart from one council in 1397, which met at Stirling, it was to Perth that the Guardian summoned almost every other meeting during the period of his domination. This centrality, and the position of the Blackfriars within it, is exemplified by its function as the location for the formal submission of Alexander Stewart, earl of Buchan, better known as the 'Wolf of Badenoch', younger brother of Robert III and

Fife, following his infamous burning of Elgin Cathedral in June 1390. Buchan made his submission before his brothers and an important cross-section of the political community at a stage-managed ceremony at the gates of the friary and again before the high altar in the church.[114]

The settings for most parliaments and councils of the period 1373–1406 are unknown. Other than those occasions when the venue was Scone or Holyrood, where the abbeys continued in their earlier fourteenth-century rôle, the locations in which meetings assembled are couched in general and often ambiguous terms,' usually simply naming the burgh in which they were held, for example, Edinburgh, Glasgow, Linlithgow, Perth or Stirling. Edinburgh appears on occasion to have been used as shorthand for Holyrood, which was described as 'the monastery of Holyrood of Edinburgh' in 1389.[115] Holyrood, however, was supplanted by the tolbooth of Edinburgh in the fifteenth century. This became the most regular meeting-place for Scottish parliaments from the reign of James II (1437–60), but may have served in a similar rôle from an earlier date. It was Perth, however, which could claim to have served in the late fourteenth and early fifteenth centuries as the nearest Scotland had to a fixed seat of legislative government.

Fife's monopoly on the exercise of royal power by virtue of his office as lieutenant for his incapacitated brother, Robert III, and from 1406 until his death in 1420 as Governor of the kingdom for his captive nephew, James I, saw the effective settlement of the meeting-place for parliaments and councils in the heart of his region of personal domination at Perth. Throughout this period, and continuing under James I after his release from England in 1424, Perth Blackfriars emerged as the replacement for Scone as both a royal residence and venue for political assemblies. It was in Perth, too, that the provincial council of the church appears to have most regularly assembled between the thirteenth and fifteenth centuries, presumably in recognition of both its significance in secular politics and its central location within Scotland.[116] The convent-church itself housed the full parliamentary sessions. In a general council held there in October 1433, James I is described as sitting 'in front of the high altar in the choir of the church' in the presence of the prelates and magnates of the kingdom.[117] This suggests that the friars' choir-stalls were occupied by the principal members of the council and that it was standard practice for the assembled members to sit facing each other 'across the floor of the house' in what appears to have been the standard European format, typified by the English Westminster parliament. [118] The friars' convent was ransacked by a Protestant mob in 1559 and its abandoned buildings were subsequently plundered for stone, leaving no upstanding remains.

Administrative business spilled beyond the convent precinct and the adjacent royal residence. As early as March 1408, the governor and members of his council met in the chapel of St Mary at the east end of Perth's High Street to receive resignations of property rights,[119] while in March 1415 a subsidiary tribunal gathered in this same 'chapel [of St Mary] next to the great bridge of Perth, in the name and on behalf of the Three Estates of the kingdom of Scotland then assembled and the council general meeting in the house of the Friars Preachers [Dominicans] of the said burgh'.[120] After the Reformation in 1560, the site was acquired by the burgh and portions of the medieval chapel were incorporated into a new tolbooth. This survived in a much-altered and expanded state until the later nineteenth century; a sixteenth-century stone building on the site was excavated in 1975–7, prior to construction of the present Marks & Spencer store.[121] The use of this chapel for parliamentary business presumably had more to do with requirements of space and the hall-like qualities of the building than with any spiritual significance in the business under discussion. St Mary's most regular administrative role, however, was as the meeting-place for Exchequer audits. Audits from the end of the reign of Robert I had been held for the most part at Scone, further emphasising the Westminster-like role for the abbey which that king had established, but when regular records of audits resume in 1359–60, Perth emerges rapidly as one of the principal meeting-places for exchequer business. Annually from 1365 to 1372 and sporadically thereafter, repairs to an unnamed chapel in which the exchequer met, evidently St Mary's, are recorded.[122] This role continued throughout the period of Fife's governorship: all audits held from 1406 to 1422 were heard in Perth. In 1406, the auditors evidently complained about the condition of the' building, for the Governor granted them 14s 10d for the repair of the chapel windows, and further repair work associated with audits was carried out in 1414 and 1416.[123] By the 1430s, Perth was bidding fair to become the permanent seat of the Scottish parliament, having housed 15 out of 19 parliaments and councils held between 1406 and 1437. Indeed, the special significance attached to the burgh by the king is

further emphasised by the unsuccessful royal petition to the pope that the University of St Andrews, which James wished to remove from the influence of the bishop, should be relocated to Perth.[124] In February 1437, however, James I was murdered in his lodgings at the Blackfriars. Perth's near monopoly as the meeting-place of parliament and incipient 'capital city' died with the king.

THE ROYAL HALL

1.7. James I with his Parliament, soon after his return to Scotland in 1424; woodcut from Holinshed's *Chronicles* (1577). (British Museum)

Although the reign of James I presents an image of conservatism and adherence to tradition in the use of the Dominican friars' convent at Perth as the most usual venue for parliaments, it was in other ways a quite revolutionary period in the development and function of government and the projection of monarchical power, in many ways harking back to the style of kingship practised by David II after 1357. Like David, James's first-hand experience of the workings of English royal government and his familiarity with both English and French seats of power had a profound effect on his vision for reconstructed royal authority in Scotland. Furthermore, both were men determined to set the crown firmly at the heart of the political life of the kingdom and to elevate it securely above the level of the magnates. For both, this involved the political emasculation of the aristocratic governing *élite* and the building of a wholly new apparatus of administration and government. It also required physical projection which would underscore the psychology of the new régimes. For David II this was made manifest in the massive tower-house which he built on the summit of the castle rock at Edinburgh, a fittingly militaristic symbol for a king whose domination of his nobility was achieved through military superiority. James, however, demonstrated the power of his new régime through quite different architecture in a structure loaded with political symbolism, the Palace of Linlithgow.[125] Here we see the first tentative uses of classical symbolism to celebrate Scottish royal and governmental power – a trend which would eventually culminate in the vast range of classically-expressed civic and national imagery of the nineteenth and twentieth centuries.

The remodelling of the old royal residence at Linlithgow began in 1425, but from 1428 the scale of expenditure on the royal works there suggests that the operation was nothing short of building from scratch. The structure which emerged over the next six years was something radically new, reflected in its description from 1429 as a 'palace', a wholly new term in the Scottish vocabulary of power.[126] Unlike David II, James chose not to project his authority through fortress-like architecture, adopting instead a relatively unfortified style which drew heavily on the classicism of early Italian Renaissance and French designs. Although primarily residential, the palace was monumental in scale and had as its focus a vast hall which filled almost the whole of what became the east quarter of the quadrangular complex developed by his successors. At the time of its completion, this hall was probably the largest such structure in the kingdom, which begs the question of its intended role. It was loaded with visual symbolism. The statues over the courtyard mouth of the gate pend depict the three main orders in medieval society, namely the nobles, clergy and labourers (groupings not quite corresponding to the parliamentary estates); and above the main entrance is a massive representation of the royal arms and crown supported by angels. These suggest strongly that James may have intended this hall to act as a venue for more than just ceremonial feasting or as a stage set on which to parade his exalted ideals of monarchy. Any plans for a more formal rôle, however, were stillborn, dying with James in 1437.

As we have seen, halls had been a central element in the traditional architectural vocabulary of royal power through the twelfth and thirteenth centuries. It was the loss of these formal ceremonial chambers to the Scottish crown after 1296, first through enemy occupation then through physical destruction, which had resulted in the shift to primarily ecclesiastical settings for national political assemblies. Although Robert I constructed a new royal hall at the heart of his 'retirement home' at Cardross in Dunbartonshire, and a hall was evidently a major component of the complex initiated by David II and completed under Robert II at Edinburgh, neither was intended to serve as anything other than a setting for displays of royalty by the Bruce kings, for whom Scone functioned as the parliamentary *locus*.[127] Provision of such formal secular settings was not a priority for Robert II, Robert III or Albany, but James I may have had just such a function in mind when he began the redevelopment of Linlithgow. The arrangements which emerged under his son and successors, however, were decidedly less grandiose.

While the evidence from royal buildings remains ambiguous, the deliberate provision of a hall as the meeting-place of councils and assemblies can be seen clearly in one highly significant non-royal instance: the Lordship of the Isles. At Finlaggan on Islay, the seat from the thirteenth century of the Clan Donald segment of the descendants of Somerled, lord of Argyll, the fourteenth and fifteenth centuries saw major redevelopment of the old stronghold under the powerful MacDonald Lords of the Isles. The Lordship has been presented in the past as a rival political force within Scotland to the Lowland, east-coast-based monarchy, a view given added strength by the evident cultural cleavage between the intensely Gaelic West Highlands and Islands and the more anglicised society of the Lowlands. The political pretensions of the Lords were further emphasised by the elaborate quasi-regal inauguration ritual which each underwent on his succession.[128] While clearly having its origins in Gaelic Irish king-making rituals, there are also close parallels with the pre-1329 Scottish

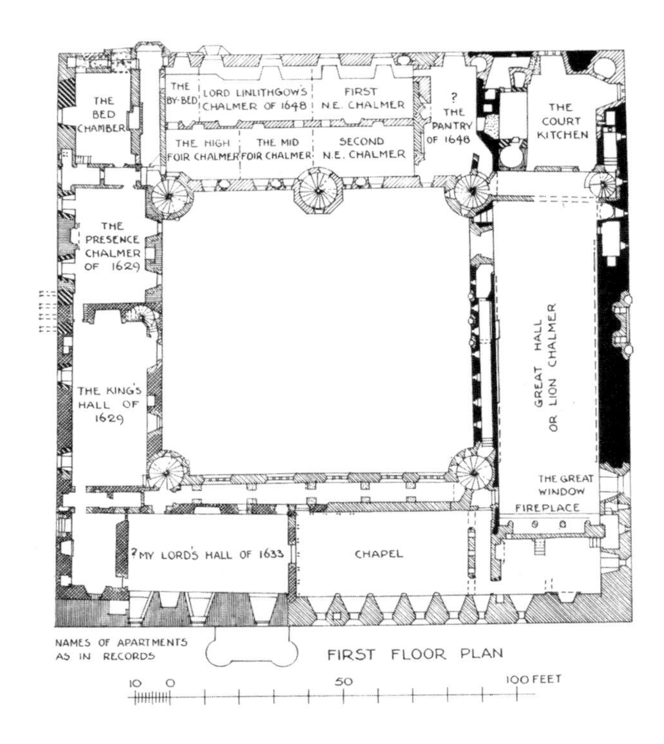
THE BED CHAMBER
THE BY-BED
LORD LINLITHGOW'S CHALMER OF 1648
FIRST N.E. CHALMER
? THE PANTRY OF 1648
THE COURT KITCHEN
THE HIGH FOIR CHALMER
THE MID FOIR CHALMER
SECOND N.E. CHALMER
THE PRESENCE CHALMER OF 1629
THE KING'S HALL OF 1629
GREAT HALL OR LION CHALMER
THE GREAT WINDOW
FIREPLACE
? MY LORD'S HALL OF 1633
CHAPEL
NAMES OF APARTMENTS AS IN RECORDS
FIRST FLOOR PLAN
10 0 50 100 FEET

ceremony. It is perhaps no coincidence, then, that the inauguration site at Finlaggan developed the dual inaugural and assembly function displayed at Scone, particularly so since Scone's dominance as the king-making and parliamentary seat was strongest during the period of consolidation of MacDonald power under the first Lord of the Isles, John (1336–87).

The seat of lordship at Finlaggan occupied two islands in a shallow loch. The larger, Eilean Mòr, contained a substantial complex of structures and evidently comprised the principal residential and industrial element of the site. The smaller island, Eilean na Comhairle (the Council Island), appears to have been the site of the original late twelfth- and thirteenth-century fortress, which was swept away and replaced in the fourteenth century by a non-defensive complex comprising three buildings. The largest of these has been interpreted as the residence of the keeper of the Council Island and dates from the period 1420–75, with the smallest serving as its store-house. The remaining building, a well-built rectangular structure measuring approximately 7m by 3.5m internally, thus appears to have housed the chamber from which the island took its name.[129] It was probably here, too, rather than in the great hall or chapel on Eilean Mòr, that the inauguration ceremony described in the sixteenth century took place. Although of good construction, it can hardly have been an imposing edifice, but since the Council of the Islands which gathered there numbered usually only some 14–16 members, it would have provided ample accommodation.[130] Despite its lack of architectural pretensions, the council chamber possessed a symbolic significance as a ritual and political focus for much of Gaelic Scotland. As a consequence of that, when the Lordship of the Isles was forcibly suppressed by James IV in 1493 the buildings on Eilean na Comhairle were carefully levelled and the site given over to cultivation.

In its functions, the Council of the Isles was both a judicial and an advisory body. The Council was described in sixteenth-century accounts as 'the supreme court of appeal in the lordship of the Isles', but there is little surviving documentary evidence to show it active in this rôle.[131] Archdeacon Monro, writing in the 1540s, commented that it 'decernit, decreitit and gave suits furth upon all debaitable matters according to the laws of Renald McSomharkle', in essence that it administered a law code attributed to Ranald son of Somerled, the late twelfth-century lord of Argyll.[132] Nowhere is it claimed that the

TOP.
1.8. Linlithgow Palace, first-floor plan, with Great Hall at right. (RCAHMS)

BOTTOM.
1.9. Linlithgow Palace, 1983 aerial view, with Great Hall at left. (RCAHMS WL/3937)

Council exercised any rôle as a legislative assembly. There is a good body of charter evidence, however, which shows it acting in an advisory capacity.[133] Here, important land grants, grants of key offices and the disposition of marriages appear to have strengthened by their arrangement through the counsel and advice of this body. In these two areas of competence, the Council of the Isles shared the characteristics of magnate councils – where they can be identified – elsewhere in the kingdom. Such functions were features of parliamentary business, too, but here the comparison ends. So far as can be ascertained, the Lords of the Isles did not seek formal advice on foreign alliances and negotiations: the 1462 Treaty of Ardtornish-Westminster, for example, was a private arrangement settled between John, Lord of the Isles, and the English crown. Essentially, the council's sphere of competence was restricted to internal matters, and even then of a primarily domestic nature.

THE EMERGENCE OF THE CAPITAL: HOUSE OF THE MAGISTRATES

A major consequence of the assassination of James I at Perth was the final shift of the seats of Scottish royal government to the country south of the Forth. It was here that the principal royal fortresses – Stirling and Edinburgh – were located, and where the dominant figures in national political and economic life had their main centres of power. This centralisation and urbanisation of political power was a general trend across Europe during the late Middle Ages. Overwhelmingly, it was Edinburgh, the wealthiest and most populous of Scotland's burghs, that acted as a political centre of gravity and became swiftly in real terms the kingdom's 'capital'. The castle, which had been redeveloped under David II as the principal royal residence, became a true seat of royal government, with both the royal archives and treasury based there and with key officials provided with accommodation within its walls. This, however, was as far as its rôle went for, contrary to nineteenth-century traditions, it did not serve as the venue for parliaments despite its possession of one of the larger royal halls.[134] From the reign of James II to James IV, the principal function of the great hall at Edinburgh was as a venue for court ceremonial, in particular for the formal banqueting which was a major feature of the great occasions of state. It was evidently in the castle that the nobility assembled, as in 1438 for the coronation of the young king when they processed down the hill to Holyrood and to which they presumably returned for the celebratory feast. Certainly, repairs in 1457–8, described as being undertaken 'on account of parliament', were not carried out in advance of any meeting of that body in the hall: the only parliament which assembled in that period, commencing 6 March 1458, met in the tolbooth.[135] Rather, it would seem that the hall was being prepared to accommodate the enlarged court which was the inevitable accompaniment to the congregation of the kingdom's political classes. We may already be witnessing the development of processual ceremonial of the kind later seen in the 'Riding of Parliament' (see Chapter 2).

The trauma of the murder of King James I in his own house at Perth had a profound impact on Scottish government. With the assassins still at large, the queen and her six-year-old son, now King James II, moved south to the relative security of Edinburgh and Stirling. So unsafe was Perth felt to be that the decision was made to shift the coronation from Scone, where all Scottish kings had been enthroned since the formation of the kingdom, to Holyrood, under the watchful eye of the royal castle. It was there that the new government and the loyal lords gathered, and on 25 March 1438 they processed from the castle to the abbey for the coronation, then assembled for a parliament which initiated proceedings against the assassins and their abettors.[136] The shift in the place of coronation from Scone to Holyrood may only have been regarded as a temporary expedient, but the circumstances of the successions of James II's descendants ensured that Scone's exclusive traditional role was ended.[137] The consequent effect of this transplanting of the king-making process was the ending of the formal link of the abbey with parliament and its business, a severance which had at its roots a continuing question mark over the security of Perth as a meeting-place.

Something more profound was taking place, however, albeit perhaps unconsciously. The break with Scone and with Perth Blackfriars marked a watershed in the development of the Scottish parliament, for it resulted in a more general ending of the role of church buildings as the meeting-places of secular assemblies. This may have been a reflection of the growing continental influence in

Scotland. In Europe, many legislative assemblies by this date tended to meet in secular, if not specialist, venues. Throughout France, for example, the regional Estates met in the great halls – *Salles des Etats* – within the walls of the chief royal or ducal castles, a position with which many of the leading figures in Scottish government would have been personally acquainted.[138] Contemporaneously, within the Burgundian territories in the Netherlands, Duke Philip the Good (1419–67) developed specialist administrative centres for his far-flung domains at Brussels, Ghent and The Hague, building on his grandfather's provision of a single such centre at Lille. The nuclei of these administrative centres were a *chambre de conseil* and a *chambre des comptes*, combining the legislative and financial functions on a single site.[139] Possible venues of this form existed within Scotland from the second half of the fourteenth century. There are, indeed, parallels in the use of Perth Blackfriars for parliaments and the nearby chapel of St Mary for exchequer audits, while James I's building work at Linlithgow Palace and Edinburgh Castle appeared to provide almost purpose-built settings with just such a rôle in mind. For some unknown reason, however, such formal settings were rejected as natural venues, and that despite the key players in the years of minority government after 1437, Sir William Crichton and Sir Alexander Livingston, controlling the castles of Edinburgh and Stirling respectively: neither stronghold emerged as a replacement for Perth. Scotland appears unique amongst the monarchies of fifteenth-century Europe in that it rejected the development of a specialist, formal and secular setting for its parliaments at the same point as it abandoned its traditional ecclesiastical settings. The reasons for this abandonment are not altogether clear, but may be a manifestation of a growing anti-clericalism in the fifteenth century, or may be in some way linked to the tensions between the papacy and the wider body of the church which had erupted into open warfare in the Council of Basel (1431–49). Many Scots played a leading role in the Conciliar movement or supported its views, including the key political figure in the kingdom at this time, James the Gross, 7th earl of Douglas, and it is possible that the influence of the reforming principles expressed in the initial stages at Basel contributed to a nascent desire to effect a clearer separation of spiritual and temporal authority. Whatever the cause of the break, it was abrupt and permanent.

After abandoning one manifestation of the basilican tradition in the churches, the expedient was adopted of housing meetings of parliaments or general councils in the civic expression of that tradition, the tolbooths of the kingdom's chief burghs, principally at Edinburgh, Stirling and Perth. These were, of course, distinctly secular buildings with already established judicial, legislative and fiscal roles as the seats of burgh government and (unlike royal palaces) open to citizens to give in petitions; we should remember that from the late fourteenth century, the commissioners sent by the royal burghs made up one of the estates of parliament. It may have been this status as *pretoria*, as they were labelled in Latin sources, meaning literally 'house of the magistrates' and identified with the attributes of coercive power, which singled them out as a potential location for parliament meetings. After the parish church, tolbooths were usually the largest public buildings in the medieval townscape, often dominating their burghs with tall towers, and contained a substantial hall in which the burghs' ruling councils met: a fuller account is contained in RCAHMS, *Tolbooths and Town Houses*, 1996. The move to hold parliaments in them may have been prompted by a reluctance on the part of many of the political community to place their persons in the hands of the wily and ambitious politicians who controlled the chief royal castles. Most likely, however, it was the result of a piece of opportunism on the part of the chief burgesses of Edinburgh, the largest and wealthiest urban community in Scotland, who, presumably recognising the economic and political advantages which would accrue from the regular basing of parliament in the heart of their town, and perhaps spurred by the obvious splendour of the civic administrations of Europe, offered their tolbooth to a distinctly shaken royal household. This was a distinctly Scottish response to a peculiarly Scottish problem. However, right across Europe in the following centuries, civic and national legislative architecture became intermingled to the point where one historian could argue that 'to the end of the seventeenth century, government buildings were . . . nearly all town halls'.

In November 1438, parliament assembled 'in pretorio' at Edinburgh.[140] A tolbooth is on record in the burgh by 1365, when David II granted the burgesses a plot of land near to the site of their old tolbooth for the construction of a new one.[141] This new building, which appears to have stood in a vennel off the High Street to the south-east of St Giles', had been constructed by 1368 but was burned during the sack of the town by the English in 1385.[142] Work on a replacement began in 1386, when Robert II granted the burgesses a new site on the north side of the market-place immediately to the north-west of the west front of St Giles'.[143] This survived, much altered in subsequent centuries, until its demolition in 1817, when Sir Walter Scott bought its main doorway and some late fifteenth- or early sixteenth-century architectural detailing for incorporation into his new house at Abbotsford.[144] Little evidence exists of its earlier fifteenth-century appearance. Most representations of the building postdate its replacement in 1561–2 by the New Tolbooth (which lay to its south within what is now Parliament Square), the demolition of its tower in October 1571 during the siege of Edinburgh,[145] the rebuilding of what was evidently the fourteenth-century western portion of the structure in 1610, and the subsequent conversion of the Old Tolbooth into a prison, the 'Heart of Midlothian'.[146]

The earliest surviving depiction, in a bird's-eye view of the town drawn by an English spy in 1544, is highly schematised; the draughtsman made no attempt to give an accurate architectural representation of the townscape and he places the tolbooth too far to the east, adjacent to the chancel of St Giles'.[147] The next oldest detailed image, James Gordon of Rothiemay's 1647 bird's-eye view of the burgh, postdates the replacement of the fourteenth-century work, but shows the eastern portion of the building, which was nearing completion in 1501.[148] Drawings and plans of the Old Tolbooth, made shortly before its demolition, show this eastern block to have been an elaborate design, its northern façade, which fronted the High Street, faced with ashlar and with richly decorated canopied and corbelled niches framing the windows on the first and second floors. Nasmyth's 1817 view of the Old Tolbooth from the south-west shows the south front of this block, with its main ogival-headed entrance-doorway in a projecting circular stair-tower at the south-east angle, set below a decorated niche and with a framed armorial panel over the first-floor window.[149] The fenestration and detailing suggest that its principal chambers were originally at first-floor level, presumably mirroring the arrangement in the older fourteenth-century block. It would have been within that older structure that parliament met, presumably in the main hall on the first floor.

There was clearly no intention in 1437–8 that Edinburgh should become the fixed seat of parliament. Where parliament was held still clearly depended on the location of the king, even when the king was a minor. In 1439, therefore, a general council was summoned to assemble in the tolbooth at Stirling, James II then being in the control of Sir Alexander Livingston, keeper of Stirling Castle. Nothing survives of this early tolbooth, the present structure occupying a site which was acquired for the burgh in only 1473.[150] In June 1445, parliament assembled in the tolbooth of Perth, which has likewise long vanished. This, however, was an expedient forced on the Douglases, who controlled the king's person at that time, for Edinburgh Castle, held by Sir William Crichton, was currently under siege. It may also have been linked to an attempt to declare the minority of the 15-year-old king at an end, possibly in some ceremony at Scone where James may have been required to take the coronation oaths which, as a six-year-old at Holyrood, he had been incompetent to perform.[151] Interestingly, however, it was still in the tolbooth rather than in the traditional assembly places at Scone Abbey or Blackfriars that the meeting was held, which shows that a conscious decision had been taken – by whom remains unknown – to break with past precedent and meet instead in secular, civic venues.

The Perth assembly of June 1445 was brief, parliament being continued to Edinburgh to receive the negotiated surrender of the castle. This marked the end of the peregrinations of the early years of the minority and, although James II held four further parliaments or councils outwith Edinburgh – two in the tolbooth of Perth and two in the tolbooth of Stirling – he held eleven within the town, which was now clearly viewed as the chief seat of Scottish royalty. But in August 1455, arrangements for the fitting-up of parliaments 'in ilk Burgh quhair Parliament or General Council sall be halden', were enacted, a wording which suggests that Edinburgh, where this legislation was passed, was still far from having monopoly status.[152]

The same act of the 1455 parliament, which is concerned mainly with the dress of the different ranks of nobles and burgess commissioners attending parliament, indicates that it was in the tolbooths of the various burghs that parliaments would convene. It gives, moreover, the first clear information on the physical layout of the assemblies, stating that in place of the 'Barre', that is, the barrier which separated the formal space of the meeting from an area near the door where non-members could be admitted to view the session or give evidence or information, there was to be a three-tiered, removeable seat on which the burgh commissioners would sit.[153] Presumably, there was already tiered seating for the noble and ecclesiastical estates, arranged in lines facing each other along the side walls of the hall. Such a face-to-face arrangement, often mistakenly seen in Britain as originating with 'Westminster tradition', was of course ultimately inspired by the classical precedent of the Roman Senate, which influenced so much of the architecture of European government in those years; but what was different now was the dominance of the king at one end of the chamber. He sat in the 'place Riale', the royal place or seat, which, like James I enthroned before the high altar in Blackfriars, would have provided a strongly directional focus for the assembly, very different from the more diffuse, oligarchic hierarchy of the Senate.[154] One late sixteenth-century account speaks of a board with a board-cloth set in front of the king and his chief advisers, presumably at which the clerks would have recorded the proceedings, and legal materials and documents would have been deposited.[155] It may have been on this table, too, that the crown, sceptre and sword, carried by three of the senior earls before the formal procession of the king, his parliamentary nobility, prelates and burgh commissioners, were set.[156] Although mostly in place only from the reign of James IV, and first mentioned in this context at the parliament of August 1524, it is probable that the presence of the regalia, by then clearly imbued with the symbolism which differentiated the abstract notion of monarchical authority from the physical person of the king, was regarded as an essential component in establishing the legitimacy and authority of the assembly, particularly when the king himself was either absent or in his nonage.[157] It was at this time that the Stewarts began to employ the imperial crown as a symbol of their authority.

The death of James II in 1460 was followed by a further shift in favour of Edinburgh. The parliaments and councils of James III's minority years all met in the tolbooth at Edinburgh, with the exception of a single meeting at Stirling in 1468. As a mature ruler, James III has been criticised for his supposed laziness and dislike of travel, which saw him rarely stir far beyond the confines of what was now indisputably the capital. This inertia may be more apparent than real, for it is based chiefly on the evidence of the place of issue of documents recorded in the *Register of the Great Seal*, with 707 out of a total of 712 enrolled between November 1469 and May 1488 emanating from Edinburgh.[158] What this more truly reflects is the more or less permanent settlement of the offices of government, particularly the writing-office, in Edinburgh Castle, as the scale of the royal administration expanded.[159] The castle had served as the main repository of the royal archive in the thirteenth century and again from the 1350s, and was the base from which the chapel, or royal writing office, operated. Clerks, if not the chancellor himself, however, had always accompanied the kings on their travels around the kingdom, to be on hand to deal with the recording of important business and to issue charters. This is very clear from any examination of the places of issue of charters of all Scottish kings before the fifteenth century, which shows a spread of locations around the kingdom with a few favoured royal residences predominating.[160] Government, however, became increasingly sophisticated from the later fourteenth century, with the evident development of a greater level of bureaucracy. This must have been particularly true during the reigns of James I after 1424 and, more particularly, James II after 1455, as a consequence of those kings' annexation of substantial lands to the crown with the forfeitures of the Albany Stewarts and the Black Douglases. Certainly, the volume of business passing through the chancellor's office increased massively in the course of the fifteenth century, serving to make this arm of government less mobile. As the executive became increasingly fixed in Edinburgh Castle, the case for continuing to move the legislature around the burghs of the kingdom must have proportionately weakened. Increasingly, too, nobles who wished to retain influence at court needed both a town house and a rural seat.

Like the writing-office and repository of the records, the Exchequer also gravitated towards Edinburgh in the aftermath of the assassination of James I at Perth. During the minority and reign of James II, most audits were seemingly held there, although Stirling put in a brief appearance. It was at Edinburgh that the first Exchequer of James III's reign was held, but in 1466 Linlithgow Palace was the venue for the audit from which the teenage James III was kidnapped by the Boyds; the palace was by then well provided with large chambers, in addition to the formal space of the great hall and the royal suites. After James III's assertion of his personal rule in 1469, followed by the effective settlement of royal government in Edinburgh, the castle there became the seat of Exchequer audits; the records, writing-office and treasury were likewise situated within what was effectively a royal administrative centre. At Falkland, building expenses for 1461–2 record repairs to the palace 'counthouse', while at Stirling, a 'compt house' is on record from 1531. Both these establishments probably functioned as the accounts office of the royal residence concerned, particularly when the household was in occupancy, rather than as the venue for full exchequer audits.

Under James IV, the position of Edinburgh as the seat of both legislature and executive was confirmed. Unlike his father, James was a prodigious traveller who undertook extensive annual forays around his kingdom. While charters continued to be issued from the various locations at which he based himself on these trips, from Tain to Whithorn, Loch Kilkerran (Campbeltown) to Coldingham, the vast majority emanated from the capital.[161] Furthermore, from 1489 – when a council met at Stirling – until 1513, all parliaments met in the tolbooth at Edinburgh. Indeed, through the sixteenth century it was only the threat of war or disease which forced parliament to assemble elsewhere than in the tolbooth at Edinburgh. Thus, in 1513, en route to the battle of Flodden, there was an assembly of the lords at Twizelhaugh, Northumberland, and after the battle, fearing an English invasion, a parliament met at Perth. In 1545 parliament assembled at Linlithgow, Edinburgh having been sacked and burned by the English army in 1544. The nunnery of Haddington was the venue in 1548, when the Scots ratified their treaty with the French which settled the marriage of Queen Mary to the Dauphin Francis, in the course of the Franco-Scottish siege of the English garrison of the burgh.[162]

The pre-eminent position of Edinburgh was further reinforced after 1488 by the division of the functions of the ancient royal council into two distinct but not mutually exclusive specialist segments, one largely judicial, exercised by the session, and the other advisory and less formal, by the body which was later formally constituted in 1545 as the Privy Council. This latter group was principally engaged in formulating royal policy, and emerged as an executive in the course of the sixteenth century. As it was still largely an advisory body, however, it tended to be mobile and could be summoned to assemble wherever the king happened to be at a given time. With kings spending an increasing amount of their time in Edinburgh, however, meetings tended to be held in either Edinburgh Castle or (from the 1530s) in the new royal palace of Holyroodhouse. In 1535–6, when James V undertook the construction of the south and west quarters of the quadrangle at Holyroodhouse, a new chapel was built in the south quarter while the old chapel, evidently in the north quarter built by James IV between 1502 and 1504, was fitted up or rebuilt as a chamber for meetings of the Privy Council.[163] The implication is that the new council was constituted on a far more formal basis than the early medieval *curia regis*. Certainly, by the mid-sixteenth century, its business was recorded meticulously and lists of those present – sederunts – were compiled, and its sessions were given added dignity by meeting in a formal setting. The model for this provision of a specialised council chamber may have been the Star Chamber at Westminster, the meeting-place throughout the later Middle Ages for the English royal council. The shared characteristics of advisory body and judicial court for both Scottish and English councils adds some weight to this possibility, but the growing influence of French royal architecture in Scotland at this time offers an alternative source in the council chambers and *salles des états* of the Loire chateaux, especially that at Amboise, built for King Charles VIII (1483–98), which functioned as the hub of French government during his reign and again under Francis I (1515–47).

In tandem with the refinement of the Privy Council, sessions of parliamentary and conciliar committees for the administration of civil justice, which can be traced from the reign of James I and evolved into 'the Session', were matured in the reign of James V. Although a more-or-less permanent corps of judges had been instituted before 1513, it was he who formalised the Session through the institution of the College of Justice, modelled to some extent on the Parlement de Paris, in 1532; in an allusion to the combined judicial and political function of the Roman Senate, the Session judges were referred to as 'senators'.[164] Parliament had always had a judicial function alongside its other roles, while the king's council had not; and so these sessions appear to have met in the tolbooth at Edinburgh throughout the fifteenth century, and James V's failure to provide his promised funding for the new College of Justice ensured that courts continued at first to sit in that building, between 1532 and 1539. After that it moved to the mansion of the President, Abbot Myln, in the Lawnmarket. From 1552 until 1560, the court sat in a range of locations, including the Blackfriars Hall, the Tolbooth, the Magdalen Chapel, and the mansion of the Bishop of Moray at the foot of the High Street.

THE REFORMATION ERA: PARLIAMENTS, CONVENTIONS, ASSEMBLIES

In the second half of the sixteenth century, we move from the era of the simple consolidation of royal power into a transitional period, in which the authority of both the monarch and the church was called increasingly into question: the time of the Reformation. In this period, religious and political reform proceeded in parallel, with a growing trend of separation of church and state. Until then, as we have seen, parliament had needed the royal consent to meet, and to make its acts legal, and its work was channelled through the heavily regulated committee of the Lords of the Articles; in effect, it served as a meeting-place for interest groups rather than as a forum for debate. The 'Reformation Parliament' of 1560 showed the potential for autonomous parliamentary action. It proceeded to exploit the weakness of the monarchy in those years by abolishing papal jurisdiction and outlawing the mass, citing an overarching interest of national community. During the rule by regent which followed the abdication of Mary, the convening of parliaments became a matter of political factionalism; during ten months in the early 1570s, six rival parliaments were called.

Since the mid-fifteenth century, other quasi-parliamentary meetings (usually under the title of 'convention') had also become increasingly common; the various estates often held their own conventions around the sessions of parliament. Additionally, the Convention of Royal Burghs (a kind of 'burghal parliament' convened by the Lord Chamberlain) met until the early sixteenth century prior to the meetings of parliament and the estates. After 1567, the title 'Convention of Estates' was increasingly used to denote a national but informal quasi-parliamentary meeting, free of the control of the Lords of the Articles, and able to pass temporary legislation and levy taxes: to some extent, the powers of these gatherings overlapped with those of the Privy Council. Such meetings became more and more frequent, with seventeen being held between 1594 and 1601; by the 1640s, with the decline in the power of the Articles (see Chapter 2), they would become virtually identical with formal parliaments. In 1587, parliament itself had been reorganised into four estates (by the addition of the lairds), a situation which prevailed until bishops were abolished in 1639.

Another consequence of the Reformation was that the General Assembly of the reformed church developed as a new national religious legislature, its members mainly ministers with some burgesses and lords. It concerned itself repeatedly with the correction of supposed royal misuse of power, and the combating of erastianism (the doctrine of state control of the church). The two assemblies shared some organisational features and sat in a similar U-shaped layout. The historian and political philosopher George Buchanan, tutor of the infant king James VI and Moderator of the 1567 General Assembly, wrote a corpus of texts advocating curbs on royal power by the nobility and the reformed clergy, adducing in support the classical constitutional precedent of the *res publica*: these books included *De Iure Regni Apud Scotos* (1567/8) and the *History of Scotland* (1582). However, on reaching adulthood in the 1580s, James VI dedicated his efforts to reversing this decline in royal prestige, citing the contrasting classical precedent of imperial Roman authority. As well as summoning full parliaments he also called conventions of the the estates, and attempted to control parliament through his appointments of bishops, and through the committee of the Lords of the Articles. By the end of the period covered by this chapter, a general conflict had begun to take shape within the Scottish elite, between monarchical and oligarchic factions, both citing antiquity in their support; this conflict had religious overtones, owing to the fact that the Reformation in Scotland had prevailed through an act of resistance against the state.

What were the architectural repercussions of this growing conflict of views and interests? Two themes in particular stand out: an expansion of permanent accommodation in the centre of Edinburgh, based on the established tolbooth pattern; and a growing tendency, during periods of emergency and civil strife, for competing or splinter assemblies to meet in a variety of *ad hoc* settings. In 1561–2, prompted presumably by the conflicting demands of parliament, court of session and the town council of Edinburgh, as well as the evidently poor physical state of the old building, Queen Mary ordered the building of a 'New Tolbooth'.[165] Overseen by master of works David Somer, this was erected to the south of the Old Tolbooth in what is now Parliament Square. It lapped around and adjoined the south-west end of St Giles's on a rough L plan.[166] It had three or more storeys, with an entrance in a semi-polygonal turnpike stair projecting from its narrow north end; accommodation included a hall or apartment on two levels, termed either the Laigh or High Tolbooth, or the Laigh and High 'counsall-hous'. The meetings of the town council were moved from the Old to the New Tolbooth, and the Lords of Session, itinerant during most of the 1550s, also took up permanent residence there; the old building was mainly used as a prison from *c.*1562 onwards, and at some date before 1610, when work began on the building of new prison accommodation, the late fourteenth-century western portion had been demolished. The New Tolbooth also became a centre for the meetings of national assemblies. Parliaments may on occasion have continued to meet in the main chambers of the late fifteenth-century eastern block, but it is more likely that their sessions moved into the New Tolbooth, which remained the primary venue for parliamentary meetings until the building of the New Parliament House in the 1630s. The New Tolbooth was used by a wide variety of other national institutions, including meetings of the 'generale Kirk' (the General Assembly – on 24 December 1565), and the Convention of Royal Burghs (1579). The exchequer likewise had rooms here until the seventeenth-century Parliament House was opened. The Laigh Hall or House (within the New Tolbooth) was decorated with oak panelling, and possibly portraits, including one said to represent Mary of Guise.

Shortly before the building of the New Tolbooth, the Reformation had opened up the possibility of subdivision of the large unitary space of St Giles', and its south-western section was now fitted out as an overspill tolbooth, containing several rooms, including the town's charter house in a room above the south door. This overspill accommodation was referred to in 1598 as the 'Outer Tolbooth' and also sometimes, confusingly, as the 'new tolbooth'. At ground level, a narrow passage between St Giles' and the New Tolbooth gave access to the kirkyard (now Parliament Close), while an upper-level link allowed easy intercommunication between the New Tolbooth and the tolbooth accommodation inside St Giles'. In 1601, the Lords of Session were moved into the three westernmost bays of the nave of St Giles', which served as a court-room annexe to the Old Tolbooth, under the title 'Outer House of the Lords', and provided their usual meeting-place until 1632; part of the remainder of the nave accommodation was used by the town bailies as a burgh courthouse.[167] This move on the one hand harks back to the earlier medieval use of church naves as court-houses, while on the other it hints at contemporary

1.10. Edinburgh Old Tolbooth, plans after Chambers and north elevation after Sime. (RCAHMS)

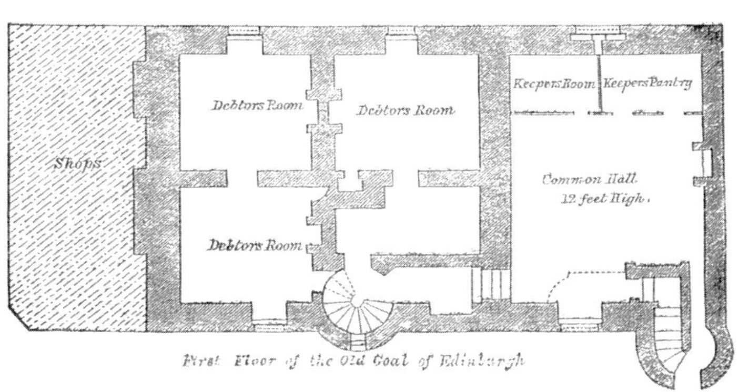

First Floor of the Old Goal of Edinburgh

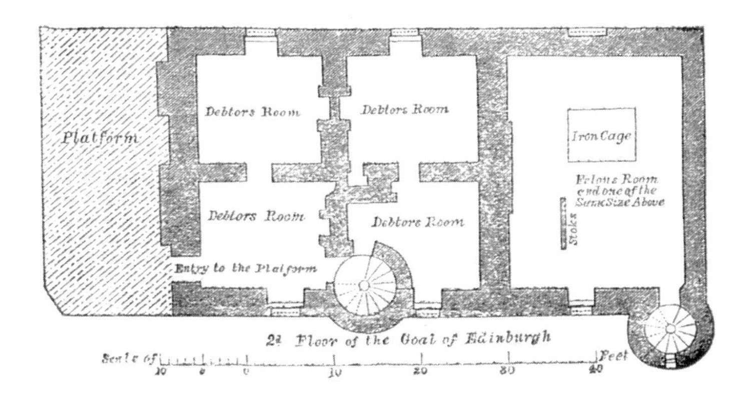

2d Floor of the Goal of Edinburgh

The Old Jail from the Lawn Market opposite Bank Street

perceptions of the architectural norms for judicial buildings, perhaps reflecting the revival of Classical models, especially the aisled basilica.

By the 1560s, therefore, Edinburgh had secured its place as 'capitall toune' and 'the first parliament toun' of the kingdom, and Scottish government had acquired a recognisable legislature and executive, although it had yet to secure the dedicated, specialist venue which would give it an institutional identity.[168] The civil war of 1570–73, while it undermined the growing cohesiveness of government, further reinforced the powerful symbolism of Edinburgh as the seat of national government, with the rival factions going to enormous lengths to establish their legitimacy to rule through the summoning and holding of parliaments in the midst of the war-zone which was the nation's capital.

Contemporary accounts of this conflict, although concerned primarily with the political and military ebb and flow between the supporters of the deposed and exiled Queen Mary and those of her young son, James VI, provide the first detailed information concerning some of the tradition and ceremonial which had built up around the holding of parliament over the preceding three centuries, and which still retained force, even in the aftermath of the upheaval of 1560.[169] The legislative powers of the assembly remained generally under the control of the ruler, whose officers and appointees dominated the committee of the Lords of the Articles, which drew up the programme of business and prepared legislation for presentation before the full sessions of parliament. But certain forms were now in place which acted as safeguards against the subjection of parliament to arbitrary royal decisions. Thus, procedures had to be gone through for the summoning of parliaments, initiated by a formal proclamation at the cross of Edinburgh in which a venue and date for the next occasion were specified. Once set, these could not be changed nor the summonses cancelled. This was the argument used in 1578 against James Douglas, earl of Morton, regent for James VI from 1572–8, and champion of an erastian and episcopalian settlement of the Kirk, when he attempted to move a parliament summoned at Edinburgh to Stirling, where he controlled the castle.[170] In 'resisting him, the chancellor, John Stewart, earl of Atholl, declared that the attempt was aganis the King's proclamatiounis and inviolable edicts, aganis all justice, consuetude and law', and 'in manifest abrogation and diminution of the libbertie and power of the thrie Estaits, the onlie

TOP.
1.11. Edinburgh Old Tolbooth and St Giles's Kirk seen from the north-west, drawn in 1817 by Daniel Somerville.
(D J Black)

BOTTOM.
1.12. Edinburgh Old Tolbooth and St Giles's Kirk seen from the south-west, drawn in 1817 by A Nasmyth.
(Mrs S Stevenson; RCAHMS EDD/579/2)

stowppis and pillers of the Crown'.

This underscores the problem which faced Matthew Stewart, earl of Lennox, regent for his grandson James VI, in May 1571. Parliament had been summoned to assemble at the tolbooth of Edinburgh, but the castle and burgh were controlled by the supporters of Queen Mary, who proceeded to hold their own parliament in the appointed place.[171] Lennox was bound by procedure, however, and could not shift the venue of 'his' parliament without first 'opening a formal session in Edinburgh and then 'continuing' it at some more convenient location. As a consequence, therefore, he and his supporters occupied the house of William Cook in the Canongate, technically outwith the burgh but claimed as lying 'within the freidome of Edinburgh', and 'fenced' or formally instituted parliament there. His purpose, as understood by one contemporary observer, was to establish it as a legitimate parliament.[172] This was a necessary step towards establishing his authority as lawfully appointed regent, both at home and in the eyes of foreign observers, and to giving credibility and force to his government and its legislation. Furthermore, it could be claimed as the 'official' parliament of 1571, denying the legitimacy of the assembly of the Queen's men in the tolbooth and thereby removing any questionmark over the authority or validity of subsequent parliaments summoned by him. Its business was brief, basically the passing of sentences of forefeiture on the 'rebels' in the castle, which had been the principal intended purpose of the parliament summoned to the tolbooth, and the announcement of its continuation at Stirling. In this, too, Lennox followed the established tradition as closely as possible, proclaiming the continuation of parliament and the date and venue for its re-assembly at the cross in the Canongate.[173]

The absence of the regalia seems also to have been a major concern for Lennox and his supporters. At his first parliament in October 1570, the new regent had failed to secure the presence of these powerful tokens.[174] The rapid descent into civil war over the following months ensured that Lennox had been unable to gain possession, and for his Stirling parliament of August 1571 he was obliged to have a new set of regalia manufactured for the ceremonial procession of the young king and his nobility from the castle to the tolbooth.[175] Interestingly, one source for this event, giving a more detailed account of the pageantry of the procession, describes how the king was 'brocht furth of the castell downe to the tolbuith with gret tryvmphe the crowne beand on his heid the vthir crowne beirand be his guidshir the regent baith borne vnder ain paill the cepture and the sword also befoir thame borne'.[176] These may have been the 'jewallis . . . maid of brace [brass] and doubill ourgilt with gold', used by the King's Men at their Edinburgh parliament of January 1572–3.[177] The reference *two* crowns, however, adds further strength to the political symbolism attached to the regalia, the crown borne by the regent, presumably, being the actual coronation crown – or in this context a facsimile of it – which carried the greater symbolic weight as the manifestation of kingly authority.

By the early sixteenth century, the public parading of the crown, sword and sceptre in the mounted procession of the king and his nobles from the castle or palace of Holyroodhouse to the tolbooth had become a central feature of parliamentary ritual. During both the minority and the personal reign of Mary, where the queen evidently did little more than attend the opening session in which the Lords of the Articles were nominated, deliver her propositioun and orisoun in parliament', and return when necessary to settle formal processes which required her authority, such as forfeitures, the regalia must already have acquired its role as a symbol of monarchy.[178] Although it is nowhere stated explicitly in sixteenth-century or earlier accounts, the symbolic role of the royal regalia in establishing the authority of seventeenth-century Scottish parliaments must represent the continuation and development of an older tradition. In the opinion of some, the fact that the 1560 'Reformation Parliament', convened without the permission of the Queen, had assembled without these powerful symbols of royal authority, brought the legitimacy of its proceedings further into question.[179] Despite Lennox's efforts in 1571, there was clearly doubt over the validity of the actions of the king's parliaments since October 1570, which had either met without the 'official' regalia, or which had assembled elsewhere than in the tolbooth of Edinburgh, but it seems to have been the latter point which was of paramount concern, presumably as a consequence of the potential illegality of the Canongate parliament of 1571. Thus, in January 1573, when one of Lennox's successors as regent, the 4th Earl of Morton, had succeeded in taking the town of Edinburgh, he convened a parliament in the tolbooth while the castle was still under siege, with the express purpose of ratifying all acts passed in the king's name since 1567.[180]

In recognition of the continuing siege – the castle's artillery fired on the burgh throughout Morton's parliament was hardly an exercise in triumphalism.[181] Although the replacement regalia was borne in procession, no trumpeters or heralds proclaimed their arrival nor the fencing of parliament, and the regent and his allies were obliged to pass through St Giles's and enter the tolbooth through a breach made in its wall. Presumably as a consequence of either the risk posed by the artillery barrage, or as a result of existing damage to the upper levels of the new building, the parliament convened in 'the laigh [low] counsall hous of the toun on the west syid of the tolbuyth'.[182] In April 1573, as the civil war moved to its close and many of the erstwhile leaders of the Queen's party sought reconciliation with their opponents, Morton, now based in Holyroodhouse, summoned a second parliament. After a ceremonial procession from the palace to the tolbooth and the formal selection of lords of the Articles, its business session was moved down the hill to Holyroodhouse, well out of range of the castle's guns.[183] There, after processing from 'the tour of the abbay', evidently the existing north-west tower built by James V, through 'the inwart clos', the regent and nobles convened in the 'north hall', presumably the council chamber which had been fitted up in the former chapel in the north quarter of the palace (see below).[184]

CONCLUSION

Throughout this chapter, the physical settings of Scotland's medieval parliaments have remained elusive. The ravages of time and warfare have today obliterated most traces of the earliest venues of government, leaving simply the frustratingly imprecise recording of the name of the location in the equally frustrating fragmentary documentary record. For the earliest of the sites, dating from the formative years of the Scottish kingdom, archaeology has added considerably to our knowledge, but this is largely through conjecture and analogy with excavated remains elsewhere in Britain and on the European continent rather than through the detailed examination of any Scottish remains. What is evident, however, even from the earliest period, is the range of influences and inspirations upon which Scotland drew. From the first emergence of a fully-fledged monarchy in the early ninth century, traditions were imported, in some cases from England, and also in the form of late Imperial Roman influences, directly from the Carolingian empire and, through the medium of the church, from Rome itself.

This multiplicity of influences continued throughout the Middle Ages. The Anglo-Norman régime in England after 1066, and the compelling exemplar of Angevin government after 1154, may have been the immediate sources of some ideas permeating Scottish political culture in the eleventh and twelfth centuries, but by the early thirteenth century powerful impulses were being received from both France and the papacy. In particular, it may have been the growing sophistication of ecclesiastical government under the emergent papal monarchy from the time of Innocent III, with which the Scottish church was intimately connected, and the key role played in Scottish royal government at this time by the senior clergy, which moulded the style of parliament – and the preference for siting its meetings in ecclesiastical venues – which had emerged by the closing decades of the thirteenth century.

More generally, the fourteenth, fifteenth and sixteenth centuries were the 'age of estates' across the whole of Latin 'Christendom': a time when the authority of rulers was widely assumed to rest on a contractual relationship with the other 'orders' of society, and representative institutions with tax-gathering, legislative and judicial powers flourished in many countries. In Scotland, this outlook was exemplified in the concept of the 'community of the realm', which, by the late thirteenth century, could be seen as partly autonomous in relation to the authority of the king. Although in some ways indebted to the Roman *res publica* concept of constitutional balance, its expression through representative government, rather than direct popular assemblies, marked a decisive departure from the patterns of antiquity, and a pointer to the world of modern government. In some countries, the idea that parliamentary approval ought to be secured for all important laws was carried much further than in Scotland: for instance, in Poland, by the late sixteenth century, the control of the Diet over legislation as complete, and the king had been reduced to a subordinate element in the legislature alongside the nobility. The position in Venice, with its figurehead ruler, was even more extreme.[185] Within

Scotland, the influence of the English system of more restricted parliamentary power remained fairly strong, as a legacy of the close political relationship between the two kingdoms in the central decades of the thirteenth century. Westminster, indeed, was the model followed in the development of Scone as the physical nexus of royalty, government and religious symbolism. Furthermore, despite the catastrophic failure of the good relationship between the kingdoms in the period after 1296, it was still partly to the Westminster tradition that Robert I returned when reconstructing Scottish government.

From 1296 until 1437, it was ecclesiastical buildings which predominated as the regular venues for parliaments and councils. Most probably, it was the essentially basilican form of the churches so employed which provided the attraction, but this may also have been influenced by the established position of church buildings – especially the basilican naves as the locations of secular courts and meeting-places. Such was the force of this tradition that long after the crown had refurnished itself with what were otherwise suitable stages on which to parade the powerful new monarchy of the post-Wars of Independence era – such as Linlithgow – parliaments continued to meet in these established ecclesiastical venues. The impact of tradition in influencing Scottish responses to the needs of government should not be underestimated, and is seen most clearly in the emergence of Perth. There, geographical location and the coincidence of the sites of the king-making ritual, the meeting-place of the provincial council of the Scottish church, and an economically influential burgess community with suitable structures within which to house the king and his household, the participating nobility and their retinues, and the officers and functionaries of government – overrode what we, with the benefit of hindsight, might regard as logical imperatives for relocation elsewhere.

The survival of Perth as the location of parliament long after Edinburgh had regained its status as the seat of government, is a powerful indication of the strength of tradition.

It took force to break that grip. The assassination of James I in 1437 appears as the single act which severed both the link to Perth and the bond with the church as a parliamentary venue. Underlying this, however, were a number of factors which contributed to an unvoiced demand for change. Growing anti-clericalism and the demands for clearer separation of the functions of church and state which issued from the Council of Basel, coupled with the practical concerns regarding the security of Perth and the political reality of the economic and governmental dominance of Edinburgh, brought about that change at a single stroke.

Colouring the scene, however, may again have been growing continental influences, where specialist settings for government were being developed in many of the states with which Scotland had close diplomatic or commercial links. Furthermore, the flow of early Renaissance principles concerning the exercise of political authority, and a reawakening of interest in the classical Roman past, evident from the reign of James I onwards, may have stimulated a conscious rejection of the medievalism of the old parliamentary tradition in favour of the secular, magistratial and essentially imperial tradition represented by the civic authority of the tolbooth. Although not a specialist parliamentary structure *per se*, the tolbooth marked a decisive step from medieval monarchy towards an architecture of modern government. But the path which linked the two would be riven with conflict; the balanced 'society of orders' of the late Middle Ages could now no longer be maintained. The legacy of the Reformation was a contest between polarised extremes of oligarchy and monarchy over the source of authority in government, a contest which would sharpen into a bitter civil war in the 1630s and '40s.

NOTES

1. S.M. Foster, 'Before Alba: Pictish and Dal Riata power centres from the fifth to the late ninth centuries AD', in S. Foster, A. Macinnes and R. Macinnes (eds.), *Scottish Power Centres from the Early Middle Ages to the Twentieth Century*, Glasgow, 1998, 1–31.
2. Foster, 'Before Alba', 10–11.
3. Foster, 'Before Alba', 16; A.O. Anderson, *Early Sources of Scottish History AD 500 to 1286*, Edinburgh, 1922, i, 50.
4. Anderson, *Early Sources*, i, 291.
5. L. Alcock and E.A. Alcock, 'Reconnaissance excavations on Early Historic fortifications and other royal sites in Scotland, 1974–84'; L. Alcock, 'Excavations and other fieldwork at Forteviot, Perthshire, 1981', *Proceedings of the Society of Antiquaries of Scotland* (*PSAS*), 122, 1992, 215–93 at 218–42; L. Alcock and E.A. Alcock, 'The context of the Dupplin Cross: a reconsideration', *PSAS*, 126, 1996, 455–7; S.M. Foster, *Picts, Gaels and Scots*, London, 1996, 48–51, 98–99.
6. D. Broun, 'The Origin of Scottish Identity', in C. Bjorn, A. Grant and K.J. Stringer, *Nations, Nationalism and Patriotism in the European Past*, Copenhagen, 1994, 35–55 at

52–4; J. Bannerman, 'The Scottish takeover of Pictland and the relics of Columba', *Innes Review*, xlviii, 1997, 27–44.

7. S. Airlie, 'The View from Maastricht', in B.E. Crawford (ed.), *Scotland in Dark Age Europe*, St Andrews, 1994, 33–46 at 35.
8. B.Hope-Taylor, 'Doonhill, Dunbar, East Lothian', *Medieval Archaeology*, 10, 1966, 175–6; I.M. Smith, 'Sprouston, Roxburghshire: an early Anglican centre of the eastern Tweed Basin', *Proceedings of the Society of Antiquaries of Scotland*, 121, 1991, 261–94. For a general discussion of lordly and royal power centres in this period, see S.T. Driscoll, 'Formalising the mechanisms of state power: early Scottish lordship from the ninth to the thirteenth centuries', in Foster, Macinnes and Macinnes, *Power Centres*, 32–58.
9. See, for example, B. Hope-Taylor, Y*eavering: an Anglo-British centre of early Northumbria*, Department of the Environment Archaeological Report, 7, London, 1977; P. Rahtz, *The Saxon and Medieval Palaces at Cheddar*, Oxford, 1979.
10. Foster, *Picts, Gaels and Scots*, 59
11. Driscoll, 'Formalising the mechanisms of state power', 43.
12. Foster, 'Before Alba', 20.
13. F.J. Byrne, *Irish Kings and High Kings*, London, 1973, 53–7.
14. Anderson, *Early Sources*, i, 224; A.A.M. Duncan, *Scotland: the Making of the Kingdom*, Edinburgh, 1978, 115; *Foster, Picts, Gaels and Scots*, 49. The certain identification of Scone as the *Caislenn Credi* of the annals is still a matter of academic debate.
15. This remained the site of royal enthronements down to the time of Robert I. For a detailed medieval description, see Walter Bower, *Scottichronicon*, D. Watt and others (eds.), 5, Aberdeen, 1990, 293–5.
16. Anderson, *Early Sources*, i, 445; Foster, Picts, Gaels and Scots, 112; A.P. Smyth, *Warlords and Holy Men, Scotland AD 80–1000*, London, 1984, 189.
17. *John of Fordun's Chronicle of the Scottish Nation*, W.F. Skene (ed.), (facsimile reprint), Llanerch, 1993, 177.
18. *John of Fordun's Chronicle of the Scottish Nation*, W.F. Skene (ed.), (facsimile reprint), Llanerch, 1993, 218
19. T. Thomson and C. Innes (eds.), *The Acts of the Parliaments of Scotland*, Edinburgh, 1814–75, i, 545.
20. Foster, 'Before Alba', 19.
21. *Registrum Episcopatus Moraviensis* (Bannatyne Club, 1837), no. 159.
22. Driscoll, 'Formalising the mechanisms of state power', 41–3.
23. For a discussion of the *curia regis*, council, its composition and workings, see A.A.M. Duncan, *Scotland: the Making of the Kingdom*, Edinburgh, 1975, 211–3, 608–610.
24. Bower, *Scottichronicon* (Watt), 4, 21.
25. G.W. S. Barrow (ed.), *Regesta Regum Scotorum*, ii, *The Acts of William I*, Edinburgh, 1971, no. 519.
26. G. Duby, *France in the Middle Ages*, trans. J. Vale, London, 1991, 255; Joinville and Villehardouin, *Chronicles of the Crusades*, trans. M.R.B. Shaw, London, 1963, 177. Joinville's account of Louis IX's court emphasises the informality of medieval government.
27. A.O. Anderson, *Scottish Annals from English Chroniclers, AD 500 to 1286*, London, 1908, 233.
28. G.W.S. Barrow (ed.), *Regesta Regum Scotorum*, i, *The Acts of Malcolm IV*, Edinburgh, 1960, 14–15.
29. For example, Duncan, *Making of the Kingdom*, 212.
30. F. Watson, 'The expression of power in a medieval kingdom: thirteenth-century

Scottish castles', in S. Foster, A. Macinnes and R. Macinnes (eds.), *Scottish Power Centres from the Early Middle Ages to the Twentieth Century*, Glasgow, 1998, 59–78 at 63.

31. For example, *APS*, i, 64, 66 (Alyth and Selkirk), J.M. Thomson (ed.), *Registrum Magni Sigilli Regum Scotorum*, (reprint), Edinburgh, 1984, i, no. 549 (Loch Freuchie in Strathbraan), no. 639 (Kindrochit in Mar); *RMS*, ii, no. 2198 (Hunthall in Glenfinglass), nos. 922, 923, 2185 (Glenartney).
32. J. Steane, *The Archaeology of Medieval England and Wales*, London, 1984, 13–4; W.L. Warren, *Henry II*, London, 1973, 473. It is known that William the Lion attended councils of Henry II of England at Northampton and Feckenham in 1176, Nottingham in 1179 and 1181, London in 1185, Oxford in 1186, and visited also the royal residences at Woodstock and Windsor.
33. A.C. Lawrie (ed.), *Early Scottish Charters prior to 1153*, Glasgow, 1905, no. 136.
34. *RRS*, ii, nos. 147, 203, 204, 331, 435.
35. Bower, *Scottichronicon* (Watt), 4, 339.
36. *A Scottish Chronicle Known as the Chronicle of Holyrood* (Scottish History Society, 1938), 168–9.
37. A.O. Anderson, *Scottish Annals from English Chroniclers AD 500–1286*, London, 1908, 300–301; *APS*, i, 70.
38. *RRS*, ii, 15, no. 326. For alternative locations and discussion, see Duncan, *Making of the Kingdom*, 212, note 54; W.F. Skene (ed.), *John of Fordoun's Chronicle of the Scottish Nation* (facsimile reprint), Llanerch, 1993, ii, 269; Bower, *Scottichronicon* (Watt), 4, 395.
39. APS, i, 66.
40. *RRS*, ii, 18–19, 103.
41. *RRS*, ii, 19, 104; Bower, *Scottichronicon* (Watt), 4, 459.
42. Bower, Scottichronicon (Watt), 4, 457 and note.
43. A.A.M. Duncan, 'The early parliaments of Scotland, *Scottish Historical Review*, xlv, 1966, 36–58.
44. Duncan, The early parliaments', l, note 5.
45. A. Grant, *Independence and Nationhood: Scotland 1306–1469*, London, 1984, 162–3, 166–7.
46. Bower, *Scottichronicon* (Watt), 5, 181 and note on 279.
47. Bower, *Scottichronicon* (Watt), 5, 181.
48. Bower, *Scottichronicon* (Watt), 5, 183–5.
49. Duby, *France in the Middle Ages*, 218, 255–6, 283, 284.
50. D.E.R. Watt, 'The Provincial Council of the Scottish Church, 1215–1472', in A. Grant and K.J. Stringer (eds.), *Medieval Scotland: Crown, Lordship and Community*, Edinburgh, 1993, 140–55.
51. Duncan, *Making of the Kingdom*, 294; G. Barraclough, *The Medieval Papacy*, London, 1968, 135.
52. J. Bain (ed.), *Calendar Relating to Scotland*, i, Edinburgh, 1884, nos. 526, 840.
53. Preparations for the war with Norway in 1263 appear to have been finalised in a parliament or council at Edinburgh in February 1263. On 18 March 1286, the afternoon before his death, Alexander III held a council in Edinburgh Castle, attended by 'a great number of his nobles', followed by an extended banquet; Anderson, *Early Sources*, ii, 690–1.
54. M. Powicke, *The Thirteenth Century*, 2nd edition, Oxford, 1962, 147, 177.
55. R. Midmer, *English Medieval Monasteries, 1066–1540*, London, 1970, 89–90. Parliaments also met in the refectory in 1296 and 1447.
56. A. Stevenson, 'Medieval Scottish Associations with Bruges', in T. Brotherstone and D. Ditchburn (eds.), *Freedom and Authority; Scotland c. 1050–c. 1650*, East Linton, 2000,

100. *APS*, i, 59; see also Duncan, *Making of the Kingdom*, 529, note 19. Gilleasbuig appears as a witness to a charter of Thomas de Colville, lord of Dalmellington, dateable to 1201/1206 (*Liber S. Marie de Melros*, Bannatyne Club, 1837, no, 192).

57. *APS*, ii, 43, where the bar was replaced by new seating for the burgh commissioners under legislation of 1455. This is the arrangement which can be seen in a late thirteenth-century manuscript illustration showing Edward I enthroned before an assembly of clerics, with scribes seated on the floor at their feet (British Library, Cottonian MS Vitellius A XIII, f.6v).
58. T. McNeill, *Castles in Ireland: Feudal Power in a Gaelic World*, London, 1997, 45–7.
59. It is possible that some structural remains of Alexander II's hall survive in the rubble-choked and overgrown ruins of Kinclaven in Perthshire. Smaller halls perhaps survive in the fragmentary remains of the royal hunting-lodges at Kincardine near Fettercairn and at Clunie near Dunkeld.
60. G. Stell, 'Architecture: the changing needs of society', in J.M. Brown (ed.), *Scottish Society in the Fifteenth Century*, London, 1977, 153–83 at 157–9.
61. W. Fraser, *The Lennox*, Edinburgh, 1874, ii, no. 9.
62. Duncan, 'Early parliaments', 37, note 5; A.A.M. Duncan, *Scotland: the Making of the Kingdom*, Edinburgh, 1978, 592–3; Bower, *Scottichronicon* (Watt), 5, 417.
63. Bower, *Scottichronicon* (Watt), 5, 291–3.
64. *APS*, i, 69, 424.
65. Nicholson, *Later Middle Ages*, 28.
66. Duncan, 'Early parliaments'.
67. *Chron. Fordoun*, ii, 357.
68. John Barbour, *The Bruce* (edited and translated by A.A.M. Duncan), Edinburgh, 1997, 79–81 and notes.
69. Robert Lindsay of Pitscottie, *The Historie and Cronicles of Scotland* (Scottish Text Society, 1899), 173–6.
70. *CDS*, ii, no. 1978.
71. Barrow, *Robert Bruce*, 112.
72. The burgh was fortified by the English after 1304 and was besieged in December 1308 by Edward Bruce; D. Macpherson and others (eds.), *Rotuli Scotiae in Turri Londiniensi et in Domo Capitulari Westmonasteriensi* (1814–19), i, 60a.
73. MacGibbon and Ross, *Ecclesiastical Architecture*, i, 372–5.
74. *APS*, i, 454.
75. Barrow, *Robert Bruce*, 183–6.
76. Barrow, *Robert Bruce*, 183–6.
77. Fawcett, *Scottish Abbeys and Priories*, 101.
78. Bower, *Scottichronicon* (Watt), 8, 3–5.
79. RCAHMS, *South East Perth: an Archaeological Landscape*, HMSO, 1994, 124–7.
80. *APS*, i, 546: '. . . in Secreta Camera predicti domini Regis in suo Secreto consilio et post in Camera sui parlamenti in publico'.
81. RCAHMS, *Stirlingshire*, i, no. 130; S. Cruden, *Cambuskenneth Abbey, Stirlingshire*, Edinburgh, 1973, 6.
82. J. Dunbar, 'The Palace of Holyroodhouse During the First Half of the Sixteenth Century', *The Archaeological Journal*, cxx, 1964, 250.
83. RCAHMS, *The City of Edinburgh*, Edinburgh, 1951, no. 86, 131; Fawcett, *Abbeys and Priories*, 101.
84. R. Fawcett, *Scottish Cathedrals*, London, 1997, 59–60.
85. *RRS*, v, 91 and no. 18.
86. *RRS*, i, no. 240.

87. Bower, *Scottichronicon* (Watt), 6, 379.
88. *Rotuli Scotiae*, i, 80a.
89. Bower, *Scottichronicon* (Watt), 6, 379.
90. *APS*, i, 73.
91. *APS*, i, 7, 81.
92. R. Nicholson, Scotland: the Later Middle Ages, Edinburgh, 1978, 129–30.
93. Bower, *Scottichronicon* (Watt), 7, 109.
94. Bower, *Scottichronicon* (Watt), 7, 117.
95. Bower, *Scottichronicon* (Watt), 7, 117.
96. RCAHMS, *Fife, Kinross and Clackmannan*, Edinburgh, 1933, no. 197, 113–20.
97. Nicholson, *Later Middle Ages*, 138–9; Bower, Scottichronicon (Watt), 143.
98. Bower, *Scottichronicon* (Watt), 7, 143–5.
99. Nicholson, *Later Middle Ages*, 139.
100. Barrow, *Robert Bruce*, 268–9; D.G. Adams, *Celtic and Medieval Religious Houses in Angus*, Brechin, 1984, 28.
101. The friary buildings, including large parts of the church, were excavated in the mid-1990s. The outline of the church has been marked in the paving of the car park behind the tenement blocks fronting the south side of the Green.
102. Nicholson, *Later Middle Ages*, 164–5.
103. *APS*, 495; J. Goodare, *Parliamentary History*, 15, 1996.
104. There does not appear to have been adequate accommodation for the king, court and household at Blackfriars before the 1380s. In 1373, Robert II hired two houses for royal use in the burgh, possibly at the time of the Scone parliament of that year. These were probably used to accommodate household departments, principally the king's and queen's wardrobe: see *ER*, iii, 442.
105. M. Brown, *James I*, Edinburgh, 1994, 114–5.
106. Bower, *Scottichronicon* (Watt), 6, 365 and note.
107. Bower, *Scottichronicon* (Watt), 8, 243 and note.
108. *RMS*, i, no. 652.
109. *APS*, i, 550; *RMS*, i, nos. 752, 770.
110. *APS*, i, 551, 553, 555.
111. *APS*, i, 500; S. Boardman, *The Early Stewart Kings: Robert II and Robert III*, East Linton, 1996, 124.
112. *APS*, i, 555; Boardman, *Early Stewart Kings*, 152.
113. *APS*, i, 556–7.
114. *Moray Registrum*, 382.
115. *Moray Registrum*, 557.
116. Watt, 'Provincial Council', 145.
117. Bower, *Scottichronicon* (Watt), 8, 289.
118. For the layout of medieval European parliaments and assemblies, see A.R. Myers, *Parliaments and Estates in Europe to 1789* (London, 1975), figs. 2, 15, 18, 28.
119. *RMS*, i, nos. 896, 908.
120. *APS*, i, 587.
121. Royal Commission on the Ancient and Historical Monuments of Scotland (RCAMHS), *Tolbooths and Town-houses: Civic Architecture in Scotland to 1833*, Edinburgh, 1996, 205–206.
122. *ER*, ii, 223, 262, 290, 309, 348, 360, 394–5.
123. I. Campbell, 'Linlithgow's "Princely Palace" and its Influence in Europe', *Architectural Heritage*, 5, 1995, 1–20; J. Dunbar, *Scottish Royal Palaces*, East Linton, 1999, 5–10; Brown, *James I*, 114–5.

126. *ER*, iv, 513.
127. Boards for the roofing to the hall at Edinburgh were purchased in 1375: see *ER*, ii, 472; Dunbar, *Scottish Royal Palaces*, 75–7.
128. *Monro's Western Isles of Scotland and Genealogies of the Clans*, R.W. Munro (ed.), Edinburgh, 1961, 95–100; *Highland Papers* (Scottish History Society, 1914–34), i, 23–4.
129. D.H. Campbell and N.A. Ruckley, 'Domestic Architecture in the Lordship of the Isles', in R.D. Oram and G.P. Stell (eds.), *Lordship and Architecture in Medieval and Early Renaissance Scotland* (forthcoming).
130. *Acts of the Lordship of the Isles, 1336–1493* (Scottish History Society, 1986), xivi–l.
131. Monro, *Western Isles*, 57; Highland Papers, i, 25; *Acts of the Lordship of the Isles*, xliii.
132. Monro, *Western Isles*, 57.
133. *Acts of the Lordship of the Isles*, nos. 42, 76, 80, 82, 89, 90, 91, 96, 119, 122, 123.
134. *ER*, vii, p.lx; Dunbar, *Scottish Royal Palaces*, 76–7.
135. *ER*, vi, 385.
136. *APS*, ii, 31; C.A. McGladdery, *James II*, Edinburgh, 1990, 11.
137. James III was crowned in 1460 in Kelso Abbey, following the death of his father during the siege of nearby Roxburgh. In 1488, James IV chose to be crowned at Scone, presumably to give greater legitimacy to a regime which had established itself through the violent overthrow and death of the old king by his son: see N. Macdougall, *James IV*, Edinburgh, 1997, 51.
138. For example, the great halls at Tours, Bois or Amboise, which had formal legislative and judicial, rather than banqueting roles. Tours was the venue for the assembly of the three Estates of France in 1468: Philippe de Commynes, *Memoirs*, trans. M. Jones, London, 1972, 168–9.
139. G. Holmes, *Europe: Hierarchy and Revolt, 1320–1450*, London, 1975, 272.
140. RCAHMS, *Tolbooths and Town-houses, Edinburgh*, 1996; N. Pevsner, *A History of Building Types*, London, 1976, 34; *APS*, ii, 31.
141. RMS, i, no. 207.
142. *Tolbooths and Town-houses*, 82; Registrum *Cartarum Ecclesie Sancti Egidii de Edinburgh* (Bannatyne Club, 1859), 2; Bower, *Scottichronicon* (Watt), 7, 407.
143. *Tolbooths and Town-houses*, 83; *Edinburgh St Giles Registrum*, 77, 170.
144. J. Gifford, C. McWilliam and D. Walker, *Edinburgh*, London, 1984, 66.
145. *A Diurnal of Remarkable Occurrents that have passed within the country of Scotland from the death of King James the Fourth till the year 1575* (Bannatyne and Maitland Clubs, 1833), 252.
146. *Tolbooths and Town-houses*, 82.
147. British Library, MSS Cotton Augustus I, vol. ii ant. 56.
148. *Tolbooths and Town-houses*, 82.
149. *Tolbooths and Town-houses*, 83.
150. *Tolbooths and Town-houses*, 188.
151. McGladdery, *James II*, 33.
152. *APS*, ii, 43.
153. *APS*, ii, 43: '. . . there be ordained quhair the Barre uses to stand, a seate of three seges, ilk ane hiare than other, to the Commissionares to sit on, under the payne of ten pounds to be raysed of the Toune, quhair Parliament or General Councel sall be halden, and the said seges un-maid, als oft als they are halden'.
154. *APS*, ii, 125.
155. *The Historie and Life of King James the Sext* (Bannatyne Club, 1825), 88.
156. For example, Robert Lindsay of Pitscottie, *The Historie and Cronicles of Scotland*, A.J.P. Mackay (Scottish Text Society, 1899), ii, 201.

157. *Diurnal of Occurrents,* 9.
158. See 'Place-dates: James III (1460–88)', in P.G.B. McNeill and H.L. MacQueen (eds.), *Atlas of Scottish History to 1707*, Edinburgh, 1996, 180.
159. The Treasurer, for example, was accommodated with a lodging in the castle by the fifteenth century. Repairs to the 'dom(us) thesaurarie' are listed in the Exchequer accounts for 1468: *ER*, vii, 424; Dunbar, *Scottish Royal Palaces*, 82–3.
160. 'Place-dates of royal charters', McNeill and MacQueen (eds.), *Atlas*, 159–76.
161. Exchequer, *ER*, v, 180; *ER*, vii, l; Nicholson, *Later Middle Ages*, 411; Dunbar, *Scottish Royal Palaces,* 23 and 200. James IV's charters: McNeill and MacQueen (eds.), *Atlas*, 181.
162. *Diurnal of Occurrents*, 46–7.
163. Dunbar, *Scottish Royal Palaces*, 68, 73. See also Pitscottie, *The Historie of King James the Sext*; or *Diurnal of Occurrents.*
164. *The Historie of King James the Sext*, 170.
165. Pitscottie, *Historie*, ii, 253; Diurnal of Occurrents, 214.
166. *Diurnal of Occurrents*, 214.
167. *Diurnal of Occurrents*, 214–5.
168. *Diurnal of Occurrents,* 191: 'It is to be notit, that in thair passing to the said tolbuyth, remayning in the same, nor yit returneing thairfra, thair wes nather croun, sceptre nor sword in this parliament borne, for thaj had nane bot quhilk wes in the castell of Edinburgh, and the capitane thairof wald not deliuer the same to thame . . .' Lennox also lacked the records and books of parliament, which the Queen's supporters had obliged the scribes of the Session to hand over to them: *Diurnal of Occurrents*, 213.
169. *Diurnal of Occurrents*, 242.
170. Pitscottie, *Historie*, ii, 262.
171. *Diurnal of Occurrents*, 324.
172. *Diurnal of Occurrents*, 76.
173. *Diurnal of Occurrents*, 61.
174. *Diurnal of Occurrents*, 324.
175. Pitscottie, *Historie*, ii, 296.
176. *Diurnal of Occurrents*, 324.
177. Pitscottie, *Historie*, ii, 301.
178. *Diurnal of Occurrents*, 330–331.
178. Dunbar, 'The Palace of Holyroodhouse', 243, 248–40; Gifford and others, *Edinburgh*, 125–6.
180. G. Donaldson, *Scotland: James V to James VII*, Edinburgh, 1965, 42, 46–8.
181. J.H. Burton (ed.), *The Register of the Privy Council of Scotland, i, 1545–69*, Edinburgh, 1877, 198–9.
182. *Tolbooths and Town-houses*, 86; Gifford and others, *Edinburgh*, 103–106.
183. Gifford and others, *Edinburgh*, 119.
184. *The Historie of King James the Sext*, 178.
185. A.R. Myers, *Parliament and Estates in Europe to 1789*, London, 1975, 31–2.

CHAPTER TWO

The Crisis of Kingship: 1603–1707

Aonghus MacKechnie

He shall build ane House for my Name,
and I will Stablish the Throne of his Kingdom for ever.
2 Samuel 6, v.13; inscribed at Holyrood, 1633.

. . . it is a striking fact that the new Parliament House,
the building of which as so intimately connected with arbitrary
policy in the affairs of Scotland, was scarcely completed before it
was the scene of a determined attack upon the royal prerogative.
R.K. Hannay and *G.P.H. Watson*, 1924[1]

During the century covered by this chapter, the old society of estates disintegrated in a succession of ruinous civil conflicts. A powerful alliance of interests, based within the landed and urban classes and the Presbyterian clergy, set out to confront a confident monarchy, energised by the growing prestige of absolutist rulers on the Continent. As this period had begun with the dynastic unification of the monarchies of Scotland, England and Ireland, these political and religious conflicts had the effect of drawing the three countries into ever more complex involvements in each others' affairs. This trend eventually led to a full political union between Scotland and England, at first under military duress in the 1650s, and then a second time by negotiated agreement from 1707 onwards. Partly as a result of this growing solidarity, it was possible for the conflict between royalists and anti-royalists to end in a very different way from the general Continental trend towards strong kingship. In Scotland and

England, it was the forces ranged against royal absolutism which eventually triumphed, at the end of the seventeenth century. These sharp political and dynastic fluctuations were played out against the backdrop of more consistent, long-term processes of economic and social change, which pointed the way to the drive for 'improvement' and modernisation in the eighteenth century: for example, it was the absolutist James VII in the late seventeenth century, not the Hanoverian Whigs in the 1750s, who first developed the idea of a separate residential 'new town' linked by bridges to the congested burgh of Edinburgh.

In this tempestuous century, national assemblies played a variety of roles in the course of Scottish history. The sharpest conflict was between the General Assembly of the Kirk, an elected oligarchy which saw itself appointed by God to represent the (supposedly) presbyterian nation and challenge royal abuses of power, and the two kings James VI and Charles I. They claimed a semi-divine personal status, which was broadcast through visual propaganda and James's philosophical tracts on kingship, and enforced above all through the executive actions of the privy council (the 'lords of secreit counsell'). The national parliament continued to negotiate its way between these two extremes in an *ad hoc* manner. During the periods of royalist dominance, the committee of the Lords of the Articles (its membership corresponding largely to that of the privy council) could be used to bolster the influence of the king, although parliaments could still be very difficult to 'control'. At other times, parliaments, or national conventions, acted in an almost completely independent and radical manner, most notably in 1639, when parliament challenged Charles's authority, triggering war in all three kingdoms; in 1689, when a national convention of estates declared the crown vacant and sent an embassy to London on its authority to offer the crown to the Prince of Orange, in the hope of securing a less interventionist monarchy; and in 1707, when it finally voted itself out of existence. The anti-royalist initiatives of this period echoed the medieval idea of the community of the realm, and of a social contract between ruler and ruled – a concept ultimately derived from the Roman *res publica*, and elaborated in the late sixteenth-century writings of George Buchanan.

The ambiguous and shifting role of parliament in the seventeenth century led to much subsequent myth-making, especially among presbyterian propagandists, who sought to downplay its role and glorify that of the General Assembly. Even as recently as 1999, Lord Hogg of Cumbernauld, opening the General Assembly as Lord High Commissioner, claimed that Scotland's seventeenth-century parliament was 'not in the least bit democratic'; the only 'democratic' legislature of 'the folk of Scotland' was the Kirk's General Assembly, which 'had the affection of the people . . . and provided the cement that made for social cohesion'. Such rhetoric, needless to say, bears little or no relation to the historical facts. The General Assembly and its Covenanting allies, far from being genuine 'democrats' in the classical Greek sense of direct popular rule, were actually an oligarchy, like the ruling elite of republican Rome – an oligarchy which defined itself through contrasts with supposedly arbitrary *regnum.* And the General Assembly met only infrequently during the early seventeenth century, and then only before the sessions of parliament, to lobby the latter – demonstrating its own subordinate status. Despite the revolutionary political changes of the time, none of those in charge were 'revolutionaries' in the twentieth-century sense – the social hierarchy was always generally upheld.[2]

When our period opened, parliament was not yet fully domiciled in Edinburgh, though it most frequently met there, in the new tolbooth. Throughout the seventeenth century, Edinburgh took active steps to enhance its civic prestige, and in 1625 the town council claimed that 'this burgh is the principall and heid burgh of this realme'. Inevitably, in the context of classically based educational and legal systems, this led to attempts to emulate aspects of antique and Renaissance Rome.[3] In the 1630s, parliament acquired a purpose-built, prestigious new home in the centre of Edinburgh, and so our story is centred there. Internationally speaking, this tailor-made new home, although more modest in scale than the triumphal parliaments and town halls of the nineteenth century, was still relatively unusual in the context of pre-modern Europe. As the building and use of Parliament House was closely bound up with the tempestuous history of the era, this chapter particularly emphasises the wider political context: this was an architecture not so much of sovereignty as of competing claims and concepts of governance. The chapter is divided into five main sections. These comprise the post-1603 part of James VI's reign; the reign of Charles I and the construction of Parliament House; the wartime period of Covenanter and parliamentary rule in 1639–51, followed by the abrogation of parliament under English military occupation; the time of revitalised monarchy under Charles II and James VII; and the final years of parliament from 1689 to 1707, in which it recovered much of its authority of the Covenanting years.

JAMES VI AND THE REGNAL UNION

Since the Reformation in 1560, Scotland's political focus had shifted from alliance with France to identification with Protestant Northern Europe. Into this pattern came James VI's marriage in 1589 to the Danish princess, Anne, and the forging of closer links with England, culminating in James's accession to the English crown in 1603. In Scotland, although James held seven parliaments and four conventions between 1603 and 1625, and returned once in person, in 1617, he was now an absentee monarch. With the departure of the court, Scottish culture lost the direct support, leadership and patronage of the crown – a trend which was only underlined after 1689 with the change to a less assertive style of monarchy. The aristocracy spilled into the vacuum, and became, together with the municipalities, *de facto* the foremost movers and patrons within Scottish culture and society, a situation which indirectly led to a rise in the prestige of parliament. As English king, James elaborated the symbolism of imperial pomp which he had already exploited at home to support his claims to divine kingship. A carefully stage-managed entry in 1603 to London saw him process through a series of elaborate triumphal arches specially constructed for the occasion. The concept of formalised procession was of course ancient, and long associated with ritualised celebration of gods or rulers. Conquering Roman emperors passed through triumphal arches in formal procession, as did Renaissance monarchs. The London entry built upon a long-established formula associated with Scottish kingship which, from at least 1469, had employed the concept and, from the 1480s, the visual imagery of classical authority; English monarchs had used similar devices from at least the mid-sixteenth century. Now, James, at the earliest opportunity, was broadcasting to his new subjects the imperial status of their new monarchy.[4] Immediately after his assumption of the English crown, James set out to extend the regnal union into a complete political union, under his own divine authority: for his Scottish subjects, he was not just 'our soverane lord' but also his sacred

Palatium regium
Chor des heyligen tempels so der West munster genant
Chorus insignis monasterij Occidentalis
Tres gladij praelati
Tubae argenteae nouem
Innumera nobilium, aulicorum, et satellitum ante fores tem
turba

majesty, a consequence of the 'cult of adoration' associated with the previous English ruler, Queen Elizabeth. In biblical language, he argued that 'What God hath conjoined then, let no man separate. I am the husband, and all the whole isle is my lawful wife; I am the head and it is my body; I am the shepherd and it is the flock'.[5] In 1604, commissioners were appointed from both countries to negotiate political union, but the project made scant progress. It was in this context, to discuss the union scheme, that James in that year convened the first parliament of the post-1603 period. It met first in Edinburgh's tolbooth, and subsequently at Perth tolbooth.[6] By this date, the procedure for calling a parliament was quite standardised. First, a parliament would be proclaimed at the mercat crosses of principal burghs, and commissioners would arrive at the allotted town. We should bear in mind that the mercat cross was the focus of civic authority in any burgh, and thus a 'governmental' structure in its own right. More ambitious towns such as Edinburgh, Glasgow and Aberdeen constructed grander crosses standing on a circular or polygonal raised base, which could be used for public and judicial proclamations, and, sometimes, executions. For instance, Angus Og MacDonald of Islay was executed at the mercat cross of Edinburgh, together with some of his supporters, in 1615, as was the Marquis of Montrose in 1650.[7] It was also the focus for expressions of civic or public festivities or celebration: as in 1600, when the king was welcomed to Edinburgh, and his deliverance from the Gowrie conspirators celebrated, when the cross was clad with tapestry. In the course of preparations for the king's 'hamecoming' in 1617, 'the Crosse of Edinburgh was taken doun; the old long stane, about fortie foots or therby in length, from the place where it stoode past memorie of man, to a place beneath in the High Streete'. A new cross or 'obelisk' was erected on 25 March, with the mason work contracted for by John Mylne and John Telfer.[8]

The holding of parliament would be preceded by the 'Riding of parliament', a state procession which (when in Edinburgh) began with assembly at Holyrood, and proceeded in formalised ranking up the length of Canongate and High Street to Parliament House, with the Honours of Scotland (the national regalia) borne by officers of state, all of whom were members of the nobility. While triumphal procession was reserved for the monarch, the Riding gave parliament a share in the glory. The ceremony was redefined by James in 1587,

2.1. The triumphal coronation of James VI as King of England in Westminster Abbey, 25 July 1603.(British Museum)

when the instructions for apparel were also laid down. Parliament had become a great spectacle, the Riding a major event for which a good view was worth money, and which was protected by elaborate temporary railings and ropes in the High Street.[9] Its route was carefully sanded beforehand, for the benefit of the horses. The Riding began with commissioners and others assembling in the forecourt at Holyrood. They were ranked *ad seniores* (with the least important first) and led by the king's commissioner, accompanied by the Honours, and by the commission itself, resting on a cushion. Edinburgh town council was also represented, and (after 1617) its mace was carried. The purpose of assembly at Holyrood was to escort the monarch – whether in person, or as symbolised by both the King's/Queen's Commissioner and the Honours – from the palace. The palace forecourt thus took on an occasional civic role, and was to be the first in a sequence of public open squares in the town. The need for a corresponding square where the Riding terminated was possibly met either simply by the wideness of the High Street, or else by the area which was in the 1630s to become Parliament Close.

The main landmark through which the Riding passed on its ascent was the Netherbow Port, the principal town gate at the foot of the High Street. Suggestive in its form of a triumphal arch, the gate was decorated for both the state entry of Queen Mary in 1561 and the 1633 visit of Charles I. As part of a rebuilding scheme of 1606, which added a clock and steeple, the town council also decided to erect on it a stone statue of their absentee king, arguing in 1607 that 'it is the custome of maist renownit cities to haif the effigie or statue of thair prynce sett up upoun the maist patent parts of thair citie'; the statue would be 'gravin in . . . maist pryncelie decent forme in remembrance of his Majestie and of thair sinceir affectioun borne unto him'.[10] This was the first post-1603 architectural act of glorification of the king, and formed part of a widespread phenomenon across Europe to raise the status of both monarchs and capital cities by evoking Roman majesty; for example, passers-by were encouraged to doff their hats to Pietro Tacca's 1610 equestrian statue of Henri IV on the Pont Neuf in Paris. The statue of James was finally made in 1615–16, spurred on by the king's impending visit – as were other projects such as repairs to roads and bridges on the royal route. The statue was begun by a Frenchman named Benjamin Lambert, and was completed by John Mylne; probably set in the inner aedicule of the port, the statue was coloured and gilded, and accompanied by an inscription which pledged 'the people's love' to James. The statue was demolished by English Cromwellian troops during the occupation of the 1650s.[11]

On the arrival of the Riding at the location of the parliament, an elaborate inaugural ceremony took place. A later seventeenth-century account, from an age of similar royal dominance, shows us its character: essentially, there were elaborate opening and closing ceremonies in which all members participated, but the processes of active decision-making and drawing-up of legislation were entirely delegated to the Lords of the Articles. The ceremony began at the conclusion of the Riding: the representative of the absent king, the Lord High Commissioner, was greeted by the Earl Marischal, keeper of the parliament building, and then seated himself on the royal throne, with 'near him the great Officers of the Crown, and in two ranks the Prelates and the Secular Peers, the Deputies of the Provinces to the right, and those of the Burghs to the left. The Honours are put on the table by the High Constable and the Earl Marischal. After prayers by the Bishop of Edinburgh the list of the Deputies is read. Thereafter, the Lord Chancellor approaches the Throne on his knee, and receives from the hands of the Lord High Commissioner the King's Commission, which he gives to a Secretary to read. Then is read the formula which is the Manner and letter of the assembly, after which the Lord Lyon King-of-Arms descends from the Throne and places the Lords and Deputies according to their rank'. The Lord High Commissioner then declared the intentions of the Crown and tendered the oath to the deputies, or commissioners (i.e. the members). A late sixteenth-century English account emphasised the shortage of space: 'the Prince beinge placit in the highest place, the Chauncellor at his feet, the Clarke under the Chauncellor, and the Dempster under the Clerke. The Archbisshopps and Bisshopps are scituate one the right hand of the Prince. The Earles on the left hand till the Rome be fulfillit, and when there is not sufficient roome in the highest degree [for] the Bissopps and Earles, [they that] getts na roome are placed in the second degree with the lords and others great barons, and the Burgesses are placed on the other side forenent the Lords, and the remanent small Barons stands on the flure'. It was not actually the Commissioner, but the Chancellor, who acted as presiding officer during the sessions themselves.[12]

At this point, the 'fencing' (the formal declaration of the opening of parliamentary business by the Lord Register) took place, and the names of the 'suitors' necessary to constitute a feudal court were read. The first day's principal business, during those years of royal predominance, was to elect the Lords of the Articles, whose duty was to work with the officers of state and the monarch or his/her representative to draw up legislation. Commonly – though this varied – the Lords comprised eight of each estate. In 1604, in place of the monarch, the Earl of Montrose was designated 'great comissionar', and in 1639 the Earl of Traquair was 'his Majesties Commissionar'. When Traquair abandoned that parliament, a new term, 'president', was coined for his replacement, elected without the king's approval: 'The haill bodie of the estats . . . conveind in Parliament Did vnanimouslie Elect and choose Robert Lord Burghlie To be precident of this meiting of estatis in parliament'. A 'continuation', or a break between the opening day of parliament and the commencement of business, to enable sifting out of the submissions, was normal. The 1617 parliament, for instance, was called 'to be haldin at the burgh of Edinburgh and to begin, God willing, [upon] the xxvij day of May nixttocome, with continuation of dayis . . . and mak publicatioun heirof be oppin proclamatioun at the mercate croceis of the heade burrowis of this realme and otheris placeis neidfull'.[13]

The complicated process of electing the Articles is illustrated by the 1633 parliament, at which, unusually, the monarch was present: 'His Majestie and estaits of parliament Being convenit in the parliament hous The Court of parliament being fensit And the suittes callit His Majestie The Clergie and nobilitie past furth of the parliament hous And his Majestie reteiret to the Inner great roume of the exchecker hous The Clergie to the litle exchecker hous And the nobilitie to the Inner hous quhair the lords of sessioun sittes And they being sett the saids noblemen electit for the Clergie the persones vnderwrittine to be vpoun the articles viz . . . And the Clergie electit the persones vnderwrittine for the nobilitie to be vpon the articles viz . . . And thairefter immediatlie the Clergie and nobilitie being convenit togidder in the said Inner hous quair the lordes of sessioun sittes And having maid publicatioune of thair severall electiones They all Jointlie togidder electit and choysed the persones following of the Commissionars of the Barounes and frie burrowes To be vpoun the articles, viz . . . And thaireftir notice of the said electiounes being given to His Majestie His Majestie enterit into the said Inner hous And in presence of the said clergie and nobilitie nominat his officiares of estate vnderwritten to be vpon the articles viz . . . And als nominat the chancellar to preside among the saids haill lords of the articles In all thair meetings And thaireftir his Majestie with the clergie and nobilitie reenterand into the said parliament hous And his Majestie being sett in his throne And the haill estaits having takin thair places Publicatioun was maid of the saids electioun and nominatione'. The Lords of the Articles were then instructed to meet at 10 a.m. each day within the Inner House – in the Over Tolbooth, where the Lords sat – until business was ready for voting. Royal influence on these deliberations was increased by the activities of other more informal bodies, such as the 'cabinet counsel' which met daily in Holyrood Abbey during 1621, to select subjects for discussion by the Committee of the Articles.

In summary: the king's commissioner (or, rarely, the king himself), the officers of state and all other members assembled in a parliamentary body; then, the two 'higher status' estates went each to a separate room, and in private, selected each other's appointees; both estates then met together – again, in private – to appoint those from the other estates, which, all the while, simply awaited conclusion of this process. At the end of the meetings of the Articles, the members all assembed once again in the parliament house, heard the findings of its deliberations and – generally – ratified them, usually following a vote. Lastly, the closing riding of parliament took place and the honours were returned to the Castle.[14]

The architectural implication of these complex procedures was that while the existing tolbooth accommodation would be adequate for most of the time, when either parliament was not in session at all or the Lords of the Articles were at work, for the grand ceremonies of opening and closing of parliament a more ambitious hall, as well as subsidiary chambers, was desirable. By the early seventeenth century, the grouping of tolbooth buildings and rooms had assumed considerable complexity. Although Robert Miller partly reconstructed the way in which the various buildings were used, the incessant changes and overlaps of uses and names make any definite conclusions difficult. Parliaments generally continued to meet in one of the two main halls in the 1560s New Tolbooth – that is, in the Laigh Council House and the Over or High Council House. The latter also seems to have been referred to as the 'Inner House', and was expensively redecorated with 'mekle tapestrie' in 1617 in preparation for James's visit, and as part of a more extended programme of post-1603 enhancements. The Lords of the Articles of the 1617 parliament met here; we saw above that it was used in 1633 by the nobility, clergy and king meeting to select the Lords of the Articles, and later by the latter themselves.[15] After completion of the new 1630s Parliament House, the Laigh House was used for the meetings of other bodies, including the Town Council and the Convention of Royal Burghs, as well as extraordinary meetings of Privy Council committees, or meetings of the executive Commission of the Kirk. The outer tolbooth (or the 'outer house of the lords' tolbooth'), located in the subdivided western part of St Giles', was mostly used for national and burgh judicial purposes: around 1618, the Benedictine Dom Alexander Baillie described this accommodation, 'towards the west end of the Church, which is divided in a high house for the College of Justice, called the session or senat-hous, and a low house called the low Tolbooth, where the baillies of the toune used to sit and judge common actions and pleas in the one end thereof, and a number of harlots and scolds for flyting and whoredom inclosed in the other'. In 1610, the outer house was fitted out with green cloth decoration, and new desks and seats for the advocates.[16]

The New Tolbooth had a courtyard, with a gallery added in 1613, and here James was lavishly banqueted in 1617. On 7 May of that year, the town council agreed to build 'ane banquating hous in the Counsalhous yaird for intertening of his Majestie and his nobles'. According to Calderwood, on 26 June 1617 there was 'a timber-hous erected upon the backe of the south side of the Great Kirk of Edinburgh, which was decored with tapestrie, where the toun prepared a banket for the king and the nobilitie. The day following, sundrie knights and gentlemen of good note were banketed in the same hous, and made burgesses. They danced about the Crosse with sound of trumpets and other instruments; throwed glasses of wine from the Crosse upon the people standing about; and endit with the King's scoll' [i.e. health, in Danish].[17] From this, it would seem that the area adjacent to the New Tolbooth and soon to be named Parliament Close was already in use as civic space.

Meanwhile, the General Assembly of the Kirk, chaired by the elected Moderator, was also in the process, gradually, of centring itself in Edinburgh, within the same building – St Giles' – as the outer

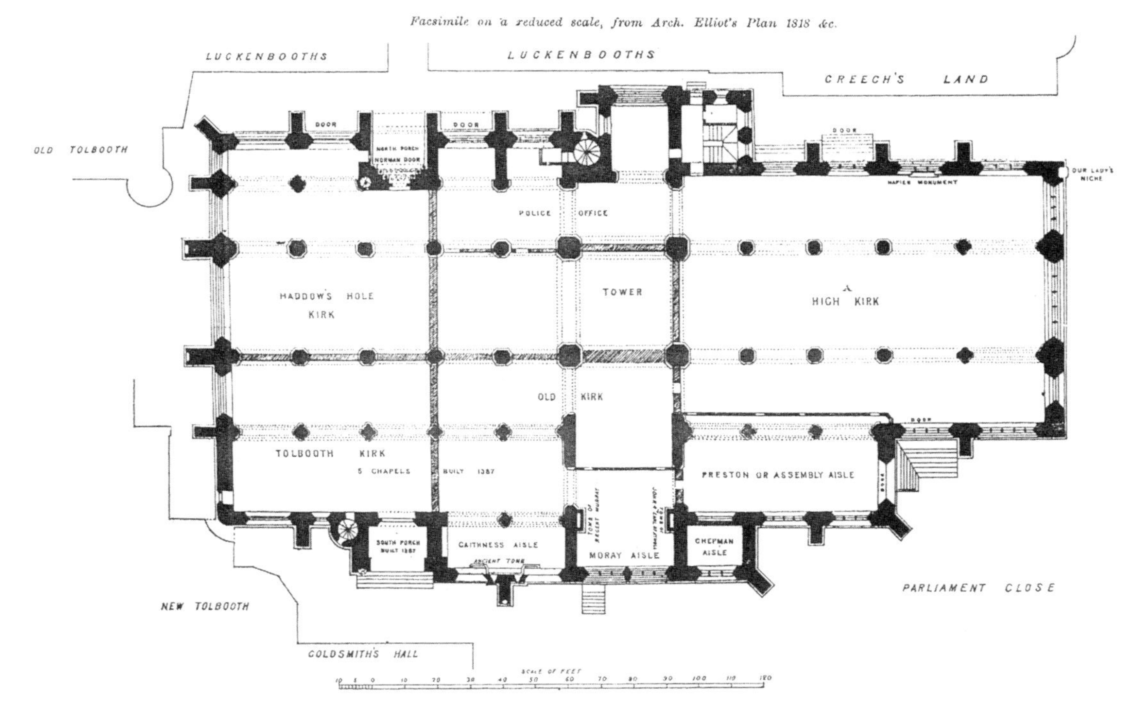

tolbooth. However, it should be borne in mind that its activities were highly intermittent during this time: between 1618 and 1638, for example, it did not meet at all. While early General Assemblies had met in Edinburgh's tolbooth, generally before parliamentary sessions (in order to lobby parliament), from 1580 the Assembly had met instead in the New Kirk, that is, the church which occupied the former St Giles' choir. Following the subdivision of St Giles', the most prestigious of the new churches, by the seventeenth century, was the High, or Great Kirk. In it were lofts (galleries) for the king, privy council, lords of session and the bishops.[18] During James's reign, some General Assemblies were held elsewhere, usually in royal or episcopal burghs, such as Linlithgow (1606 and 1608 – in St Michael's Kirk), Glasgow (1610), Aberdeen (1616) and Perth (1618). These non-Edinburgh meetings always seem to have been held in churches. The Perth Assembly, held apparently in St John's Kirk, was especially significant, for there James's demands for adoption of English liturgical practices (the 'Five Articles of Perth') were ratified under duress.

2.2. 1818 ground plan of St Giles' Kirk, Edinburgh, showing its great diversity of uses prior to Burn's reconstruction in 1829–33; the Preston Aisle, used by the General Assembly, is at lower right. Adapted from Archibald Elliot's plan of 1818. (RCAHMS SC426649)

BUILDING A CAPITAL: CHARLES I AND THE PARLIAMENT HOUSE PROJECT

The Scottish parliament's most significant architectural legacy of the seventtenth century was Parliament House, built in the 1630s to the designs of Sir James Murray of Kilbaberton, the king's master of works. Although subsequently partly demolished, stripped of most of its original decoration and engulfed in nineteenth- and twentieth-century additions, much of the original structure nevertheless survives or can be reconstructed on paper. The context in which Parliament House was built was the reign of Charles I, a time of confrontation and destructiveness within Scottish government, yet a time which paradoxically brought great benefit to the *architecture* of Scottish government. King Charles's calculated escalation of his father's strategy of absolutist monarchy was a significant factor in the ruinous political and religious conflicts which engulfed Scotland, England and Ireland during the 1640s and '50s. Yet he was also the catalyst for a significant enhancement of the status of Edinburgh as 'capital', by centring there all national administrative, executive, and legislative functions, and the supreme judiciary, and as the focus of an episcopalian religious system. These innovations had far-reaching implications for both civic and religious architecture. Charles demanded that St Giles' should be converted from its subdivided post-Reformation state, containing four congregations and a tolbooth, into a unitary cathedral. This, in turn, created a need for new churches as well as a shortfall in civic accommodation. Accordingly, at the same time, Charles also demanded of the town council that it should provide a new parliament house – a project which was fully implemented against a background of impending civil war, and which would witness some of the great movements and events of the decades of turmoil, the 1630s and '40s.

Taken in total, the architectural works instigated by Charles in the 1630s represented the first coherent programme of urban improvement in the history of Edinburgh, providing the town not only with a parliament building but with its first Renaissance civic square (Parliament Close), an episcopalian cathedral, new churches, and an updated royal palace and royal church nearby. The king's strategy was strongly influenced, as elsewhere in Europe, by the continuing authority of Rome as the 'universal' city, a city which, with

2.3. Charles I pictured with Edinburgh as background; engraving by Cornelius van Dalen, probably executed in 1638. (British Museum)

The high & mighty Monarch CHARLES by ye grace of GOD King of Great Brittaine France & Ireland Defendor of the Faythe. etc.
EDYNBURGH
Cd. v. Dalen sculp.

its layers of monuments, remained a cultural paradigm across Europe despite challenges to its political and religious authority. In Scotland, the conception of Edinburgh as a Northern Rome was of some importance to its development as a capital, and added a visual element to the Scottish intellectual and legal dependence on Roman culture – although the connection was complicated by the Reformation, and later obscured by the early nineteenth century's preference for an 'Athenian' image. In the same way that, as we saw in Chapter 1, king Domnall macAilpin chose to promulgate his new legal code in *c.*860 at Forteviot, symbolic focus of Pictish monarchy, the Stuarts now hoped that by elaborating Edinburgh into a symbolic historical landscape, studded with monuments to the Scottish sources of their present British dynastic glory, they could make a virtue of the migration of real royal power to London. However, the creation of the Edinburgh historical landscape was a much longer-term process, and was not confined to the years of kingly dominance and Catholic leanings. For example, the positioning of the out-of-town houses of the wealthy on alignments orientated towards the historic skyline of Edinburgh, in the same way that Renaissance Rome's suburban villas and their gardens were aligned on the city, had begun even in the late sixteenth century, when Aberdour Castle, country seat of the episcopalian Regent Morton, was built looking out over terraced gardens across the Forth to Edinburgh; and in 1622–3, when the architect of Parliament House, Sir James Murray, built his own villa, Kilbaberton, he was careful to align its flank upon Edinburgh Castle.

Charles's strategy of enhancing the architecture of Edinburgh as a symbol of divinely ordained monarchy was heralded, in microcosm, in the temporary decorations for Charles's coronation visit in 1633; Edinburgh, not Scone, was again the site of the ceremony. For that visit, as for James's visit of 1617, Edinburgh decked itself out as the capital, with elaborate festivities, and a parliament held in the tolbooth, which the monarch attended in person. Extensive repairs and reconstructions were made to the royal palaces by Sir James Murray and Sir Anthony Alexander, the king's masters of works, and Holyrood Abbey Kirk was reconstructed specifically for the coronation. The Edinburgh visit began on 15 June 1633, processing eastwards along the traditional High Street route through a series of triumphal arches. Like all attempts across Europe, right up to this century, to express nationalistic pride through classical forms, the imagery on the arches was torn between pro- and anti-Roman themes. In one painting, Roman soldiers, identified by S.P.Q.R. on their ensigns, were seen being repulsed by Scottish warriors, whereas elsewhere inscriptions in the name of the 'Senate and People of Edinburgh' hailed Charles in the style of a Roman emperor.[19]

The centrepiece of Charles's reconstruction programme, the drive to build a new Parliament House, was, however, prompted as much by practical as by symbolic considerations. The town council minutes of a crucial meeting of 13 March 1632 showed evidence that the royal pressure for the building of a new cathedral, and a replacement parliament, privy council, civic and court accommodation, was having some effect, as was the council's own fear of loss of status and income. They recorded that '. . . regraitting that a pairt of thair grit churche which was apointed for divyne service sould be applyet to secular uses and withall considdering that the laick of convenient and fitt roumes within this burgh for keiping of parliament, sessioun and counsall-hous and uther publict meittings may procure the same to be abstracted furth of this burgh to the grett lose and prejudice of the whole inhabitants of all degries; for remeid querof it is thocht fitt and expedient that thair be buildit and erected such spacious and necessarie housses within this burgh in such plaices as the counsall sall designe be advyse of the maist skilfull architectouris as may with credit and conveniencie befitt the honour of the hie estaittes of justice within this kingdome'. The meeting agreed to investigate how far the townsfolk ('honest nichtbours') might be agreeable to contribute to such a scheme.[20]

A week later, on 20 March, the town council reported to the Privy Council, then meeting at Holyrood House: 'The whilk day the provest and bailleis of Edinburgh, assisted with some of the town counsell, compeirand personallie before the Lords of Privie Counsell declared that they wer of purpose and intentioun for the ease and conveniencie of the Estaits and credite of the kingdome to build and raise ane Parliament Hous and Counsel hous and Session hous, and thairfoir desired the saids Lords to assist thame with thair best advice and directioun both anent the contryving of the hous and choise of the place where the same sall be seated. The Lords after hearing and consideratioun of the bussines allowed of the propositioun and gave thame hearty thankes for so worthie ane offer tending so muche to the credite of the kingdome; assuring thame that they would not be wanting to further and assist the bussines by thair best advice whenever the toun sall draw the platt and modell of the hous and consult the Lords tuiching the fabrick and maner of contryvance of the same'.[21]

Thus, the Privy Council expected from the new work a Parliament House, Council House (for the Privy Council), and a session house for the lords (later, court) of session. We will see that this evolved into a plan for two buildings, though in the end only one was built. The site for the new parliament house was officially confirmed in June 1632, after trial excavations for foundations. Two separate projects were at first intended: new privy council accommodation, to occupy a site on the High Street beyond the tolbooth, and the parliament and college of justice building, containing 'such spatious and competent roumes as may sufficientlie serve both for the parliament hous and colledge of justice, in that plaice quhair the ministers' houses doe now stand'.[22]

The site chosen for the parliament house lay close to the tolbooths, within the then-obsolete St Giles burial ground; it sloped steeply downward towards the Cowgate, to the south. It was the intention originally to build on the foot of this slope, on the Cowgate, but the upper level was in the event used, affirming the area around the west end of St Giles' as the location for continued civic/legislative development. The old burial ground had already lost favour by 1566, when Queen Mary authorised the Greyfriars gardens, outside the town, to be made over as a new burial place. A chapel built on this slope shortly after Flodden by the printer Walter Chepman, dedicated to the Holy Rood, had been demolished in 1559, its stones used for the new tolbooth. The principal buildings remaining on the site were three ministers' manses, which were demolished in 1632 to make way for the new Parliament House.[23] Although the awkwardness of the site was no novelty to Edinburgh builders, Parliament House was different in the scale of underbuilding necessary: one end of the hall was at street level, while the other, alongside the jamb rear wall, was set three storeys high. The ground level was dictated by that of St Giles and the tolbooths, and the building's linear orientation also indicated a desire to fit into, rather than rupture, the existing context.

The architect was identified in the town council minutes of 1 February 1633, when it was decided to 'pay to James Murray, Maister of Worke to his Ma., for his bygane travellis takin be him in the

Tounes workes and for drawin of the modell of the workes of the parliament and counsalhous presentlie intendit the soume of ane thousand pundis'. Murray made two designs ('modell' presumably denoting a drawing rather than a three-dimensional model), one for the parliament house that was built, and one for the unbuilt council house. The fact that a large, round sum was paid, rather than a quantified bill, may indicate other services to the council, over a longer period.[24]

James Murray, the king's master of work from 1607 until his death in 1634, was selected for this key project because of his status as the country's 'maist skilfull architectour[is]'. He was descended from an aristocratic family, the Murrays of Falahill and Traquair. His father, James Murray the elder (d.1615), had been a wright in the royal works from at least 1575, becoming master overseer in 1601; he was promoted, and evidently well regarded, by William Schaw (d.1602), at that time the' king's master of works. James Murray the younger was employed in the royal works by 1594, as a wright, selecting timber at Leith for a building project at Stirling – presumably for the Chapel Royal. He was soon also serving the king in more esoteric ways: for instance, in 1597, he was paid for 'transporting of xxviii deir' to Falkland, while in 1603 he was paid for 'making of daskis and saittis about the pulpet in the chapell of Halierudhous' and – by James's 'special command' – providing billiard balls for the king. In December 1607, following the death of Sir David Cunninghame of Robertland, Murray was appointed 'principall master of all his majesties warkis and buildingis' – the first holder of this post known to have had an artisan background. In all probability, he had been *de facto* master of work since 1603, when Cunninghame was taken to England by the king. In official documents, Murray was described both as 'magister operum' (overseer of works) and as 'architect[us] suo' (king's own architect, or master-builder). His appointment was ratified by Charles on the latter's accession in 1625. In 1629, Murray was conjoined in his post – although retaining seniority – with Anthony Alexander, second son of the Earl of Stirling, who had been promoted to Secretary for Scotland by Charles.[25] Alexander had prepared for the post, having travelled abroad for the specific purpose of studying architecture, but there is nothing to suggest a plan to substitute him for Murray.

In 1612, Murray received the first of a series of charters of the lands of Kilbaberton (present day Baberton), where he built his own house; a modest-scaled suburban U-plan classical dwelling. In his first major documented work, Dunbar House in Berwick (left uncompleted in 1611), Murray was already enjoying the patronage of one of the foremost courtiers of the new unionist monarchy, and he later worked for the king himself in reconstruction schemes at Edinburgh Castle (1615–17) and (from 1618) the Linlithgow north quarter. Besides the vital link with Dunbar, clearly, Murray was, at least, known to, and in some cases, close to, a wide circle of other political, aristocratic and commercial grandees, including not only establishment figures such as Alexander Seton (Chancellor from 1605) and the future 1st Earl of Haddington, whom he accompanied on a journey to England in 1611, but also some who later took up anti-royalist positions, such as the wealthy businessman, Sir William Dick of Braid, prime sponsor of the covenanters and generous benefactor to causes including Parliament House. Anthony Alexander seems to have been part of this wide social circle: Murray was a godparent to at least one child of Sir Henry Wardlaw, royal receiver of rents and Alexander's father-in-law. When he eventually died in December 1634, 40 years after he first appeared on record, Murray was a wealthy man. His annual income at that date, over and above his official salary, included almost £500 from property he rented in Edinburgh. His estate totalled approximately £37,000, including debts of £28,000, owed mostly by the crown.[26] This debt, which was never repaid, included not only salary arrears, but also the direct expenses of some royal building works, which Murray had personally financed when official support was not forthcoming.

In his work for the visits of James in 1617 and Charles in 1633, Murray was involved in a number of highly symbolic projects. Preparations for the 1617 'hamecoming' included an important transformation of the chapel royal within Holyrood Palace; the institution of the chapel royal had been relocated from Stirling in 1612 as part of the royal centralisation process. Over a number of years after 1612, the chapel was rearranged for episcopal worship, and ornamented with imagery and woodwork by craftsmen brought from England. The project involved Murray in liaison with his English counterpart, Inigo Jones, who supervised the woodwork of Nicholas Stone for the chapel. In this Holyrood project, James was able to try out in a controlled, elite setting his liturgical strategy, which was subsequently put into effect nationally by the 1618 Perth General Assembly, ratified by parliament in 1621, and celebrated architecturally in a 'model' church at Dairsie, built by John Spottiswoode, Archbishop of St Andrews, also in 1621. The interiors of the Holyrood chapel and of Dairsie were both stripped out by Presbyterian iconoclasts in the early 1640s.[27] For the 1633 coronation visit, Murray – and Alexander – were given their first major tasks for Charles. Once again Holyrood Palace, site of the coronation ceremony, was reconstructed. The Abbey Kirk was transformed, its east gable given its present giant, traceried window and the west gable likewise altered dramatically, with a bell-cast cupola over the north-west steeple.[28]

In view of this pedigree of architectural works and establishment connections, it would have been odd had the town council done other than approach Murray to design its parliament house. The fact that on the same day in 1632, Charles wrote to the Privy Council encouraging work on Parliament House to proceed, and also to the Chancellor – Hay of Kinfauns – authorising that Murray be knighted, on grounds of his 'qualitie and sufficiencie' and 'affection to doe ws good service', may imply that the king himself had a hand in his selection. The conferring of the knighthood was delayed a year until Charles could perform the honour himself, at Seton Palace.[29]

Although built and owned by the town council, Parliament House, as conceived by Charles, was an architectural expression of his royalist, centralised view of government (an approach generally seen as a mark of progressiveness across Europe in those years) and of Edinburgh's status as one of the historic sources of the pan-British Stuart monarchy. The parliament building was to overlook a new civic square which, like a Roman forum, would be fronted by prominent religious and public buildings. In those terms Parliament House, in its originally intended multi-purpose governmental role, accommodating the parliaments and conventions of estates, and the judiciary, was conceived less as a *curia* than as a basilica, with its general hall space for meetings and trials. This was not a single-purpose, monumental parliament building, as was normal in the nineteenth- and twentieth-century period of mass suffrage. But it was, nevertheless, a new building constructed *mainly* to house a national parliament – something unique in pre-eighteenth century Britain and Ireland, and highly unusual even in European terms. And more specifically, in terms of the inevitable comparisons with Westminster, we should remember that the latter was to remain a jumble of feudal palace buildings for another two centuries.[30]

In its relationship with its surroundings, the parliament project was one of a small group of ambitious Scottish urban initiatives during the first half of the seventeenth century; the largest of these was Glasgow College, also commenced around 1632. The immediate context of the new civic square, its level payed fore area contrived by massive underbuilding at the south end, was especially important in ceremonial terms, to facilitate the holding and viewing of the riding of parliament, and (later, if not originally) the accommodation of dismounted horses. In contrast with the more private royal connotations of the outer close at Holyrood, this new formal square, or hilltop piazza, celebrated the status of parliament and of the town.

But the new parliament building also fitted into a wider conception of civic planning, focused on the visual and symbolic relationships between key monumental buildings of the town. In contrast to the classical or romantic-picturesque townscapes of the nineteenth and twentieth centuries, whose interrelationships were of a relatively free, fluid kind, the Scottish Renaissance city and its symbolic landscape was more rigidly structured by concepts of geometry, especially as interpreted by freemasonry. We will see later that the design of Parliament House itself, outside and inside, was governed by the use of 30, 45, 60 and 90 degree angles. The square, or 90-degree angle, the angle of dressed ashlar, was of supreme importance within the masonic craft, whose badge set a square with compasses interleaved; freemasonry as a whole had been reorganised and codified in 1598–9 by one of Murray's predecessors as Master of Work, William Schaw.[31] The two other key town planning initiatives of early seventeenth-century Edinburgh were Murray's reconstructed Palace of

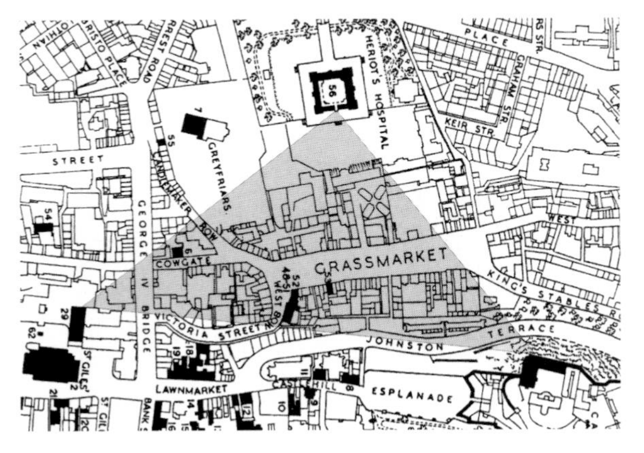

RIGHT.
2.4. Map (with south at top) showing the geometrical relationship of the south façade of Parliament House, the main north entrance of George Heriot's Hospital and the south-west corner of the palace block at Edinburgh Castle – all projects with confirmed or probable attribution to royal architect James Murray. (RCAHMS EDD/1/7, adapted by A MacKechnie)

OPPOSITE.
2.5. Detail of Gordon of Rothiemay's 1647 map of Edinburgh, showing Parliament House, St Giles' and their surroundings from the south. (RCAHMS C 48619)

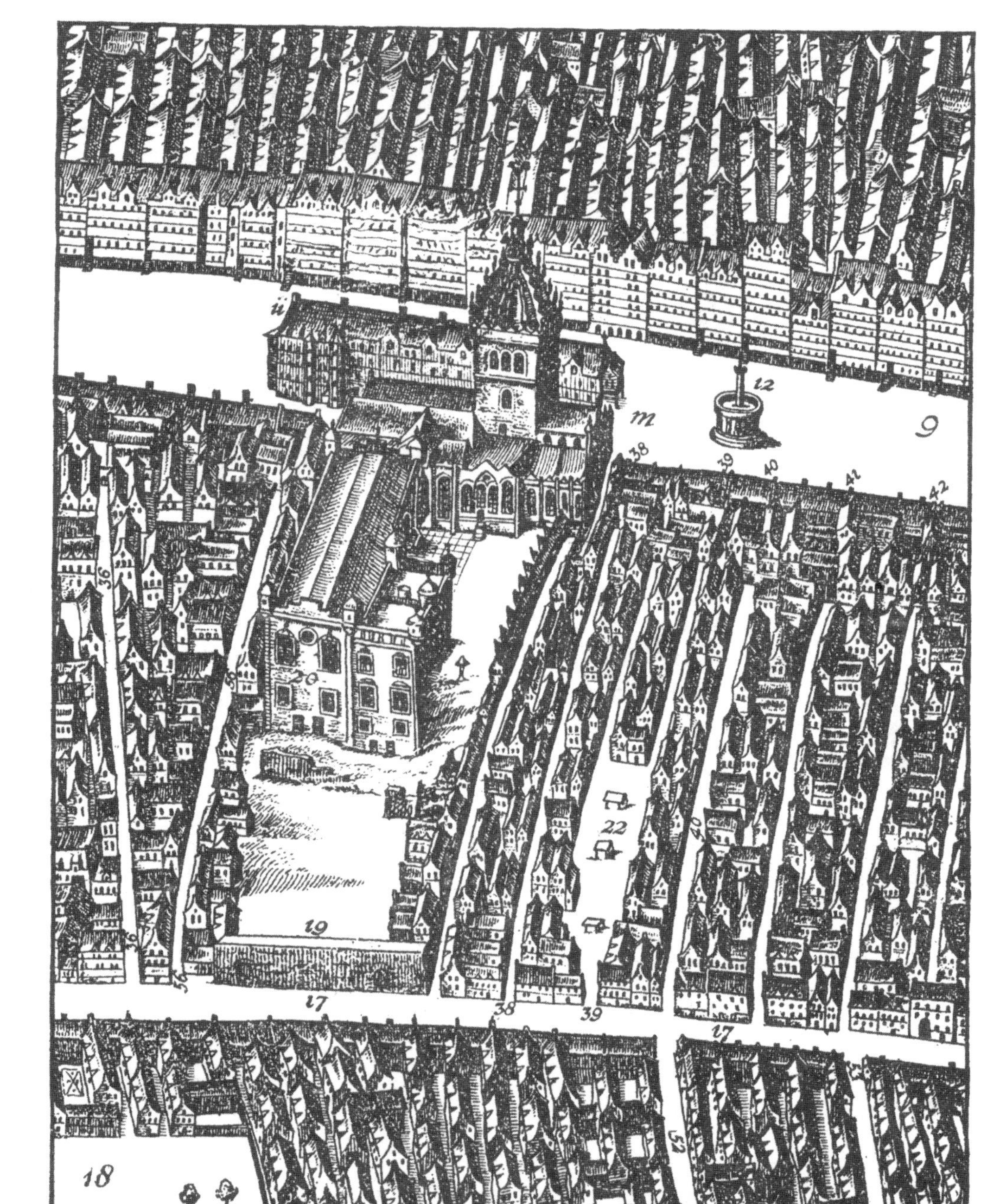

ii
12
m
9
38
39
40
41
42
36
20
22
19
17
38
39
17
52
18

1615–17 within the castle, aligned on the courtyard of Holyrood Palace at the far end of the Royal Mile, and Heriot's Hospital (begun 1628), facing the hollow between castle and town, with an axially planned approach and bridge. The new Parliament House was carefully positioned in relation to the two other monuments; the main north façade of Heriot's occupies the apex of a right-angled triangle, whose other angles (of 45 degrees) correspond to the south gable of Parliament House and the south-east corner of the castle. Within the parliament hall, the castle palace block and Half-Moon Battery were represented on one of the ceiling corbels, and a three-towered building reminiscent of Heriot's on another. More research is needed on the possible links between geometry and masonic/biblical symbolism in town planning during this period.

Knowledge of the original plan and appearance of Parliament House derives from a number of views, notably those by Rothiemay and Elphinstone. This evidence is supplemented by three groups of sculptural fragments, salvaged when the building was re-fronted after 1806, and by remaining evidence within Parliament House today. The building, as erected, was an L-plan structure of two main storeys and partial basement, with a main block running north-south, and a subsidiary south-east jamb; the main frontage faced east, across the new civic square. Its main west block contained the great hall of the 'outer house' for parliament and the Lords Ordinary, with the 'Laigh Hall' below it. In the south-east jamb, an entrance lobby and the Inner House (Court of Session) occupied the ground floor, with the Court of Exchequer above; further vaulted basement accommodation lay below these at the south extremity of the building. In effect, the L plan reflected the division between full-height and horizontally divided interiors.

TOP.
2.6. View of Parliament House from the east, in its original state, *c.*1646. (From de Wit's engraving of a drawing by Gordon of Rothiemay; reproduced in *Book of the Old Edinburgh Club*, 13, 1924, 220; RCAHMS D49011)

BELOW.
2.7. 1967 view of the surviving west wall of Parliament House and the Laigh Hall, with nineteenth-century law-courts and library accretions, and recast windows to Parliament Hall. (RCAHMS ED/2161)

The main east façade of the building was made up of the north section of the hall, and the jamb. The frontage to the hall was of three bays, with a grand entrance direct into Parliament Hall at the north end, and two window bays to the south: the idea is seen in vernacularised form at the nearby and slightly earlier Gladstone's Land, and in doubled, symmetrical form in Murray's palace block at Linlithgow. The two-storey façade – set opposite single-level fenestration on the west wall – implies that an internal gallery was located at that point, extending to the door at the north end of the east wall. The ground-floor windows had triangular pediments, and those above had

CVRIA Supremj Conventus Ordinum Regni Scotiæ
Vulgo Domus Parliamentj
The Parliament House in Edinborrowgh by I.G.

strapwork heads; the windows themselves had timber shutters beneath fixed leaded upper panes. A turreted staircase tower projected from the junction of the main façade and the jamb. The east façade of the jamb was almost symmetrical and five-bayed, with central stair-tower and some rectangular classical windows; its three-bay north façade had a central doorway, framed by channelled pilaster strips, voussoirs and obelisks. The south gable wall of the main hall had two tall broken-pedimented windows (mostly destroyed by a later large central window) and the upper levels of the jamb had pedimented window heads; the line of this south wall was perhaps intended to read as part of the same plane as the Castle south wall. The capping stone of the south gable parapet is a 1639 dated sundial. On the west wall, the six hall windows had single mullions and transoms, while the laigh hall windows on this wall were differently spaced. The north gable wall of the hall originally had a door leading out towards the tolbooths (now marked by a 1636 datestone on the inner wall of the present Signet Library). The roof was very low-pitched, indeed almost flat, and concealed behind balustrading; the latter was pierced to the east and crenellated to the west (facing the Castle). At all the angles were bartizans to denote status and power, and containing small viewing chambers; they are square, as at the nearby royal palace, and one has a large sundial. On the south gable, these sat above pilaster strips. Some of the sparse visual evidence suggests similar pilasters on the east façade, which would have constituted the earliest use in Scotland of a giant Order (the idea otherwise remaining unused until or after the late 1670s at Drumlanrig).

The overall architectural treatment of Parliament House was typical of the work of Murray and Alexander in its combination of profuse classical detailing and strapwork-type decoration with a regular, although not necessarily symmetrical, general disposition. Murray and the other contributors to its design had to consider both its practical functions and its symbolic role, and to choose between the free classicism of the Scottish Renaissance tradition and stricter Italianising models. Although, for Charles, England was doubtless the foremost model in constitutional terms, architecturally it would have been difficult to transplant the features of the bicameral English parliament to unicameral Edinburgh; nor would the makeshift old structures at Westminster in any case have seemed an attractive model. In Edinburgh, 'lords' and 'commoners' shared the same chamber, and

TOP.
2.8. The south-east bartizan of Parliament House. (RCAHMS D42931)

BELOW.
2.9. The south wall of Parliament House, showing the remains of the original pedimented window-surrounds flanking the large central nineteenth-century window. (RCAHMS D42929)

the composition of the estates prevented a division either of landowners and others, or of nobility and others; for bishops would most probably be commoners, and barons or even burgesses might be landowners. A grand space was therefore necessary, as the monarch would always be represented or potentially present, and the nobility would always be present. Among possible classical sources, a straightforward giant-columned basilica-hall (such as the spinal-arcaded Palais de Justice in Paris) was not attempted at Edinburgh, nor was there any direct attempt at reproduction of Italian classicism or of Inigo Jones's Italianising royal works in England, which would be especially well-known to the nobility and to Murray. The most ambitious 'parliament' building of the age, Jacob van Campen's Amsterdam Town Hall (from 1648), had not yet been commenced. Its vast two-storey *Burgerzaal* would celebrate not royal but city-state power; but in 1630s Scotland, a giant-size hall still denoted or implied royal or religious authority. Linlithgow's great hall (1424) had introduced the concept in relation to royal works, while that at Stirling was of comparable scale to Parliament House, and must have presented itself as a reference point. But this was a different age and different building type, and different symbols were required. In general, across Europe as a whole, the architectural setting of legislative-judicial activity was changing from the 'great hall' to the classical palace.[32]

Perhaps the most significant single design decision at Edinburgh was the choice of an almost flat rather than steeply pitched roof. This can be interpreted in at least two ways. In the most immediate sense of purely visual precedent, it was a motif that was to some extent associated with English late sixteenth/early seventeenth-century aristocratic houses, and had been employed almost certainly at Dunbar House and by Lord Kinloss – a naturalised Englishman – at Culross Abbey House (1608), before being used by Murray in his royal palaces, both within Edinburgh Castle and at Linlithgow. More generally, across Renaissance Europe a balustraded flat roof, with its connotations of antique stateliness, was used to denote buildings associated with authority and government. The most prestigious examples were naturally in Rome, whether secular (the government buildings on the Capitoline Hill) or religious (the buildings erected by Pope Paul III at St Peter's). In England, the royal architect Inigo Jones had used the idea – in unambiguously Italianate style – on two major

TOP.
2.10. Detail of top of blocked window at lower level of Parliament House south gable, now incorporated inside sub-basement level of courts complex. (RCAHMS D42956)

MIDDLE.
2.11. Dated door-pediment from Parliament House, relocated in the early nineteenth century under the arcade of Robert Reid's new façade. (RCAHMS D42926)

BELOW.
2.12. Door pediment and frieze from main entrance to Parliament House, with royal arms, relocated by Sir Walter Scott as part of a garden doorway at the rebuilt Abbotsford (1817–23). The initials 'CR' inside the pediment appear to have been gouged away, perhaps by Covenanters. (RCAHMS D62188/CN)5

OPPOSITE.
2.13. Gateway in walled garden, Arniston House, assembled out of fragments of Parliament House. Above the door is a window pediment from the courtyard front, flanked by corbels from the main parapet. Flanking the opening are diamond-pointed stones from the main door pilasters, topped by upside-down pilasters from an armorial frame, probably from the jamb overdoor. (RCAHMS D58825)

ABOVE.
2.14. Bridge in sunken garden, Arniston House; another collage of Parliament House fragments. From left to right: diamond section of door pilaster; finial, probably from jamb door; corbel or console; window-pediment, probably facing close; voussoir, possibly from main door; and another diamond-pointed pilaster segment. (RCAHMS D58804)

early seventeenth-century projects for the monarch, the Banqueting House and the Queen's House. In the Scottish and North European context, the use of a flat roof was a clear repudiation of the civic architectural tradition of narrow, tall tolbooth buildings with steep roofs and towers, in which the main public halls were on the first floor above prison cells (for which, see *Tolbooths and Town Houses*). Closely comparable was Salomon de Brosse's Parlement de Rennes of 1615–18, built for the autonomous Breton parliament: although this was a fully detached palace-like block with regular arched classical façades, it had high roofs and a main hall on the first floor. Likewise, Elias Holl's Augsburg Town Hall of 1615–20, also with a first-floor great hall, had tall gables; and the later Amsterdam Town Hall, although more regular in its classical exterior and plan form, still had a high roof and central tower. In comparison with the huge palace at Amsterdam, Scotland's more modest Parliament House, with its angle stair turret, looked rather more like a substantial country house; its principal floor was entered at ground level, more like a religious building, or like the royal halls at Stirling and Edinburgh. Although the new parliament was still a multi-purpose building, it at least no longer had to double as a prison, and the Italianate horizontality of its architecture emphasised the fact.

Other individual aspects of the design undoubtedly had their own particular connotations. Some, such as the thistle and rose sculptures expressive of Stuart unionism, are unambiguous in their meaning, but others are more difficult to interpret today. For example, was the use of ashlar symbolic of more than wealth and stability? Perhaps it alluded to Roman architecture, and the learning associated with Rome. But equally, in a post-Reformation context, for a nation which had played a key role in the revitalisation of Freemasonry around 1600, perhaps biblical imagery also had a role; Solomon's Temple had been an explicit architectural ideal since at least the time of James IV. The main parliament house portal on the east façade was laden with potentially symbolic features. Its Doric order was composed of boldly projecting, diamond-pointed square blocks, executed with an Italic boldness unmatched in Scotland until the Argyll Lodging gateway was built, *c.*1674. There was no close parallel or prototype in these islands, although many of the components of the formula were used elsewhere, for instance at the Vigna Panzani, in Rome. Above the portal were two allegorical sculptural figures flanking a royal coat of arms. While the general concept of placing figures above a door is ancient, a trend of more informal poses began in the work of Michelangelo. The two Edinburgh figures (now repositioned within the present Supreme Courts complex) were straightforwardly upright and devoid of dramatic gestures. 'Justice', seen since Plato's *Republic* as the chief of the four cardinal virtues, is a laurel-wreathed, bejewelled figure, with classical folds to her clothing, and originally holding in her right hand a large palm, symbol of triumph or victory, and in her left, the scales of justice. 'Mercy', a statue inferior in quality to 'Justice', bears an imperial crown, entirely wrapped in laurel, symbolising a merciful Christian government which deferred to the integrity and intellectualism of antiquity. An accompanying inscription stated: 'Stant his felicia regna' ('The rule of kings prospers through these virtues'). Between the figures was placed the royal arms; the original was destroyed in 1652 by Cromwell's army, and later replaced.[33] The smaller centre door of the jamb north façade seemed to have a more civic character, with the town's arms above it, and the motto 'Dominus custodit introitum nostrum' ('The Lord guards our entry'; from Psalm 121 v.7).

The primary dimensions of the building, especially those inside the main hall (which measures 40.1m in length by 12.8m in width), appear to have been set by the same framework of geometry which determined its wider town-planning relationships. The outline ground plan and length of the whole building, together with the length and cross/long sections, was made up of a series of 30, 45, 60

and 90 degree angles. For example, the cross-section of the hall from floor to ceiling was an equilateral triangle, while the section from floor to corbel height was a right-angled triangle; the long section of the hall was made up of four equilateral triangles; and the plan of the hall provided a ratio close to *pi*. Here again, we should probably look to a combination of Renaissance humanism with a masonic conception of biblical geometry: it was the great masonic reformer William Schaw himself who had attempted to reproduce the supposed proportions of Solomon's Temple in the design of the new Chapel Royal at Stirling in 1594, while by the 1630s Napier of Merchistoun's invention of logarithms may have further enhanced the appeal of geometry-based design within Scotland. Within Murray's period, the system was used on the elevations and plans of royal and aristocratic projects, including the Linlithgow palace block; it was still influential in the decades around 1700, in the designs of James Smith and William Bruce, as at Hamilton Palace, Holyrood and Hopetoun.[34]

Internally, the main hall and the laigh hall each formed a single space, with the gallery probably stretching along part of the main hall's east wall. The wide span of the main hall's heavy floor determined the

2.15. The Justice and Mercy statues from Parliament House, relocated in a corridor inside the nineteenth-century Supreme Courts complex. (RCAHMS D42941)

layout of the laigh hall below, by necessitating intermediate supports for the joists. At Stirling and Edinburgh, the joist problem had been dealt with by cross-walls and vaulting. The laigh hall, by contrast, was designed to be as open as the main hall above, and its roof was supported by a round-arched spinal arcade, running from north to south along the centre of the hall. This feature could possibly have been inspired by French precedents, such as the *salles des états* at both Blois and Amboise, which featured one or two lines of central columns – a layout also adopted in some of the larger halls of the ancient world. However, the French examples were principal rather than subsidiary halls. The laigh hall was not linked directly to the main hall above, but was accessed by a doorway in the north wall. The jamb had two equal-sized ground-floor rooms, with a turnpike stair on the east wall. The north room was a lobby, and the south room (situated nearer the throne) was used as the Inner House of the Lords of Session. Writing in the 1790s, Lord Cockburn recalled that 'the den called the Inner House then held the whole fifteen judges. It was a low, square-like room. It stood just off the south east corner of the Outer House, with the Exchequer, entering from the Parliament Close, right above. The Barons [judges of the Exchequer], being next the sky, had access to the flat leaden roof, where I have seen my father, who was one of them, walking in his robes . . . There was a gallery over the bar'.[35] Rothiemay's view from the east shows mezzanine windows at this point, implying that the room had a gallery, accessible from the east central turnpike. The two exchequer rooms on the upper floor, immediately beneath the roof, were also used intermittently by the privy council. At the basement level, the building had a cross-shaped arrangement of walls, creating four rooms; a doorway from the main laigh hall leads into the northern part of the jamb, whose floor level is approximately the same. There are two large vaulted chambers in this northern part, whose vaulting may not be original. Each of these vaults gives access to the southern part of the jamb, which has different floor levels, and which relates to a four-storey elevation shown by Rothiemay. Of these, the south-eastern vault appears original, with a narrow chamber occupying the eastern end. Some window/door bands, lintels and sills, and part of the south-eastern angle pilaster, can still be seen, encased within the extensive nineteenth-century additions to the south.

The chief element of the hall interior which survives today is the roof, which was constructed by John Scott, the king's master wright. Whether he or Murray was responsible for its design lacks specific documentation, but Murray was almost certainly the real designer: after all, he had risen to prominence as a wright. If so, this was not only by far the widest single-span flat roof associated with Murray (the palaces at Edinburgh and Linlithgow, for instance, were supported mid-span by spine-walls), but was also probably the widest yet built in Scotland. The decorative treatment of the roof's members disguises the essential simplicity of its basic constructional formula, which is that of a series of timber arches of polygonal form, rising from the stone corbels and kept stiff by a series of radial members and triangles butting up against them, including very shallow, full-width triangles immediately under the roof, which also provide some tying force between the wallheads. The radial struts, linked by curved fins, continue downwards to project below the arches, forming a five-cusped section similar to that of windows installed by Murray at Holyrood Abbey in 1633; perhaps this feature symbolised royal antiquity, echoing as it did the arches of the sixteenth-century Stirling palace block. Almost all the weight of the flat roof is transferred to the arches and corbels, through these varied members, rather than applied to the wallhead. This arch-span arrangement is articulated lengthways for window-bay spacing and is topped by a flat 'lintel' which simultaneously ties the wall-heads and (assisted by the lead platform) compresses the walls vertically, countering the outward thrust which its infrastructural frame transmits via the arch to the wall-heads. The impressive ornamental effect is achieved by the roof's seeming complexity and skeletal openness, by the visual force of the downward-thrusting radials and by the contrast between the oak and the gilt finials.[36]

By choosing this arched structure, a number of other possible options were ruled out. These included the flat-ceilinged, trussed pattern, with its potential for Italianate coffering and wider spans, such as tha used by Inigo Jones in England at the Banqueting House, or sometimes used by Christian IV at the Danish palaces. Jones had also designed an arched ceiling for the Westminster House of Lords: but it was set firmly above a deep cornice, the timberwork concealed, the ceiling ribbed.[37] An old-fashioned hammer-beam construction would have necessitated an extremely high roof, something obviously ruled out on the exterior. Yet there was obviously a desire to combine the stately modernity of the outside with an inside roof structure that would generally recall the great halls of the ancient palaces. The Parliament Hall roof, as executed, inspired a similar internal roof design by John Scott at John Mylne's nearby Tron Kirk, with arched structure and intermediate framing, but in that case combined with a high external roof profile.

In its detailed design and finishes, the main hall itself was treated in a stately yet sumptuous manner. Where the walls are now plain, with a haphazard-looking series of portraits, statues and niches, originally there were square tiles or flagstones on the floor, and ornate timber furnishings, including a royal throne which surely matched in grandeur other seventeenth-century thrones in Scotland and England, including that installed by James Smith in the Chapel Royal (1688), and known from an illustration in *Vitruvius Scoticus.* The 1617 chapel royal at Holyrood, over whose construction Murray had presided, was another recent illustration of the lavishness demanded by royalty. The allegorical programme was carried inside, doubtless to a degree far beyond what is now known, for interior ornament or sculpture is now confined to the roof and its stone corbels. The latter mainly bear representations of heads, but there are also towers or gates, including the triple-towered castle of Edinburgh's arms; the symbolic or allegorical significance of most of these awaits discovery. One sculpture on the west wall depicts Edinburgh Castle, including the Half-Moon Battery and the palace built in 1615–17 by Murray. According to James Grant, the hall 'was hung of old with tapestry and portraits of the kings of Scotland, some by Sir Godfrey Kneller. These were bestowed, in 1707, by Queen Anne, on the Earl of Mar, and are now said to be among the miscellaneous collections at Holyrood'.[38]

Despite the scanty surviving evidence of the original arrangement of Parliament Hall, it seems reasonably clear that it was arranged in a hierarchical manner, as appropriate to a unicameral legislature of the age of estates. The progression in status was linear, rising from north to south. The main entrance door was as close as practicable to the north end, given the external orientation of the building to the east, while the grand royal throne, for the use of the monarch, the King's or Queen's Commissioner, or whoever else presided, was placed centrally on the south wall, flanked by two windows (replaced by the present large central window in the nineteenth century). The processional aspect of the design was closely related to contemporary trends in Scottish church building in the 1620s and '30s, which also emphasised strongly linear, processional planning.[39] As to the detail of the layout, it would be desirable to be able to differentiate between the early and mid-seventeenth century, the late seventeenth century, and the years after 1707, but the evidence is insufficiently specific. What seems generally clear is that the most prestigious seating for the estates was arranged in fixed rows in Roman Senate fashion, face-to-face along the side walls, while other less prestigious seats were arranged transversely: in other words, a typical estates-legislature layout, with the 'monarch' facing a U-plan of permanent or movable seats.

For more specific detail as to the internal arrangement of the hall, we have to rely on the accounts of a number of later witnesses and historians, from the late seventeenth century onwards. The most important single piece of evidence is the engraving of parliament in session in 1685, reproduced by Nicholas de Gueudeville in 1708; a translation of the accompanying text, and a commentary (both by Dr Athol Murray) are included as an appendix to this book. Of the other significant written accounts, the earliest is that of 1689 by Thomas Morer. He wrote that 'Within the room on the south [of the main entrance] is an high throne, and on each side several benches one above another, the uppermost whereof is level with the throne, and the lowest reaches the pit, well furnished with forms, for the conveniency and ease of the members. Opposite to the Throne, and without the area, is a pulpit, for sermons in sessions of Parliament, upon special occasions. Behind the pulpit is a large partition, where strangers stand and hear the sermon . . .'[40] In 1779, Hugo Arnot recorded that while the north end of the hall was now occupied by booksellers' stalls, the remainder of the hall retained its pre-1707 layout: 'On the south end of the room is an high throne, erected for the sovereign, now the Lord Ordinary's bench. Round the room are wooden seats, where the bishops and nobility sat, now occupied by those who have business before the court. In the midst of the floor, there were forms for the representatives of the counties and boroughs. On the outside of a wooden partition is a pulpit, where sermons used to be preached to the parliament, and behind that, a small gallery, where those who were not members might hear the debates of the house. These now serve no other purpose but to accommodate the band of musick which performs on his Majesty's birth-day, when the Lord Provost of Edinburgh is entertaining the nobility and gentry with wine and sweet-meats . . . Off this apartment

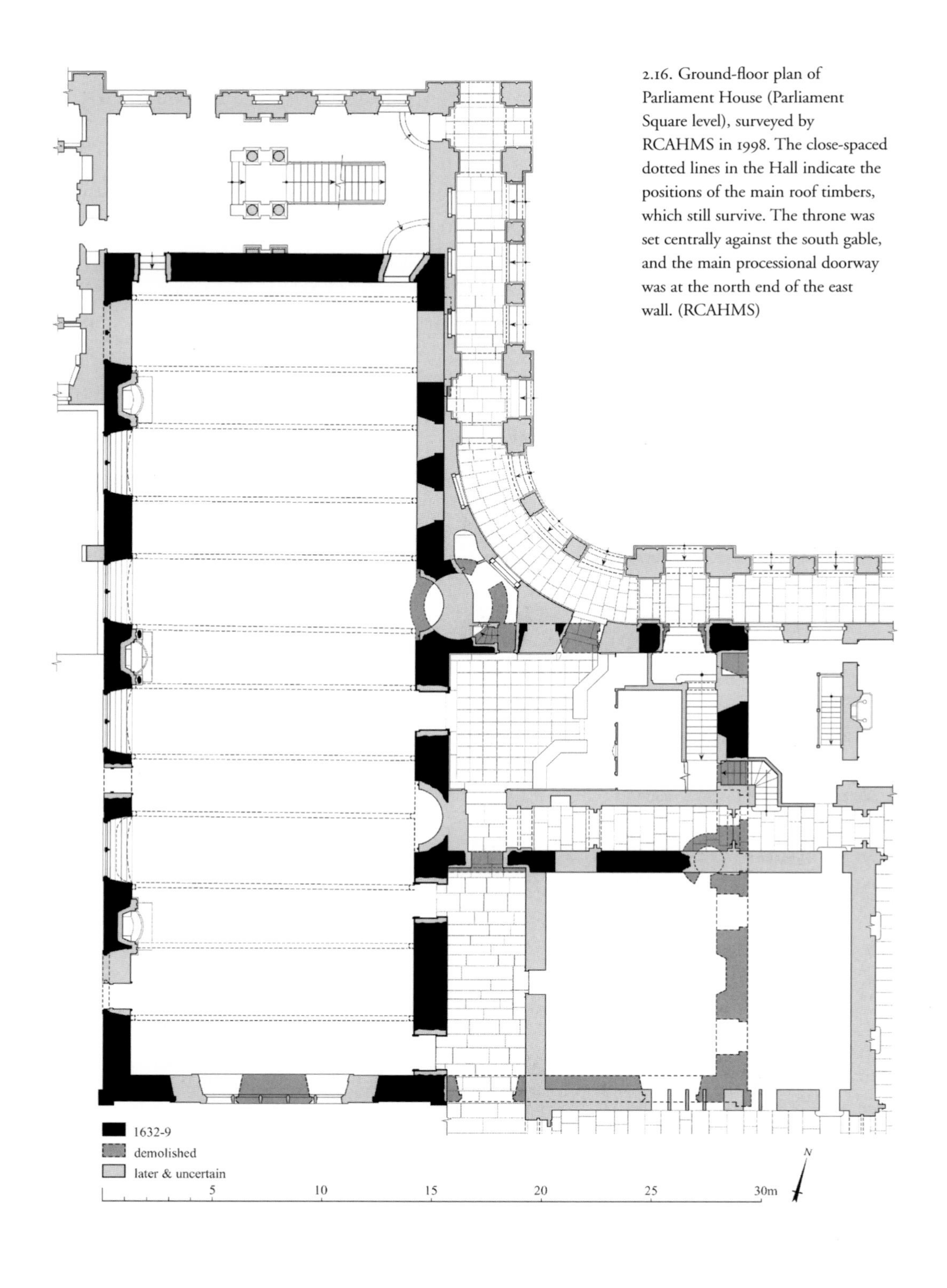

2.16. Ground-floor plan of Parliament House (Parliament Square level), surveyed by RCAHMS in 1998. The close-spaced dotted lines in the Hall indicate the positions of the main roof timbers, which still survive. The throne was set centrally against the south gable, and the main processional doorway was at the north end of the east wall. (RCAHMS)

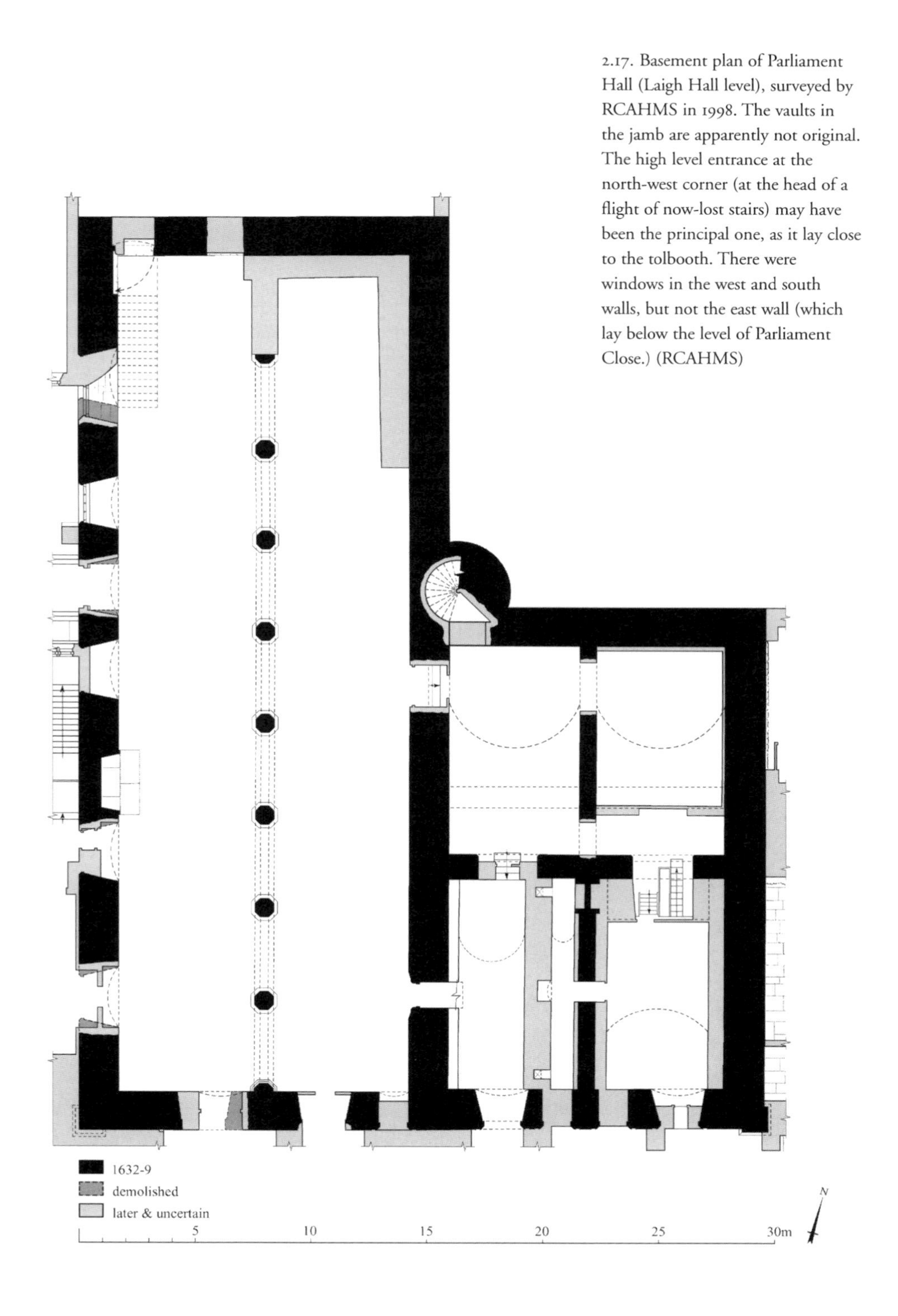

2.17. Basement plan of Parliament Hall (Laigh Hall level), surveyed by RCAHMS in 1998. The vaults in the jamb are apparently not original. The high level entrance at the north-west corner (at the head of a flight of now-lost stairs) may have been the principal one, as it lay close to the tolbooth. There were windows in the west and south walls, but not the east wall (which lay below the level of Parliament Close.) (RCAHMS)

is the Court of Session, with its lobby and robing room for the judges. The court-room is nearly square, well-lighted, and, besides the seats for the judges, is accommodated with benches for the advocates and writers to the signet, and galleries for spectators. This court, in the size of the room, and dress of the judges, makes a better appearance than the courts of Westminster-hall. Above this room are the Court of Exchequer, and other apartments for the Barons, and other officers of that court, who, besides, have further accommodation in apartments in an adjacent building, called the Treasury chambers; because, formerly, the Lords of the Treasury used to meet in them, and also, the Lords of the Privy Council'.[41] And in 1884 J. Balfour Paul wrote that 'The whole Parliament sat as one chamber, like the States-General of France. On the steps of the throne were congregated the officers of state. On either side of the upper end of the hall there were raised and decorated benches for the use of the nobles and higher barons. At a table in the centre the Judges and the Court of Session with the Clerks of Parliament were seated, while the commissioners of burghs and the lesser barons were ranged on plain benches lower down. Beyond these, at the end of the hall, such of the general public as had gained admittance and the retainers of the various members assembled. Distinguished strangers were either accommodated with seats at the extremities of the burgess's benches, or were admitted into a small gallery, which was possibly situated above the present entrance door, where a projection may be seen in the wall. A pulpit stood below the gallery, from which sermons were occasionally preached to the House . . . The walls were then, as now, decorated with pictures, but these, which were portraits of sovereigns and statesmen, have long ago disappeared, though portions of the early decorations, including fragments of ancient tapestry, were only removed at the end of the last century'.[42]

2.18. Drawings of Parliament House (based on 1998 RCAHMS survey) demonstrating the geometrical compositional framework, governed by use of 30/60 and 45-degree triangles: (a) ground-floor plan; (b) plan at Laigh Hall level; (c) longitudinal section (north-south) through Parliament Hall and Laigh Hall; (d) latitudinal section (east-west) through Parliament House, with halls at left. From the centre of the Hall floor, a 45-degree triangle defines the roof-corbel height, and an equilateral triangle defines the roof-height.

The interior of Parliament Hall thus seems to have been used in a fluid and intermittent manner. When parliament was in session, the hall could be opened up as a single large space, but more normally it was divided by a timber partition reaching halfway up the height of the wall; the main, or furnished, parliamentary meeting area was to the south of this partition, and was used by the Court of Session at these times. The intermittent usage of the hall led to its outer area being soon invaded by 'kramers', or shops, but it is not clear when this first happened.[43]

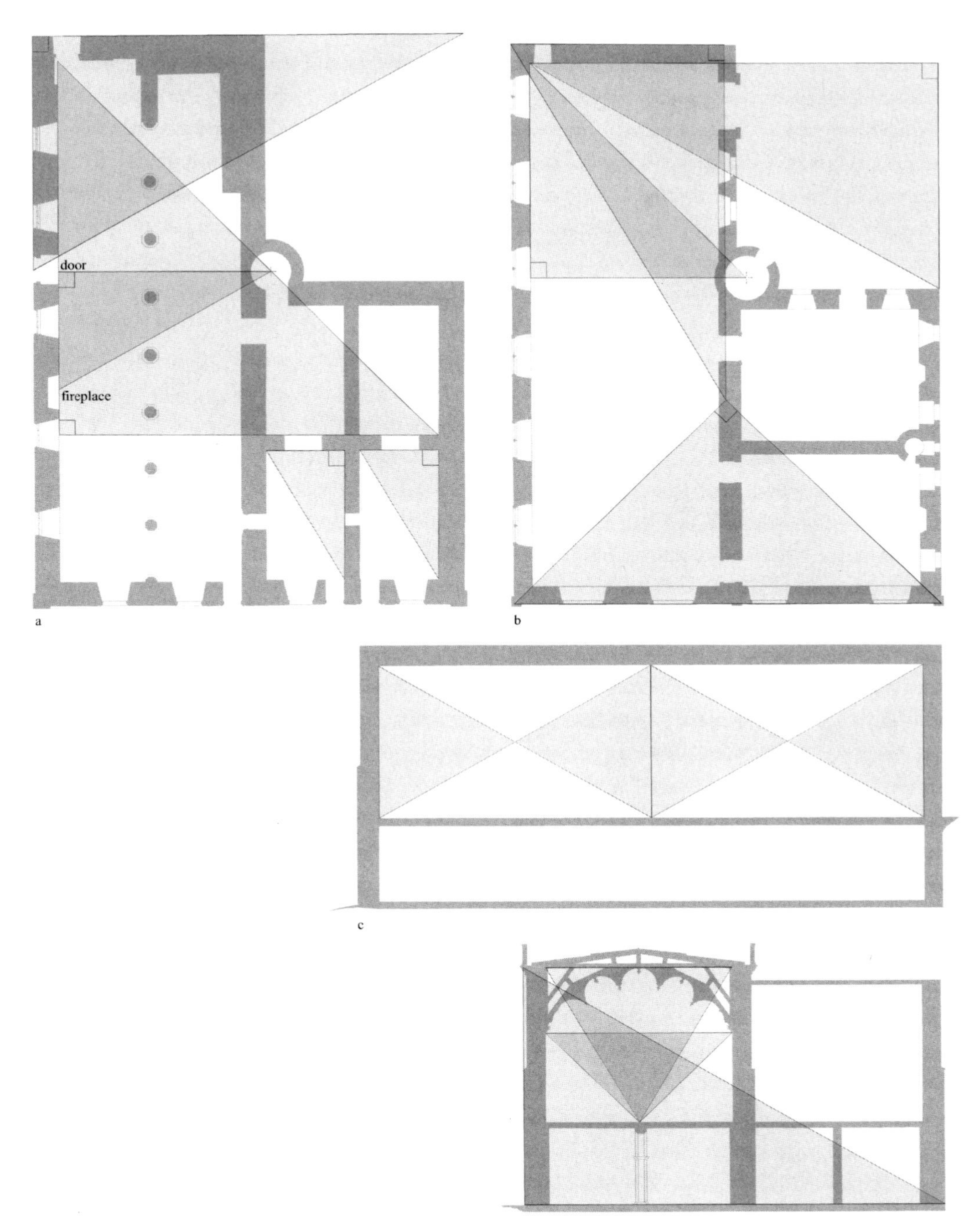
door
fireplace
a
b
c
d

The throne at the south end, which evidently reached a substantial height, had six steps before or around it and the bench of the Lord Chancellor. Facing were the two tables for the Clerk Register and his deputies, and the Lords of Session. On either side of the throne were tiered benches, ultimately stemming from the *curia* arrangement but also recalling episcopal choir stalls. The relationship of the throne to the areas for the estates recalls the arrangement of pulpit and seating within a three-armed church. The benches were tiered along either side of the long-wall, facing one another and reaching quite high up the wall: the bishops' bench was originally on the right hand and the nobility's on the other. This arrangement created the sense of a cavernous central area (Morer's 'pit'), where the clerks' table stood, and also the table on which the Honours of Scotland were placed; in 1703, these benches were recorded as laid out in 'three steps and rows'. Many of these fittings would have been permanent. Opposite the throne, between the fixed benches, stood two ranges of 'forms', or stools, for the lesser-status estates, those on the right being for the commissioners of shires, and those on the left for the commissioners of the burghs. According to Morer, a pulpit was placed directly opposite the throne, that is, north of it and in the middle of the hall; presumably it stood in front of the partition which divided off the northern part of the hall.[44] It seems likely that it was not envisaged in the original design, but was the result of an intervention during construction by the covenanting ministers who (as we will see) were, in the event, the first to use the completed building. This may have been the same pulpit that is today preserved in the Museum of Scotland, and known, significantly, as 'John Knox's Pulpit'. This close interrelationship between mighty and the Almighty was matched in churches, where a laird's loft was often set directly opposite the pulpit. The fact that this pulpit stood in the centre of the hall (albeit probably backed by the removeable timber partition), rather than directly against a stone wall with back-lighting windows, contrasted with the presbyterian norm. Here the position was the opposite: it was the royal throne which had that dignity, and was clearly much larger and more elaborate. During meetings, whilst the officers of state and the estates occupying the benches could easily view all proceedings, whether at the throne or the pulpit end, the estates occupying the forms must have had to turn to face first one way, then the other. There was also, according to Arnot, a small gallery behind (that is, to the north of) the pulpit. Arnot and

2.19. Parliament Hall seen during the official inauguration ceremony of the new parliament, 1 July 1999. (D65684 CN)

others state that its purpose was to permit visitors to view the proceedings of parliament. Certainly, it seems unlikely to have been there as part of the proceedings themselves, as the commissioners of the estates seem all to have been housed within the area down below. Such a gallery can hardly have extended over the full width of the hall at its north end, and still have been called 'small'. Its most likely location would therefore have been (as Balfour Paul suggests) on the east wall, for if placed there it would facilitate both audibility and a clear view. That would also explain why on the front to Parliament Close, the façade is two-storeyed, the hall being otherwise treated as a single storey.

The documented presence of a programme of paintings and tapestries in Parliament Hall is intriguing, and underlines how much has been lost. Mention of paintings of monarchs suggests the time-honoured sequence drawn from the *Scotichronicon*, stretching back to Fergus I; such a sequence adorned an archway on Charles's processional route in 1633 (conceivably, using the same pictures). James VII was later to install a series of portraits painted by De Witt, and again from Fergus onwards, within the gallery at Holyrood. This old imagery remained a key part of Stuart kingship until the time of that last Stuart king. The six-bay interior lay-out of Parliament Hall would have lent itself well as a division of 120 (if the number were rounded up), but window and other interruptions make this postulation less probable. In the light of the destruction of royalist images in the 1640s/50s and around 1689, more likely the monarchs' portraits were of later date; one of King William II (of Orange), for instance, is recorded.[45]

THE BUILDING AND INAUGURATION OF PARLIAMENT HOUSE

The new Parliament House was never used in exactly the way originally intended by Charles and his supporters on the town council, chiefly because it was completed in the course of a revolution against the king's rule, and controlled from the beginning by his opponents. Let us now briefly trace the sequence of events which led to that unexpected outcome. On 3 August 1632, the ground stone of Parliament House was laid. Ashlar blocks came on sleds and carts

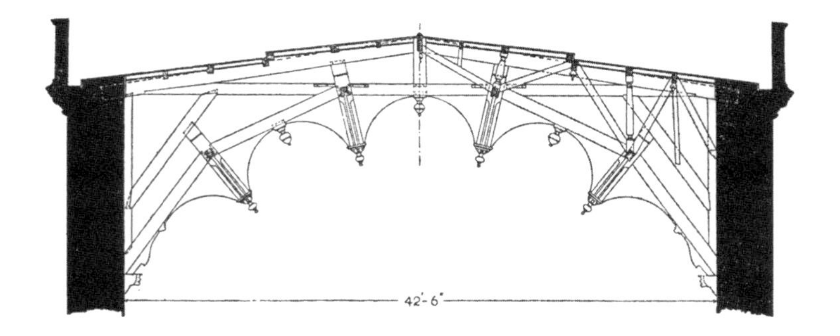

from Ravelston quarry, supplemented, later, with ashlar from Culross; other stones came from the Society Quarry on the Burgh Muir and elsewhere. In February 1633, the town council decided to proceed with clearing and other operations at the site beyond the tolbooth, that is, the site previously identified for the second civic building, the council-house for the use of the Privy Council and Lords of Exchequer – a project which, in the event, was destined never to be built. Men from Parliament House were engaged also at the tolbooth, presumably in anticipation of Charles's arrival. The master mason, and most likely the general overseer of works, was John Ritchie, who also worked at Glasgow College and St Giles', and for Linlithgow town council. Although an important individual, he (unlike Murray and Alexander) was also an operative; the mason Thomas Paterson may have been

TOP.
2.20. Section of the roof of Parliament Hall. *(Book of the Old Edinburgh Club*, 13, 1924, 3)

BELOW.
2.21. Transverse view of the roof of Parliament Hall. (RCAHMS D42939)

next in the chain of command. It is not clear to what extent, if any, Murray was involved with the project after the design stage.[46]

When Charles eventually arrived in Edinburgh and proceeded to convene a meeting of parliament, this new civic forum area must have resembled a building site. Screens, apparently, were set up for his benefit at Parliament House. James VI's 1621 parliament had already seen the beginnings of a polarisation of opinion between 'court' and opposition 'country' factions, and this polarisation had increased in the interim. Therefore the procedure for the election of the Articles followed the precedent of 1621, in an attempt to ensure royal control; bishops – whose careers depended on royal favour – chose eight nobles, nobles chose eight bishops. They in turn chose eight each from the shires and the burghs. Charles appointed Chancellor Hay to preside over the articles, and went beyond the draconian procedures laid down in 1621, by dictating events personally, confining proceedings to ten days only, and suppressing debate and unauthorised meetings; the Convention of Royal Burghs, whose gathering usually coincided with parliament, was banned from meeting.[47] At this stage, there was no wish for a re-run in Scotland of Charles's dissolution of the English parliament in 1629 (where rule by the crown replaced the function of parliament), but the 1633 parliament, held in the old quarters of parliament, showed how the king anticipated that the new Parliament House would be used: as a theatre for the confirmation of his own power. Nevertheless, opposition to the king had now reached such a pitch that the most unpopular measures of religious and taxation reform were almost defeated. After his departure, construction work on the new building continued. In October, he wrote to the town council demanding faster progress not only with the clearance of St Giles', but also with the construction of the 'New Tolbooth' – presumably referring to Parliament House. In 1634, the 'laigh hous' was ready for its joists, and its iron windows were painted. Frustrated by what he regarded as unacceptably slow progress, Charles sacked the Edinburgh magistrates, disregarding supplications made on the council's behalf by Sir John Hay, Lord Clerk Register, and the Earl of Stirling.[48]

Following the king's departure, sustained pressure upon the town council to pursue building contributed, alongside Charles's religious innovations, to the building up of resentment within the town, as taxation was increased, while the crown contributed nothing. In

October, 1635, for instance, 37 masons were employed at Parliament House, and in February 1636, their total was 47, some on overtime. Eventually the burgh, its situation worsened by the demand that it should also build two new parish churches, was forced to go into debt, and the treasurer was instructed in 1636 to borrow 10,000 merks, at 8 per cent interest: the first of a sequence of massive loans. Safeguarded by these financial injections, building work continued apace. The joisting of the laigh hall continued into 1635, while the south-east jamb, with its spinal and interior walling, was evidently built secondarily, for it was not until March 1635 that drinksilver was distributed, following completion of the entire foundations. It seems improbable that the jamb was an afterthought, to avoid construction of a second building, and the design was probably erected more or less as conceived. By the beginning of July 1635, the frame of the Parliament Hall floor was completed, while in August the Inner House flooring was being joisted, and the 'gryt lyntill' of 'the for entry of the jame' (one of the fragments now preserved at Arniston House) was set in place.[49] The years 1636 and 1637 brought further financial crises and *ad hoc* subsidies to rescue the project. In June 1636, it was feared that the original design would have to be simplified, until the Bishops of Edinburgh and Dunblane (the latter, James Wedderburn, being also Dean of the Chapel Royal) lent between them 28,500 merks on

2.22. Corbel of Parliament Hall roof, depicting the palace block of Edinburgh Castle (along with Heriot's Hospital, one of the two buildings located in a triangular pattern with Parliament House). (RCAHMS ED/8862)

2.23. Present-day view inside Laigh Hall from south-east. (RCAHMS B42945)

favourable terms, and the Town Council agreed that the original plan could proceed. In August and September, 'knappald' (wainscot) was ordered to be obtained from Copenhagen ('Coupmaholme'), followed in the autumn by Baltic oak for the roof, some from a Jutland wood-merchant named Lasene or Lawson. With much of the walling nearing completion, Alexander Mylne was occupied from 1636 carving exterior decorative ornament, including the royal arms, for which Robert Telfer was paid for 'cullouring the Kingis airmes with quhyte leid'. In 1637 Alexander Mylne agreed to carve 'the twa picturis and lyoun and twa wing pieces'. The lion appears to have been that shown by Elphinstone as the topmost overdoor feature; the 'picturis' were the allegorical statues of Justice and Mercy above the entrance. Whatever Alexander Mylne's role, the sharp disparity in quality between the two demonstrates that they cannot both have been made by the same sculptor. Thereafter, paintwork by John Sawers, who had worked under Murray at the Linlithgow north quarter, included 'the Kingis armis and pictures', and two 'great yettis', presumably the main doorways. In January, 1637 John Scott was appointed 'maister wricht to the guid toun in thair workes of the Parliament hous and repairing of the queir' [in St Giles']; for St Giles', simultaneously, was still being fitted out as Charles's new cathedral, and in August, John Mylne contracted to repair the 'gritt eist vindow in the queir . . . for hewing and setting vp of the staine worke thairof conform to the plett [plan] schewen'. Timber was now arriving on the parliament building site from several sources, and the jamb roof was leaded over, its interior to be decorated the next year.[50] During early 1637 the finances were still difficult, and workmen were temporarily laid off. However, these difficulties had increasingly political overtones, as the balance of power in the town and the country began to shift against the king: Wedderburn, for instance, reacted to the riot of 23 July in St Giles', against the introduction of the English liturgy, by reclaiming his loan.

In the two years that followed, as the opposition to Charles's policies escalated into an oligarchic revolution, the king's architectural strategy for Edinburgh, far from being abandoned, was taken over by the revolutionaries and pursued for their own purposes, demonstrating the extremely loose fit between architecture and politics, as well as the potentially symbolic national role of the new parliament building. Parliament House was near-complete, and a meeting of the Estates was set for May 1639.[51] But the balance of political power in Edinburgh was now tilting sharply away from the king, who had alienated landed interests through his scheme of 'revocation' of customary property rights, and presbyterians through his episcopalian and erastian policies.

The redoubt of Charles's power in Scotland at this time was the privy council, whose membership Charles continued to augment with bishops and aristocrats favourable to his interests. Up to 1636, it met usually at Holyrood, but sometimes in the tolbooth, in the laigh council house. Like Parliament and the town council, it appointed committees, which sometimes also met in the laigh council house. The town council had in 1636 resurrected its intention to build a new privy council meeting-house, but this could hardly be started while construction of Parliament House was still in full swing.[52] Following the July 1637 riot at St Giles', privy council meetings at first alternated between Edinburgh and Holyroodhouse, but by September a wave of protests from parishes and burghs began pouring in to the council; the emphasis of James I and Charles I on the capital status of Edinburgh had ironically made it the natural focus for popular representations. After that, the king moved its meetings away from Edinburgh.

Following the wave of protests in autumn 1637, a huge election meeting was convened on 15 November, possibly in the near-completed Parliament House, at which four commissioners were chosen from the nobles, lairds, burgesses and ministers to negotiate with the privy council. There was an obvious potential overlap between this group and the work of parliament and the Lords of the Articles, and indeed its popular name, the 'Tables' or 'green tables', seemed to refer to the green cloth-covered tables used during parliamentary sessions. Meeting in the rooms of the nearly completed parliament house, the Tables developed rapidly from a protest group to a provisional government which, in effect, began to replace the privy council and the Articles, and to serve as the kernel of a reformed parliament. In this, they were encouraged by Charles's instruction to the privy council and court of session to move away from Edinburgh. In October 1637 it was decided that 'Forsamekle as it hes pleased the King's Majestie upon diverse great and good consideratiouns knowne to his Majestie to remove his Counsell and sessioun from the citie of Edinburgh to the burgh of Dundie, and whereas it is inconvenient at this time to remove it so far, his Majestie is graciouslie pleased that this nixt session sall be haldin at the burgh of Linlithgow, and the nixt after the ordinarie vacance at the burgh of Dundie, and there to remaine during his Majesteis pleasure'. On 14 November, the council met at Linlithgow, either at the palace or the tolbooth, and fixed future meetings at Dalkeith and (in February 1638) at Stirling, 'and accordinglie, the saids Lords gives warrant to his Majesteis Treasurer for preparing of the castell of Stirline in a comelie and fitting way for accommodation of the Counsell and Session.. and to continue there during his Majesteis pleasure'. As the Stirling great hall would have been too big, it seems likely that a room in the palace was used; subsequent meetings were held at Dalkeith Palace and Linlithgow Palace.[53]

The logical next step of the anti-royal political-religious alliance was to attempt to bind the wider community formally to its aims. This was done by subscription to a written manifesto, the National Covenant, prepared by several people including Alexander Henderson and Johnston of Warriston. On 28 February 1638 it was first read and signed inside Edinburgh's Greyfriars Kirk, and then (even more significantly) outside the church in the open air, the flat tombs serving as tables, following which it was distributed across the country. By the device of mass open-air signature, the covenanters were able to legitimise their oligarchic, elite movement with a degree of direct popular participation (albeit secured partly by coercion), and further undermine royal authority.[54]

The first formal gatherings within the new parliament building appear to have been anti-royalist meetings and sermons, well before parliament met there. One of the first, if not the first, was recorded by Johnston of Warriston in a diary entry for 1 July 1638: 'upon Sunday in the neu Parliament house, I heard Mr James Bonner' (minister at Maybole). The new building was embroiled, from the beginning, in the escalating political and ecclesiastical tensions, and was evidently judged a suitable place within which to preach. Prudently anticipating an outbreak of open hostilities, the town council in August designated the 'westmost laich house under the jame' as an armoury for the burgh.[55] In October 1638 William Dick of Braid – a one-time friend of Murray – was elected provost of Edinburgh, and the townsmen were ordered to receive military training.

2.24. Portrayal of the signing of the National Covenant in Greyfriars Kirkyard in 1638; the 1903 painting by William Hole is one of a series of murals in the Edinburgh City Chambers dining room. (City of Edinburgh Council; RCAHMS EDD/372/91)

Work on the parliament building continued against the backdrop of these dramatic events, and in February 1638 payment was made for plastering four rooms in the jamb, while in March the 'twa over roumes' were washed, coloured, varnished and gilded. The main roof was progressing with deliveries of oak, while 4,500 stones of lead were bought between July and September, and timbers for ribs were delivered in August. Where, less than two years previously, the bishops had subsidised the project, now General Alexander Leslie, commander of the covenanting army, personally supplied timber to help maintain progress. From October 1638, work began, or re-commenced, on the windows: this included 384 feet of glass for what was referred to as the two 'exchequer housis', indicating that the building's intended uses were changing during construction; 504 feet for the two 'laich roumes', beneath; 324 feet of glass and 336 feet of 'wyre' (glazing-bars) for the four 'great laich south windowis'.[56]

In November and December 1638 the crisis deepened when a General Assembly of the Kirk was convened in Glasgow – its first meeting since the Perth Assembly of 1618.[57] Glasgow had previously been loyal to the king, and the town council had built their new town house (begun in 1626) with a tall steeple capped by an imperial crown spire. But contrary to Charles's hopes for a respectful atmosphere, the Glasgow General Assembly provided a forum for both branches of the anti-royal alliance to vent their discontent. The Presbyterian clergy pushed for reversal of the king's religious innovations, and the aristocracy for an end to absolutist rule and for a 'return' to a golden age of consensus between ruler and ruled. Following an abortive attempt by the king's commissioner, the Marquis of Hamilton, to dissolve the meeting, it sat without him during December and passed a programme of measures reversing Charles's religious innovations, abolishing episcopacy and excommunicating the bishops. This was, in effect, a declaration of religious war against Charles.

For this event, Glasgow Cathedral, or rather the High Kirk within it, was elaborately fitted out. James Colquhoun, wright, was responsible 'for the making of the sait of the assemblie approaching, repairing of the fluir of the vter kirk, taking doun certaine windowis in the iner kirk, biggit vp with stone, and putting glas thairon, and vther warkis'. A contemporary account by Robert Baillie, minister of Kilwinning, describes the scene during the assembly proceedings; in some ways, there was a considerable similarity to the arrangement of the secular parliament (to which the revived General Assembly generally deferred, as at the beginning of the century). The Marquis of Hamilton, prior to his departure, sat at the east end of the nave in his 'chair of state', with the principal members of the privy council 'at his feet and on both sides'. Also, 'at a long table in the floor [sat] our noblemen and barons, elders of parishes, commissioners from presbyteries . . . Few barons . . . of note, but were either voters or assessors; from every burgh, the chief burgess; from all sixty-three presbyteries three commissioners, except a very few; from all the four universities also; sitting on good commodious rooms, rising up five or six degrees, going about the low long table. A little table was set in the midst, foreanent the Commissioner, for the Moderator and Clerk. At the end a high room prepared chiefly for young noblemen . . . with huge numbers of people, ladies, and some gentlewomen, in the vaults above'.[58]

It was only at the beginning of 1639 that the Estates and the Edinburgh town council both finally moved into open defiance of Charles; the council took the symbolic step of voting to reinstate the eastern partition wall within St Giles'. During this time, despite the outbreak of the first Bishops' War, work on the new parliament pressed ahead, as both sides saw it as symbolically important to them; as he marched north to war, Charles issued orders for the commissioning and fencing of parliament in July. Building work at Parliament House was now concentrated upon the great hall and its roof. By early May, the roof timberwork was complete, and the decorative finials ('knappis'), turned at Leith, were in position. These were gilded and painted by Sawers, who also varnished the hall, along with any furnishings or timber wall-panelling (presumably including the above-noted 'knappald'). Operating to a new target completion date of 24 June, the plasterers finished in the hall, dismantled their scaffold, and moved to the laigh hall. In the event, after two preliminary meetings, the session was formally convened in the 'New Parliament Hous' on 26 August, and was prorogued until 31 August, when the Riding took place. As normal, it was decided 'the whole esteates of parliament To attend and await the said Johne Erle of Traquair . . . his Majesties Commissionar with all due reverence in maner vsit to otheris having the lyke chairge of befoir At his Majesties palice of Halyrudhouse Betuixe Nyne and Ten houres befoir Noone That his hienes commissionar and estates of Parliament may ryd solemnelie ffra the said Palace in Parliament the said day To the Parliament house at Edinburghe. And ordeanes the saidis estatis to attend whill the Parliament Conclud . . . And ordeanes Proclamatione to be made heirof At the mercat Croce of Edinburghe'.[60] However, the procession lacked any bishops (owing to their abolition by the 1638 General Assembly).

The Earl Marischal met the Earl of Traquair at the main door of

Parliament House, from where he was conducted to the throne. The house was effectively complete, the close had been levelled and, at least partly, paved, though details such as finials remained to be added. Although the throne was evidently ready (presumably, the throne used in 1633 was serviceable and possibly re-located here), ecclesiastical 'furmes and buirds' – possibly elaborate choir pews – were carried from the 'Auld Kirk' to Parliament House, and returned afterwards. 254 ells of green baize had been obtained, 'for covering the whole parliament and assembly houses', whilst a saddler was paid for 'dressing' the parliament house. Proceedings began with divine service and a sermon by Alexander Henderson, one of the framers of the National Covenant, and Moderator at the Glasgow General Assembly, his subject being 'the institutione, power, and necessitye of magistracye'; presumably he made use of the new pulpit.[61]

After attempts to reform the method of election of the Lords of the Articles in the interests of the 'reight and libertie of ane frie Parliament' and the preparation of a covenanting legislative programme by the Articles (sitting in the new Inner House), Traquair adjourned the parliamentary session in November under vociferous protest. In the recess, the finishing works to the building – joinery, stone paving, copper roofing – were pressed forward, and during 1640 the Parliament House was finally completed, at an eventual cost of nearly £127,000. From May 1640, massed assemblies of townspeople were ordered to convene in Parliament Hall each Tuesday because of the deteriorating political situation.[61] When the Estates eventually reassembled in June 1640, further royal attempts at adjournment were disregarded and a comprehensive range of reformist laws was passed. As parliament itself was to be the Covenanters' main weapon against Charles, parliamentary reform was clearly the first priority. The reforms of 1640–1 envisaged a directly elected presiding officer in place of the King's Commissioner, direct election of the Articles by each estate and of the officers of state by parliament, consideration of each item of legislation 'in open parliament', and provision for regular triennial parliamentary sessions. In between these full sessions, a Committee of Estates would exercise authority in military and taxation matters. Thus revitalised, parliament would be able to act as a buffer against the attempts by King Charles to pressure it in 1641, and it could mobilise the country for war in 1643–8. Like Versailles a century and a half later, the royal redoubt had become the seat of the revolution.[62]

Parliament now had its permanent new home, and in the short term it enjoyed an unprecedented authority and autonomy under the covenanters' system of committee government. But as the logic of civil strife continued to unfold, parliament was at first displaced to meet elsewhere, and then, during a period of English military occupation from 1651 to 1660, suppressed altogether. By 1660, two decades of government by committee would leave most Scots ready for a return to the old pattern of rule by king, council and royalist parliament.

In this chapter, we cannot trace in detail the complex course of mid-century politics and warfare, other than where relevant to the built settings of governmental and national decision-taking. In 1641, following the 'Bishops' Wars' of the previous two years, Charles left London, reaching Edinburgh on 14 August, taking up residence in Holyrood. He was banqueted in the new Parliament House – presumably the Hall – by the Town Council. He had intended to attend the third session of his second parliament when it opened on 15 July, but was delayed by English parliamentary business. He was present however, at a new session which opened on 17 August, at which the attendance swelled to 163.[63] The governmental changes, and the beginnings of a tradition of free speech in parliament, were acknowledged in procedural reforms within parliament, including the introduction of individual reserved seats for members, and the insistence that all dialogue be carried on through the President. Members swore to uphold the 'power and privileges of Parliament and the lawfull lives and liberties of the subjects'.

King Charles therefore saw, and presided in, the completed Parliament House upon whose construction he had insisted. He doubtless would also have used its other principal rooms, perhaps even taking in the view from the roof platform. But the political situation was worsening, with warfare spreading to Ireland and England in 1641–2, and the covenanting government took sides against the king. A Convention of Estates met in Parliament House between June 1643 and June 1644. On 25 September 1643 a 'Solemn League and Covenant' was agreed between the Convention and the English parliamentarians. Seamlessly, the first triennial parliament opened in June 1644, and the following month a confederation of Scots covenanters and English parliamentarians defeated a royalist army; the two countries were being pulled closer together by their own political and social tensions. However, increasing revulsion at covenanting radicalism and desire for a return to 'normality', in the form of a balanced rule by a figurehead king and a sovereign parliament, fuelled a royalist counter-rebellion that was only crushed at Philiphaugh in 1645.

Because of this spreading conflict, a trend began for parliaments to convene elsewhere than in Edinburgh. The parliament which had opened in 1644 met, as already usual, within Parliament House. But because of plague in Edinburgh, for its third session (the terms 'session' and 'member' having been adopted in the early 1640s from English parliamentary usage) it assembled elsewhere: from 8 to 11 July, at Stirling; from 24 July to 7 August, at Perth; and from 26 November 1645 to 4 February 1646, at St Andrews. At Stirling, repairs costing £500 were carried out at the Castle for the 1645 session. The ordering of substantial quantities of timber deals (planks) and green cloth suggests that benches were to be built and the interior decorated in a way reminiscent of the Edinburgh Parliament House. Whether the Stirling session used the Great Hall, one or more of the state rooms (perhaps for committees), or the Chapel Royal, is uncertain. The Perth meeting presumably again occupied the tolbooth; Perth had been where Lord Elcho's government forces were raised to deal with Montrose's royalist rebellion, and the victorious Montrose returned to make a show of strength outside the town to alarm the assembled parliamentarians.[64] For the St Andrews session, the venue was the new 'Public School', completed in 1643 through a £1,000 benefaction by covenanting leader Alexander Henderson. The St Andrews General Assembly of July 1641 had met in the schools of St Salvator's College. The school building used in 1645–6, now called 'South Street Library', lies east of the gateway to St Mary's College. Built in 1612–43, its street front was altered by John Gairdner in 1764–7, and extended two bays westwards by Robert Reid (who, coincidentally, also re-fronted Edinburgh's Parliament House), in a style matching Gairdner's façade. The Parliament Hall (lower hall, or public school), is that on the ground floor; the library is above. On 17 November 1645 the Committee of Estates dispatched an order to the provost and bailies of Dundee, to send a dozen of their best wrights to prepare a room at St Andrews University for the use of parliament. Cant stated that, as completed in 1643, the temporary hall had three tiers of fixed benches facing each other across a centre area. This was perhaps in conscious imitation of the Edinburgh Parliament Hall, as it was likewise to serve for 'solemne meetings', but given that – as at Stirling for the previous session – much timberwork would be necessary for the hall to accommodate a meeting of parliament, perhaps this arrangement derived not from 1643 but from the 1645 intervention. The interior was stripped in 1817; however, two pieces of furniture used at, but not made for, the meeting, survive: the chair used by the president of the parliament, and a long table used by the clerks. In 1646, the final session of the first triennial parliament was held for the last time within Linlithgow Palace: having 'satt doune' on 3 November 1646, it rose on 27 March 1647.[65] As at Stirling, the Great Hall was a possible venue, while committees would presumably have used rooms elsewhere.

In November 1647, following his capture and committal to Carisbrooke Castle, on the Isle of Wight, Charles agreed terms with a Scottish delegation, comprising the Earls of Loudoun, Lanark and Lauderdale; this agreement, known as the Engagement, was signed on 26 December 1647, and resulted from a shift in landed opinion away from the growing covenanter extremism. In February 1648, Edinburgh Town Council appointed commissioners for the forthcoming parliament, and shortly afterwards, perhaps in a spirit of conciliation, authorised repairs to the imperial crown spire of St Giles'. This second triennial parliament opened in early March, and its sessions were all held at Edinburgh but for the last three (two at Perth in November 1650-March 1651, and one at Stirling, in May–June 1651). Although royalists at first enjoyed a 2:1 majority in the Edinburgh sessions, the defeat of the Engagers' army at Preston in England undermined their position, and parliament once again moved into alliance with the English parliamentary armies. The leader of the latter, Oliver Cromwell, entered the country in September 1648 and took up residence in Moray House, being formally welcomed by Edinburgh's town council. Chancellor Loudoun and other dignitaries, then in session in the Laigh Parliament House, communicated with Cromwell from there. The laigh hall, high-ceilinged, big-windowed and containing large fireplaces, would have been capable of providing well-lit, comfortable accommodation, with both west- and south-facing windows. Parliament House was protected from royalist 'malignants' by two horse regiments under the English military commander Lambert, while Cromwell was banqueted at Edinburgh Castle, presumably within the Great Hall.[66] Thus Moray House, a 1620s aristocratic town house with extensive ornamental gardens, and built in the same architectural style as Parliament House, found a new function: as a political headquarters, as the Scots and English parliamentary administrations negotiated a way forward together.

On 30 January 1649, Charles I was executed in London. The Scots parliament, still in session, proclaimed his son successor as Charles II, and the fragile alliance with England ended. Charles II arrived at Garmouth, at the mouth of the Spey, on 23 June 1650, and on 2 August 1650 he was entertained in Edinburgh within the Upper Exchequer House – that is, an upper room within the jamb of Parliament House – on his way to Dunfermline. At the same time, Cromwell was in the south-east, where he stayed in Pinkie House, the former home of Chancellor Seton, which, significantly, overlooked the site of the Scottish defeat of 1547. Following his victory at Dunbar, Cromwell's army entered Edinburgh, and Parliament Hall immediately began to take on other uses: English troopers sermonised in the hall, as covenanting ministers had done before; prisoners were confined in the laigh hall – all but two of whom escaped in May 1654 by cutting a hole in the floor of the hall above. Following the surrender of Edinburgh Castle in December, 1650, Cromwell made his headquarters there, doubtless using the royal palace for himself, and taking governmental decisions there.[67] Now parliamentary sessions were forced away from Edinburgh. Charles II was crowned at Scone, on 1 January 1651. In April, Charles and the Committee were at Stirling (presumably in the castle once more, rather than the tolbooth; Charles would certainly have used his palace), but Charles left thereafter for Dunfermline. After the Scottish defeats at Inverkeithing and Worcester and the capture of Perth by Cromwell in August 1651, all effective Scottish government ended and the Committee of the Estates was reduced to a peripatetic existence. During August they had travelled from Stirling and met in the small Perthshire burgh of Alyth. There, on the night of 27 and 28 August 1651, while the English army was attacking Dundee, the Committee of Estates was surprised by a force of 500 troopers under a Colonel Aldrich, and all its members – 39 commissioners and ministers (of whom there were perhaps eight), and about 70 others – were captured and dispatched to London.[68]

Other sites where attempts were made to hold parliaments in 1651 included Rothesay (presumably within either the 1614 tolbooth or the castle), and even Finlarig Castle, near Killin – a remote castle built in 1609 which was one of the two principal seats of a covenanting family, the Glenorchy Campbells. The idea of parliament meeting in a Highland rural environment would have seemed astonishing only a few months previously, but access to the more important centres was now impossible, and even public proclamations were hardly possible in safety. In the event, only three commissioners turned up at Finlarig, underlining the fact that in a situation of full-blown English occupation there could not be such a thing as a Scottish parliament. The Honours of Scotland, a key symbol of parliamentary ritual as well as of national sovereignty, had been removed by Act of Parliament from Edinburgh to Dunnottar Castle, one of the last remaining strongholds in Scottish hands, but just prior to its fall in May 1652, they were smuggled from the castle, to spend the remainder of the period of occupation concealed beneath the floor of Kinneff Church.[69]

Architectural interventions by the English forces concentrated on the building of military fortifications, while sites associated with the monarchy, including Parliament House, were symbolically slighted. For example, John Nicoll related that in February 1652 'by ordouris from the Commissioneris of the Parliament of England now sittand at Dalkeith, thair wer maissones, carpentaris and hammermen direct to the kirk of Edinburgh quhair the Kingis sait wes erectit, and to the mercat croce of Edinburgh quhair his airmes and unicorne with the croun on his heid wes set; and thair pulled doun the Kinges airmes, dang doun the unicorne with the croun that wes set upone the unicorne, and hang up the croun upone the gallowis. The same day, the lyke was done at the entrie of the Parliament Hous and Nather Bow, quhair the Kinges airmes or portrat wes fund. The lyke, also, in the Castell of Edinburgh, and Palice of Halyrudhous'.[70]

Between 1650 and 1661 the College of Justice was in abeyance, and was replaced by 'Commissioners for Administering Justice' appointed by Cromwell; this body held its meetings at a large table in the centre of Parliament Hall. In 1655 the English commonwealth leaders were entertained at a banquet in the hall. Considerable expense was devoted at this time to the enhancement of the main interiors of Parliament House with tapestries and other decorations, to compensate for the removal of royalist and episcopalian symbols

2.25. The Great Seal of England, 1651, showing the English republican parliament in session with thirty Scottish representatives. (By permission of the British Library)

(including, for example, the creed, hung on the walls of the laigh hall), and for the building's much more fundamental loss, that of its legislative role. Nicoll related how 'the Preses and the remanent memberis of the great counsall did caus alter much of the Parliament Hous, and did caus hing the Over hous with riche hingeris, in Sepytember, 1655, and removit these roumes thairintill appoyntit for passing of the billis and signeting of letters. So wes also the Lower Hous diligatlie hung'. During the years of military occupation and enforced union, Scotland was given modest representation within the English parliament, in London. In January 1652 the commissioners of the Commonwealth required the burghs and shires to elect parliamentary commissioners. They were summoned by General Monck to a convention at Dalkeith, where the English army was encamped, and agreement to union with England obtained. In August 1652 the 'Commissioners for this Kingdome were chosen at Edenboroughe for to goe up and sitt with the Parliament of England viz. 14 for the gentrie and 7 for the burrows 21 in all'. Parliament House was surely the venue for that election. Amongst the nominees was John Mylne, the master mason, one of the two Edinburgh representatives from the burghs, who left for England on 16 September. Mylne again performed state duties on 12 May 1653, 'upon a stage of Timber next beneath the Court of Guard', hung with tapestry, when Cromwell was proclaimed Lord Protector at Perth. The act of union was not passed formally by the English parliament until April 1657, but Scottish representation existed at all the parliaments from 1652 to 1659: thirty was the number allocated under the Instrument of Government, although fewer attended the earlier parliaments. For the first time,

Scottish parliamentarians assembled at, and had their country ruled from, Westminster.[71]

PARLIAMENT RESTORED: 1660–1688

From Covenanters with uplifted hands
From remonstrators with associate bands
From such committees as govern'd this nation,
From kirk-commissions, and their protestation,
Good Lord deliver us.
[on an arch at Linlithgow, 1661 anniversary of the restoration][72]

With the ending of the republican regime in 1660 came the restoration of rule by king, council and parliament, more or less in their pre-1638 form. Together with re-assertion of the royal prerogative came the re-introduction of episcopacy and the Lords of the Articles, both of whom might, as before, facilitate greater royal control over parliament. The first parliament of 1661 passed a Rescissory Act, which abolished all public general statutes enacted since 1633. A standing council on Scottish affairs, with a permament English majority, was established in Whitehall, headed by Edward Hyde, Earl of Clarendon.[73] Scotland, therefore, remained controlled from London, the power of the re-convened parliament dramatically reduced from what the covenanters had made it. This would again change, especially after 1688/9 and the abolition of absolutism, bishops and the Articles.

Parliament returned to its purpose-built home in Edinburgh, where it would continue to meet for the remainder of its existence. But our story of the seventeenth-century architecture of parliamentary and governmental power does not end there. Architecturally, the most important aspect with which the location of parliament was associated was the civic enhancement of Parliament Close, one of several improvements to Edinburgh carried out in approximately the last quarter of the century. At Parliament House, where the College of Justice was restored in 1661, the hall was returned to its former state, with the bars, seats, tables and hangings all put back. In the organisation of parliament, however, there were significant changes from the pre-1638 pattern. Sessions were now much longer, and for the first time in Scotland, a parliamentary opposition began to establish itself, utilising parliament as a debating forum within which royal policies could be challenged – although both sides, or 'parties', were still essentially oligarchic groupings headed by aristocrats. Some of the fiscal advances made by the covenanters, amongst whom had been skilled businessmen, were also retained. Aristocratic power was not simply restored, but moved on to a different plane, and many of the one-time leading covenanters or covenanting families were installed in positions of power. John Maitland, 2nd Earl (later 1st Duke) of Lauderdale, emerged as the foremost political figure, along with other aristocrats who accumulated much wealth from government office, investing much of these riches in architecture. The power given these great aristocrat-politicians, amounting to ministerial or viceregal government by permission of Charles, marked a new departure in Scottish politics.[74] Lauderdale was King's Commissioner to the 1669 parliament (which involved another attempt at effecting union); and when the opposition made the 1673 session difficult, parliament was dissolved until 1681. In that year, the next phase in parliamentary history opened, with the King's brother, the Duke of York (who became King James VII in 1685), present as commissioner. From 1679 until 1688, Scottish politics was shaped by James's interests.

Charles II's first parliament, which opened in 1 January 1661, had three estates: nobles, barons and burgesses (with twelve of each on the Articles); the fourth estate of bishops was added later that year, on the restoration of episcopacy. New seating arrangements were made in 1662, and it was ordained that 'non presume to sit upon the benshes save the nobilitie and clergie'; officers of state sat on the steps of the throne, and commissioners of shires and burghs sat in the 'furmes' appointed for them. Entertainment and socialising evidently played an important part in the parliamentary process: at the conclusion of that first parliament, the Earl of Tweeddale invited the king's commissioner and most of the nobility to a 'splendid entertainment' at Pinkie. The pre-revolutionary pomp of the regalia was fully reinstated: in 1663, the Riding procession was 'ordored to returne from the Parliament hous to the Abay, to convoy the Commissioner, according to the ancient custome . . . Upone the morne thaireftir, being Settirday, the tent day of October . . . 1663, the Honouris wer honorablie convoyit from the Abay to the Castell . . . in a kotche, the trumpet sounding before thaim, and ane great pairt of the oleaff gaird gairding thame, quho wer saluted with a number of cannoun schot from the Castle'. This settlement provoked a gradual revival of armed presbyterian opposition from the mid-1660s onwards. Lacking any national institutional focus, this movement was forced to concentrate its energies in the holding of secret open-air prayer assemblies, or 'conventicles', in remote rural areas. From 1673, a phase of toleration gave way to repression, and in 1678 a Convention of Estates authorised the sending of a 'Highland Host' to repress conventiclers in the disaffected areas of the south and west; the following year saw full-scale battles at Drumclog and Bothwell Brig, and the herding of covenanter prisoners into Greyfriars Kirkyard, scene of the signing of the Covenant. The Laigh Hall of Parliament House was used for the summary trials of some presbyterian rebels by the privy council.[75]

Architecturally, this revived monarchical confidence expressed itself especially in a renewal of the efforts to enhance Edinburgh as one of the seats of the Stuart dynasty. The overall strategy of monumental projects set in a historical landscape, on the model of Rome, was the same as before. Its dual focus on the royal and the civic was expressed in the two key projects of the period: the reconstruction of Holyrood Palace as a fitting centre for viceregal government of Scotland, and the attempt to create a far more elaborate civic and royal square on a 'Capitoline' model outside Parliament House. This recovery in royal patronage stimulated the emergence of a new generation of architects and designers, notably the royal architects Sir William Bruce and James Smith, and the king's master mason Robert Mylne; these key figures also benefited from Edinburgh town council's continuing practice of commissioning architectural advice from the royal designers. Their input to architectural development in the coming decades was thus very great. Bruce's career began in politics, where he reportedly played a key role in effecting the Restoration. He maintained a middle-rank political profile, and was then appointed royal architect, or 'Surveyor', for the specific purpose of rebuilding Holyrood, which the Cromwellian army had maltreated. Lauderdale, who had obtained the position for Bruce, also engaged him to reconstruct or build for himself a series of buildings – notably Thirlestane, as his chief country seat – but then in 1678/9 sacked him. Robert Mylne was the son of Alexander Mylne (sculptor at Parliament House), and nephew of John Mylne, king's master mason, whose post he inherited in 1668. James Smith, son and namesake of a Forres

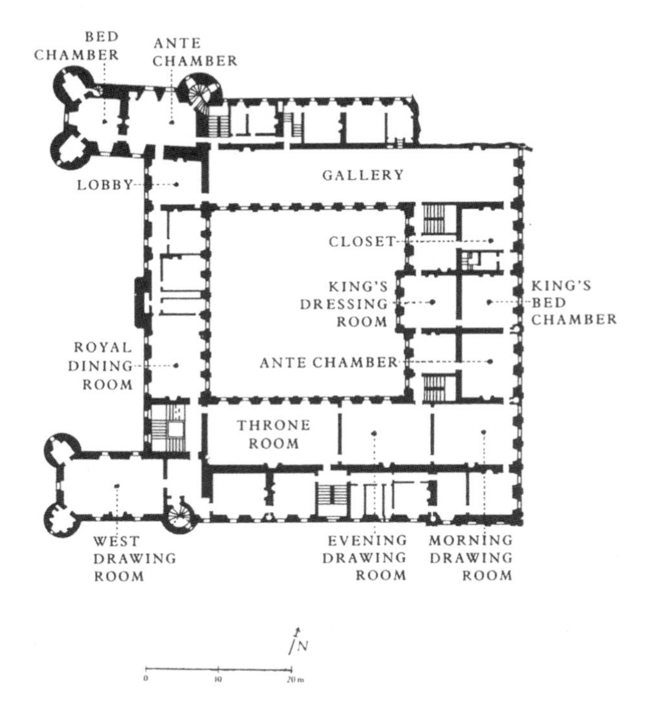

2.26. Plan of first floor of Palace of Holyroodhouse, as rebuilt 1671–9; the 'West Drawing Room' was originally the Privy Council chamber. (*Buildings of Scotland*)

mason, had travelled to Rome *c.*1670 to train for the priesthood, but returned instead as an architect. His career began in 1679 when Bruce employed him to help in the rebuilding of Holyrood; he married into the Mylne family, became a prominent Edinburgh burgess and freemason, and established good relations, as a fellow Catholic, with James, Duke of York (later James VII).[76]

The first major project of governmental architecture under Charles was, as one might expect, not parliamentary but palatial in focus: Holyrood Palace was to be almost completely reconstructed, to designs by Bruce, and at the instigation of Lauderdale. The palace, which had been damaged and maltreated during its use as a barracks in the Cromwell years, would now become a practical and symbolic centre of the revived viceregal government system of the Stuarts. Initially, in 1661, the privy council had proposed a modest scheme of repair, in which the north-west tower would be restored for the use of the King's Commissioner to parliament. A more ambitious plan for complete rebuilding followed the failure of a scheme for political union with England in 1669–70, when commissioners met in Somerset House, London. Bruce, who had been one of the commissioners, was appointed royal architect in June 1671, and instructed by the king to 'designe and order the building thereof in pillar worke conforme to and with the Dorick and Ionic orders and style'.[77]

What was needed in the reconstructed Holyroodhouse was living accommodation for the king's commissioner, and for the king and other royal family members, if they were to visit, apartments for other officers of state, and meeting accommodation for the privy council, which up to then met in Parliament House. This would have to be done in a generally classical, symmetrical manner, with interiors arranged in grand 'apartments' of enfiladed rooms. Thus far, the model was the stately classicism of the French palaces and country houses of the Louis XIV era, with their vast axial vistas on all sides. But rather than pull down the complex altogether and build a completely new palace, the neo-chivalric cult of Stuart heritage which loomed so large in post-1660 Scotland dictated the retention of the original towered block, largely built in the early sixteenth century by James IV and James V and containing the royal apartments associated with Queen Mary. This would be 'reformed' and incorporated into a symmetrical composition. To this end a second, matching south-west tower was therefore built. This was linked to the old north-west tower, in a development of the design in 1676, by a flat-roofed, balustraded classical entrance range not unlike Parliament House in appearance, but with a central giant-columned entrance doorway; a new classical courtyard block was added behind.

Inside the rebuilt palace, a stone-built, cantilevered staircase led up to royal apartments on the *piano nobile*: the king's on the south and east of the courtyard and the queen's to the west. A separate door from the head of the staircase gave direct access to the new meeting chamber of the privy council, which was to occupy the symbolically prominent location of the new south-west tower. Both this and the king's Great Apartment, with its sequence of presence chambers, antechamber, bedchamber and closet, were used alike for the activities of regal government, as were the apartments of the other officers of state, such as the Lord Privy Seal and Lord Treasurer. Both the council chamber and the other main interiors were sumptuously decorated by eminent craftsmen, including woodwork by the Dutch carver Jan van Santvoort and ceilings by the English plasterers, George Dunsterfield and John Houlbert. Already in 1668 the council's previous chamber, elsewhere in the building, had been refurnished by Lauderdale,

including several dozen turkey work chairs. The council chamber ceiling, dated 1674, comprises a large rectangular central panel and subsidiary outer panels; the present decoration of the room, with seventeenth-century style oak panelling, is of 1910–11 and designed by government architect W.T. Oldrieve. Lauderdale, as king's commissioner to parliament, took up residence in 1672. Building work at the palace started in 1671 and was largely complete by 1679. In 1685 the council chamber was completely refurbished, including a crimson velvet chair of state and 48 turkey work chairs.[78]

In the meanwhile, the civic and parliamentary area further up the High Street was not being neglected by the renewed royalist regime. Parliament House itself was provided with new seating of 'bars, tables and chairs' in 1661–2, and the old privy council chamber was repaired 'with a Bar betwixt the south and north doors'. In 1668 the Court of Session chamber was hung with a new set of tapestries depicting the story of Cyrus (the king who first unified the Persian Empire), ordered from London for £160. More importantly, the paved civic square of Parliament Close entered a new and major stage of development, following a fire in 1676 which destroyed buildings to its east. The recent precedent of the great London fire (1666) and ambitious, if largely unfulfilled, plans for subsequent rebuilding may have helped inspire reconstruction plans in Edinburgh. The resulting square was

2.27. The Privy Council chamber/West Drawing Room at Holyroodhouse *c.*1900, before the present classical wood panelling was installed on the walls. (Royal Incorporation of Architects in Scotland; RCAHMS ED/10999)

hailed by contemporaries as 'the Pride of Edinburgh'. But although both the town council and privy council were closely concerned with the improvement of the close, its actual development was largely dealt with by a private individual, Thomas Robertson (d.1686), one of the pioneers of 'speculative housebuilding' in Scotland. Robertson, a businessman and burgess, launched into building projects after 1671, working with Bruce, Mylne and Smith. Both of the latter had themselves engaged in speculative building, in a range of projects including Mylne's Court (1690), a grand tenement project arranged around an open square.[79] The centrepiece of the enhanced civic area was a new merchants' Exchange built by Robertson in 1680–2. The site for this major public building was at the east end of the – lengthened – southern part or quarter of Parliament Close. It was designed by Sir William Bruce, with Smith as consulting mason, and largely financed by Robertson, who went to 'extraordinary expenss in ornamenting and bewtifieing of the said exchange'. Owing to its destruction in 1700 in a fire which devastated the immediate area, its appearance is not directly known. The original plan appears to have envisaged a courtyard layout with front colonnade. In 1680 Bruce's 1676 design, which he had probably already altered, was agreed. The colonnade was infilled and a 'foir work' was built above, to provide additional accommodation, including the exchequer house. The

2.28. Parliament Close following the late seventeenth- and early eighteenth-century rebuildings, as seen from north-east; to the left of Parliament House is the classical Treasury building (built after the 1700 fire). (Hugo Arnot, The *History of Edinburgh*, 1788, 293; RCAHMS C77000)

original design was 70 feet square, its 'laigh' level having an open court and walks both covered and uncovered. The arcaded courtyard formula had both antique and more recent precedent, notably in Amsterdam and London.[80] The heightened, un-arcaded façade, further altered and possibly designed by James Smith, may have been contrived to balance the façade of Parliament House at the corresponding west corner of the Close.

The building of the Exchange was only a part of a more ambitious town-planning scheme of improvements to the Parliament Close area, projected by both the town council and the privy council. In February 1678 the latter directed that Parliament Close should be enlarged 'for the conveniencie of his Majesties leidges attending the supream judicatories of this kingdome as for the ornament of the city of Edinburgh'. Taking the opportunity presented by the recent fire, the passage between it and the High Street was to be enlarged into a 30ft-wide thoroughfare, including a 10ft-wide pavement, running immediately to the east of St Giles', extending southwards as far as the site then intended for the Exchange.[81] Parliament Close was to be a 'square', implying it was to be made regular; and so, of effectively the proportions which it retains today. Regarding the buildings destroyed in the fire, in view of their occupying 'so eminent a place in the citie they should be rebuilt in ane uniforme way and als splendidlie as is possible for the greater decorment of the citie'. All buildings were to be high status, 'polished aisler [ashlar] founded upon fyne piaches ['piazzas', or arcades]', and heritors who would not build were to sell their interests to the magistrates of Edinburgh. In 1683 Robertson was authorised to pave the entire space. Much of the building work involved Robertson and Mylne, while at the direction of the privy council Mylne rebuilt a fire-destroyed site at the entrance to Parliament Close in 1678 as a six-storey ashlar-faced tenement. South of that tenement were others built in the 1680s by Robertson. In 1699 the Bank of Scotland moved its headquarters from Mylne's Square to the east quarter of Parliament Close, above John's Coffee House. There were aspirations to smarten up the new square further for parliament: on 4 June 1685 'the Lord Provost did signifie to the Counsell that the Lord High Comissioner and the Lord Chancellor and severall others of the Lords of the parliament declaired to his Lordship that the chops in the parliament closs upon the south syde of St geills Kirk of necessity most be taken down In respect they deface

the bewtay of the Kirk'. In the event, the shops were not, apparently, removed.[82]

There were four possible monumental models for the Parliament Close improvement project, each of which might have influenced what was built. Antique precedent suggested the Roman forum or Greek agora; more immediately, there was Rome's Capitoline Hill, known well by James Smith and others who had made a 'grand tour'; thirdly, there was St Mark's Square in Venice, a forum more accessible to Protestants than Rome during the years of the Inquisition; and finally, there was the 'place royale', the model of stately square evolved in seventeenth-century France. Roman fora lay generally in the valleys; in Edinburgh, a valley site in the Cowgate was first considered for the new parliament house, but rejected, in favour of a site more akin to that of the Capitoline Hill. Eighteenth-century maps indicate the close to have been slightly asymmetrical; and roughly of the rectangular 3:2 proportions recommended for a forum by Vitruvius – although the precipitous slope to the south in any case precluded a more elongated plan. Elements evocative of the Roman and Venetian forum models included the arcades around it, the juxtaposition of governmental and legislative buildings with commercial and religious structures. As in the case of the *tabularium* adjacent to the Forum Romanum, even the national archives were housed here: in 1661, following their recovery from England, they were placed in Parliament House, and stored for many years within the two vaulted rooms in the jamb, beneath the Inner House. Even in the next century, when

2.29. Present-day view of Piazza del Campidoglio, Rome. (A MacKechnie)

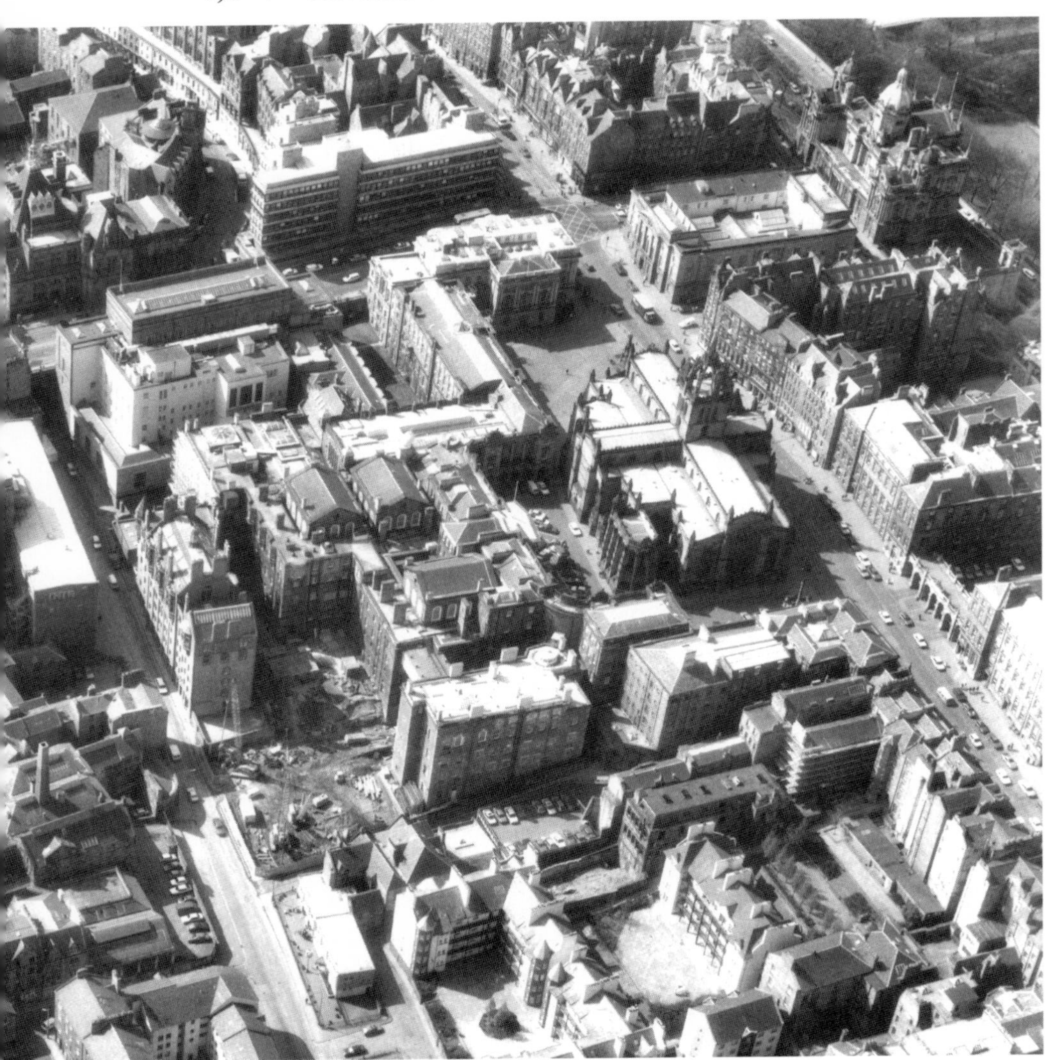

2.30. 1989 aerial view of Parliament Square from south-east; the roof of Parliament House is visible running southwards immediately to the left of St Giles'. (RCAHMS B21821)

subscriptions were sought for a new exchange, it was argued that the project would provide 'a handsome Exchange or publick forum'. At the same time, Parliament Close had, from the outset, affinities with Rome's Capitoline Hill, as it too was a paved hilltop courtyard bounded by balustraded classical governmental and royal architecture, and a church alongside.[83] The Capitoline certainly influenced other Scottish civic monuments of this period, including the rebuilt Linlithgow tolbooth, with its similar façade treatment, recessed steeple and balustraded flat roof. But to be fully complete and up to date, the new Close also needed a statue of the monarch – a pattern which suggested the 'place royale' formula of absolutist France. The idea and this location had reportedly been decided upon by the 1650s, but the subject of the statue was to have been Oliver Cromwell. A rough-hewn ashlar block, eight feet high, arrived in Edinburgh for completion by a sculptor, but Cromwell's death and the Restoration ended that scheme. In January 1685 – only days before Charles's death – it was reported to the town council that 'the Kings majesties statu in metall is raddie to be pute up in the parliament closs'. It was 'necessarie ther be ane handsome and fyne pedestall put up whereupon the statu is to stand And that ther most be ane handsome ravell [decorative railing] of good iron work pute about the same'. Agreement was sought with James Smith, who set about ordering and securing delivery of the statue; the scheme was to be 'done speidilly . . . that the statu may be erected befor his royal highnes [the Duke of York's] arriveall at this Cittie'. Robert Mylne was responsible for construction of the pedestal, and George Mitchell, deacon of the hammermen, for the railing 'and an appropriate Latin inscription was added'.[84]

The statue is a version of one erected at Windsor in 1678–90, said to be the design of Grinling Gibbons. It represents the monarch, for perhaps the first time in civic Scotland, in classical dress, following a formula which derives from the antique statue of Marcus Aurelius on the Capitol. As used here, it continued and elaborated the long-standing attempts to identify the Stuart dynasty with the Roman principate, and its combination of power and constitutional trappings. Now, rather than a feudal ruler wearing a semi-classical imperial crown, the king was explicitly represented as a Roman emperor wearing a laurel wreath. The most important and immediate precedent for this all *antica* formula came not from Rome nor from England but from the France of Louis XIV: at Versailles in 1685, the Fountain of the Crowns, constructed 1669–72 by Jean-Baptiste Tuby and Etienne Le Hongre, had the French crowns removed and substituted laurel wreaths. The Edinburgh statue project converted the enlarged Parliament Close into a 'miniature' *place royale*: that is, a square, centred upon a statue of the present king. The Place des Victoires (1685–90) and the Place Louis Le Grand (begun 1699) are famous Parisian examples, while throughout France, between 1684 and 1688, there were proposals (mostly unexecuted) in sixteen cities for *places royales.* [85]

Thus Edinburgh set out to create a hybrid, a microcosm of forum, capitol and place royale. The visitor Thomas Morer reported in 1689 that 'The pride of Edinburg is the Parliament-Yard or Close, as they call it. In the midst whereof is the effigies of King Charles II on horse-back, a well-proportioned figure of stone, and natural enough. The Yard is square and well-paved, beautified with good buildings round about it; and the only fault is, that it is no bigger, the height of the houses bearing no correspondence to the dimensions of the area. Its western boundary is the Parliament House, a large room and high roofed. East of this House, but south of the Square [i.e., in the jamb], is the Privy-Council Chamber, and not far from it, the Royal Exchange . . . The northern boundary is the wall of the High Church, which, with a few shops joining to it (leaving room for coaches to pass to the Parliament House) concludes the figure of this close, the beauty of their city'. As we will see later, the privy council chamber had been displaced back to Parliament House from its newly established location in the south-west Holyrood tower in 1686 by James VII', and took up residence in Parliament House from 1689'.[86]

2.31. Statue of King Charles II, Parliament Square. (RCAHMS ED/435)

While the enhanced status of Parliament Close was partly a consequence of the 1676 fire, the area suffered two further destructive fires in 1700 and 1824; in each case, Parliament House survived, but massive rebuilding was necessary in the immediate proximity. Following the 1700 conflagration, Duncan Forbes of Culloden lamented that 'All the pryde of Edenr. is sunk; from the Cowgate to the High Street all is burnt, and hardly one stone left upon another . . . These babells, of ten & fourteen story high, are down to the Ground, and their fall's very terrible'. The Close was rebuilt after this disaster, again, with prestigious buildings and a new exchange, two designs for which were presented for consideration to a committee on 12 March 1701. The next month, it was decided to rebuild the south part as chambers for the council and clerks.[87] East of, and adjoining, Parliament House, the symmetrical, classical Treasury building was erected (presumably after 1700); Maitland related in 1753 that 'in the lower and western part . . . is held the Court of Session, and in the upper part, formerly, the Courts of privy council and Exchequer, with the Office of Treasury; but the first and last being dissolved by the Union, it now serves to accommodate the Court and Office of Exchequer, and the Barons or Judges of the said Court'. At the 'upper end' of the court which had served the Exchange was 'a very spacious and noble room for the Convention of Royal Boroughs to meet in, denominated the Borough room'. This 'Borough room' or 'Burrow-Room' is dealt with in greater detail in Chapter 3. Next door was a tenement described by Maitland as 'the highest private building probably upon Earth, the Northern front whereof in the Parliament Close, is seven stories in height, and the Southern part regarding the Cowgate, is twelve stories high'.[88]

The 1680s also saw another classically inspired project in Parliament Close: the formation of a library by the Faculty of Advocates and the Lords of Session, initially in a house in one of Robertson's tenements at the south east corner of the Close, beside the Exchange (from 1682), which was converted with advice from James Smith. Following the fire of 1700, it was agreed that the Laigh Hall could be used: 'the house below the outter Parliament House and long hall'. The privy council, ever-conscious of the legacy of Guy Fawkes, stipulated that 'the library be always lyable to be viewed and searched by the Lord High Constable . . . as the rest of the parts of His Majesty's Parliament House are in use to be viewd or search the tyme of sitting of ane Parliament'. From 1702, The library was allocated the southern part of the Laigh Hall, from the gable to the fourth pillar. The northern part of the Laigh Hall then comprised the 'ward', or city lumber room, in which were stored miscellaneous artefacts such as fire-fighting equipment, and the 'maiden', a beheading machine'. During the same years, the courtroom accommodation upstairs in Parliament Hall was steadily expanded, from one single 'side bar' in 1661 to three by 1685.' Various structural changes were made, including in 1702, when Sir William Bruce received payments for professional services. A chimney piece and new furniture were acquired at the same time.' The national records were kept on the lower storey of the jamb, beneath the Inner House.'[89]

From the end of the 1670s Holyrood Palace, its reconstruction nearly complete, became the seat not just of a viceregal administration but of a satellite royal court. The king's commissioner to parliament had, traditionally, deputised for the king by hosting a 'court' at the palace; but now the commissioner himself was a member of the ruling dynasty. This was James Stuart, Duke of Albany and York, brother of King Charles II, who arrived in Edinburgh with his young wife, Mary of Modena, to escape opposition to their Catholicism in England. They were resident only intermittently, between November 1679 and March 1682; James was a privy council member from 1679 and High Commissioner to parliament from 1681. The impact of their stay, direct and indirect, was very considerable, and extended into the years during which the couple were King and Queen, in 1685–9. Under their oversight, a conception of government and society as a patriarchal family hierarchy was fostered during the 1680s. The contribution of James and Mary to the cultural advancement of both Edinburgh and Scotland included the extensive advancement of the professions and of learning. James also began formulating plans for a dramatic expansion of civic improvement from the core of the town, around Parliament Close, into a large-scale scheme of town extension. Those plans were cut short by the failure of his religious and political strategies as king, notably his attempt to achieve religious toleration for Catholicism, but were eventually revived and realised under a very different political regime in the next century, in the form of the Hanoverian New Town.

On James's arrival at Holyrood, most of the nobility, familiar to royal absence, who had been allocated apartments in Holyrood, were moved back out again, with the exception of the Chancellor and the Duke of Hamilton. As the natural leaders of the (then established)

episcopal church, the landed classes and the Royalist establishment, James and Mary were generally well received in Edinburgh, and for those three short years Holyrood took the role of a working royal palace, where the couple held the first resident court in the country since 1603. The duke occupied the great apartment and the duchess the queen's apartment, although they travelled elsewhere (for example, Linlithgow Palace was fitted out for them, and they visited the battle site of Bothwell Bridge). The period coincided with the fall in 1680 of the Duke of Lauderdale, Charles's one-time Secretary of State for Scotland. Lauderdale, more powerful than parliament, had effectively ruled Scotland on Charles's behalf, and in the spirit of absolute monarchy. He had also, of course, been Bruce's patron, before

2.32. James, Duke of York (later King James VII).

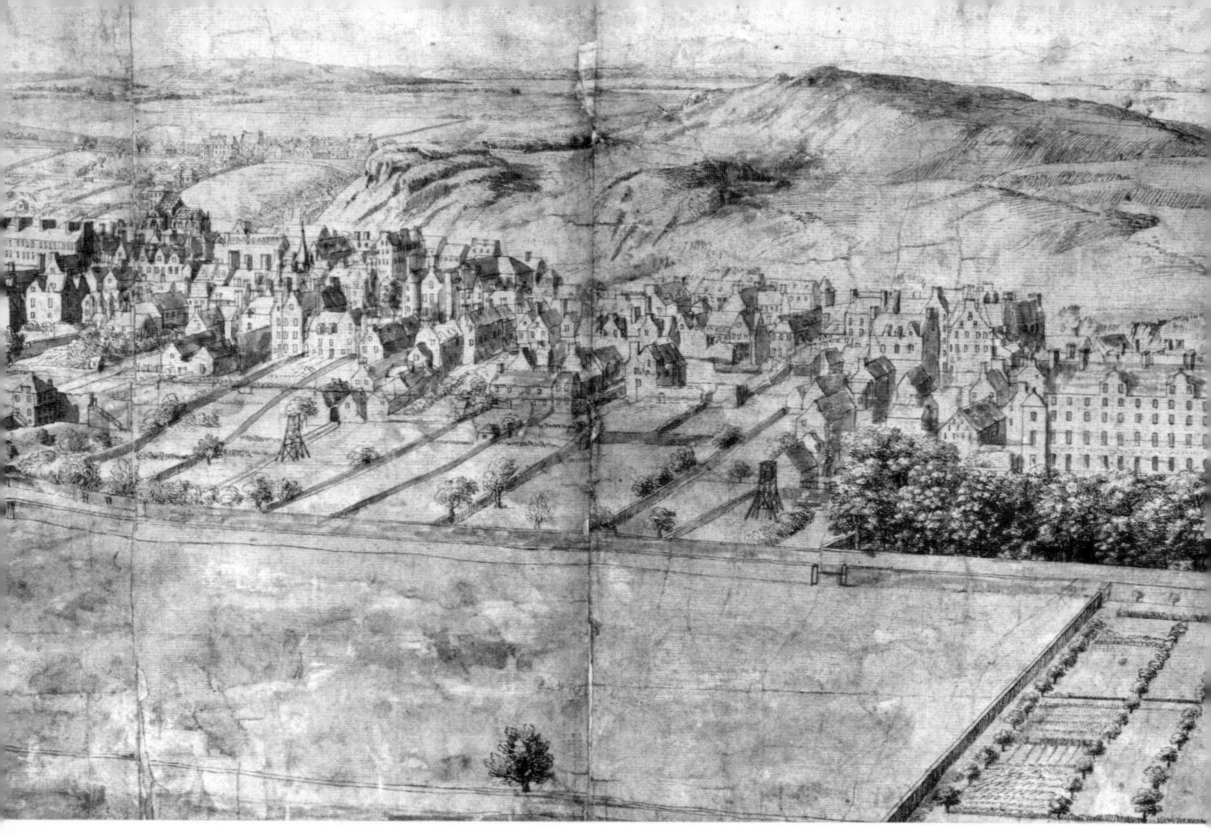

dismissing him. When in turn Lauderdale was sacked, it was James who was to fill the resultant power vacuum. Having free use of the royal palaces, he hardly needed a series of new dynastic houses as had Lauderdale; his architectural requirements and patronage were therefore different.

The royal couple's first architectural intervention was in the intended Queen's Presence Chamber, which was converted as a Catholic chapel for Mary.[90] James and Mary held numerous balls, plays, masquerades and so on; Mary, allegedly, introduced tea to Scotland. Of other more lasting effects of James's stay in Edinburgh, and of his continued interest in Scottish affairs after becoming king in 1685, Ouston has observed that 'The years between his first arrival and the collapse of his government in December 1688 saw a remarkable range of personal and institutional patronage, in most of which James himself was directly or indirectly involved. The Royal College of Physicians, the Advocates' Library and the Order of the Thistle were instituted, the Physic Garden and the Royal Company of Archers encouraged. New charters were prepared for both the City of Edinburgh and its College. Patronage was provided for surgery, cartography, mathematics and engineering, and individuals who benefited

2.33. Mid-eighteenth-century Sandby panorama of the Canongate, showing Holyrood Palace at right and Queensberry House at the centre. (The National Gallery of Scotland; RCAHMS EDD/1/116/2 and 3)

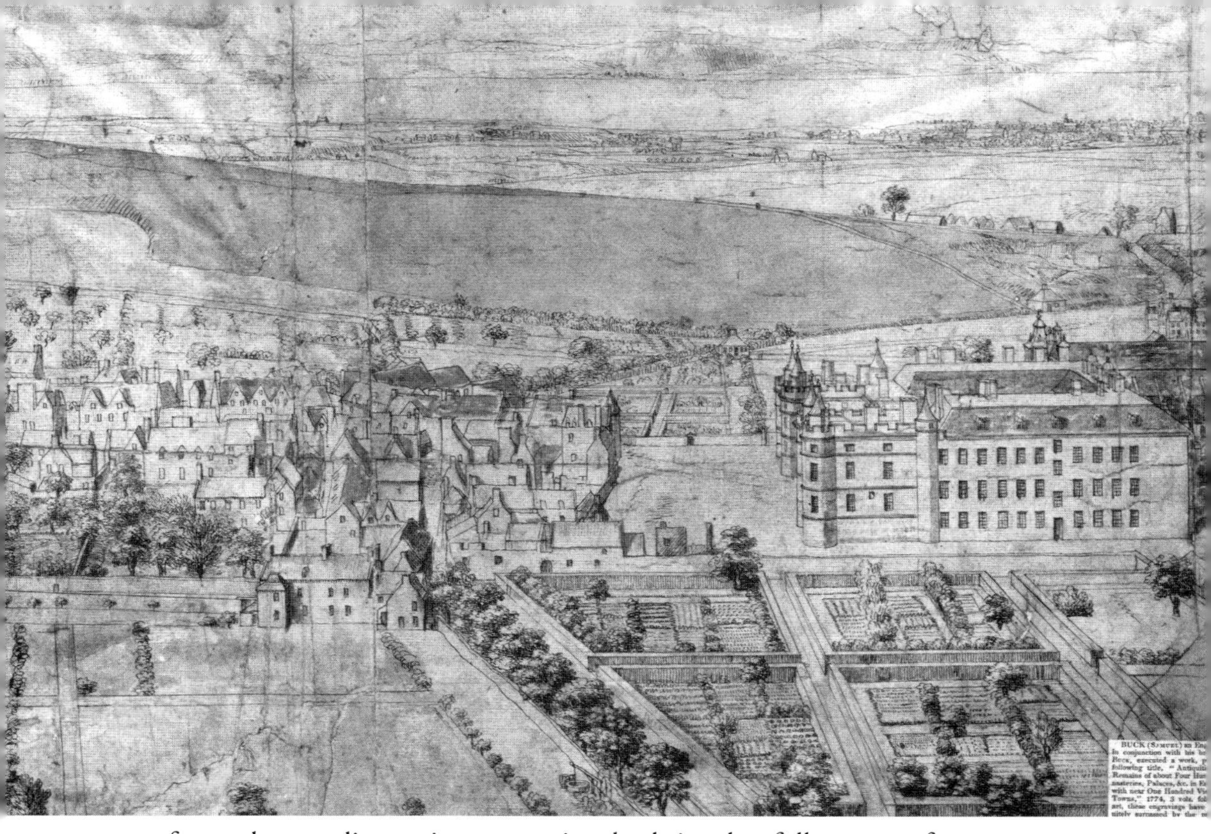

from the royalist regime were involved in the full range of seventeenth-century intellectual activities, from the medicine of Harvey and the philosophy of Newton to numismatics and weather recording'. In particular, the rise of the professions proved to be a key element in paving the way for the eighteenth-century Enlightenment and in intellectualising Scottish political culture. One of the potential beneficiaries of this trend was James Smith, who succeeded Bruce as royal architect in 1683, and whose catholic leanings chimed in well with James's leaning towards an absolutist grandeur.[91]

On 10 February 1685 the Lord Chancellor proclaimed James king at the Cross of Edinburgh. 'Traine bands in ther armes in ther best apperill' lined the route from Parliament House to the Cross; robed dignitaries processed, with the Honours carried in front, from the council house (probably at or beside the south-west corner of St Giles'), to Parliament House, on to the cross, where a platform was erected. Festivities followed, with a warning of punishment to any 'disaffected'. Soon, fears of the restoration of a Catholic monarchy prompted Protestant uprisings, and Smith apparently travelled to Argyll and Tarbert to supervise the demolition of enemy castles.[92] When James was crowned in 1685, Queensberry (builder of a

Holyrood-inspired dynastic house at Drumlanrig) was the foremost politician in the country. He would not convert to Catholicism, and James soon conducted his Scottish affairs through James Drummond, Earl of Perth, whom he made Chancellor, and his brother John, Lord Melfort, both of whom did convert.

The royal presence in Holyrood, following so closely upon the palace reconstruction, had other architectural consequences throughout the late seventeenth century. The Canongate thorough-fare was a principal venue for the Riding of parliament, and had in any case for long contained prestigious houses, close to the palace. The Dukes of Hamilton had an apartment at Holyrood, but Macky (1710) noted other palaces in the Canongate, such as those of the Earls of Winton, the Duke of Roxburgh and the Earl of Panmure.[93] In 1679, the year in which James moved to Holyrood, a great new town house – the largest in the country – was begun by Lord Hatton, brother of the Duke of Lauderdale, remodelling what had been the Maule of Balmakellie mansion. In 1686 it was acquired by the first Duke of Queensberry, who continued assembling plots, enabling the second Duke to enlarge it further into a U-shaped plan, in a phase of work beginning in the late 1690s. The architect in both cases appears to have been James Smith. In the style of Italianate buildings such as Baldassare Peruzzi's Villa Farnesina, a viewing tower, or *altana*, was set at the top of Queensberry House's roof, above the main stair; from this viewing platform, the eastward view overlooked Holyrood Palace directly. The roof was almost certainly clad in West Highland slates – an early and important example of this subsequently ubiquitous roof covering. Queensberry House also commanded its own extensive parterres and landscaping stretching south-east towards Arthur's Seat.

As king, James's own interventions at Holyroodhouse emphasised both the divine-right conception of government, and the promotion of Catholicism in the religious field. In 1684, the Scottish royal origin myth was resoundingly endorsed once again, when de Witt was commissioned to paint representations of all the kings from Fergus I onwards for the great picture gallery, and 'The Finding of Moses' (an allusion to Scota, an apocryphal pharaoh's daughter claimed as an ancestor of the royal line) for the overmantel of the King's closet. Whereas Louis XIV in 1661 had replaced the fire-destroyed gallery of portraits of French kings at the Louvre with a gallery devoted to Apollo, to James a more national evocation of

antiquity seemed preferable, given the sensitivities over his religious reforms. At the same time, he pressed ahead with the latter, in the architectural field as in others. In 1686 he decided to convert the newly refurbished privy council Chamber in the south-west tower to a Chapel Royal, as part of his wider ambitions for Catholicism. He instructed the Duke of Hamilton to deliver to Lord Perth the keys of 'that great Roome in our . . . Palace which formerly was designed to have been the [privy] Councell Chamber . . . to be made use of hereafter as our Chappell'; a dedication service was held on St Andrew's Day. The room, elaborately decorated with plasterwork by Houlbert and Dunsterfield, was further enlarged in 1687, by removal of the east wall; and in the same year James instructed the Chancellor's lodging to be given over to the 'Society of the Jesuits, to be made use of by them as a College'.[94] In May 1687 James announced his intention to make the Abbey Kirk the home of a revived Order of the Thistle. This chivalric order, like crown officers in parliament, would be composed of parliamentarians; political figures of James' choice. The plan was justified with evocations of the familiar Scottish royal origin myth: his aim was to restore 'his ancient Kingdom . . . to its former [pre-Reformation] splendour and reputation'. In December 1687

2.34. The Gallery at Holyrood Palace, lined with de Witt's paintings of Scottish monarchs (1684). This 1884 view shows the gallery laid out with a dining table for the General Assembly of the Church of Scotland. (National Trust for Scotland; RCAHMS B67521)

James directed that the abbey was also to become 'our own Catholic Chapel'. James Smith inserted twelve Corinthian-columned stalls projecting from the aisle arcades and a spectacular throne at the west end, with carved representations of the lion and unicorn, topped by a canopy with the royal escutcheon and other motifs. The hierarchical arrangement of a leader and twelve followers, with its obvious biblical overtones, recalled Louis XIV's villa at Marly, with its twelve 'satellite' villas (begun 1679).[95]

The new use of Holyrood Abbey required the displacement of the Canongate parishioners, who had used it since the Reformation. The idea of displacing the congregation dated from *c.*1682, and so was, presumably, initiated within the satellite court of the Yorks. In August 1688 the council was informed by the Lords of Treasury that a replacement church with churchyard was to be constructed in the Canongate. Smith's design for the new church, emerging as it did from a period of Catholic monarchy, naturally employed a Latin cross plan and curvilinear gabled frontage, in a radical departure from the centralised two- or three-armed presbyterian formula exemplified by John Mylne's nearby Tron Kirk. The layout, with its single roomy hall-like space, somewhat reminiscent of early Christian basilicas, reflected the Catholic reformation doctrines of greater accessibility enunciated at the Council of Trent (concluded 1563).[96]

By the time the Holyrood chapel was ready for consecration in December 1688, however, James's religious reforms had provoked a breakdown of his authority in both Scotland and England, and an invasion and occupation of the latter by the Dutch army of the Prince of Orange. James's attempts to install Catholics in place of the existing Protestant officers of state within parliament, and the magistrates of Edinburgh, had provoked general opposition, and the Court of Session now acted as though the established government had ceased. On 3 December the Edinburgh students burnt an effigy of the Pope, and demanded parliamentary reform. Parliament was not sitting, and the privy council's attempts at control were slight. A presbyterian mob sacked the Abbey Kirk and wrecked Smith's fittings and decorations. On 23 December James left for France, and the privy council made an address for the Prince of Orange, their example followed immediately afterwards by the Lord Provost and council; they offered their services and support, and declared for a parliament free of royal control.[97] James was given use by King Louis of the ancient chateau of St

Germain-en-Laye – St Germains, as it became known to Jacobites. This house, largely a Francois I building, with gardens by André Le Notre, overlooked Paris, and had also been the childhood residence of Queen Mary. The exiled Jacobite court attracted other exiles or enthusiasts, such as Anthony Hamilton, author of *Memoires du Compte de Grammont* (1703). It also became the focus for political intrigue against the new settlement. In 1824, the remains of James and Mary were re-interred in an aisle of the church of St Louis (built *c.*1765), commemorated by a monument erected on the instruction of George IV.

James's own architectural ambitions ended abruptly at that point, and some aspects never revived – above all, the emphasis on Holyrood as a focus of personal royal government linked to Catholic worship. But his wider civic improvement campaign lived on. Especially significant was a new charter which he proposed to the town of

2.35. Interior of Holyrood Abbey as refitted by James Smyth as Chapel Royal and chapel of the Order of the Thistle (1686–8); plate from *Vitruvius Scoticus.* (RCAHMS EDD/4/116)

Edinburgh in 1688. It provided for the expansion of Edinburgh with, in effect, powers of compulsory purchase over recalcitrants; it lauded the achievements of both magistrates and community; it renounced some royal rights in favour of the burgh; and it advocated the building of bridges linking the old town to new suburbs, streets and new ports for the extended perimeter. James's plans for the development of Edinburgh, which might otherwise have been his greatest architectural legacy, and were to be ratified in his next parliament, were instead stalled for upwards of a half-century.[98]

THE INDIAN SUMMER OF PARLIAMENT

The 'Revolution Settlement' of 1689 was a reassertion of parliamentary power and political dominance, as absolutism and 'divine right' gave way to a limited monarchy, and a renewed ascendancy of Presbyterianism. But the boldness and independence gained by parliament was, paradoxically, to be its downfall. The period began with a convention seizing the initiative, by offering the crown – with conditions attached – to William and Mary, leaving parliament free to pursue its own agenda. The first formal meeting in this process was in London, but Parliament House remained the meeting-place of conventions and parliament. The 'Prince of Orange' called to Whitehall the Scottish nobles and gentry then in London, to plan for the future, and what was regarded or presented as the restoration of Scotland's laws, liberties and faith. Thirty peers and approximately eighty noblemen met on 7 January 1689, and were received by the prince 'in a Room at St. James's'. Thereafter, the lords and gentry went to the Council Chamber at Whitehall. There, with the Duke of Hamilton elected as 'president', they advised the prince to 'take control of the government of the country and call a meeting of the Estates'. The assembled group had taken the role of a convention.[99] Back home in Edinburgh, Parliament House was the venue – and must have been filled – on 1 March 1689 when election was made by poll of commissioners to the Convention which William had called. It met in Parliament House from 14 March onwards. The Duke of Gordon held the Castle on behalf of King James, and attempts to dislodge him by diplomatic means failed, as communications from or on behalf of James held hope of a successful invasion in his interest.

Over the next few months there were occasional exchanges of fire, while some soldiers escaped down the castle walls. The Bass Rock, commanded by Sir John Maitland, also held a garrison on behalf of James. War, again, was probably inevitable, and Parliament House was once more at the centre of affairs.[100]

Both James and William of Orange, here denoted 'the King of England', had written to the Convention, prompting debate about how to react to the situation. Prior to James letter being opened, the Convention passed an Act declaring that, regardless of its contents, the meeting was free and lawful, and would not dissolve until it had secured 'the Protestant Religion, the Government, Laws and Liberties of the Kingdom'. The reply to William was sent for signature to the houses of absent commissioners, namely the Duke of Queensberry, the Marquis of Atholl and the Earl of Tweeddale. Thereafter, a 'Grand Committee' was formed to settle the government in the protestant interest. Edinburgh Town Council was to be purged. On 28 March, it was decided that the Town Council would take oaths of fidelity to the Estates that same afternoon, and later enacted that the burgesses should meet within St Giles Kirk on 10 April to elect 25 people, to be magistrates and ordinary council.[101] Similar elections were held in other burghs.

The Convention met in Parliament House on 14th March, the date authorised by the prince. 'The Lords Spiritual and Temporal, and the Commons being Assembled at Edinburgh . . . in Obedience to the King of England's Letters, all in one House, according to the Custom of the Kingdom. And the Bishop of Edinburgh having said Prayers, in which he prayed God to have Compassion on King James, and to restore him, they chose their President and Clerks. The Bishops and others were for the Marquess of Athol's being President, but it was carried for Duke Hamilton by 40 Voices. [The voting system was oral] The first thing they took into Consideration was the Security and Safety of the Meeting, for the Town of Edinburgh . . . is at the Mercy of the Cannon of the Castle, which is still in the Hands of the Duke of Gordon, a Roman Catholick'. On 27 March, the Committee for considering the state of the government was agreed: eight lords, eight knights and eight burgesses. Following their deliberations, the convention declared the crown forfeit (only five peers voting against) and agreed to offer the crown to William and Mary.[102]

The Lord Lyon proclaimed William and Mary king and queen at

the market cross on April 11th, the same day as their English coronation. The letter, setting out the convention's proposals and offering the crown, was taken by a delegation representing the three estates: Argyll for the lords, Montgomerie of Skelmorlie for the barons, and Sir John Dalrymple for the burgesses. The oath was taken on 11 May in the Banqueting House in Whitehall, with the king and queen enthroned. The Scots delegation emitted positive signals about the proposal for union, and William agreed to convert the Convention meeting to a parliament. Thus, the convention met daily until 24 May, adjourned to meet as a parliament on 5 June.[103] It was a meeting of the convention which had steered Scottish policy throughout this period of dramatic and radical change, pronounced the throne to be vacant, issued (following the English model) the Claim of Right – an assertion of ancient liberties, and of Protestant zeal – and offered the throne to William and Mary: technically, overstepping its legal powers.

Further preparations were made by the convention to secure its revolution, by establishing garrisons across the country, most notably at Fort William. On 14 June, Edinburgh Castle capitulated, and three days later the estates formally met as a parliament, with the Honours sent from the Castle. Following the defeat of armed opposition by 1690, the parliamentary revolution was safe. Absolutism was gone, and the power of parliament, therefore, was correspondingly enhanced. Presbyterian worship was established; ministers who did not accept the new order to pray for William and Mary as King and Queen were ejected; bishops would not sit again in parliament; and parliament could now do, within reason, more or less what it chose to do. In 1690, overruling protestes by the king and queen, it proceeded to abolish the Committee of Articles, as 'a great grievance to the Nation', and to declare that all committees would be 'freely chosen by the Estates'; legislative proposals would now be considered directly by parliament itself.[104] For the second time in sixty years, action taken within Parliament House, followed by military action in the field, and involving a host of documented or still-existing buildings, had moved from defiance of a Stuart king to the establishment of parliament as, effectively, the sovereign power. The first period ended with military conquest; the second was to end in peaceful union, as the Scottish and English governments began to work increasingly closely together.

While the Stuarts – as seen at Parliament House and their palaces

– had clear ideas which they wished to broadcast through architecture, William, by contrast, had little or no interest in creating architecture in Scotland, other than military strongholds to secure the new settlement. Among the landed elite which supported or acquiesced in the new regime, the old Scottish origin-myth of lineal antiquity, so cherished by the Stuarts, became less popular, now that the direct royal line had been broken, and led to a move away from the restoration or adaptation of castellated 'seats', and towards a more thoroughgoing cosmopolitan classicism.[105]

During these years, Parliament House entered a period of stability, with only relatively trivial changes. By the early 1700s, the normal parliamentary day was quite standardised, beginning (usually at 10 a.m.) with the saying of prayers, the calling of the rolls, and the reading of the minutes of the last sederunt, and ending with the ordering of an adjournment by the Lord High Chancellor, under the authority of the queen's High Commissioner. Committees were dealt with in the same way. What was now referred to as 'this house' had been regulated by Acts of 1662 and 1685. At the beginning of a parliamentary session, the house was fenced in the normal way by the Lyon King of Arms after calling of the rolls, and an opening address was read by the Lord Clerk Register. Votes were taken by roll-call: 'When the rolls are called for a vote of Parliament all the Members Stand upright in their places and give their votes audibly. And that none presume to answer for another.'[106] Acts of parliament were made law by being touched by the royal sceptre. From 1689 the privy council's meetings were moved from Holyrood to Parliament House, into the exchequer chambers on the upper floor of the jamb.

From 1693 the physical condition of Parliament House was overseen by two keepers, their appointments made alternately by the Lords of Session and the privy council. Everyday duties connected with ceremonial and fittings were the responsibility of the royal wardrobe keepers: for example, in March 1707, Robert Morrison, Under-keeper of Her Majesty's Wardrobe, petitioned for an allowance in respect of his 'great Expenses in upholding and dressing the Arras-hangings and Carpets for the use of the Parliament-house and General Assembly, and in attending and covering the Cros at Parliament, Council, Thesaury and Exchequer Proclamations, and carrying the Chair of State, Carpets and Chairs, &C. from the Parliament-house to the Kirk and back again each Sabbath-day, dureing the sitting of parliament'.[107] In William and Mary's reign the hall was still hung with portraits of the 1655 taspestry, as well as the creed and the ten commandmentws, along with portraits of kings and statesmen by Sir Godfrey Kneller. A garden had been created, perhaps for the commissioners' use, as was, surely, the roof promenade. In March 1662, John Thomson, gardener, was given a 19-year lease of a plot of ground on the side of the hill to the south-east of Parliament House; this was to be enclosed and 'laid out in Walks. and to be planted with Trees, Herbs and Flowers, exclusive of Cabbage and other common Garden Stuff'. Two principal walks were planned, one greater and one lesser, and a wide range of fruit bushes, fruit trees and flowers. However, on 11 June following, the council agreed to build shops along the south side of the Close, each to be 16 feet square. And later, waste ground on the south side of Parliament Close, east of Parliament House, was planted with flowers and trees.[108] Among the objects stored in the Laigh Hall in 1700 were fittings required for the chamber: these included forms, tables, cushions and chairs, 'all for tyme of parliament', and a 'lairge partition wall of dales and branders of timber painted green which crosses the Parliament House in tyme of Parliament'. This confirms that the area within which parliament sat was not only paritioned off during sessions, but that the partition was green, matching the cloth or hangings used even in the old tolbooth. The court of session had to rise to permit parliament to meet. Repairs to Parliament House roof were carried out in 1704. The jamb roofs, above both the council room and treasury room, were upgraded.[109]

The final two decades of Scottish parliamentary life saw the beginnings of a 'party' system of oppositional politics, and a growing willingness on the part of parliament to exploit its autonomy by fostering a growing range of schemes of commercial and industrial 'improvement'. These built directly on the experience of the later years of James VII's reign. For example, in his 1686 parliament – attended by both Bruce and Smith – there were Acts for rebuilding the Bridge of Ugie (on the Aberdeenshire/Banffshire boundary) with stone and lime, for cleaning the streets of Edinburgh, by then denoted the 'Capital City of the Nation', and an Act in favour of John Adair, geographer, 'for surveying the Kingdome of Scotland and navigating the Coasts and Isles thereof'. This process continued, and from 1690 onwards parliament had unprecedented opportunity to develop the country. Industry and commerce, and a general aim for commercial, industrial and more general 'improvement' became favourite issues for paraliament's involvement. Actitivities as diverse as ceramics, textiles, drainage, Nisbet's book on heraldry, Adair and Slezer's surveys, coal, salt, molasses, sugar and other areas of manufacture and trade were all supported and encouraged.[110] These initivatives, however, could not prevent the fiasco of the ill-prepared scheme for an overseas trading colony at Darien, in Central America, whose collapse in 1700 destabilised the political system.

During the first thirteen years following the Revolution settlement, the parliament originally gathered in 1689 as a convention of estates continued in being; the sole riding of parliament after 1689 took place in 1703, on the accesssion of Queen Anne. After that, tensions with England grew over the possibility of Scotland choosing a different successor to the childless queen, especially after the 1704 Act for the Security of the King prohibited a common succession with England unless previously 'there be such conditions of Government settled and enacted as may secure the honour and sovereignty of this Crown and Kingdom, the freedom frequency and power of Parliaments, the religion liberty and trade of the nation form English or any foreigne influence'; otherwise, administration would rest in the hands of the estates of parliament and the privy council.[111] Eventually, after protracted negotiations and machinations from April 1706 onwards (well documented in a range of standard histories, and so not dealt with here), the court interest succeeded in securing the acceptance by the Estates of a voluntary political and parliamentary union with England. The calculation of the 'Equivalent' (the national debt Scotland would inherit) was entrusted to a special committee, which met in the Inner Session-House. For the finalisation and signature of the Treaty of Union, because of the intense popular hostility and rioting against the proposal, the authorities reportedly returned, appropriately, to Moray House, now residence of the Lord Chancellor, James Ogilvy, Earl of Seafield; the formalities were concluded there in a garden pavilion which survives to this day.[112]

CONCLUSION

This chapter opened with parliament already more or less centred in Edinburgh, although occasionally meeting elsewhere, notably Perth.

Parliament was dominated by the king, and the general assembly of the Kirk, which had developed its power during James's minority, was likewise losing ground to royal power. Already parliament was increasingly linked to the development of Edinburgh as 'heid burgh of this realm', with the ceremonial 'Riding' of parliament reserved for Edinburgh meetings alone. The town's tolbooth provided the architectural setting – presumably inadequately after 1592, when shire representation was admitted to parliament. The interventions of Charles I encouraged yet further the link between parliamentary progress or change and civic development of Edinburgh, but also ended the Solomonic peace so carefully set in place by James. From here on came the intermittent link between parliament or government and civil warfare.

In the years that followed, we saw first the attempts by the crown to govern by remote control (attempts dogged by the often fierce divisions within parliament); then, from 1639, direct government by parliament itself, in collaboration with a compliant presbyterian general assembly; then, in the 1650s, rule by military occupation and a quasi-colonial parliamentary representation in London; then, from 1660, a reversion to a mostly absentee, viceregal system; and lastly, a rediscovered final period of autonomy in 1689–1707. What was clear for almost the whole of this period was that the power of parliament was constantly defined and constrained by a *force majeure* located outside Scotland, where that force was an absentee, and would-be absolutist, monarch or a rampant Cromwellian army. Whereas the pre-1603 Scottish monarchy and system of estates had constituted a more or less sovereign system of government, the acceptance of regnal union with a much larger neighbour, during an era when absolutist monarchy was gaining in prestige across Europe, was a recipe for the dominance of absentee government – something which '1707' would not substantially change. Nor, conversely, would the parliamentary union disturb the growing diversity of the national and local institutions of 'government'.

That diversity was reflected in the architecture of parliament and other government institutions during the seventeenth century. At first it was Edinburgh's tolbooth which was improved for parliament, emphasising the link which already existed in Scotland, as in other European countries, between civic and national assembly buildings. The association between the town council and parliament continued in the patronage and building of the latter's own new purpose-built home in the 1630s. In the last quarter of the seventeenth century, the focus moved from Parliament House itself to its urban setting, and the creation of a civic square which was simultaneously a forum, capitol and *place royale*. Of the other arms of government and assembly, the privy council, close to the monarch, usually met at first in either Holyrood or the tolbooth, until new provision was made within the jamb of Parliament House. Logically – unless meeting in Edinburgh, in the closing part of our period, when it had its own room in Parliament Close – the Convention of Royal Burghs met in the burgh tolbooths, while parliament's religious counterpart, the General Assembly, attempted to underline its separateness from the secular world by meeting in churches. As we will see in the next chapters, those varied institutions of government and assembly would continue to flourish even in the absence of a 'national parliament', during the eighteenth, nineteenth and twentieth centuries.

NOTES

1. R.S. Mylne, *The Master Masons to the Crown of Scotland*, Edinburgh, 1893, 149. See also A. Macinnes, *Charles I and the Covenanting Movement*, Edinburgh, 1991; David Mathew, *Scotland under Charles I*, London, 1955; R.K. Hannay and G.P.H. Watson, 'The Building of the Parliament House', *Book of the Old Edinburgh Club*, 13, 1924, 75.
2. *Life and Work*, 1999, 21.
3. *Extracts from the Records of the Burgh of Edinburgh*, 13 volumes (Scottish Burgh Records Society and Edinburgh, 1869–1967; hereafter *Edin. Recs.*), ed. J. Marwick and others, *1604–26*, Edinburgh, 1931, 281
4. J. Wormald, 'James VI and I: two kings in one?', *History*, 68, June 1983, 190 and 204.
5. Bruce Galloway & Brian Levack, 'The Jacobean Union: six tracts of 1604' (Scottish History Society, fourth series, volume 21), xix–xxvi and 48.
6. *Acts of the Parliaments of Scotland*, 12 volumes (T. Thomson and C. Innes, eds.), Edinburgh, 1814–75, iv, 258 and 266.
7. D. Calderwood, *The History of the Kirk of Scotland*, 8 volumes (Wodrow Society, 1843–9), 243–4; J. Drummond, 'Notice of some stone crosses', *Proceedings of the Society of Antiquaries of Scotland*, iv, 1863, 110.
8. Calderwood, 243–4.
9. *Edin. Recs., 1604–26*, 141, 168. C.R. Foster, 'Staging a parliament in early Stuart England', in P. Clark *et al* (eds.), *The English Commonwealth*, Leicester, 1979.
10. *Edin. Recs., 1604–26*, 24 and 28.
11. R.S. Mylne, 'The Netherbow Port', *PSAS*, x (fourth series), 1892, 379–88; D. Howarth, *Images of Rule*, Houndmills, 1997, 35; J. Grant, *Old and New Edinburgh*, i, London, n.d., 218; *The Register of the Privy Council of Scotland 1616–1619*, xi, 1894, 42; J.D. Mackie, 'The order of the holding of the court of Parliament in Scotland',

Scottish Historical Review, xxvii, 1948, 191–3; J. Scally, 'Constitutional Revolution, Party and Faction in the Scottish Parliaments of Charles I', in C. Jones *et al* (eds.), *The Scots and Parliament*, Edinburgh, 1996, 66.

12. Mackie, 'The order of . . . parliament', 191–3; Scally, 'Constitutional Revolution', 66, R.S. Rait, *The Parliaments of Scotland*, Glasgow, 1924.
13. *Acts of the Parliaments of Scotland*, v, 259.
14. *Acts of the Parliaments of Scotland*, v. 9–10, and 594 (25 July 1621); J. Goodare, 'The Scottish Parliament of 1621', *Historical Journal*, 38:1, 1995, 29–51.
15. *Edin. Recs., 1604–26*, 69, 12 December 1610, and 152, 8 January 1617.
16. *Edin. Recs., 1604–26*, 52, 61, 67; N.Q. Bogden and J.W. Wordsworth, *The Mediaeval Excavations at the High Street, Perth, 1975–6*, 1978, 10–13; Robert Miller, *The Municipal Buildings of Edinburgh*, Edinburgh, 1895, 54–6, 60, 70; *Edin. Recs., 1604–26*, 62, 8 July 1610, and 118; *Acts of the Parliaments of Scotland*, 527.
17. *Edin. Recs., 1604–26*, 158, 383; Calderwood, vii, 257.
18. Duncan Shaw, *The General Assemblies of the Church of Scotland, 1560–1600*, Edinburgh, 1964, 169–70; *Edin. Recs.*, 1604–26, 96, 152, 175.
19. Macinnes, *Charles I*, 1; *Acts of the Parliaments of Scotland*, v (1625-41), 166, 208–9; G. Donaldson, *Scotland: James V–James VII* (Edinburgh History of Scotland, volume III), Edinburgh, 1965, 316; L.E Kastner *et al* (eds.), *The Poetical Works of William Drummond of Hawthornden*, i, Edinburgh, 1913, 113-36, 358.
20. A. Ian Dunlop, *The Kirks of Edinburgh, 1560–1984* (Scottish Record Society, New Series, 15 and 16), Edinburgh, 1989, 17; *Edin. Recs., 1604–26*, 103.
21. *Register of the Privy Council of Scotland*, iv, (second series), 1630–32.
22. Compare, for instance, Hendrick de Keyser's churches such as the Zuiderkerk, Amsterdam, 1611; D. MacGibbon and T. Ross, *The Ecclesiastical Architecture of Scotland*, iii, 1897, 455; *Edin. Recs., 1626–41*, 109.
23. J. Balfour Paul, *Handbook to the Parliament House*, Edinburgh, 1884, 2; T. Ross, 'The Tailors' Hall, Cowgate', *Book of the Old Edinburgh Club*, xi, 1922, 129 (also called the 'Chapel of the Crucifixion'); *Edin. Recs., 1626–41*, 109, 29 June 1632.
24. *Edin. Recs., 1626–41*, 119.
25. *Acts of the Parliaments of Scotland*, v, 466; *Letters to King James the Sixth* (Maitland Club), Edinburgh, 1835, lxxxv–lxxxvi; J. Imrie and J. Dunbar (eds.), *Accounts of the Masters of Works*, ii, 1616–49, Edinburgh, 1982, lviii; *Registrum Magni Sigilli Regum Scotorum*, viii (1620–1633), 1984 reprint, 1402.
26. *Edin. Recs., 1626–41*, 52–3, 159, 175, 184–5, 243; Hannay and Watson, 'The building of the parliament house', 36–7; A. MacKechnie, Scots Court Architecture of the early 17th Century (Ph.D. thesis, University of Edinburgh), 1993, 110.
27. *Register of the Privy Council of Scotland*, x, 517; MacKechnie, Scots Court Architecture, 243.
28. *Register of the Privy Council of Scotland*, iii, 497–8.
29. James Brown, The social, political, and economic influences of the Edinburgh merchant elite, 1600–1638 (Ph.D. thesis, University of Edinburgh), 1986, 23; information from J. Gifford; *Registrum Magni Sigilli*, ix, 62, 346–7; R.K. Hannay and C.P.H. Watson, 'The building of the Parliament House', *Book of the Old Edinburgh Club*, xiii, 21; H.Colvin, *Biographical Dictionary of British Architects, 1600–1840* (third edition), New Haven, 1995, 674.
30. The following account of the construction of Parliament House is based largely upon that by Hannay and Watson. The documents in the City Archives were re-examined by Dr Grant G. Simpson, who found little material had been missed by Hannay and Watson. I am indebted to Dr Julian Goodare for discussing the building with me and sharing his knowledge. In October 1633. Charles also wrote demanding that the records

be held near the courts: R.C. Rogers (ed.), *The Earl of Stirling's Register of Royal Letters relative to the Affairs of Scotland and Nova Scotia*, Edinburgh, 1885, 685.

31. D. Stevenson, *The First Freemasons*, Cambridge, 1988, 80–2; D. Stevenson, *The Origins of Freemasonry*, Aberdeen, 1988, 20–1. A. MacKechnie, 'Geometrica Scotica', *ARCA: The Jounral of Scottish Architecture*, 5, October 2000, 10–13.
32. Emmanuel Le Roy Ladurie, *The Ancien Regime: a History of France, 1610–1774*, Oxford, 1998 edition, 18; J.H. Shennan, *The Parlement of Paris*, London, 1968, 16.
33. *I Kings*, 7, 8–9, Paul, *Handbook*, 4; Grant, *Old and New Edinburgh*, i, London, n.d.
34. A. MacKechnie, 'James VI's architects', in J. Goodare and M. Lynch (eds.), *The Reign of James VI*, East Linton, 2000.
35. Miller, 81–3.
36. Information from Ted Ruddock. The cusped framing may also owe something to the medieval roof at Darnaway.
37. David Yeomans, 'Inigo Jones's roof structures', Journal of the society of Architectural Historians, 29, 1986, 85–101; John Harris and Gordon Higgot, *Inigo Jones: complete architectural drawings*, New York, 1989, figure 52.
38. Grant, *Old and New Edinburgh*, 158, 166.
39. Nicolas de Gueudeville, *Atlas Historique* (7 volumes, Amsterdam, 1714–21).
40. P. Hume Brown, *Early Travellers in Scotland*, Edinburgh, 1891, 280–1.
41. Hug Arnot, *The History of Edinburgh*, London, 1779, 293–4.
42. Paul, *Handbook to the Parliament House*, 6–7, 72 (Laigh Hall 'restored' in 8170).
43. Robert Chambers, T*raditions of Edinburgh*, Edinburgh, revised edition, 1868, 119; G.M. Ditchfield, D. Hayton and C. Jones, *British Parliamentary Lists*, 1660–1800, London, 1995, 143.
44. D. Wilson, *Memorials of Edinburgh in the Olden Time*, i, Edinburgh, 1891, 276; F.F.B. Thomson, *The Parliament of Scotland, 1670–1702*, 121.
45. Wilson, *Memorials.*
46. Hannay and Watson, 'The building of the Parliament House', 23, 25.
47. Macinnes, *Charles I*, 86–9.
48. M. Lee, *The Road to Revolution*, Urbana (III.), 1985, 132–5; J. Goodare, 'The Scottish Parliament of 1621', *The Historical Journal*, 38:1, 1995, 29–51.
49. Hannnay and Watson, 'The building of Parliament House', 39–40, 41–2, 45, 47, 26.
50. *Edin. Recs.*, 1626–41, 186 and 178; D. Butler, *The Tron Kirk of Edinburgh*, Edinburgh, 1906, 107–115; Hannay and Watson, 'The building of the Parliament House', 46, 49, 50, 54–5, 59. The Town Council agreed on 10 June 1636: 'Ordanis the parliament hous to goe on as the samyn wes first ordaynit and that with diligence.'
51. Hannay and Watson, ''The building of the Parliament House', 63.
52. *Register of the Privy Council of Scotland*, ii, 113, 13 November 1627: 'whairas we were formerlie pleased to appoint the meetings of our Counsell to be keeped at our palace of Halyrudhous as best becomming the stait and dignitie thairof, seing yow desire during the winter seasoun that your meetings be at Edinburgh, we remitt the doing thairof for that tyme to your own discretiouns'; *Register of the Privy Council of Scotland*, iv, 189, 31 March 1631: 'the place of meiting to be in his Majesteis hous of Halyrudhous, except some urgent occasoun draw the same to some other place or part of the kingdome'; *Register of the Privy Council of Scotland*, iv, 574, 22 November 1632: 'the Lords of Secreit Counsell hes found it meit and expedient for the ease of the subjects in this unseasonable tyme of winter that the meitings of the Counsell during this winter seasoun sall be in the laich counselhous of the burgh of Edinburgh'; *Register of the Privy Council of Scotland*, 363; *Register of the Privy Council of Scotland*, vi, 165, 12 January 1636: 'in presence of the Lords of Secreit Counsell compeared personallie George Suttie,

ane of the bailleis of Edinburgh, and Mr Alexander Guthrie, toun clerk thairof, for thameselffes and in name and behalfe of the provest, failleis and counsell . . . and declared that thair toun wes of intention to build ane Counselhous for his Majesteis service and desire the saids Lords to appoint some of thair nomber to visite and consider of the mos convenient place where the same sall be built.'

53. *Register of the Privy Council of Scotland*, vi (second series), 1635–7, 537, 546–7, 753; J. Dunbar, and J. Cornforth, 'Dalkeith House, Lothian', *Country Life*, 19 April 1984, 1062.
54. R. Mason, *Glasgow Cathedral: the Glasgow Assembly of 1638*, Glasgow, 1988, 9–10.
55. David Stevenson, T*he Scottish Revolution, 1637–44*, Newton Abbot, 1973, 170; Hannay and Watson, 'The building of the Parliament House', 61–2.
56. Hannay and Watson, 'The building of the Parliament House', 60.
57. Roger mason, *Glasgow Cathedral: the Glasgow Assembly, 1638*, Glasgow, 1988, 5.
58. George Eyre-Todd (ed.), *The Book of Glasgow Cathedral*, Glasgow, 1898, 154 (citing Glasgow Burgh Records, I, 392); Mason, *Glasgow Cathedral*, 4; *The Letters and Journals of Robert Bailie*, i (Bannatyne Club), 118.
59. *Acts of the Parliaments of Scotland*, v, 250.
60. Hannay and Watson, 66.
61. Hannay and Watson, 65–75; Miller, 85.
62. John Young, 'The Scottish Parliament and National Identity from the Union of the Crowns to the Union of the Parliaments', Association of Scottish Historical Studies, Annual Conference papers, 1994, 43–4; J.J. Scally, 'Constitutional Revolution . . . in the Scottish Parliaments of Charles I', in C. Jones (ed.), *The Scots and Parliament*, Edinburgh, 1996, 54–73; see also J.R. Young, *The Scottish Parliament*, 1639–1661, Edinburgh, 1996.
63. *Edin. Recs., 1626–41*, xxiv; John Young, *The Scottish Parliament 1639–1661*, Edinburgh, 1996, 32–3.
64. D. Stevenson, *Government under the Covenanters, 1637–51* (Scottish History Society), Edinburgh, 1982, 174; Imrie and Dunbar, *Accounts of the Masters of Works*, ii, 1616–49, Edinburgh, 1982, 445–6. R.S. Rait, *Parliaments*, 341; Edward J. Cowan, *Montrose: for Covenant and King*, London, 1977, 159, 161–2, 214.
65. Ronald Cant, *The University of St Andrews*, Edinburgh, 1970, 67; J.B. Salmond (ed.), *Henerson's Benefaction*, St Andrews, 1942 (University of St Andrews, library publications, ii), 45; Stevenson, *Government*, 51; George Waldie, *A History of the Town and Palace of Linlithgow*, Linlithgow, 1879, 78.
66. *Edin. Recs., 1642–55*, 143, xxi, xx, 172; Stevenson, *Government*, 64, 70–1, 93; Thomas Carlyle, *Oliver Cromwell;s Letters and Speeches with elucidations*, London, 1888, 326.
67. Grant, *Old and New Edinburgh*, i, 159; Stevenson, 1982, 119, 122, 124; *Edin. Recs., 1642–55*, xxv; Donaldson, *Scotland*, 342.
68. Stevenson, 1982, 106, 133; John Nicoll, *A Diary of Public Transactions and other Occurrences chiefly in Scotland from January 1650 to June 1657* (Bannatyne Club), Edinburgh, 1836, 56–7; Maurice Lee Jr., 'Autobiography, 1626–1670, of John Hay, 2nd Earl of Tweeddale', *Miscellany*, xii (Scottish History Society, 5th series, 7, Edinburgh, 1994), 83; Francis H. Groome (ed.), *Ordnance Gazetteer of Scotland* (new edition) (London, n.d.), i, 48. Amongst those captured were the elder Leslie, Earl of Leven, and the Reverend James Sharpe, the future archbishop. The prisoners were mostly set free in November–December 1652 (Nicoll, *Diary*, 103).
69. 'Parliament . . . being adjourned to sit in Stirling in November last 1651, the Estates durst not meit nor convene thair, be ressoun the Englisches haid now takin the Toun and Castell of Sterling, and possest the haill land besyde; so that thai wer forcit to meit quyetlie in the Hielandis, first at Roothsay and thaireaftir at Finlarich': Nicoll, *Diary*, 74–4; Donaldson, Scotland, 343; *The Black Book of Taymouth*, Edinburgh, 1855, ic;

D. MacGibbon and T. Toss, *The Castellated and Domestic Architecture of Scotland*, iii, Edinburgh, 1889, 583–5.

70. J.G. Fyfe, *Scottish Diaries and Memoirs: 1550–1746*, Stirling, 1928, 178–9.
71. Grant, *Old and New Edinburgh*, 159; Wilson, *Memorials*, i, 275–6; Donaldson, *Scotland*, 344–6; Rait, *Parliaments*, 234; cited in R.S. Mylne, *Master Masons*, 145; Carlyle, *Cromwell*, viii, 1.
72. George Waldie, *A History of the Town and Palace of Linlithgow*, 1879,82.
73. John Young, 'The Scottish Parliament and National Identity from the Union of the Crowns to the Union of the Parliaments', Association of Scottish Historical Studies (Annual Conference Papers, St Andrews, 1994), 47–8.
74. Helen Armet, 'Notes on Rebuilding in Edinburgh in the last Quarter of the Seventeenth Century', *Book of the Old Edinburgh Club*, 29, 1956, 111; Donaldson, *Scotland*, 359–60, 375–6; *Acts of the Parliaments of Scotland*, vii, 371.
75. J. Goodare, 'The Esates in the Scottish Parliament, 1286–1707', in Jones, *The Scots and Parliament*, 27; Donaldson, *Scotland*, 361, 363, 359, 372; Nicoll, *Diary*, 402.
76. *Edin. Recs., 1689–1701*, 64. Smith: M. Glendinning, R. MacInnes, A. MacKechnie, *A History of Scottish Architecture*, Edinburgh, 1996, 74–5, 100, 556, 585, 595.
77. *History of Scottish Architecture*, 79.
78. J. Gifford, C. McWilliam, D. Walker, Edinburgh, London, 1984, 126–8 and 141–5; I.R. Gow, *The Palace of Holyroodhouse*, London, 1995, 9; R. Fawcett, *The Palace of Holyroodhouse*, 1988, 20–2; *History of Scottish Architecture*, 79. M. Swain, *Tapestries and Textiles at the Palace of Holyroodhouse*, Edinburgh, 1988, 4.
79. Swain, *Tapestries and Textiles*, 55; Miller, *Municipal Buildings of Edinburgh*, 86; J. Goodare, 'The Estates in the Scottish Parliament', *Parliamentary History*, 15, 1996, 277; Hume Brown, *Early Travellers*, 280–1; I.G. Brown, *Building for Books: the Architectural Evolution of the Advocates' Library, 1689–1989*, Aberdeen, 1989, 24; *Edin. Recs., 1681–9*, xlvi, 122; *Book of the Old Edinburgh Club*, 1925, xiv; Armet, 'Rebuiding in Edinburgh', 128.
80. *Edin. Recs., 1681–9*, 397, 404; Miller, *Municipal Buildings of Edinburgh*, 128; W. Kuyper, *Dutch Classicist Architecture*, Delft, 1980, plates 461, 423, 441; M. Girouard, *Cities and People*, New Haven, 1985, 170.
81. *Register of the Privy Council of Scotland*, v (third series), 1676–8, 358–61.
82. The 1621 Act of Parliament requiring houses to be roofed in 'sklaith skailyie lead tyld or thack stane' was supplemented by another Act on 16 September 1681 to replace thatched roofs within the year. A fire in 1674 prompted the Town council to pass an Act requiring stone for walling. Houses were to be of uniform height, regular, and arcaded; Armet, 'Rebuilding in Edinburgh', 111–3, 115–7, 124; R.S. Mylne, 237; Miller, *Municipal Builidngs of Edinburgh*, 128; Alan Cameron, *Bank of Scotland, 1695–1995: very singular institution*, Edinburgh, 1995, 26–7; *Edin. Recs., 1681–9*, xlvi, 145.
83. Brown, *Building for Books*, 21, 28; John St Clair and Roger Craik, *The Advocates' Library, etc.*, HMSO, 1989, 31; Miller, *Municipal Buildings of Edinburgh*, 128; Wilson, *Memorials*, 274.
84. E.J. MacRae, 'Charles II Statue, Parliament Square', *Book of the Old Edinburgh Club*, xvii, 1930, 82–90; Wilson, *Memorials*, i, 127; *Edin. Recs., 1689–1701*, xxxiii, 134.
85. F. Pearson (ed.), *Virtue and Vision*, Edinburgh, 1991, 29; R.W. Berger, *A Royal Passion: Louis XIV as Patron of Architecture*, Cambridge, 1994, 60.
86. Hume Brown, *Early Travellers*, 280–1 (the author cited was Thomas Morer in 1689).
87. Brown, *Building for Books*, 24; Cameron, *Bank of Scotland*, 28; *Edin. Recs., 1689–1701*, xxxii, 285–6.
88. William Maitland, *The History of Edinburgh*, Edinburgh, 1753, 185–7.

89. Brown, *Building for Books*, 24, 31–2.
90. J. Gifford, C. McWilliam, D.M. Walker, *Edinburgh*, 1984, 128.
91. H. Ouston, 'York in Edinburgh', in J.Dwyer *et al* (eds.), *New Perspectives on the Politics and Culture of Early Modern Scotland*, Edinburgh, n.d., 133; on Smith, see *History of Scottish Architecture*, 73–5.
92. *Edin. Recs., 1681–9*, xiii, 135–6; RCAHMS, *Argyll 7*, 1990, 411.
93. J. Macky, *A Journey Through Scotland*, London, 1723, 63–4.
94. Gifford *et al*, Edinburgh, 144; J. Harrison, *The History of the Monastery of the Holy-Rood and of the Palace of Holyrood House*, Edinburgh, 1919, 218–9; Rev. C. Rogers, *History of the Chapel Royal of Scotland*, London, 1882, ccxix–ccxxi.
95. Rogers, *Chapel Royal*, ccxxv–ccxxxvi; Harrison, *Monatery*, 215–6, 220; Maitland, *History*, 153.
96. *Edin. Recs., 1681–9*, xxxi, xxxii; G. Donaldson, 'Covenant to Revolution', in D. Forrester and D. Murray (eds.), *Studies in the History of Worship in Scotland*, Edinburgh, 1984, 61–2.
97. Keith M. Brown, *Kingdom or Province? Scotland and the Regal Union, 1603–1707*, MacMillan, 1992, 171–2; G. Chalmers, *Caledonia, An Account, historical and Topographic, of North Britain*, ii, London, 1810, 706–7.
98. *Edin. Recs., 1681–9*, 277–9; Berger, *Royal Passion*, 27.
99. M. Lynch, *Scotland: A New History*, 1991 (edition reprinted London, 1992), 300; Chalmers, *Caledonia*, 707; H. Scott, *Fasti Ecclesiae Scitcanae*, v, 1925, 206; E.W.M. Balfour-Melville (ed.), *An Account of the Proceedings of the Estates in Scotland, 1689–90* (Scottish History Society, third series, xlvi–xlvii, Edinburgh, 1954–5), ii, Appendix, 295.
100. *Edin. Recs., 1681–9*, xlv; Balfour-Melville, *Account*, i, 5, 10, 21.
101. Balfour-Melville, *Account*, i, 5, 16, 20, 28.
102. Balfour-Melville, *Account*, i, 1, 21–2, 26; *Edin. Recs., 1689–1701*, vii; Brown, *Building for Books*, 173; *Acts of the Parliaments of Scotland*, ix, 33–4.
103. *The Life of William III Late King of England and Prince of Orange, etc.*, London, 1705, 225; William Ferguson, *Scotland: 1689 to the present* (Edinburgh History of Scotland series, volume iv), Edinburgh, 1968 (1977 reprint), 6; *Edin. Recs., 1689–1701*, vii, x.
104. Balfour-Melville, *Account*, i, 41–2, 54–5, 105–6, 133, 142, 169, 179; Balfour-Melville, *Account*, ii, 38, 53, 64, 112, 262, 275, 286; S.H.F. Johnston, *The History of the Cameronians (Scottish Rifles)*, i (1689–1910), Aldershot, 1957, 25, 97; C. Tabraham and D. Grove, *Fortress Scotland and the Jacobites*, Edinburgh, 1995, 40–5; MacGibbon & Ross, *Castellated and Domestic*, iii, 585; I. MacIvor, *Edinburgh Castle*, Edinburgh, 1993, 87; *The Decision of the English Judges during the Usurpation*, Edinburgh, 1762, 75.
105. *Edin. Recs., 1701–18*, 124.
106. Wilson, *Memorials*, i, 276; *Acts of the Parliaments of Scotland*, xi, 1702–7, and 1705, 215; *Acts of the Parliaments of Scotland*, 45, 26 May 1703, and xi, 1702–7.
107. *Edin. Recs., 1689–1701*, xxxiii; *Acts of the Parliaments of Scotland*, xi, 141–2; E.E.B. Thomson, T*he Parliament of Scotland, 1690–1702*, London, 120–3.
108. Maitland, *History*, 186; *Edin. Recs., 1689–1701*, xxxiii; Miller, *Municipal Buildings of Edinburgh*, 128.
109. Miller, M*unicipal Buildings of Edinburgh*, 97; *Register of the Privy Council of Scotland*, vii (third series), 153; *Edin. Recs., 1701–18*, 74–5.
110. *Acts of the Parliaments of Scotland*, viii, 577–8, 587, 595, 603; *Acts of the Parliaments of Scotland*, xi, 78–85, 103, 111, 131, 152, 195, 203–4, 289.
111. *Acts of the Parliaments of Scotland*, xi, 136–7.
112. C.B. Boog Watson, *Some Notes on Moray House, Edinburgh*, Edinburgh, 1915, 2, 7. Their account is, however, refuted in C.A. Malcolm and J.N.W. Hunter, *Moray House: A Brief Sketch of its History*, 1948, 11.

CHAPTER THREE

'Very Little of Government': 1707–1885

Miles Glendinning

... no State-aided institution, but the citizens' own,
to be erected with their money, to be dedicated to their use,
and to pass under their exclusive control.
William Young, referring to Glasgow Municipal Buildings, 1890[1]

INTRODUCTION

In this chapter, we trace a period of nearly two centuries during which 'national government' had almost no presence in Scotland – a phase which was brought to an end in 1885, with the establishment of devolved government administration. Under the union settlement of 1707, Scotland's dual identity was elaborated into a status unique in Europe. The external alliance with England was deepened into a merging of governmental and economic systems, creating the largest free trade area in the continent. Scotland was welcomed into a joint enterprise of Protestant empire-building, projecting Scottish values across the world, sometimes with idealism but also often with cruel force. At the same time, the autonomy of Scottish civil society was expressly safeguarded, especially in several key areas of 'governmental' activity. These included the law, local royal burgh administration, and, above all, religion: the system of 'two kingdoms' continued unimpeded, despite the transition of temporal sovereignty. Indeed, over the next 180 years, in the view of one commentator, Scots were among 'the least governed people in Europe'. The Scottish privy council was brought to an end in 1708, and the post of Secretary for Scotland was abolished between 1725 and 1742, and again after 1746. Shortly after the union the Lothian laird, Sir John Clerk, remarked that 'by taking away the privy council, there is very little of government to be seen amongst us'. This situation was underpinned by the fact that, in their worsening confrontation with French state absolutism, both Scotland and England emphasised the private and individual rather than the public and the centralised, a viewpoint which was reinforced by the eighteenth-century Scottish Enlightenment, whose rationalist scepticism undermined all traditional authority structures. In the view of Scots Whigs around 1800, 'the growing happiness and prosperity of Scotland' was 'not equalled in any corner of Europe'.[2]

Until 1761, 'North Britain' was loosely managed on London's behalf by the house of Argyll, and from the later 1770s to 1828 by Henry Dundas (1st Viscount Melville) and his son. An early move towards the English party system of Whigs and Tories following the union was undermined by the outbreak of the Jacobite conflicts from 1715 onwards. Financial oversight in Edinburgh was the responsibility of the Court of Exchequer, and the Lord Justice Clerk, an Argyll appointee, handled government business; the Lord Advocate handled Scottish members at Westminster as well as overseeing the legal system. Beneath that light umbrella, the exercise of power was at once oligarchic and highly dispersed, even after the Home Secretary was given general oversight over Scottish government in 1782.[3] In early and mid-eighteenth century Scotland, there was little bureaucracy as such. Government and politics remained just as much a personal, face-to-face matter as in antiquity, although, in Roman terms, the 'state' in Scotland in those years was not so much a *res publica* as a *res privata.* Prior to reform in 1832, authority in the burghs rested with the town councils, while in rural areas the landed classes dominated administration and law-enforcement: especially before the abolition of heritable jurisdictions in 1747, the country house remained a very real seat of government. The franchise was restricted to landowners and town councillors, who totalled no more than 4,000 voters. The Kirk, reconciled to the monarch by Principal William Carstares and to the Treaty of Union by its entrenched constitutional status, oversaw not only religious affairs but also parish-based education and poor relief. The later system of administrative boards for Scottish government business was foreshadowed in 1727 in the creation of the Board of Manufactures, charged with the distribution of the compensatory grants awarded Scotland in 1707 so as to foster industry. And the system of Scottish civil and criminal law, established in the seventeenth century, was still administered from Edinburgh. Only in the early nineteenth century would this finely balanced oligarchic system finally collapse under the impact of accelerating economic and social change, including growing demands for 'democracy', and the interventions of 'national assemblies' of a religious, rather than secular, kind.

THE ARCHITECTURE OF MANAGED AUTONOMY

The eighteenth and early/mid-nineteenth centuries are arguably the period of Scottish history furthest removed from our present-day preconceptions of the appropriate architectural expressions of government and national sovereignty, focused on specialised legislative and administrative types. In many ways, what was *not* built during this century and a half period is more significant than what *was*. In sharp contrast to the grand state buildings of monarchical and revolutionary Europe, the Hanoverian monarchy had given up the trappings of absolutist power and emphasised a more modest image in keeping with deference to parliamentary authority; never again in Scotland would the architectural expression of 'government' be a royal palace. That change was enthusiastically supported by the Presbyterian Covenanting tradition, which memorialised its heroes and martyrs in a succession of monuments, including Greyfriars Kirkyard (1706) and the site of the 1666 battle of Rullion Green (1738); these were paralleled in England by monuments to 'British freedom' at locations such as Stowe.

The buildings associated with the public functions of government were highly decentralised, with the country houses of the landed classes among the most important. While country-house architecture remained generally faithful to the international and originally French tradition of the classical exterior and the grand internal sequence of public rooms, even here there was a reining-in of ostentation. The suddenness of the change was underlined especially in the utopian architectural projects designed in 1718–28 by Lord Mar,

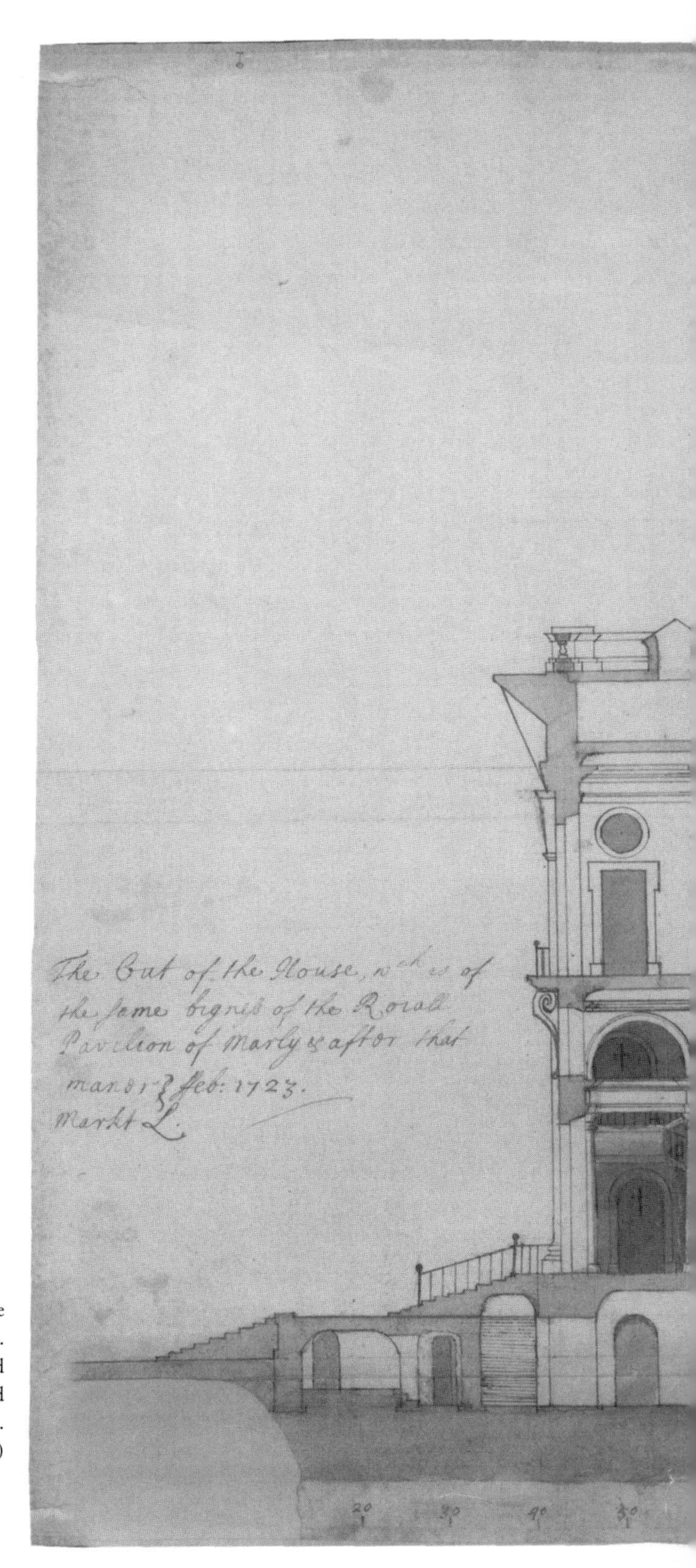

3.1. Cross-section of design by Lord Mar for a 'House for the King in the Padocke in Kensington', 1723. Conceived as the London palace of a restored Jacobite monarchy, its centralised plan was modelled on the Royal Pavilion at Marly-le-Roi, 1679. (National Archives of Scotland, RHP 13256/9)

80
90
100
110
120
130

the military leader of the Jacobite forces in the 1715 dynastic war, following his defeat and exile to the Continent.[4] Dominated by vast Baroque palaces intended for royal government in London following the hoped-for overthrow of the Hanoverians, these exuded a Versailles-like grandeur and Continental cosmopolitanism which were totally alien to the businesslike Protestant ethos of the new, Whig Britain. The 'country seats' of Scotland's oligarchic elite, such as Arniston (built from 1726 by William Adam), home of the Dundas dynasty, combined a degree of classical pomp with external severity and restraint. What was also at first downplayed by the new rulers was the old emphasis on the Scottish royal and baronial heritage, and especially the origin-myth traditions that had been incessantly exploited by the Stuarts to bolster their absolutist claims. Rather, the focus shifted to a concept of Protestant modernity underpinned by antique probity. The principate of Augustus still seemed the most appropriate classical precedent, but now because of its success in reconciling oligarchic government with modesty and constitutionalism, rather than (as with the Stuarts) for its imperial might. Thus, one of the first architectural effects of 1707 was a negative one: the decay or utilitarian re-use of the monuments of Stuart royal power. This process, which lasted just over a century, was concentrated in the area around Edinburgh's Holyrood Palace, closely associated as it was with the absolutist regimes of Lauderdale and James VII.

Within Holyrood Palace itself, the discontinuation of the privy council left the council chamber redundant, although, by the nineteenth century, the room (now known as the Picture Gallery) was used before the opening of each new parliament at Westminster, for an assembly of the Scottish peers to elect representatives to the House of Lords. With the abolition of the Scots parliament, there was no longer any Commissioner to occupy the great apartment in state. The palace was subdivided into a tenement of noblemen's grace and favour apartments, and after its brief state occupation by Prince Charles Edward Stuart (who used the Duke of Hamilton's apartment) in September 1745, it fell into a faded obscurity, broken only by the semi-royal state held for a fortnight each year by the Lord High Commissioner to the Kirk's General Assembly, giving banquets in its halls and holding levées in the gallery. The attics were occupied by small tradesmen and debtors. Following botched repairs to the Chapel Royal in 1758–68, the roof collapsed. From 1795, the apartments on the east side of the courtyard were occupied for four years by Charles, Comte d'Artois, exiled heir-presumptive of the Bourbons, who claimed debtor's sanctuary after a disastrous military campaign in Northern France; the government paid the firm of Young, Trotter and Hamilton £2,613 to refurbish the royal apartments for him. After six years on the French throne as Charles X, he would eventually return in exile to Holyroodhouse again in 1831. The Canongate saw several more decades of declining prosperity as a centre of aristocratic town houses. The final phase was marked in 1754–8 when William Adam built a small, elegant villa (Milton House) there for Lord Milton, one of the oligarchs of Scottish law and administration. Queensberry House gradually descended in fortune. From 1761 to 1773 it was leased to the Earl of Glasgow, and from 1773 to 1803 to Sir James Montgomerie. In 1803, it was purchased by the Board of Ordnance and converted to a barracks, including the insertion of a new central staircase, the addition of another storey, and removal of the original interior finishings; from 1832, it became a poorhouse. At the other end of the High Street, the Castle was taken over for military use, culminating in the wartime construction of the vast, utilitarian five-storey block of the New Barracks in 1796–9; the vaults under Crown Square were used for prisoners-of-war until 1814.

In contrast to this decay at the extremities of the Royal Mile, the area at its centre, around Parliament Square, witnessed a continued prosperity. Its symbolic power had been contested during the dynastic wars, when the Mercat Cross was chosen by the Jacobites as the site for the proclamation of James VIII in September 1745. Subsequently, it witnessed the consolidation of the new agencies of domestic government in Hanoverian Scotland. Parliament House itself, although still owned by the Town Council, was now increasingly taken over by the legal profession, a change slightly reminiscent of the way in which the Roman Senate, under the principate, accrued legal powers to compensate for its loss of political power. Following the abolition of Parliament, the southern part of the Upper Hall, already used intermittently during the seventeenth century as the Outer House of the Court of Session when parliament was in residence, was now used exclusively by that court, all of whose 'senators' were now (since 1688) lay judges. The Inner House of the court continued to occupy the ground floor of the jamb of Parliament House, with the fifteen judges sitting around a curved amphitheatre-like bench. Two doors led directly from the Inner House into the Outer House. There, the principal bar (the Fore-Bar) adapted the fittings of the old Parliament, with the presiding throne of the King's Commissioner, against the south wall, used by the Lord of the Outer House; there were two subsidiary bars on the side walls. Up until 1779, the hall retained many of the other furnishings and features (except the royal portraits) from its days as a national legislature; it also served as the scene of the 'solemnisation' of the King's birthday each year. The partition still screened off the northern part of the hall, with the old pulpit of Parliament standing beside it. In 1787 the benches were renewed and the partition, now only about 15 feet high, was moved north, extending the Outer House to 89 feet in length. After the 1740s, the north-west corner had been screened off to house the Bailie (burgh) Court; the remaining north-east section housed shops, stalls and even a coffee house. The bailies left in 1798 for accommodation in the new Royal Exchange.[5] By 1805, the courts had obtained the use of the whole hall, and another bar was set up. Below, the use of the Laigh Hall as the Advocates' Library from 1701 was gradually extended. Its stock of books increased tenfold between 1692 and the 1770s, and reached 60,000 by the early nineteenth century; from 1790 it was extended to occupy the rooms under the Inner House.

Immediately adjacent to Parliament House, the southern section of St Giles' Kirk, as partitioned since the Reformation, was the focus of the continuing regime of the two kingdoms: the Parliament of the one had departed, but that of the other continued in being. Here was the seat of the General Assembly of the Church of Scotland, and of the Commissioners who exercised authority between the annual sittings of the Assembly. In the 1720s Daniel Defoe recorded that seats for parliament, high commissioners and nobility were retained in the church, while the General Assembly held meetings in a consistory room on the south side, as did the Commission of the Assembly during the remainder of the year. Elsewhere, the Preston Aisle at the south-east corner of the church was normally identified as the Assembly location, whereas an imprecisely drawn view of the 1787 Assembly by David Allan shows a meeting taking place in the subdivision of the church immediately to the west of there: the so-called Old Kirk.[6] As appropriate to a body which was both legislative and judicial in character, the assembly layout and furnishings in this 1787 view resemble both contemporary galleried Presbyterian

TOP.
3.2. The Laigh Hall in the late nineteenth century, when in full use as the Advocates' Library. (RCAHMS C21626)

BELOW.
3.3. The General Assembly of the Church of Scotland, seen in the Assembly Aisle of St Giles' Kirk, 1787. The Earl of Dalhousie presides (right); the orator at the bar (left) is James Boswell. (British Museum; drawing by David Allan)

BAR
The General Assembly of the Kirk of Scotland 1787

churches and law courts. There is a U-shaped, tiered layout of box-pews surrounding a bar, a central enclosure and a throne-like raised dais with canopy for the Lord High Commissioner, standing against the centre of the south wall, as in Parliament House. This plan-form, with its compressed, promiscuous spaces, was less hierarchical and linear than the medieval royal parliaments. But it also lacked the sense of unified openness later associated with amphitheatre-plan legislatures.

The medieval centre of Edinburgh also remained the seat of royal burgh power. The Town Council continued to use parts of the Laigh Hall and the north section of Parliament Hall to store municipal equipment, such as street lamps and public gallows. Since the 1700 fire, owing to the cramped conditions in the New Tolbooth, it had held its own meetings, and (from 1709) that of the Bailie Court, in the new 'Burrow-Room and Council Chamber' built in 1701 immediately to the south-east, near where the First Division and Justiciary courtrooms stand today. This room was adorned with full-length royal portraits to emphasise the council's Hanoverian loyalism. After 1742 it fell into disrepair and was demolished; from that point, council meetings were presumably held either in the Lord Provost's lodgings or back in the New Tolbooth. Some council functions, such as the town clerk's office and a police office, were retained in St Giles' Church until the early nineteenth century, and the old and new tolbooths stood nearby until their demolition in 1810–17. An 1818 drawing prior to rebuilding showed St Giles' divided into four churches, General Assembly meeting hall, police office and fire engine house. The Burrow-Room also served as the meeting-place for the annual Convention of Royal Burghs. The power of these authorities was upheld across the country by the post-1707 system: during the nineteenth century, there were over seventy of them. Where, before the Treaty of Union, they had sent commissioners to Parliament, now they elected members to 15 seats at Westminster, and held their Convention in Edinburgh.

3.4. Dundee Town-House, elevation and first-floor plan by William Adam, 1730–1 (*Vitruvius Scoticus*, Plate 104; RCAHMS AND/159/1)

In general, the buildings of civic administration across Scotland still combined council chambers, courthouses and jails: up to 1839, royal burghs remained responsible for maintaining burgh and, in some cases, county prisons. However, as the word 'tolbooth' increasingly had the connotation of a stinking prison in an old-style tower, new all-purpose civic buildings were usually now called 'town houses'.

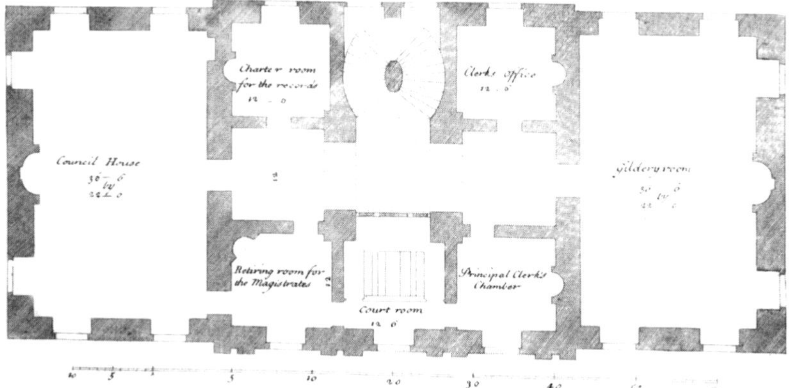

The Plan of the Principall Floor & Elevation of the Town House of Dundee Is most humbly Inscrib'd to Alexr. Robertson Esqr. Ld Provest & the other Magistrates of the sd Burgh.

3.5. Glasgow Tolbooth and town hall, view from south-east by Paul, *c.*1760; the 1626–7 tolbooth steeple is incorporated at the right-hand side. The building was replaced by Stark's new municipal building by Glasgow Green in 1814. (RCAHMS GWD/19/3)

The townhouse was still the unchallenged focus of secular authority in the burgh; where up-and-coming mercantile burghs built large new townhouses, the tradition of the tall clock steeple was jealously upheld, and combined with more regularly classical plan-forms. These regular exteriors sometimes concealed a considerable complexity of different public and commercial activities. In Dundee, for example, the architect William Adam condemned the old 1562 tolbooth and, in 1732–4, built a new townhouse at a cost of over £4,000. It had a seven-bay rusticated front with central pilasters and pediment, and steeple above recast in a Gibbs style: there were shops on the ground floor, a symmetrical layout of council and guildry chambers on the first floor, and a prison in the attic. Where older tolbooths were re-used, new extensions were clearly differentiated from them. In Aberdeen, the castellated 'wardhouse' of 1616 was reconstructed and extended in 1750–6, to form an approximately symmetrical, classical group with the tower at its centre, the townhouse and courtroom in a wing to the west, and a tenement, inn and masonic lodge in a wing to the east. And in Glasgow, the five-storey tolbooth was enlarged with regularly pilastered classical extensions in 1736–40 (containing a new town hall over a merchants' exchange) and 1758–60 (an assembly room) – extensions that were destined soon to fall out of council use in the nineteenth century, as the booming town traded one municipal headquarters for another in rapid succession. For a more detailed account of townhouse architecture during this period, readers should consult *Tolbooths and Town-houses.*[7]

In the capital, attempts to extend civic improvement beyond the existing dense town had limited success at first, as was shown by the halting progress of the Royal Infirmary project in the 1730s. What was lacking was not entrepreneurial spirit on the part of the Town Council or individuals, but political stability. Once the Hanoverian-Jacobite dynastic clash had been finally resolved by the latter's defeat, the way was open to investment and planning. A new and dramatic phase of Town Council innovation was signalled in a series of civic improvements pushed forward in the 1750s/60s by Lord Provost George Drummond, following pressure by the Convention of Royal Burghs. It began with a bold stroke in the heart of the town, opposite the religious and civic headquarters: the building of a new exchange building for the town's merchants. The Exchange, constructed in 1753–61 to a plan by John Adam (as amended by a group of tradesmen headed by architect John Fergus), was an imposing U-planned group laid out around an arcaded courtyard, with a one-storey arched screen across the front. Built of Craigleith ashlar, the building was four storeys high to the front but as much as twelve on the steeply falling ground to the north. The town council retained ownership of the centre block, which would be taken over in the next century as a new townhouse.[8] There were also schemes in the mid-1760s to build a replacement for the Burrow-Room, to house meetings of the town council and Convention of Royal Burghs, but these came to nothing; the meetings of the Convention were held in the Exchange or in one of the new courts in Parliament House.

Large-scale improvement in Edinburgh could only proceed by breaking out from the constraints of the city rock, and linking the existing town by bridges to a new planned settlement outside – a concept first suggested in 1688 by James VII, and realised at last in

James Craig's competition-winning scheme of 1766 for the grid-planned New Town. As first built, the New Town seemed like a built embodiment of the British Hanoverian rejection of centralist government. Where earlier Continental versions of such grand, axial plans invariably focused on the palaces of absolutist rule, this was a purely residential suburb symbolic of the supposed freedom of the individual. Indeed, the street layout initially proposed by Craig had been in the shape of a British flag. In practice, however, Hanoverian state power lay just below the surface: we should remember that the very concept of new planned settlement was closely bound up with the practice of colonial plantation town-planning, often using grid layouts, in Ireland and the colonies.[9] And much closer to home, the vast programme of agricultural improvement and reordering was underway, as was the programme of planned defence works associated with the pacification of the Highlands in the wake of the 1745–6 war. The architecture of mercantile 'liberty' in Edinburgh was only possible because of the fearsome architecture of authority that culminated in Fort George, a fortified town designed by Colonel William Skinner and built by the Adam family in 1748–69, with classical barrack squares set inside overlapping polygonal bastions. Soon, the Edinburgh New Town began to change from its residential origins, and started to attract buildings of national government power. Initially, national status was to be evoked by individual interpretations of the international language of antique classicism. This paradoxical link between classicism and nationality had first been established in the seventeenth- and eighteenth-century French debates between the 'ancients' and 'moderns', and by 1740 Claude Perrault could describe the colonnade of the Louvre as 'le portrait du caractere de la Nation'.[10] At first, each country tried to become a Rome, by building monuments of antique grandeur. In Scotland, this approach had been foreshadowed in Mar's utopian projects of the 1710s and 1720s, but it was only in the work of Robert Adam, backed by first-hand archaeological recording of antique remains, that it could begin to be realised. Adam applied the symbolism of antique grandeur to a range of public buildings of the early 1790s, including the triumphal-arch façades of the Edinburgh University College and the Infirmary and Trades House in Glasgow. These were commissioned by a wide variety of agencies, as public architectural patronage remained highly decentralised and voluntary. But alongside these there began, in his work, a tentative new lease of life for the government architect, now no longer as the servant of an absolutist monarch but as a part-time official.

Robert Adam, despite his cultivated image of dashing cosmopolitanism, was uniquely fitted for this new role by his family background, which was steeped in organisational support for Hanoverian power. His father, William Adam, had been 'Mason to the Board of Ordnance in North Britain', and Robert and his brothers had cut their architectural teeth in the building of Fort George and the fortifying of castles. In 1761 he was appointed, along with his rival William Chambers, to one of the two newly created posts of Architect of the King's Works. In this capacity he was awarded the commission for the first important government building to be started in Scotland or England since the London Horse Guards complex fifty years before: Register House, located at the east end of Edinburgh's Princes Street, planned in 1771 and commenced in 1774. The site was gifted to the state by the Town Council, as a spur to development of the Eastern New Town. Adam's plan was focused on a domed, Pantheon-style reading room rotunda, which was set in the centre of a rectangular courtyard formed by a quadrangle of offices; the offices all faced outwards, with a corridor running round the courtyard. The building, fronted by a sober, almost neo-classical porticoed façade, was completed in 1822–34 by government architect Robert Reid.

Register House, and its function of record-keeping, was one of the foundation-stones for the expansion of state administration activity in Scotland, especially in the next century, with its passion for censuses and statistics; the expansion of modern bureaucracy depended both on places to store records, and on offices in which to use them. At the centre of the Hanoverian Government system, in London, the story was the same: the pragmatic and anti-absolutist values of the British state ensured that the largest government building of those years was a vast office complex, designed by Adam's colleague as government architect, William Chambers: Somerset House (from 1776). By comparison with these substantial buildings for the 'tail' of Hanoverian government, the 'head' – comprising the legislature, and the head of state – was addressed only through theoretical projects for the rebuilding of royal palaces and the Westminster parliament. The most important of these proposals were drawn up in the 1760s by Robert Adam and his brother James. They considerably overlapped with the Register House design, as specialisation of government

APPENDIX.

B

PLAN of the Entrance Story *of the* OFFICE *for the* Public Records *of* SCOTLAND.

The floor shaded dark shews what is finished, the light floor shews what remains to be finished

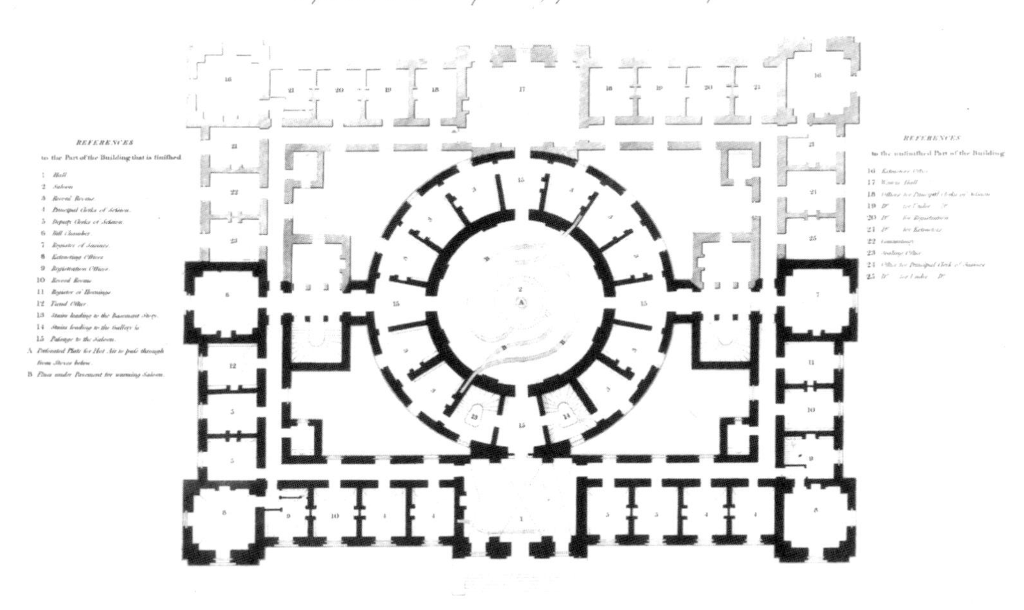

building types was still relatively embryonic. Significantly, while the royal palace designs envisaged relatively prosaic arrangements of courtyards and extensions to existing buildings, the Westminster designs were of great size and splendour, and full of significance for future parliamentary architecture.[11]

The proposals of the Adam brothers for Westminster did not emerge out of a vacuum. Instead, they formed one stage in a succession of attempts in Western Europe and America, during the eighteenth and early nineteenth centuries, to design legislative buildings for constitutional government systems, which combined the grandeur of classical antiquity and royal palace architecture with elements of Enlightenment rationalism. The older kinds of national assemblies had not needed special, purpose-designed buildings; as we saw, even the seventeenth-century Scottish parliament building was a somewhat 'loose-fit', multi-function complex. Now, especially within the anglophone world, a new type of symbolically planned parliament building evolved, with a bicameral layout echoing the political ideal of a Roman-style balanced constitution, in opposition to the hierarchical palaces of absolutist royal power. Owing to poor knowledge of classical architecture (and almost complete ignorance of Greek remains), these ideals were often expressed using classical precedents, such as the Pantheon, that had in reality not been assembly halls at all. If the Renaissance age had seen a change in the architecture of assembly and justice from great hall to palace, now the model began to change again from palace to classical temple. The new Irish parliament building of 1728–31, in Dublin (by Edward Lovett), was the first major example; it was axially planned around an octagonal House of Commons, topped by a Pantheon dome, but the off-centre placing of the House of Lords diminished the bicameral symmetry. In England, attention soon focused on the old medieval buildings of Westminster which, like those in Edinburgh, had muddled together legislature, law-courts and church, with the House of Commons housed since 1547 in a converted chapel fitted with side galleries. In 1732–9, government architect William Kent made a series of proposals for rebuilding in a restrained palatial style, featuring a central square hall with a Pantheon dome, flanked by the two chambers; externally, there would have been monumental colonnades, porticos and domed angle towers.[12] The Adam brothers' proposals of the 1760s, at a time of renewed discussion about rebuilding of this outmoded complex, also

TOP.
3.6. Plan of General Register House, Edinburgh, 1800, showing the portions of Robert Adam's original 1771 design that were completed (in black), and those yet to be built, at that date (in grey). (RCAHMS C47450)

BELOW.
3.7. General Register House in its completed state, seen from the south-west; photograph taken *c.*1925. (RCAHMS ED/9676)

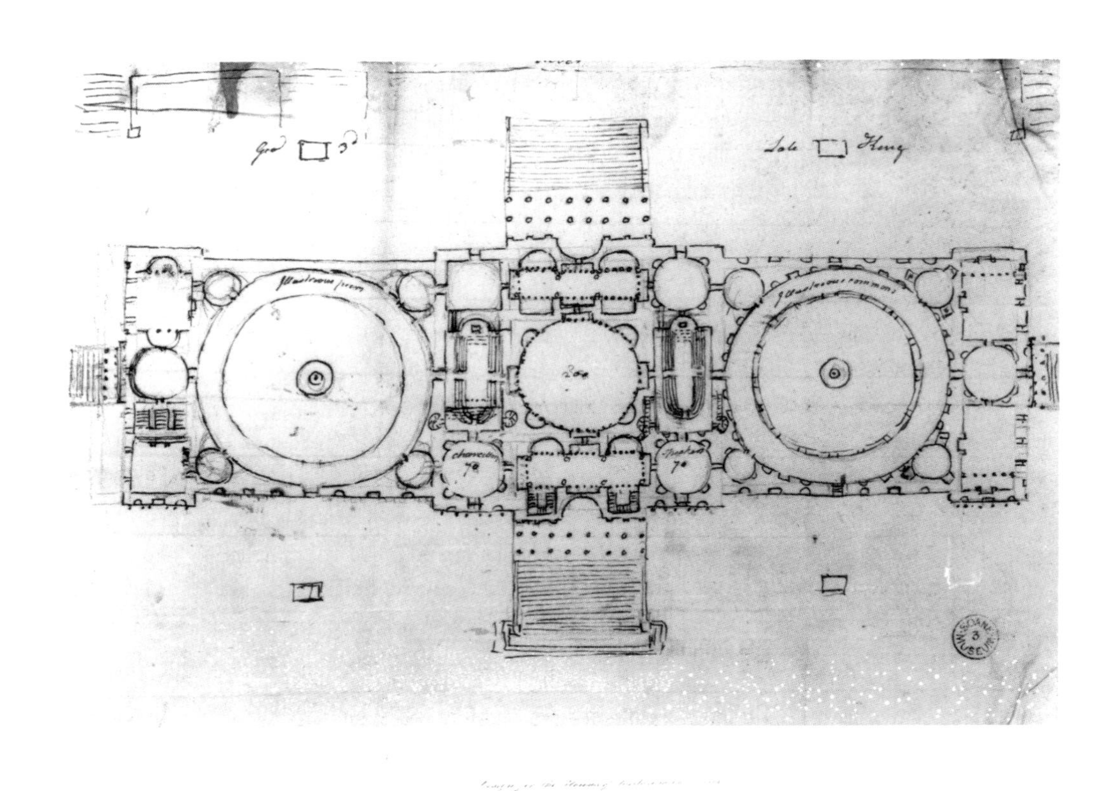

envisaged a symmetrical and highly monumental treatment, centred on a Pantheon-domed, column-ringed rotunda; the building was still to house a combination of legislature and law-courts. James Adam's last and most developed design for Westminster elongated the main parliament block into a broad rectangle, whose central rotunda was flanked by Lords and Commons chambers, and large outer open courtyards. The two chambers were shown with elongated 'U' layouts of facing seats, not dissimilar to that of the existing Commons chapel building, and to the Roman *curia* pattern. The design was articulated externally as a central porticoed block, with main and subsidiary domes, and colonnades linking to outer pavilions and triumphal arches; the scope of British power was asserted by the naming of the four porticoes: British, American, Irish and French. James Adam also designed a new 'Britannic Order' for use on the building.

Although this London parliament design was never built, it influenced later projects in Scotland, such as Register House and Gosford House. More importantly – and ironically, in view of the prominence of its 'American' portico – it was in post-revolutionary America that the classical palace-cum-temple planning ideas it embodied were decisively brought into alignment with the developing ideas of representative constitutional government. During the late eighteenth and early nineteenth centuries, the United States pioneered a wide range of design solutions for the giant legislative building, or 'Capitol'. The unicameral arrangement was addressed, for example, through a temple-like design for the Virginia State Capitol in 1784, by Thomas Jefferson and the French architect Charles Clérisseau. At the federal Capitol at Washington DC, the palace formula of the Adams was modified into a more explicitly 'antique', neo-classical style influenced by contemporary French developments, in order to distance the constitutionally balanced US bicameral legislature from Westminster, and echoing the Roman 'capitol' in its elevated site. The US Capitol was built originally to the designs of amateur architect, painter, and physician William Thornton, assisted from 1803 by Benjamin Henry Latrobe. Thornton (born 1759), a native of the British Virgin Islands who had been educated at Aberdeen and Edinburgh Universities in the 1780s, won the 1793 competition for the Capitol with a plan which articulated the bicameral US constitution through Adam-like juxtapositions of geometrical spaces, and was hailed by George Washington for its 'Grandeur, Simplicity and

TOP.
3.8. James Adam, *Plan for the Houses of Parliament, Westminster, c.*1762. One of a series of proposals by James Adam for reconstruction of the Westminster complex in a grandly 'antique' palace/temple style. The central rotunda is flanked by Lords and Commons chambers, and outer courtyards. There is strict bilateral symmetry, with two main porticoes (the 'British' and 'American'), and two side ones ('French' and 'Irish'). (By courtesy of the Trustees of Sir John Soane's Museum, AV VII, f.3)

BELOW.
3.9. After James Adam, elevation of a 'Design for the Houses of Lords and Commons', *c.*1762; a modified elevation, probably prepared by C L Clérisseau, derived approximately from the plan in illustration 3.8. (By courtesy of the Trustees of Sir John Soane's Museum, AV XXVII, f.2)

3.10. The original US Capitol building, Washington, D.C. (built from 1793 to the designs of William Thornton, with assistance from Benjamin Henry Latrobe), pictured following its sacking by British troops in 1814. (United States Capitol Historical Society, *We The People*, 1978, 28)

Convenience'. There were to be two Pantheon-like rotundas at the centre, flanked by a semi-circular Senate and a rectangular House of Representatives containing an elliptical colonnade; a vaulted supreme law court was later added. The likely conduits of influence of the Adams' work on the US Capitol project included not only Thornton's own Scottish education, but also the more direct link provided by the master mason for the construction of the White House, Collen Williamson (1727–1802); he and John Adam had remodelled Moy House, Morayshire, in the early 1760s, at exactly the time James and Robert were busy with their parliament designs, and he emigrated to the United States in the year before Thornton drew up his design.[13]

The US Capitol building underwent incessant changes and extensions, notably following its burning by British troops under Rear-Admiral Sir George Cockburn in August 1814 – an attack which Thornton himself vainly tried to prevent, by standing in the soldiers' way and denouncing them as 'Goths and Vandals!' – but the overall themes of bicameral symmetry and antique temple monumentality were maintained and even accentuated. Most importantly, Latrobe reconstructed the House as a semicircular tiered auditorium, on the model of Jacques Gondouin's anatomy theatre at the Ecole de Chirurgie, 1769–75, in Paris, which had been the first to combine a half-Pantheon ceiling with a tiered Greek amphitheatre plan. This precise combination of elements was found nowhere in antiquity, and was no more 'authentic' or intrinsically 'democratic' than the 'U' plan of the Presbyterian meeting-place or the *curia* plan of Westminster; but that did not diminish its power as an authoritative image of *res-publica* constitutionalism. When Palladio, in the sixteenth-century age of monarchy and oligarchy, first revived the classical theatre and

roofed it in, at the Teatro Olimpico at Vicenza (1580–4), the political association of the amphitheatre plan-form with Athenian democracy had remained dormant; and in fact, subsequent theatres and public auditoria, such as the Teatro Farnese at Parma (1617–28, by G.B. Aleotti) or the St Cecilia's Hall in Edinburgh (1762, by Sir Robert Mylne), had rapidly moved away from the shallow amphitheatre plan towards a more elongated 'U' or ellipse form.[14] But now, with the dawning of representative constitutionalism in countries much larger than the Greek city-states, the need for places of egalitarian mass assembly reawakened the association between the wide amphitheatre and 'democracy'.

3.11. Paris, Les Tuileries: the former *Salle des Machines*, transformed in 1793 into an assembly hall for the post-Revolution *Convention nationale*. To fit the seating into this wide and shallow space, architect J. P. Gisors designed a tiered amphitheatre on a half-oval plan, facing a tribune along the back wall. This plan became one of the most popular layouts for nineteenth- and twentieth-century parliament chambers across the world. This view, from F. L. Prieur's *Collection complète des tableaux historiques de la Rèvolution Française* (1798), shows the assassination of a deputy in the early 1790s.

During the French Revolution of 1789, the newly constructed Salle des Etats-généraux, a long room like a banqueting hall, with tiered seats running round the sides, was at first rearranged for the new National Assembly merely by moving the tribune from its royal position at one end of the hall to the middle. But in 1792–3, to house the 750-strong Convention Nationale, the lofty theatre at the Palais des Tuileries was remodelled by J.P. Gisors with a tiered semi-oval of benches, constructed in temporary wood and papier-maché, facing a stepped tribune, with public galleries set into the side walls.[15] This space, and its successors, including the Salle des Cinq Cents (1795–6) at the Palais Bourbon, authoritatively re-established the old, egalitarian Athenian connotations of the broad, curved amphitheatre, in opposition to the hierarchical connotations of long, narrow halls laid out with seats all facing one end. But it was the US federal Capitol that was the first to incorporate this influential 'antique' pattern into a building of palace-like plan and scale, allowing the legislature and its supporting bureaucracy to be combined in the same complex. During the mid- and late nineteenth century, the spread of these patterns in continental Europe was associated with unicameral as much as with bicameral planning. What all these large buildings had in common, however, was the stress on the parliamentary institution as a community in its own right.

BUILDING FOR THE AGE OF REFORM

After the war victory in 1815, the character of Scotland's classical architecture of government power changed, as the pace of urban development accelerated to a frenzy. In the words of Henry Cockburn, after 1815 'there were more schemes, and pamphlets, and discussions, and anxiety about the improvement of our edifices and prospects within these years after the war ceased, than throughout the whole of the preceding one hundred and fifty years'. The British empire now encompassed 20 per cent of the world's population, and Scotland was beginning to feel confident enough to assert a place in that triumph. Architecture was an important means of expressing that confidence, owing to its ability to integrate past and future, but its contribution was now re-assessed, especially in Edinburgh. The classical expression of the 'national' changed from Rome to Greece: Britain as a whole could be seen as the 'Periclean' liberator of Europe, while many Scots saw Edinburgh as a pure, intellectual Athens to London's powerful but decadent Rome. On the other hand, there was a growing romantic appreciation of the importance of landscape and untamed wilderness in the definition of *genius loci*.[16] This new cult of the romantic sublime contributed to the development of national consciousness not only in Scotland but right across Europe and North America; the 'Ossian' poems published by James Macpherson in 1760–3 powerfully invigorated the German romantic movement, and their martial heroism fired Napoleon's imperialistic campaigns of conquest.

The association of nationality with Grecian purity, temple architecture and sublime landscape had its most striking architectural impact in Edinburgh, where the whole city and its natural landscape was now praised as a single work of art by commentators such as Sir Walter Scott and Lord Cockburn. The New Town became merged with the Old, in a single historical landscape. The Calton Hill mediated between the two and became a national pantheon, symbolising Scotland's dual identity with its mixture of monuments to British military prowess and Scottish intellectualism. Chief among these were the half-built facsimile of the Parthenon constructed in 1826–9 (to the designs of C.R. Cockerell and W.H. Playfair) to commemorate the Scottish contribution to the Napoleonic Wars, and the Royal High School built by the Town Council on the south flank of the hill in 1825–9 (designed by Thomas Hamilton), its interpenetrating temple and stoa forms acting as an agora-like foil to the acropolis behind.

Within this framework of growing confidence and wealth, the demand grew for more specialised government buildings, expressed externally in an austere Greek style. Robert Reid followed Adam as official architect (as Master of Works to the King in Scotland, between 1824 and 1839), but, on the whole, private architects were used for the most innovative projects. For example, 1822 saw the commencement, at last, of a permanent headquarters for the Board of Manufactures, whose original task as a government agency for industrial promotion was now being supplanted by new initiatives to raise the quality of design. Located on a site at the foot of the Mound, commanding Princes Street, the building (now the Royal Scottish Academy) was designed in a columned Greek Doric style by William H. Playfair, who was brought back subsequently to enlarge it and add new colonnades in 1832–5.

In other towns across the country, central government architecture also began to make its presence felt – for example, in the massive Doric block of Greenock's Custom House (1818), by William Burn. In general, however, the most prominent administrative buildings remained those of the town councils. Here there was a growing tension between the traditional steepled tolbooth pattern with its mixture of law-enforcement and administrative uses, and the horizontal dignity demanded of a neo-classical public building. Still with one foot in the former camp was David Hamilton's Port Glasgow Town Buildings of 1813–16, built at a cost of £12,000 to house council

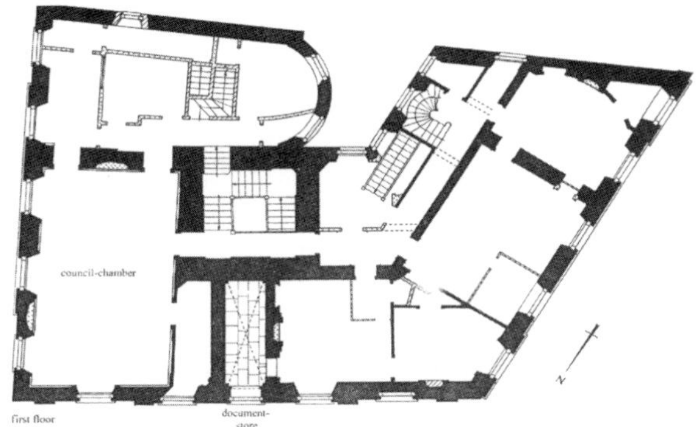
council-chamber
first floor
document-store
N

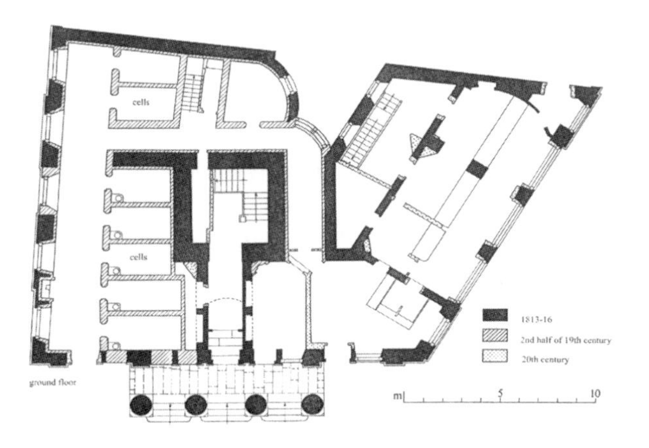
cells
cells
1813-16
2nd half of 19th century
20th century
ground floor
m 5 10

accommodation, courthouse and prison; fronted by a Doric portico and steeple, the building's first floor originally contained both cells and coffered council chamber. Thomas Hamilton's townhouse and assembly rooms of 1828–30 in Ayr (the 'Town's New Buildings') remained faithful to the steeple tradition, by including a specially tall and monumental tower to ensure the sound of its bells could be heard at a distance; but it eliminated the law-enforcement functions. William Stark's Glasgow town and county buildings, built in 1810–14 at a cost of £34,811 to replace the old tolbooth, unambiguously presented the image of a grave public building, with its massive hexastyle Doric temple portico and channelled wings, and banished its prison accommodation to a courtyard at the west side. Ironically, after the municipal offices moved on again in 1844, this building was employed exclusively for law-enforcement purposes, and was later reconstructed for national judicial use as the Justiciary Courts in 1910-13 by J.H. Craigie.[17]

The high status of old Scottish heritage within Romanticism dramatically threw into reverse the post–1707 neglect of the Stuart legacy. At the very time that the pressure for rationalistic modernisation was accelerating further, a new, emotional nostalgia was popularised by Sir Walter Scott. The 3rd Duke of Argyll had paved the way for this by following the military defeat of Jacobitism in 1746, by rejecting classicism when commissioning a new country seat at Inveraray. Instead, he co-opted the Stuart concept of baronial lineage as a new support for Hanoverian rule, by building a new Gothic castle. This stood in close juxtaposition to a classical planned village, to which tenants displaced by the castle were moved. From that point, a medievalising architecture of dynastic heritage, and associated Ossianic imagery of Highland romance, rapidly gained popularity in country-house architecture, so that in the 1820s David Hamilton's vast classical enlargement of the viceregal Hamilton Palace seemed distinctly old-fashioned. In the building of Walter Scott's own country villa, Abbotsford (1817–23), these ideas were given an architectural shape which was both more antiquarian and more suitable for reproduction in middle-class villa form: for the first time, there was explicit use of the corbels and crowsteps of Scottish Renaissance palaces and houses, motifs later to be used in a more archaeologically correct manner in the mid-century 'Scotch Baronial' style. This historical precision, already seen in classical architecture in the use of

TOP.
3.12. Port Glasgow Town Buildings (David Hamilton, 1813–16), view from north. (RCAHMS B47632)

BELOW.
3.13. Port Glasgow Town Buildings, ground and first-floor plans. (RCAHMS)

accurate Greek styles, was increasingly important to architects as a way of conveying meaning and a sense of tradition in new building types: under this system, called 'eclecticism', specific historical styles, or combinations of several, would be used to convey the values associated with a building.

Scott also introduced the imagery of Highland romance to the capital. During the visit of George IV to the city in 1822, he orchestrated a series of ceremonies intended to imbue the present-day Hanoverian monarchy with the romantic prestige of Edinburgh's royal heritage. Already, in February 1818, authorised by a royal warrant, he and the Scottish officers of state had recovered the regalia, walled up in the Castle since 1707. For the king's visit, clad in an adaptation of highland dress, the city was laid out as a theatrical arena of living history. At Holyrood, the king held a levée and reception, for which the royal suite was reconstituted; William Trotter was paid £1,470 for furniture and upholstery work. King George participated in Presbyterian worship at St Giles' Kirk, bringing the latter into a new prominence. At the Castle, he arrived in grand procession to view the regalia, following which they were placed on public view – the beginning of the gradual takeover of the Castle by heritage interests. And at Parliament Hall – which, sixty years previously, had witnessed the beginning of Ossianic romanticism, in the form of a subscription dinner to finance James Macpherson's Highland researches – a banquet for the king was held, attended by three hundred tartan-clad aristocrats, with forty-seven toasts, highland music, and elaborate conviviality.[18]

The key question posed by the works of Scott was that of the impact of modernity on Scottish society. In his novels, modernity was represented by the post-1707 dual identity of Scotland, with its domestic autonomy controlled by the lairds, clergy and professional classes. Now that order, in its turn, was imperilled, by the challenge of furious urbanisation and social change. Although Scott himself was vehemently opposed to the dilution of landed privilege, his novels made the idea of national identity available to everyone, at a time when its eighteenth-century supports were beginning to collapse.

The 1815 victory brought expansion and urban growth not only in Edinburgh but also in Glasgow, whose industries and proletariat began to offer a new and turbulent model of the city, and created the bipolar Central Belt we know today: as early as 1816 Scott could

contrast 'our metropolis of law, by which I mean Edinburgh', and 'our metropolis of mart and gain, whereby I insinuate Glasgow'.[19] The complacent assumptions of Edinburgh ascendancy, and the image of 'Modern Athens', were both shattered in 1833 when the Town Council became insolvent; but the expansion of Glasgow continued and gathered force. The most prized institutions of the old cultural autonomy, such as the 'democratic intellect' tradition of education, had become sclerotic: a royal commission of 1826 exposed corruption and low academic standards in the universities, and the system of parochial schooling and poor relief administered by the Kirk was in disrepair. The new urban boom spawned not only an impatient commercial bourgeoisie but also, from the 1830s, its own political radicalism in the form of the Chartist movement, which invoked both Jacobite and Covenanting imagery. The American and French revolutions had already re-invigorated the *res publica* ideal of balanced constitutional government, and undermined the prestige of the old oligarchic system. A struggle began between ideals of oligarchy and democracy, with each side accusing the other of factionalism, as had Aristotle in Ancient Greece.

3.14. The banquet given by the city of Edinburgh to King George IV in 1822 in Parliament Hall; drawn and engraved by W. H. Lizars. (RCAHMS EDD/168/14)

In tackling this crisis, the initiative was decisively taken by the central state. The Reform (Scotland) Act of 1832 revitalised the parliamentary system by enfranchising the emergent bourgeoisie: the electorate was expanded at a stroke from 4,000 to 65,000. Although the new system was dogged by electoral corruption, the transition from oligarchy to representative democracy had begun. Although reviled by Tory traditionalists such as Scott, who declared that his heart had been broken by the 'democratic ascendancy', representative democracy was sharply distinguished from Athenian direct democracy by a range of stabilising buffers interposed between electors and rulers.[20] As in the Roman system of controlled oligarchy, the delegates remained largely autonomous elite, accountable to the people solely at elections, but now there were new and additional factors, reflecting the greater complexity of society. The political elite's continuity and cohesion were protected by the discipline of party organisation (something which only became a full-blown reality now) and by the services of a supporting bureaucracy; and the national system was bedded into an extensive network of municipal and local politics.

Under the new Whig government elected in 1832, a succession of centrally driven changes followed, which reformed the legal system and the universities, and, in the Municipal Reform Act of 1833, reorganised the oligarchic town councils. The system of central government in Scotland had been overhauled in 1828, with the abandonment of 'management' through grandees, and the substitution of a new administrative regime under the authority of the Home Secretary, advised by the Scottish Lord of the Treasury and the Lord Advocate, based in Parliament House. Government from Parliament House continued through the 1830s and '40s.[21] This new system of limited representative democracy, with its supporting structures of civil service, local government and judicial administration, was unified, and given hierarchical authority, by a new emphasis on the absolute primacy of the Westminster parliament over all other structures. This was a substantial revision of the entrenched provisions under the 1707 Union settlement, which had supported the North British establishment.

What was the appropriate architectural expression of reformed government? That question came to the fore immediately after the passage of the 1832 parliamentary reforms, when Scottish architects were presented with an opportunity to help celebrate them architecturally – not in Edinburgh, but of course in London – after a large part of the Westminster parliament complex was gutted by fire in 1834. Since the Adams' projects, there had been other less ambitious plans, by Sir John Soane and others, for rebuilding the bicameral legislature in symmetrical, classical form. The opportunity to do so properly now seemed to have arrived. The 1835 competition following the fire called for a purpose-built legislative complex adjoining the surviving law-courts. The new accommodation, fitted on an awkward elongated site along the River Thames, had to include the two debating chambers of the Westminster system, along with extensive service and committee rooms, and club-like rooms for members' relaxation. The potential complexity of the site was increased by the medieval Westminster and St Stephen's Halls, which competitors could retain if they wished, but a symmetrical palace-like solution like the Adams' plan or the Washington Capitol would still have been eminently possible.

The reformist aspects of this new British capitol project were overlaid and modified by complex symbolic overtones, some of which made the competition a considerable challenge for Scottish competitors. To be sure, there was a desire to celebrate the 1832 constitutional reforms as a break from tradition: the new building must be 'worthy of being the palace of the constitution which its authors boast of having effected so great an improvement on the old English government'. But this break was not a revolutionary rupture, as in America and France. And there was also a desire to reassert a specifically English tradition, and to remould it by making Westminster, rather than Canterbury, into the spiritual heart of the English nation; to make London the true capital of England for the first time. This had direct implications for the parliament's architectural appearance, in view of the growing use of historic styles to signify meanings, including national identity. These styles, and the meanings attached to them, both shifted rapidly. In early nineteenth-century Scotland, national sentiment could be conveyed by a range of premodern styles, including neo-Gothic and Baronial castellated elements, as at Abbotsford. In contemporary England, there was a more vehement insistence on Gothic, but this was defined to include both the grid-like late Gothic 'Perpendicular' and hybrid Gothic-Renaissance 'Elizabethan' variants specific to that country. For example, in 1831 the influential *Quarterly Review* praised the latter as 'exclusively English' in its 'rich irregularity . . . reminding us of the glorious visions that flitted across the imagination of the immortal bard of the same age'.[22]

The Westminster competition accordingly specified that the new buildings must be either Gothic or Elizabethan in style. Although this requirement may have deterred Scottish architects accustomed mainly to classical work, a number of prominent designers familiar with neo-medieval styles, such as Gillespie Graham and David Hamilton, did participate. Graham, like the eventual winner of the competition, the English architect Charles Barry, delegated the drawings and design of details to the fertile imagination of his young English collaborator, A.W.N. Pugin, who had worked with him since 1829 on a number of projects. Most competitors chose a Perpendicular Gothic style, but a few selected Elizabethan, including David Rhind, whose entry ('*Pro patria semper*'), including parapets indebted to Audley End and turrets to Hertford House, was acclaimed by the *Gentleman's Magazine* as 'decidedly magnificent' in its detail and arrangement; his later Daniel Stewart's Hospital, Edinburgh (1848–53) used the same general style. The English architect Anthony Salvin, conversely, based his entry very largely on a Scottish Renaissance precedent: the towered style of Heriot's Hospital.[23]

In their general planning principles, the Westminster entries divided into two groups. There were those who simply extended the existing informal agglomeration of the existing complex. And on the other hand, there were those who designed the new building as a unified composition, with a regular roofline and a symmetrical or axial arrangement of the two chambers – in other words, as a bicameral Washington-style capitol in Gothic dress. Graham's sumptuously drawn entry was the most extreme example of the agglomerative approach, treating the two chambers as separately articulated hall blocks, surrounded by lower gables and turrets: the whole composition was crowned by a tall lantern tower like St Ouen, rivalling the adjacent towers of Westminster Abbey. Although its detailing was French, its general massing owed much to Hollar's seventeenth-century view of Westminster. Both Charles Barry and David Hamilton – who won third prize under the pseudonym 'King, Lord and Commons' – submitted plans for a loose grid layout interspersed by courtyards, with a main west-east entrance route intersecting a main north-south axis in a lobby between the two symmetrically placed chambers, and carrying on to a second north-south axis of committee rooms and libraries along the river front.

Barry's winning entry was less satisfactory than Hamilton's in strict planning terms, as its slanting alignment to the river resulted in

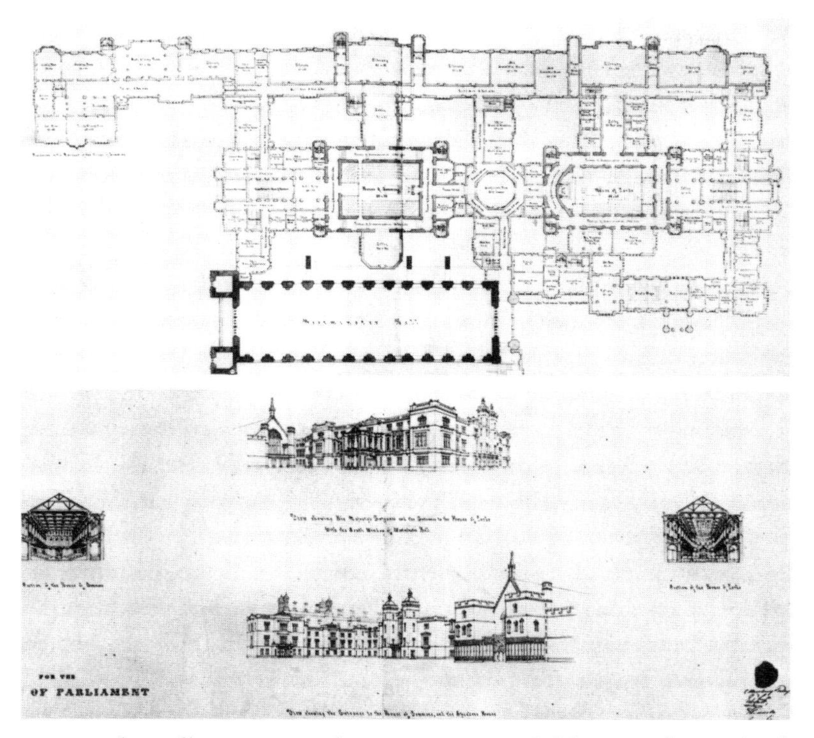

TOP.
3.15. Competition design by David Hamilton for new Westminster parliament complex, London, 1835 (awarded third prize): plan of principal floor. Hamilton's layout, with its grid-layout and octagonal central hall between the two meeting chambers, substantially influenced the eventually built plan by Charles Barry (from 1840).

BELOW.
3.16. Competition design by David Hamilton: Perspectives of Old and New Palace Yard, and sections of the two assembly chambers.

some awkwardly compressed spaces at one end. However, he retained Westminster Hall, and stylistically, his highly unified Gothic design, richly detailed by Pugin and dominated by a huge south-west state entrance tower, made a far greater impact than Hamilton's relatively low and heavily massed Tudor-cum-Jacobean exteriors, which were similar in their overall arrangement to contemporary country houses designed by him, such as Lennox Castle (1837–41) and Dunlop House (1831–4), and lacked the vertical accent of a tower. On his appointment, however, Barry adjusted his plan to incorporate some of the best features of the runners-up. His revised plan of 1836 adopted two key features from Hamilton: the river front was straightened out, regularising and loosening the whole layout; and the focal space of the central lobby between the chambers was changed to an octagon. Construction eventually began in 1840, with Pugin closely harnessing his decorative talents to Barry's plans to produce neo-Gothic external detail and interiors of unprecedented richness. The legislative chambers differ in their internal layout: the House of Commons follows the face-to-face plan of the Roman *curia*, while the House of Lords is arranged in a 'U' shaped plan, to evoke not democratic equality but the hierarchical heritage of the medieval royal parliaments. Both seating plans were generally similar to those in James Adam's earlier project.

THE ARCHITECTURE OF DISRUPTION

While this triumphal celebration of reformed English/British constitutionalism was getting underway in London, some of the same individuals, and the same architectural ideas, were involved in a 'parliamentary' building project of a very different sort in Edinburgh: a building to house the assembly of the 'Church of Christ' in Scotland, a church which was about to split violently asunder in reaction to the demands of absolute parliamentary sovereignty. The turmoil of social and economic modernisation was approaching its climax, a climax that would focus, architecturally, on buildings of religious assembly. However, in contrast to the English Gothic Revival, architecture did not take up any partisan positions in this controversy.

Almost all commentators were agreed that the vigorous state interventions of the years around 1830 had virtually torn apart the old dual identity of 'North Britain'. In the view of Henry Cockburn, up to that point 'almost the whole official state, as settled at the Union, survived; . . . unconscious of the economical scythe which has since mowed it down'. Where the critics disagreed was in how to react. Among antiquarians, the prevailing mood was at first one of resentful opposition. Cockburn argued that 'the great modern object has uniformly been to extinguish all the picturesque relics and models of antiquity, and to reduce everything to the dullest and baldest uniformity'.[24] Architecturally, the furious modernisation now seemed to have arrived in the heart of Old Edinburgh, in a series of invasive reconstruction schemes which prompted visceral opposition from Scott and his circle. These projects bore no exact relationship to political or economic reform, and actually anticipated them, but that was almost incidental to their emotional impact, as the heart of the eighteenth-century 'hotbed of genius' and of the seventeenth-century Scottish polity was physically excised.

The campaign began with the rebuilding of the Parliament House complex into a modern group of purpose-designed law courts.

Internationally, the evolution of the modern law courts building-type during the nineteenth century ran in close parallel with the emergence of the parliamentary capitol type, both having the same general character of self-contained institutions focused on debating and administration. In Scotland, this relationship was expressed not through completely new buildings but through a process of superimposition within the existing built heritage: the new national law courts were physically built into, and around, the site of the old legislature. As early as 1804–11, the government architect Robert Reid had begun remodelling the Inner House, adding a new courtroom in 1808–9 following its split into two Divisions; he also built a new Exchequer Court, jail accommodation and library. From 1809 the Signet Library was begun, with interiors by Stark. As part of this scheme, Parliament Square was rebuilt and refaced by Reid in a stolid Adam-like style in 1807–10, and the New Tolbooth was demolished in 1811. Cockburn nostalgically recalled the old façade as 'venerable and appropriate; becoming the air and character of a sanctuary of Justice', and bemoaned its removal for 'the bright freestone and contemptible decorations that now disgrace us'. Lord Chief Baron Robert Dundas recovered cartloads of architectural fragments from the exteriors of Parliament House, where they 'were treated as mere rubbish', and incorporated them into his walled and sunken gardens at Arniston House. Other fragments were included in the renovated Abbotsford by Sir Walter Scott: for example, a window pediment from the main Parliament House façades which was combined with a door salvaged from the old Tolbooth and set into Abbotsford's exposed south-west wall. In 1817–19, two new Outer House courts were built by Archibald Elliot outside Parliament Hall. From that point, the hall was increas-

3.17. James Caldwell's view of Robert Reid's refaced and rebuilt Exchequer and law-courts buildings in Parliament Square (1807–10). (RCAHMS EDD/167/2)

3.18. The ruins of Parliament Square following the November 1824 fire. (From a contemporary etching; reproduced in *Cassell's Old and New Edinburgh*, n.d., 173)

ingly used for public events and meetings, including a series of 'Edinburgh Festival' concerts, as well as a grand dinner for George IV during his 1822 visit, served with much Highland pageantry, with the royal dais at the south end of the hall in the traditional place of the pre-1707 King's Commissioner to Parliament.[25]

Following a second 'Great Fire' in 1824, which destroyed Assembly Close and the east side of Parliament Square, including some of Reid's buildings, the Parliament House complex was extended to the south and east with a curved façade completing Reid's scheme. New courtrooms were built in a severe neo-classical style: each had arched windows, high compartmented ceiling, pew-like benches on a rectangular U-plan layout, and galleries all round; the judges' bench was arranged on the traditional curved plan. The new east range, completed in 1830, included the civil courtrooms of the First and Second Divisions of the Court of Session (1830), obliterating the old Inner House, and the south range, completed in 1838, the supreme criminal courtroom of the High Court of Justiciary (1835); the mace in the First Division courtroom (the Old Exchequer Mace) is also carried in the procession of the Lord High Commissioner of the Church of Scotland General Assembly. After 1844, four further Outer House courtrooms were built to the south by government architect William Nixon, bringing to an end the regular use of Parliament Hall for court sittings and completing the transformation of the complex. From this point, high courts, with their national status, became a specialised building type, distinct from 'government' as such, and outwith the scope of this account. However, the increasingly functional separation of courtrooms, legislative chambers and Presbyterian church halls was not mirrored exactly within architecture. The rectangular auditorium plan of these new courtrooms was little different from that of Presbyterian churches or, for that matter, that of the *ekklesiasterion* of fourth-century BC Priene; the seventeenth century layout of Parliament Hall itself had of course been a U plan, but on a single level.[26] Certainly, Scottish courts paid no regard to the theoretical type-plans by Durand (1809) for grid-layouts of courtrooms planned like small apsed basilicas, or to Latrobe's unconventional design for the US Supreme Court (1803–12) as a low, massively vaulted space with flanking benches facing one another across the desks of officials.

At the same time as the law-court rebuildings, St Giles' Kirk, which had become dirty and dilapidated, was reconstructed so as to create a more unified, cathedral-like form, reversing the Reformation and covenanting alterations by reducing its internal subdivisions, recladding it with new ashlar and tearing down the external excrescences; this work was subsidised by the government to the tune of £12,600, over half of the total cost.[27] As part of this campaign, presaged in a report of 1817 by Elliot and executed by William Burn in 1829–33, the Town Council demolished the Old Tolbooth in 1817, to the protests of Scott, who immortalised it as the 'Heart of Midlothian' in his novel of that name the following year.

In the 'restoring' modernisation of St Giles', we arrive at the architectural eye of the great national storm that was now approaching its height. The foundation of the 1707 treaty settlement had been the guarantee of autonomy of the Church of Scotland. This autonomy was seen from the Kirk's viewpoint not so much in terms of secular constitutional federalism but as a continuation of the doctrine of the two kingdoms, temporal and spiritual, that had been first enunciated by Pope Gelasius I in the fifth century, and had later been recast by Scots Calvinists in anti-erastian form. The 'spiritual' was still assumed to be something that could override or intervene in the secular: the Kirk's parish system claimed control over the substantial social responsibilities of education and poor relief. When, under its lax eighteenth-century control by lairds, this system began to disintegrate, it was challenged from within by a new, activist grouping, the evangelicals.

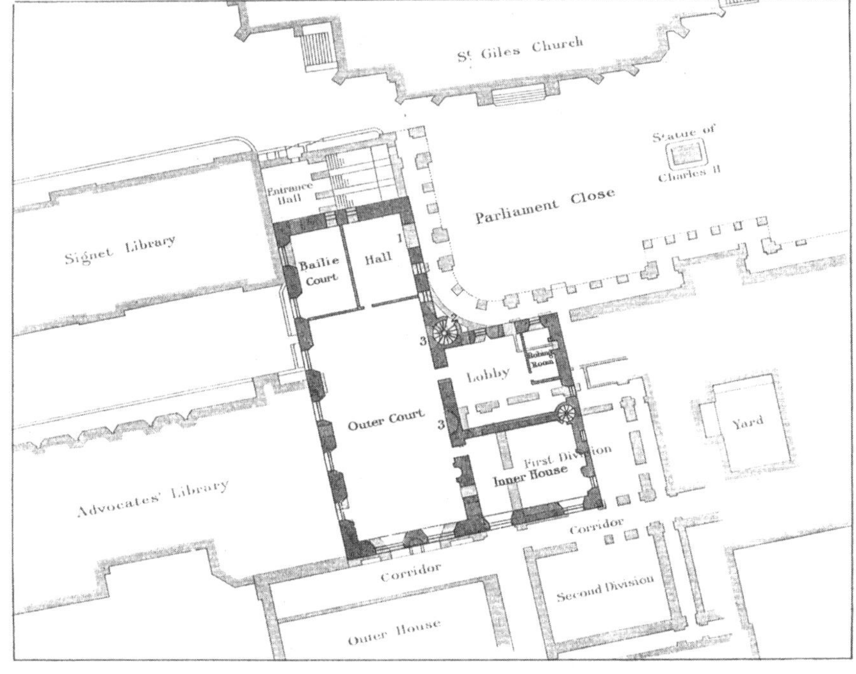

St Giles Church
Statue of Charles II
Entrance Hall
Parliament Close
Signet Library
Bailie Court
Hall
1
3
Lobby
Outer Court
3
Yard
First Division
Inner House
Advocates' Library
Corridor
Corridor
Second Division
Outer House

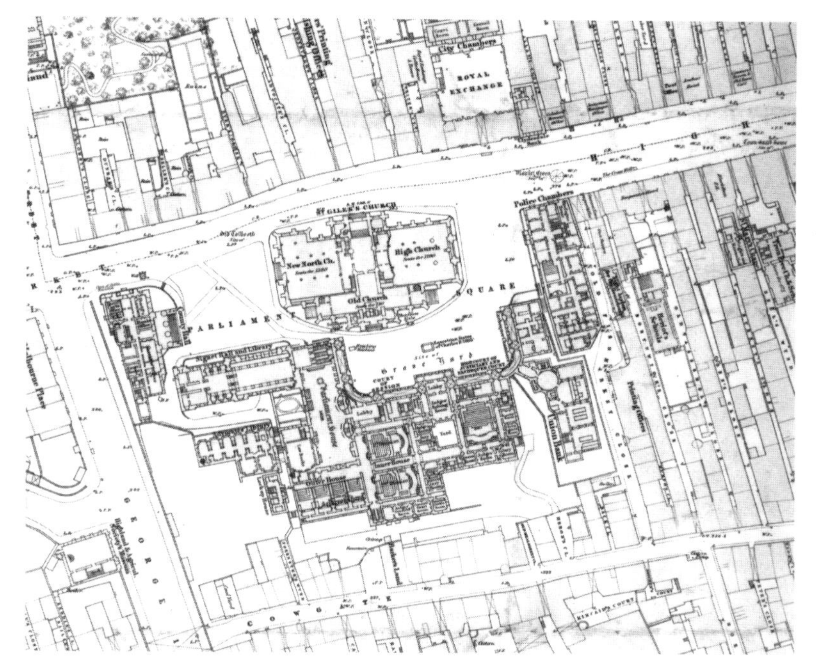

Their views were a mixture of social modernity and religious fundamentalism. Far from meekly accepting the withdrawal of religion from public secular life into the personal sphere, they believed that the rural-oriented parish system must be reinvigorated to combat urban social and religious disintegration. As part of their campaign the evangelicals, led from 1831 by Thomas Chalmers, tried to use the Kirk's parliament, the General Assembly, to stop the appointment of ministers by landowners against the wishes of the parish ('intrusion'), while at the same time expanding the number of evangelical ministers in the Assembly by including the ministers of provisional parishes in urban areas. But their opponents successfully appealed to the Court of Session, and Westminster, to overrule the General Assembly decisions, setting the scene for an irreconcilable clash over the relationship of church and state.

In this context of mounting crisis, the question of the physical accommodation of the General Assembly came to the fore. Initially, Burn had made provision for the Assembly to remain in the southern part of St Giles', creating an enlarged hall for it as one of the three subdivisions of his scheme.[28] However, with the rapid rise in the number of ministers entitled to attend to nearly 1,200, even this was no longer large enough, and the 1841, 1842 and 1843 General Assem-

OPPOSITE TOP.
3.19. 1990 aerial view of Parliament Square from north-east, showing the new unified classical facades of the early nineteenth century. (RCAHMS B49058)

OPPOSITE BELOW.
3.20. 1895 layout plan of Parliament House with 1640 plan (in black) superimposed. (R. Miller, *The Municipal Buildings of Edinburgh*, 1895, 81)

ABOVE.
3.21. Part of the 1st Edition Ordnance Survey 1:1,056 map of Edinburgh, surveyed in 1852 and published in 1854. The map shows the internal layout of the Parliament Square courts complex, and the simplified internal subdivisions of St Giles' following Burn's alterations. (RCAHMS EDD/1/178)

blies were held in St Andrew's Church, George Street. To deal with this sudden growth in the Assembly, the evangelical ascendancy in the Kirk began to plan something altogether more ambitious. In 1835, James Gillespie Graham had been engaged to draw up plans to restore the roofless Holyrood Abbey, last used by James VII as a chapel for his Order of the Thistle, as a hall for the assembly, but the scheme proved too expensive. Now, attention returned to the upper end of the Old Town, where an improvement scheme conceived in 1824 by Thomas Hamilton had begun to advocate the opening up of new bridges and vistas, with buildings in a 'Flemish' neo-Gothic medieval style, including an abortive proposal of 1829 for an openwork-steepled 'John Knox Church' at the head of the 'Earthen Mound' ascending from Princes Street. In the late 1830s, the Church of Scotland leadership eventually decided to build a new assembly hall on an adjoining site at the top of the Lawnmarket. In view of the national status of the Kirk, the building was to be called the Victoria Hall, and would be paid for out of public funds. Of the total cost of £16,000, the Town Council paid £6,000 and the Treasury the rest, including £3,600 for the site; it was erected under the provisions of the Edinburgh Improvement Act of 1827. Despite its economical cost, this would be no ordinary assembly hall, but a vast, two-storey structure with a 241 ft (73m) high steeple, 153m above sea level, that would trumpet the spiritual independence of the 'Church of Christ' across city and nation and, by its axial position commanding Dundas Street, would continue the integration of the New and Old Towns. Gillespie Graham was its architect, and the master builder was John Lind; but the working drawings for the rich Gothic detail which disguised this essentially utilitarian hall building were by none other than Augustus Welby Pugin, the helper of Barry (and Graham) at Westminster. That the same hand should be engaged in drawing out rival temporal and spiritual parliaments was an irony indeed – not least as Pugin had converted to Catholicism in 1835, and was thus a religious outsider to both camps. Pugin was violently hostile to 'the scotch kirk', which he regarded as 'the abomination of desolation', so unsurprisingly he took pains to conceal his role in the building of its national assembly hall.[29]

3.22. Victoria Hall, Edinburgh (by J. Gillespie Graham, 1839–44): photograph of *c*.1900. (Scottish Colorfoto Lab, RCAHMS Box 5/ED/9340)

The new Victoria Hall was symmetrically planned, with the tall steeple at the front. The steeple, whose richly profiled shape echoed and outdid the earlier John Knox proposal, was closely related to Pugin's second design for a church in Southwark, London: it had a

ARMS

TO THE GLORY OF GOD IN HONOUR OF THE QUEEN

ON THE 3d DAY OF SEPTEMBER IN THE YEAR OF OUR LORD

MDCCCXLII.

The Day of our Most Gracious Majesty

Queen Victoria

VISITING THE CITY OF EDINBURGH,

The Right Honourable Sir James Forrest of Comiston, Bart.

LORD PROVOST.

The Revd. David Welsh, D.D. Moderator of the Assembly

THE FOUNDATION STONE OF THIS SUPERB STRUCTURE TO BE CALLED

Victoria Hall

FOR THE USE OF THE

GENERAL ASSEMBLY OF THE CHURCH OF SCOTLAND.

WAS LAID BY

The Right Honourable Lord Frederick Fitz Clarence, G.C.H.

GRAND MASTER MASON OF SCOTLAND.

IN PRESENCE OF THE GRAND LODGE & OTHER MASONIC LODGES.

JAMES GILLESPIE GRAHAM, ESQUIRE, OF ORCHILL ARCHITECT.

JOHN LIND, MASTER BUILDER OF THE HALL.

Length of Building from East to West 141 Feet
Height of Spire over the Entrance 241 Feet

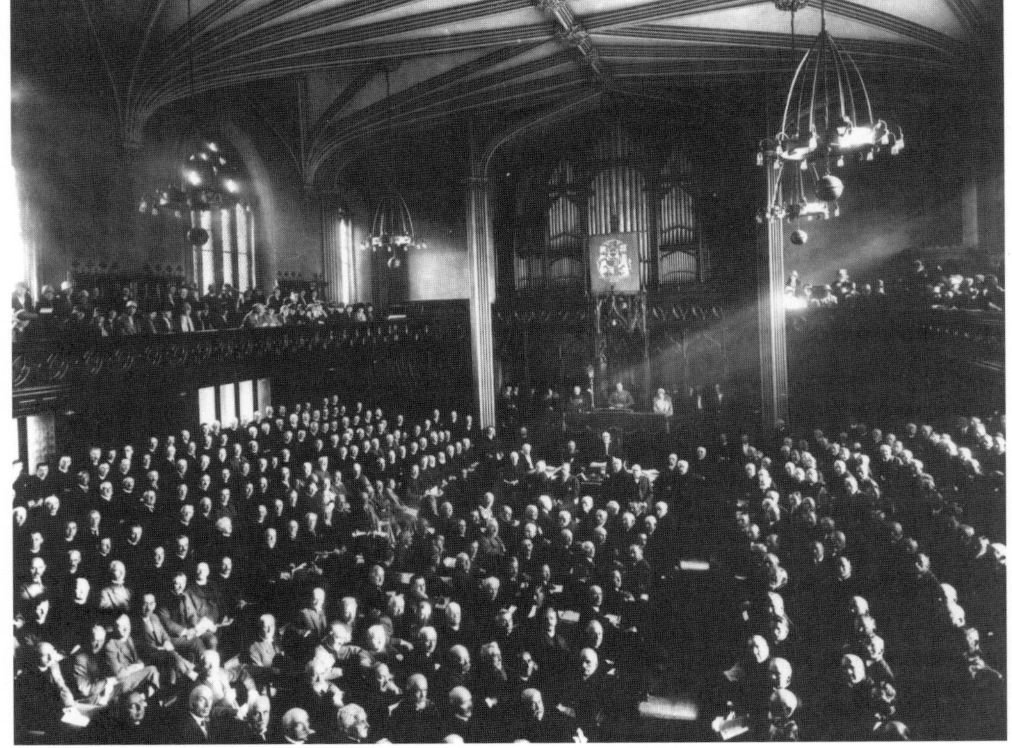

gableted clock stage and an octagonal spire above. The building is entered by a rib-vaulted vestibule and inner vestibule, leading to ground-floor committee rooms and the main hall above; as part of the continuing evacuation of St Giles', the latter was also used for worship by the Tolbooth Kirk congregation. The hall is a tall, aisleless box, roofed in a single span with flat plaster rib-vault, lit by wide windows. The seating followed a rectangular, galleried 'U' plan, perpetuating the St Giles tradition but greatly elongated and deepened: it was seven rows deep at the sides, and with room for about eighty delegates seated in the centre. Fittings designed by Graham and Pugin included a richly traceried screen running across the arched east bay, and a platform intended as a throne bench for the Lord High Commissioner.[30]

The foundation stone of the new hall was laid on 3 September 1842 by Lord Frederick FitzClarence, the Grand Master Mason of Scotland, in the presence of the Lord Provost, Sir James Forrest, and the Moderator, Rev. Dr David Welsh; and the building was duly completed in 1844. But between those dates the project was dramatically sidelined by the disintegration of the institution it was meant to house. At the General Assembly of 1842, the majority approved by 241 to 110 votes a 'Claim of Right' which repudiated the concept of parliamentary sovereignty over the 'Church of Christ'. In echoing the name of the original Claim of Right made against James VII, a century and a half before, the non-intrusionists evoked the secular tradition of anti-tyrannical constitutionalism stretching back to ancient Athens and Rome, but combined it with the specifically Christian doctrine of the two kingdoms. But with the breakdown of cohesion of the 1707 settlement, this two-pronged argument by the Kirk's supreme legislature, once so effective in the hands of the Presbyterian opponents of the Stuarts, could no longer count on the support of the judiciary, newly modernised and re-housed; the courts overruled the Claim of Right and amended the voting system in future General Assemblies against the evangelicals.[31]

The result of this decision was inevitable. At the opening of the 1843 Assembly on May 18 in the temporary location of St Andrew's Church, George Street, the retiring Moderator (David Welsh) denounced the court interventions as intolerable erastianism, and led out 40% of the clergy: 474 out of the 1,195 present. The sombre column of seceding ministers marched down the grand classical streets

TOP.
3.23. Victoria Hall, notice of 1842 foundation-stone laying. (Richard Emerson; RCAHMS EDD/49/1)

BELOW.
3.24. Victoria Hall: the final assembly meeting, presided over by the Duke of York, immediately preceding the reunification with the United Free Church in October 1929. (RCAHMS C44487)

© Benjamin Tindall Architects 1998

OPPOSITE TOP.
3.25. The interior of Victoria Hall, as converted into The Hub (Edinburgh Festival Centre) by Benjamin Tindall Architects in 1997–9. (Benjamin Tindall)

OPPOSITE BELOW.
3.26. Tanfield Gasworks, Edinburgh, site of the signing of the Act of Separation and the Deed of Demission at the May 1843 Disruption; view prior to demolition in 1986. This pioneering gasworks had previously been visited, on grounds of its technological interest, by the renowned Prussian architect K.F. Schinkel on his 1826 tour of Scotland. (RCAHMS B7497)

LEFT.
3.27. '*The Disruption!*': one of the collection of Disruption cartoons, produced by two unknown artists between 1840 and 1845, and now in the collection of New College Library, Edinburgh. The procession of the seceding ministers out of the General Assembly in St Andrew's Church on 18 May 1843 is portrayed as a carnival parade. (University of Edinburgh)

named after the old regime – Hanover, Dundas, Pitt – to a temporary assembly place in a gasworks at Tanfield Hall, where they signed a 'Deed of Demission' giving up their livings, and convened the first General Assembly of the Free Church of Scotland. Mixing religious fundamentalism and modernity, the Free Church claimed to be the true Church of Scotland, invoking the Reformation and the National Covenant; yet its chief supporters came from the modernising commercial and professional middle classes – although we should also bear in mind that a substantial proportion of Scots already belonged to voluntary churches with no link to the state, such as the United Presbyterian Church.[32]

Lavishly financed by its wealthy supporters, the Free Church was able to build up a complete shadow infrastructure with incredible speed. Within four years it had built over 730 places of worship, and had raised enough money to begin construction of a permanent theological college in Edinburgh, replacing temporary premises in the city's George Street; the permanent building was to incorporate a new General Assembly hall. Following a competition, the commission was awarded to W.H. Playfair, whose closest friend, Lord Rutherford, the Lord Advocate, was a prominent Free Church member. In the capital, ever since the 1820s, the classical styles favoured for churches in Glasgow had been generally rejected as 'pagan', and some form of medieval style, Gothic or Romanesque, was demanded: here the Free Church especially favoured Gothic as a way of emphasising its claims

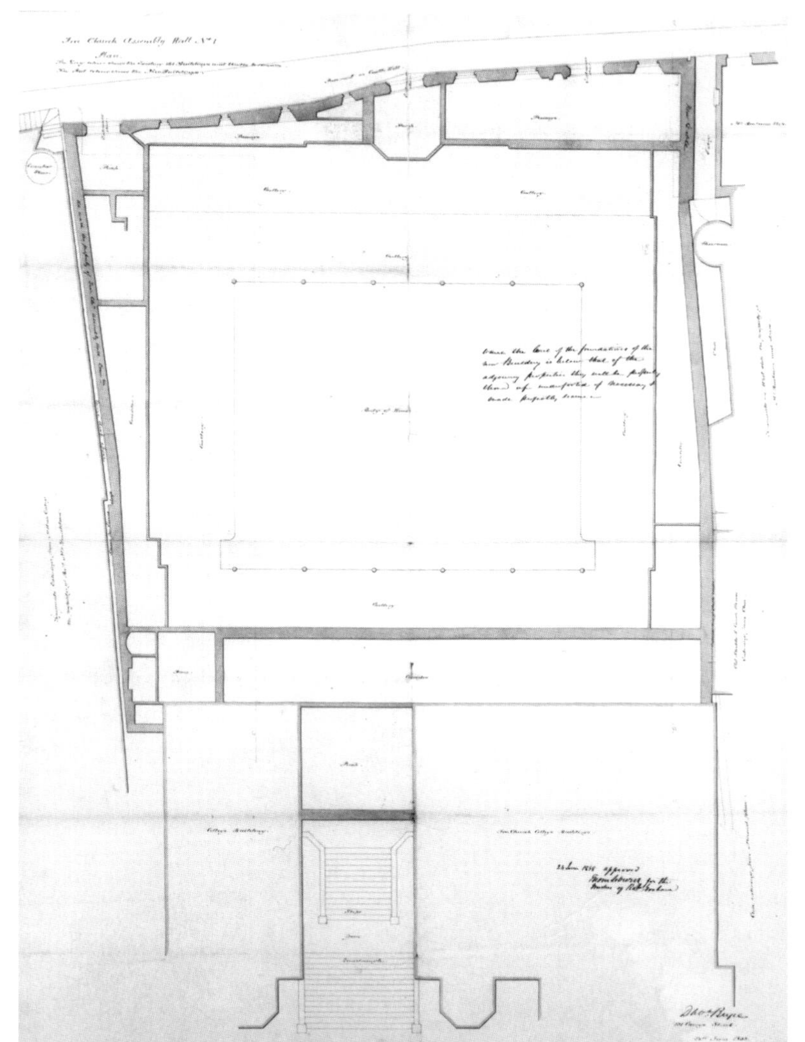

OPPOSITE TOP.
3.28. 1930s view of the quadrangle of Free Church College (New College), Edinburgh, by Playfair, 1846–50, with the steeple of Victoria Hall seen behind. (NMRS B66765)

OPPOSITE BELOW.
3.29. The view in the opposite direction, looking north from the Victoria Hall steeple across Free Church College courtyard and down Dundas Street/Pitt Street directly towards Tanfield Gasworks – the latter being the route of the 1843 Disruption procession. (RCAHMS, 1999)

LEFT.
3.30. Plan for the new Free Church Assembly Hall, Edinburgh, by David Bryce, July 1858. The hall was fitted into the space between Free Church College and the Lawnmarket; after the reunification of 1929, it became the General Assembly hall of the Church of Scotland. (City of Edinburgh Council; RCAHMS EDD/236/6)

to be the true Church of Scotland. But, as always now in central Edinburgh, the way that the new theological college building fitted into the overall ensemble could be as significant as its own design in isolation.

The site chosen was that of the old Guise Palace, set axially at the head of the Mound. Therefore the college had to establish an eclectic contrast with the classicism of the New Town, and the horizontal Doric dignity of Playfair's own government building for the Manufactures at the foot of the Mound. More important, however, was its relationship with the steeple of the newly completed Victoria

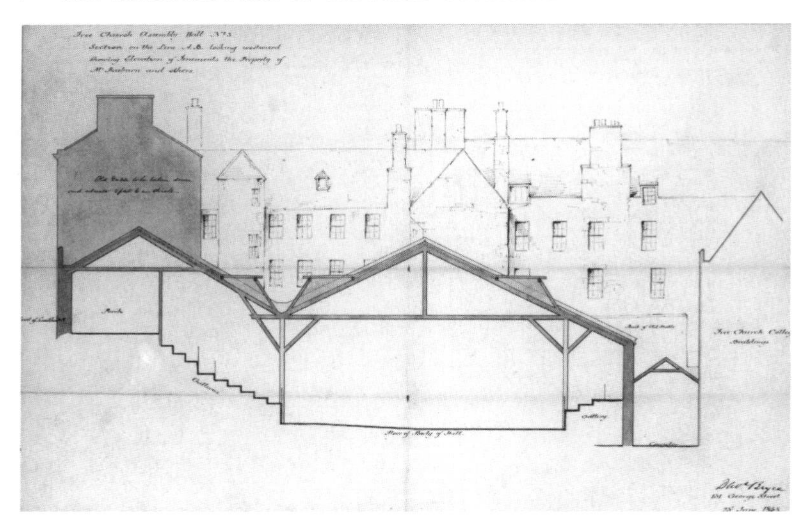

RIGHT.
3.31. Cross-section of Free Church Assembly Hall, 1858. The relatively utilitarian timber roof construction of this large space is clearly shown. (City of Edinburgh Council; RCAHMS EDD/236/4)

OPPOSITE TOP.
3.32. The last General Assembly of the Free Church of Scotland, preceding the union with the United Presbyterian Church in May 1900. (Church of Scotland; painting in New College)

OPPOSITE BELOW.
3.33. The state carriage of the Lord High Commissioner to the General Assembly of the Church of Scotland outside the main west front of Holyrood Palace in May 1884. (National Trust for Scotland; RCAHMS B67520)

Hall just behind, a hall commissioned by the evangelicals but now in the hands of their depleted opponents. The solution devised by Playfair was a brilliant *coup de théatre*. The new building was designed as a Gothic façade centred on twin steeples that would capture the assembly hall spire, and claim it once again for the 'Church of Christ' when viewed in axial vistas from the north, both near and far. Seen from the distant foot of Pitt Street, at the site of the signing of the Deed of Demission, the dramatic composite tower seemed to preside like a Free Church 'cathedral' (if such a thing were possible) over the processional route taken by the seceding ministers in 1843: Playfair's design disguised the fact that Graham's and Pugin's steeple was slightly off the central line of this axis.

The foundation stone of the new college building was laid in June 1846 by Thomas Chalmers; it was completed in 1850 at a cost of £36,000. The accommodation comprised a quadrangle fronted by the 121-ft-high twin entrance towers. On the east side of the court was the Free High Church, expressed externally by a third, slightly lower tower. The complex, as originally completed in 1850, contained classrooms, senate hall, students' hall, and library. On the south side of the quadrangle a staircase ascends steeply to an arched cloister giving access to the new assembly hall, with the steeple of the old hall looming up behind. The new hall was added in 1858–9 to the designs of David Bryce, the leading Edinburgh establishment architect after Playfair's death in 1857. Its cost, £7,000, was entirely collected by 'ladies of the Free Church'. Owing to the need to evoke church

tradition, the time-honoured galleried U-plan layout around the Moderator's dais was employed yet again. The hall comprises a broad, low nave and aisles covered by a giant brown-stained roof; the plan is wider and shallower than that of Victoria Hall. The roof is supported on utilitarian square timber columns with cantilever brackets, carrying huge trusses which divide the roof into four sections.

The Disruption marked the final dissolution of North Britain's old balance of state sovereignty and Scottish civil autonomy. But it was not so much a victory of Westminster over Scotland – after all, the state's victory was pyrrhic, since what it meant to control slipped through its fingers – as a revolution *within* Scottish society, a revolution brought about by the very success of 'improvement'. It was precisely because Scottish society had become so much wealthier and more confident that the old, privilege-ridden institutions of North British autonomy eventually corroded and collapsed. For example: the middle classes might well wish to pursue urban social reform, but it was now clear that this could not be done through a 'national church'. This represented the beginning of a long process of democratisation and diversification. But the destruction of the old idea of a cosy 'commonweal' of all Scots would require a new balance to be struck between external allegiance and domestic community.

THE ARCHITECTURE OF CIVIC PRIDE

The increasing wealth and confidence of society provided its own answer to this dilemma – or, more precisely, two linked responses. Both were defined by Scotland's new, mainly middle-class Liberal elite of the Disruption era, an electorate which expanded further in 1868 to 230,000; the Third Reform Act of 1884 greatly extended the rural franchise. These responses, in combination, would create a new dual identity for the nation. The first response was externally orientated: to transform the Scottish commitment to British imperialism from a narrow ruling-class affair into a mass movement, whose militaristic energy would galvanise and unite the middle and skilled working classes. It was argued that Scotland, through her own efforts, was now an equal partner in empire. The second response was internally orientated: to reinvigorate Scottish civil society around an agenda of material and social progress, led both by voluntary groups and by the rejuvenated municipalities. In both cases, the Presbyterian ethos of probity and meritocracy was elaborated into a new 'secular religion' of national pride, and combined with imagery of the romantic Highlands.

This heady mixture of imperialism, capitalism and Presbyterianism was firmly based in economic reality, in the task of creating and exploiting the commercial opportunity to make Scotland one of the richest countries in the world. But it led on from there in an unexpected direction, towards the beginning of demands for greater governmental autonomy – in other words, for a kind of home rule. As early as 1826, Scott had argued that Scots, English and Irish 'would not become better subjects, or more valuable members of the common empire, if we all resembled each other like so many smooth shillings'[33] Increasingly, such complaints assumed a political form, focusing on the question of how to administer the domestic apparatus of Scottish home government, whose reform in the 1820s had created a loose network of central boards and local agencies. As these began to proliferate, the system gradually grew more unwieldy. For example, following the effective breakdown of parish-based poor relief, an 1845 Poor Law Act set up a Board of Supervision, ruled by lairds, which supervised the administration of disabled poor relief by parochial boards of property owners; from 1839 the Prisons Commissioners inspected the inadequate county and burgh jails; and from 1857 the Board of Lunacy worked with local boards to erect new asylums. The 1872 Education Act created a rather more centralised body, the Scotch Education Department, charged with supervising the local power of elected school boards.

The 1850s saw the beginnings of agitation, led by the short-lived (1853–6) National Association for the Vindication of Scottish Rights, for an increase in the Scottish share of parliamentary representation to allow for the nation's allegedly growing status as an 'imperial partner', and for the handling of domestic government by an administrative assembly or the revival of the office of Scottish Secretary. However, the NAVSR was essentially still a romantic anti-modernisation campaign against state control, with much thundering against industrialisation, the loss of authentic culture, and so forth. Decisive moves towards administrative devolution would have to wait until the 1880s.[34]

In the built environment, these two trends were each expressed in their own appropriate way. The external solidarity with British power was voiced through a limited symbolic architecture of national grandeur, centred in Edinburgh. The 'home' autonomy was expressed in an architecture of civic dignity, organically linked with a vast increase in local governmental activity and pervading the entire country.

The symbolic national architecture was especially associated with the Scotch Baronial style. In it the romantic national legacy of Sir Walter Scott was reconciled with modern society: Baronial buildings juxtaposed crowsteps and corbels in machine-cut ashlar with modern plate glass and upholstery. Some of the elements of George IV's 1822 visit were elaborated into a fully developed cult of the monarchy: here the role of Baronial was guaranteed by the rebuilding of Balmoral Castle in 1853–5 to the designs of William Smith and Prince Albert. The 1850s and '60s also saw a growing emphasis on militaristic imperialism, perhaps influenced by the contemporary claims that Scotland was a 'Teutonic' or 'Germanic' nation. This trend was exemplified in the building of J.T. Rochead's spectacular Wallace Monument at Stirling (1859–68), whose rock-faced rubble and imperial crown spire trumpeted the hero as a forerunner of laissez-faire empire-building. These ideas were combined with a growing veneration for old remains and a desire to enhance them by 'restoration', especially in Old Edinburgh. Calton Hill, showpiece of the previous, 'Periclean' period of national pride, now declined in status, with the construction of further prison buildings on its flank: in the 1850s Henry Cockburn dismissed it as the site of 'everything that was too abominable to be tolerated elsewhere'. Edinburgh Castle began to change from an active military headquarters to a touristic setpiece dressed in military imagery. Abortive plans of the 1850s for the recasting of its main buildings like a bristling chateau, and of 1864 by Bryce to build a 165-ft-high keep at the top of the rock as a 'Scottish National Memorial to the Prince Consort', were followed by extensive Baronial-style restorations by Hippolyte Blanc, including the rebuilding of the Great Hall in 1887–91 as a banqueting hall and showcase of old weapons. Holyrood Palace, virtually cleared of grace and favour apartments by 1860, saw increasing use by the monarchy, but was at the same time re-framed as a historic relic, with the opening to the public of the historical apartments in the tower (1854), and the building of Baronial lodges and ancillary buildings by government architect Robert Matheson in 1857–62. Other buildings symbolic of

TOP.
3.34. The former Free Church Assembly Hall in 1998, prior to conversion into the interim chamber of the new parliament. (RCAHMS)

BELOW.
3.35. 1851 view of the interior of Parliament Hall, in use as a waiting-room for the courts. (RCAHMS EDD/168/10)

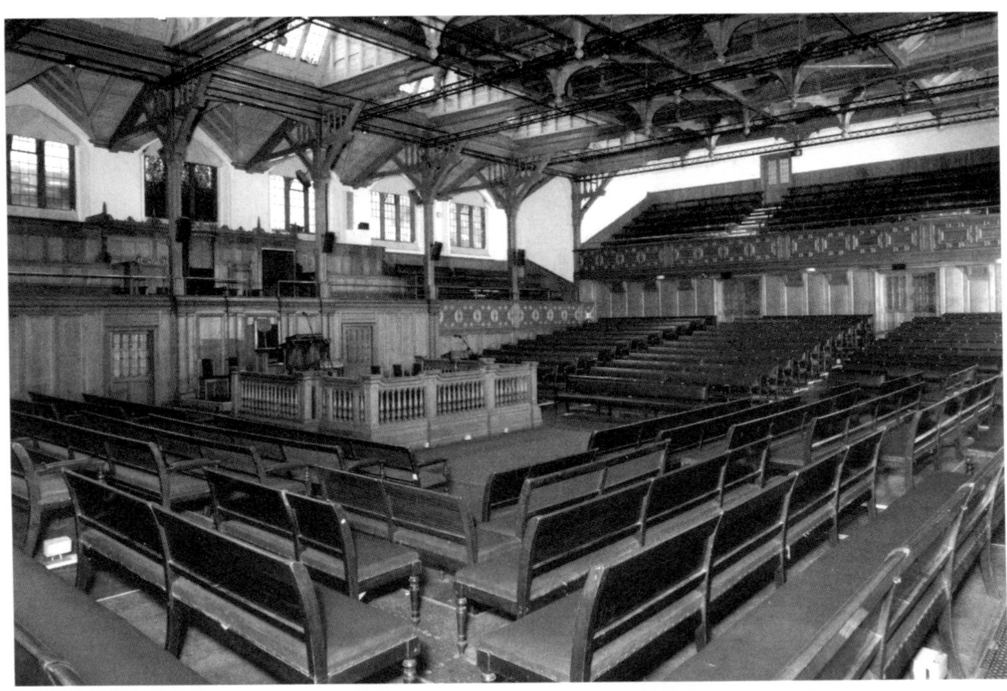

IN DEFENCE
NEMO ME IMPUNE LACESSET

national dignity were given the same treatment. These included Parliament House, which now served mainly as a monumental waiting-room for the courts. It was now rapidly turned into a pantheon of the Scottish legal tradition, stuffed with heraldic stained-glass windows, portraits and statues from the Faculty of Advocates collection. The Great (South) Window was installed in 1868 at a cost of £2,000 to the designs of Wilhelm von Kaulbach and Maximilian Ainmuller (Inspector of the Bavarian Royal Glass-Making Institution) of Munich, depicting the inauguration of the Court of Session by James V in 1532. The king was shown presenting the papal charter to Abbot Alexander Mylne, the first Lord President of the court, while Archbishop Gavin Dunbar, Lord High Chancellor, gave his blessing. The faces in the painting were based on people connected with the Court of Session in 1868.[35]

A much more diverse picture was found in the architecture of local government. In rural areas, where the county administrations were steadily extending their remit, the continuing power of the landed classes ensured that Baronial became the preferred style for building types involved with administration of the law, such as country houses and sheriff courthouses. But Scotland had become one of the world's most urbanised countries, and the 1833 Act had revitalised municipal government, and shifted the balance of power and energy to the industrial west. There was a proliferation of agencies of a private and semi-public kind: boards, trusts, commissioners, each with its own building, with its own balance of administrative and 'legislative' accommodation. As the nineteenth century went on, this variety of bodies was gradually drawn together under municipal control: the townhouse became more and more central in the life of the burgh. Most large nineteenth-century municipal buildings contained not only meeting rooms and bureaucratic offices and archives but also police and prison accommodation, and burgh courtrooms, responsibilities inherited from the tolbooth days. These building projects had equivalents in the town halls of other countries, such as the neo-Renaissance enlargement of the Paris Hotel de Ville in 1837–46 (by E.H. Godde and J-B-C Lesueur), Cuthbert Brodrick's Leeds Town Hall (1857–68), or, much later, Haller & Lamprecht's Hamburg Town Hall (opened 1897–8). But there were a number of significant organisational differences. In contrast to the party-politicisation of local government in England, Scottish town councils were

3.36. The new south window of 1868 in Parliament Hall; the stained glass, by Wilhelm von Kaulbach and Maximilian Ainmueller, depicts the institution of the Court of Session by James V in 1532. (RCAHMS B66686)

dominated by looser, non-party groupings, which allowed the evangelical, idealistic ethos full rein – although the Liberal Party became increasingly dominant in urban areas during the century. And unlike their French counterparts, whose local strength was offset by the interventive powers of central government, Scottish cities were rather more autonomous, something perhaps ultimately inherited from the royal burghs' pre-union autonomy. Indeed, one turn-of-century Glasgow commentator argued for an even older precedent, that of the imperial Athens of antiquity: 'The modern City is reverting in importance to the City-state in classical antiquity'.[36]

Architecturally, the general design programme of a large nineteenth-century city hall, with its mixture of meeting halls and offices, bound together within a hierarchy of stately and utilitarian circulation spaces, was fairly similar to that of a parliament building or US state capitol. Freestanding new buildings were generally planned with symmetrical, axial layouts around courtyards, with the main public halls on a *piano nobile* accessed by grand staircases, and the legislative chamber(s) located either on a central or side axis. For example, Hamburg Town Hall and the Prussian provincial *Abgeordnetenhaus* (both 1890s) each had one fan-shaped chamber, located in the centre in Berlin and at one side in the Hamburg complex (whose centrepiece was a grand hall). Stylistically, an 'international' Renaissance classicism remained dominant, within which the meanings and purposes of the building were conveyed by classical principles of stately arrangement and decoration. But there was, by the late nineteenth century, a significant counter-trend towards specifically 'national' styles which could more arrestingly convey the supposed cohesion and historical roots of the modern nation. Within Scotland, the choice between the two approaches was conditioned by the cultural polarity between the 'historic' east and the thrustingly 'modern' west. Paradoxically, it was the 'modern' west which continued to rely on the now more old-fashioned classical approach, while the east, as we saw above, showed more interest in 'national' concepts of architecture – in the form of the Scotch Baronial style. However, in the planning of Edinburgh's own municipal headquarters, special circumstances dictated an extreme contextual and classical conservatism. Here, despite a tripling in population and a vast extension in boundaries between the mid-eighteenth century and the 1880s, the Town Council did not build a new townhouse, but,

3.37. 1990 aerial view of the City Chambers, Edinburgh, showing the original arcaded courtyard and the massive later extensions, mostly of 1898–1904. Parliament Square and Parliament House are at the bottom right. (RCAHMS B49055)

instead, concentrated on regaining control over the Royal Exchange, and internally reconstructing it. This policy began to take shape in 1809 when, prompted by the inadequacy of the existing accommodation in the New Tolbooth and the north aisle of St Giles', the council decided to convert the part of the Exchange they owned into a municipal headquarters, or City Chambers. The council chamber was housed in the former Customs House on the first floor, with its panelled walls and coved ceiling, and the east wall of an anteroom was opened up into a columned screen; in 1811 the Lord Provost, magistrates and council walked in procession to their new home. Between 1857 and 1891, the remainder of the building was re-acquired, and a proposal for complete redevelopment was vetoed in 1887 by a plebiscite of the electorate. Eventually, from 1898, the Edinburgh City Chambers was reconstructed by City Architect Robert Morham, who completed the front quadrangle by redeveloping an old tenement that had been stranded there at the building of the Exchange; the west wing was reconstructed with a stately courtroom on the ground floor (1898–9) and a new, Baroque council chamber at the north end of the first floor (1901–4).[37]

In Aberdeen, the years 1867–74 saw the construction of another major municipal headquarters on the east-coast incremental pattern: the County and Municipal Buildings, won in competition by Edinburgh architects Peddie & Kinnear. But this, in contrast to Edinburgh, was a largely new building, in a grand Scotch Baronial form; costing £50,000, it set out to express the growing power of local authorities in the country as well as the city. This complex function was disguised by the unified grandeur of the exterior, clad in Kemnay granite after local protests at original plans to use sandstone. Behind this façade, no fewer than four public authorities had to be housed – the town council, the Aberdeenshire county authorities (the Commissioners of Supply), the Commissioners of Police (responsible for many aspects of urban regulation, including water supply, and amalgamated with the town council in 1871) and the sheriff courts – as well as lettable office chambers on two floors; each of these functions had to have its own separate entrance. Originally conceived by the county authority, but decisively promoted by Lord Provost Sir Alexander Anderson, the project had to be authorised by a special act of parliament, to apportion the costs, and it was managed by a board of commissioners.[38]

3.38. Edinburgh City Chambers, Old Council Chamber. Originally the eighteenth-century Customs House, this room was converted for municipal use, and opened up at the end with a Corinthian screen by David Cousin in 1859.(RCAHMS C04185)

The Aberdeen site was in even more direct continuity with the burgh heritage than that of Edinburgh, as it physically incorporated the original, castellated tolbooth, or wardhouse. Around and to the rear of this the law-enforcement requirements, including courts and cells, were concentrated; the seventeenth- and eighteenth-century classical extension to the wardhouse was ingeniously incorporated in the new fabric. The main part of the new Aberdeen County and Municipal Buildings was dominated by an elaborate balance of functions and symbols between the town and county authorities: even its Baronial style was a judicious compromise which reconciled the pride of aristocratic rural interests with the desire of Aberdeen's Free Church bourgeoisie to associate themselves with burgh tradition. The town accommodation, concentrated at the west and north sides, was entered through the great 60m-high corner tower, dominating Aberdeen's city centre and containing the Lord Provost's chamber and the fireproof, galleried charter-room, the 'hearth-stone of the burgh', and symbol of the continuity of municipal order in the Granite City over seven centuries. The building was constructed in two phases; first, the west section was built for the town, and after they had vacated the old townhouse, the east section was redeveloped for the county authority. The latter's accommodation was reached through an externally less imposing, but internally grander sequence of spaces culminating in a stone imperial staircase. A minor rearrangement of 1906 made the town section easier to use, by opening out direct access to its circular staircase hall. The main sequence of public rooms, on the principal upper floor, was ingeniously shared between the two authorities, and was adorned with royal and aristocratic portraits commissioned by the Town Council for the eighteenth-century townhouse. At the centre, the Town and County Hall, with its arched timber ceiling and minstrels' gallery, and its array of old military flags, was intended for civic and royal receptions. It was flanked by a sumptuous Baronial council chamber on either side, with stencilled wallpaper, the western room being the Town Council's and the eastern that of the Commissioners of Supply; in practice, however, the latter held their meetings in the Town and County Hall, and the adjoining chamber was used as a committee room. The county meetings were held on the basis of landowner qualification, and several dozen members usually attended. A montaged photograph of 1897 shows the furnishing and arrangement of the town council chamber, not in its

TOP.
3.39. 1989 aerial view of the Aberdeen municipal complex, seen from the south. The towered County and Municipal Buildings (1867–74, by Peddie & Kinnear) are visible at lower centre, with the original tolbooth on their right; immediately behind is a densely packed warren of nineteenth-century administrative and judicial accommodation. To the north-west are the post-1945 extensions of those functions. Immediately behind the tolbooth and courthouse is the Grampian police headquarters, while behind the civic building is the Town House extension (1975–7), and, across Broad Street, the administrative slab block, St Nicholas House (designed by the City Architect and built from 1965). (RCAHMS B22546)

BELOW.
3.40. View of the Aberdeen County and Municipal Buildings, *c.*1900; the original seventeenth-century tolbooth steeple is visible at the right. (RCAHMS A33181)

original state but at a time when the council had just been enlarged following the 1891 boundary extension, with 31 members rather than the original 19. The members are provided with individual desks and chairs, arranged in semicircular rows to face the magistrates' desk below the main north window. With its dispersed furniture and flat floor, the room is less densely architectonic than that of the old pattern of parliamentary, Presbyterian or judicial assembly, with its tiers of pews; the impression is, rather, that of a library in a gentlemen's club.[39] The new House chamber at the US Capitol (completed 1857), with its 237 separate seats, had only recently underlined the principle of individualised desks for legislators.

The position in the burgeoning industrial west was very different from the east's sometimes suffocating sense of heritage. Mid-nineteenth-century Glasgow had developed a highly diverse civic culture, looking overseas and to other British west-coast port cities rather than to Edinburgh and the rest of Scotland; its most talented citizens, far from seeing municipal office as the first step towards a Westminster career, devoted their Presbyterian evangelical zeal to the building of a reformist municipal liberalism which would tackle the class divisions and squalor of urbanisation with bold initiatives of community intervention. The most symbolic of these new utilities, prompted by the cholera outbreak of 1848–9, was the project to bring the drinking water of Loch Katrine to the city through many miles of tunnels and aqueducts, tapping the purity of the Highlands to fight urban degradation. But municipal power also had a secular as well as religious context. The proliferating responsibilities of the Town Council fuelled a territorial expansion that was analogous to British imperialism, with its twin governing values of Christian 'civilising' zeal and technocratic efficiency. As Glasgow surged ever outwards, first infiltrating surrounding burghs with its tramways and then gobbling them up altogether, and as it tackled its savage underworld by surgical redevelopment, it came to see itself as a microcosm of the empire.[40]

Architecturally, Glasgow's pride in its civic and capitalist modernity was expressed not through the 'national' imagery of Baronial but through an eclectic Renaissance classicism. The Second City of the Empire had no patience with Edinburgh's make-do-and-mend philosophy, which its leaders regarded as a mark of outmoded conservatism. On each occasion that Glasgow town council outgrew its premises – which happened four times during the nineteenth

TOP.
3.41. The Town and County Hall, principal public space of the Aberdeen County and Municipal Buildings; flanked by city and county council chambers, it was intended for civic and royal receptions. (RCAHMS D41726)

BELOW.
3.42. 1897 photograph of the Aberdeen City Council Chamber, with montaged figures of the magistrates and councillors to depict the newly-enlarged council in session; the individual desks are arranged in semicircular rows. (Aberdeen City Council; RCAHMS D41742)

century – the response was to discard it immediately, and build a brand-new headquarters somewhere else. And there were numerous other public bodies who fearlessly embarked on large premises for themselves, including both offices and assembly rooms: for example, the monumental Beaux-Arts classical headquarters built from 1882 by J.J. Burnet for the Clyde Trust, overseers of the city's harbour infrastructure. The grandest of all these projects, however, was undertaken by the Town Council themselves in 1883, when they commenced construction of a huge new municipal capitol in George Square.

ABOVE.
3.43. Glasgow Municipal Buildings (1883–8, by William Young) seen just after its completion. (RCAHMS GW/2113)

RIGHT.
3.44. The ground and second (principal) floor plans of Glasgow Municipal Buildings, in its newly-completed state. (RCAHMS)

Glasgow Municipal Buildings, the last of the city's nineteenth-century civic centres, was also the climax of Scotland's entire municipal administration building boom of the nineteenth century, and, including its furnishings, cost £578,000 – vastly more than the Aberdeen building. The new headquarters in fact pre-dated the most decisive reorganisation of the municipal system in 1897; it was originally conceived in 1877, only three years after the completion of its predecessor, the Wilson St complex designed by Clarke & Bell.

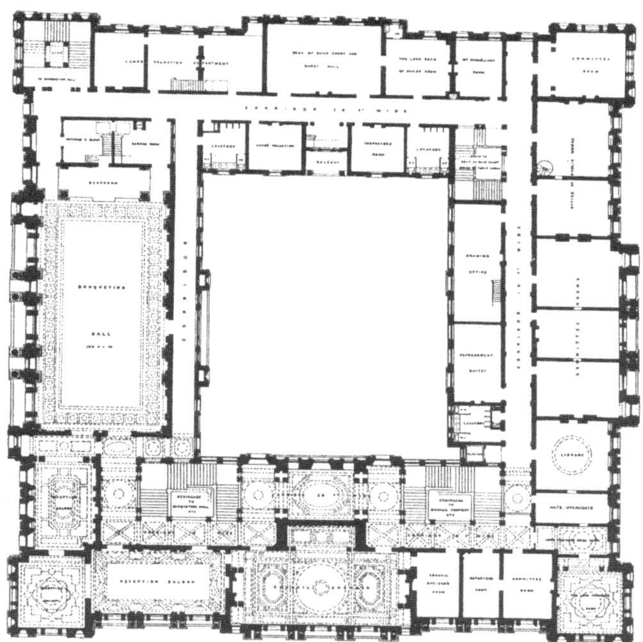

PLAN OF FLOOR UP TWO STAIRS

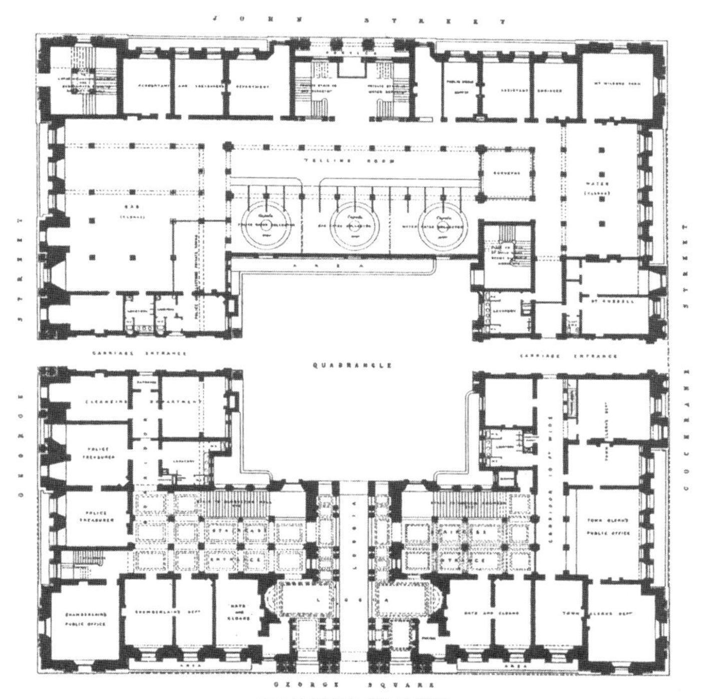

PLAN OF FLOOR ON LEVEL OF STREET

Despite the slump which followed the crash of the City of Glasgow Bank in 1878, a two-stage competition was organised in 1880-2: the assessor was the English architect Charles Barry Junior, working with City Architect John Carrick in the second competition. The brief was based on highly specific sketch plans by Carrick, which arranged accommodation in a hollow square. The results of the first competition, in which the first three prizewinners were all English firms, were set aside. The second competition attracted 110 entries, of which the most prominent, such as those by J.J. Burnet, William Leiper, James Salmon, and James Sellars, showed a decisive move away from congested mid-nineteenth-century eclecticism towards a more spacious, rationalistic classicism.[41]

The winning design, by William Young, set out to achieve a 'free and dignified treatment of the Italian Renaissance . . . hitting a mean between over-bearing pomposity of style and excess or floridness of detail'. Its front façade to George Square comprises a 'grand rusticated base' of two storeys, with a centrepiece in the style of the Arch of Constantine, and two upper storeys surmounted by a pedimented centrepiece and tall central tower on a rusticated podium. Inside, the main sequence of public spaces is overpowering in its grandeur and sumptuousness. A column-lined ground-floor entrance loggia, two storeys in height, leads to matching open staircases (the Council Hall Staircase to the south, the Banqueting Hall Staircase to the north), entirely clad in alabaster and marble, and ringed by 'tier upon tier of pillars, arches, and cornices . . . of surpassing splendour'.[42] These give access, on the principal (second) floor, to the columned and recessed council chamber, set centrally immediately above the loggia, and to other lofty saloons, committee accommodation and a large banqueting hall with arched ceiling and suspended electroliers. The four huge committee rooms, where much of the council's active work was done, are reached from a corridor lined with faience, with separate small domes in each of its eight bays.

The colossal, square building, completed in 1888, was entirely faced in Polmaise and Dunmore stone but with much use of steel reinforcement: it contained over 9,905 cubic metres of stone and ten million bricks. Industrialised efficiency was epitomised by the extensive use of stone-moulding machinery, which converted the masonry building process to one of assembly of pre-worked components. Glasgow Municipal Buildings was Scotland's only civic

TOP.
3.45. Glasgow Municipal Buildings: detail of pediment on main west facade. G. A. Lawson's sculptural group depicts Queen Victoria, ringed by figures symbolic of Scotland, England, Ireland and Wales, receiving 'homage' from subjects across the world. (RCAHMS A59894)

BELOW.
3.46. Glasgow Municipal Buildings: the council chamber *c.*1890 in its original state, with separate double desks. (RCAHMS B64056)

complex by wallpapering grand neo-Renaissance façades, similar in style to Glasgow's, around the outer edge on the south, west and north sides, a strategy which left the interior of the site a warren of brick buildings and irregular courtyards. The first floor, which contained the principal interiors (above a zig-zag internal carriage drive across the site), was pulled together through the device of a cruciform, columned 'grand corridor', linking the members' accommodation to the south and west with a circular lobby and council chamber on the north; the 'tolbooth' part of the complex, including a galleried, skylit courtroom, was set apart in the north-eastern corner of the site. The high-ceilinged, rectangular council chamber is laid out around a continuous D-plan members' desk, now broken in the middle of the curved (entrance) side; the provost and magistrates were seated along the straight arm.

Externally, Greenock's attempts at a monumental regularity to rival Glasgow were compromised by the constraints of the site. Only on the western side is there an uninterrupted façade. On the south, the town council was unable to acquire part of the site, and thus could

3.49. Greenock Municipal Buildings: view of the council chamber from west. (RCAHMS D34032)

only build the left-hand eleven bays of what should have been a palatial sixteen-bay, arched, arcaded design; ironically, the offending south-east angle building ('Cowan's Corner') was bombed in World War II, leaving an even more incongruous gap. The proudest feature of the Greenock Municipal Buildings is the Victoria Tower, a domed steeple nearly 250ft high with aedicules and banding reminiscent of Alexander Thomson's church towers, and rising from the yawning arched entrance to the carriageway. Close up, the tower's situation, sandwiched between Cowan's Corner and another existing building, seems jarringly disjointed. But seen from a distance, for example from Helensburgh across the Clyde, its height and silhouette are what counts, providing a theatrically effective signal that one of Scotland's most important towns is centred in this dramatic place, between the steep hills and the water.

CONCLUSION

Summing up Glasgow's ethos of dynamic grandeur at the celebratory banquet that followed the 1883 foundation stone-laying of the Municipal Buildings, Lord Provost Ure looked forward to a time 'when in the course of centuries the needs of Glasgow shall again outgrow the limits set for them – when even these wide foundations shall sustain no fabric spacious enough to embrace the multifarious requirements of her gigantic civic life – and when my successor at the head of that vastly greater municipality performs a like ceremony to that which you have witnessed today'. (46) But within fifty years, that confident combination of civic and imperial pride, in Glasgow and across Scotland as a whole, would have almost completely disappeared.

NOTES

1. W. Young, *Municipal Buildings, Glasgow*, Glasgow, 1890, 11.
2. J.S. Shaw, *The Political History of 18th Century Scotland*, London, 1999; H.J. Hanham, 'The creation of the Scottish Office', *Juridical Review*, October 1965, and *Glasgow Herald*, 23 March 1807, both cited in D.S. Forsyth, *Scottish Geographical Magazine*, January 1997; J.S. Gibson, *The Thistle and the Crown*, Edinburgh, 1985, 8.
3. Gibson, *Thistle and the Crown*, 7.

4. Glendinning *et al*, *History of Scottish Architecture*, 102–8.
5. J. Grant, *Cassell's Old and New Edinburgh*, 157; Miller, *Municipal Buildings of Edinburgh*, 80–2. Swain, 'Tapestries and Textiles', 5.
6. J. Cunningham, *The Church History of Scotland*, ii, 1859; J. Cameron Lees, *St Giles', Edinburgh*, Edinburgh, 1889, 253; Grant, *Cassell's Old and New Edinburgh*, ii.
7. *Tolbooths and Townhouses*, 202, 24–31, 100; Corporation of Glasgow, *Municipal Glasgow*, 1914, 26–7.
8. Miller, *Municipal Buildings of Edinburgh*, 112–125.
9. R. Home, *Of Planting and Planning*, London, 1997.
10. J-M Perouse de Montclos, *Histoire de l'architecture française: de la Renaissance a la Révolution*, Paris, 1989, 399.
11. A. Tait, *Robert Adam, Drawings and Imagination*, Cambridge (England), 1993, Chapter 2.
12. N. Pevsner, *A History of Building Types*, London, 1976; M. Wilson, *William Kent*, London, 1984, 168–71.
13. P. Scott, A.J. Lee, *Buildings of the District of Columbia*, New York, 1993; S. Maroon, *The United States Capitol*, New York, 1993; L. Aikman/United States Capitol Historical Association, *We The People*, Washington, DC, 1978; H. Colvin, *A Biographical Dictionary of British Architects*, 1995 edition, New Haven, 1060.
14. Maroon, *Capitol*, 27; M. Forsyth, *Auditoria*, London, 1987; Pevsner, *History of Building Types*, 67.
15. J-M Pérouse de Montclos, *Histoire de l'Architecture Française, de la Renaissance a la Revolution*, Paris, 1989, 459–61; Assemblée Nationale, *Landmarks in the History of the French Parliament*, Paris, 1997.
16. H. Cockburn, *Memorials of his Time*, Edinburgh, 1910 edition, 275. J. Lowrey, 'National and regional identity', lecture of 23 April 1998 to Edinburgh University Architecture Department. T.A. Markus, *Order in Space and Society*, Edinburgh, 1982.
17. *Tolbooths and Townhouses*, 172, 42, 101; Corporation of Glasgow, *Municipal Glasgow*, Glasgow, 1914, 27.
18. J. St Clair, R. Craik, *The Advocates' Library*, Edinburgh, 1989, 29. Swain, *Tapestries and Textiles at the Palace of Holyroodhouse*, Edinburgh, 1988, 5.
19. Sir W. Scott, *Old Mortality*, 1816 edition.
20. M. Fry, 'Millennium Project', *Herald*, 3 September 1998.
21. Gibson, *Thistle and the Crown*, 10–11; S. Brown and M. Fry (eds.), *Scotland in the Age of the Disruption*, 1993.
22. M.H. Port, *The Houses of Parliament*, New Haven, 1976, 21, 31.
23. Port, *Parliament*, 39; C.L. Eastlake, *A History of the Gothic Revival*, Leicester, 1970 edition, 173.
24. R.J. Finlay, in *Scottish Geographical Magazine*, January 1997; Cockburn, *Memorials*, 274.
25. Cockburn, *Memorials*; Historic Scotland List, Temple Parish; G.W.T. Omond, *The Arniston Memoirs*, 1887, 297–8; Miller, *Municipal Buildings of Edinburgh*, 91.
26. Lord Cullen, *Parliament House, a Short History and Guide*, Edinburgh, 1992.
27. I.A. Dunlop, *The Kirks of Edinburgh*, Edinburgh, 1988.
28. National Monuments Record of Scotland (NMRS), plan reference EDD/6/1, 2, 5.
29. NMRS, plan reference EDD/49/1; Rosemary Hill, 'Pugin and Scotland', *Architectural Heritage*, 8, 1997, 17; G.A. Haggart, A.W.N. Pugin and the ecclesiastical architecture of Edinburgh, M.A. thesis, Edinburgh University, 1989.
30. Dunlop, *Kirks of Edinburgh*.
31. Brown and Fry, *Age of the Disruption*.
32. Brown and Fry, *Age of the Disruption*.

33. Sir Walter Scott, *The Letters of Malachi Malagrowther*, 1826 (1981 edition), 143; G. Morton, *Unionist Nationalism*, East Linton, 1999.
34. D.S. Forsyth and R.J. Findlay, *Scottish Geographical Magazine*, 113:1, 1997; R J Findlay, *A Partnership for Good*, Edinburgh, 1997.
35. Cullen, *Parliament House*. Calton Hill: Markus, *Order in Space and Society*.
36. James Hamilton Muir, *Glasgow in 1901*, Glasgow, 1901, 46–7; I.S. Sweeney, The Municipal Administration of Glasgow, 1990, Ph.D. thesis, Glasgow University, 4 (source: Ranald MacInnes).
37. Miller, *Municipal Buildings of Edinburgh*, 112–25; *Tolbooths and Town Houses*, 87.
38. Aberdeen: information from Iain Gray.
39. F. Wyness, *City by the Grey North Sea*, Aberdeen, 1966, 246.
40. Sweeney, *Municipal Administration*, 831–6. Loch Katrine: information from Ranald MacInnes. R.J. Finlay, *Scottish Geographical Magazine*, 113:1, 1997.
41. R. Emmerson, *Winners and Losers*, Edinburgh, 1991, 16.
42. William Young, *Municipal Buildings, Glasgow*, Glasgow, 1890, 13.
43. Young, *Municipal Buildings*, 27.
44. Young, *Municipal Buildings*, 18–19.
45. Glasgow Town Council, *Description of Ceremonial on the Occasion of Laying the Foundation-Stone of the Municipal Buildings*, Glasgow, 1885, 2, 9, 11, 20; Young, *Municipal Buildings*, 11.
46. Glasgow Town Council, *Description*, 60. Greenock: D. Walker, 'Designing the Royal College, Glasgow', in D. Mays, M. Moss, M. Oglethorpe (eds.), *Visions of Scotland's Past*, East Linton, 2000, 110.

CHAPTER FOUR

Social Nation: 1885–1997

Miles Glendinning

We do not want to be like the Greeks, powerful and prosperous wherever we settle, but with a dead Greece behind us. We do not want to be like the Jews of the Dispersion – a potent force everywhere in the globe, but with no Jerusalem.
John Buchan, 1932[1]

THE ARCHITECTURE OF IMPERIAL MIGHT

Among all the competing 'Great Powers' in the decades leading up to World War I, imperialism abroad went hand-in-hand with a more unified, socially cohesive policy at home. Nineteenth-century laissez-faire individualism was given up in favour of a search for national unity and community. In Scotland, this new conception of secular national community was at first seen in the context of an overarching commitment to the British Empire – but an empire which was beginning to be redefined as a family of nations, of which Scotland was one. In the 1880s, the demand for greater political autonomy for Scotland began to resurface. Already, in a speech at Dalkeith in 1879, the Liberal leader William Gladstone had suggested all-round devolution within the United Kingdom as a possible solution to the 'Irish problem'. But the reason why many Scots now began to support devolution was not a wish to follow Ireland in separating from the union, but a desire to secure greater recognition for their role within the union, as an 'imperial partner'. Groupings

OVERLEAF.
4.1. The proclamation of King George V in 1910 at the Mercat Cross, Edinburgh; the City Chambers is in the background. (Scottish Colorfoto Lab; RCAHMS ED/9296)

such as the Scottish Home Rule Association and the Scottish Patriotic Association sprang up. The latter's journal, *The Scottish Patriot*, combined a fervent love of empire with demands for 'restoration of the Scottish parliament'. Before 1914, home rule to Scots meant not the dilution but the reinforcement of their British commitment, through firmer foundations at home. The 'national question' was articulated above all in terms of imperialism, with its mixture of moral missionary zeal and technocratic efficiency. This could be linked to the local and municipal pride that had built up in the nineteenth century: in 1914, on the eve of war, Glasgow's Lord Provost Daniel Macaulay Stevenson wrote that municipal power was 'still in the morning of the times', and called for general devolution of power to municipalities as an integral aspect of 'home rule all round'. A different, less bellicose city-state culture was promoted by reformist-planner Patrick Geddes in Edinburgh. He argued that Scotland should see itself not as an 'imperial partner' but as 'one of the European Powers of Culture', and that Edinburgh citizens should 'share in that wider culture-movement which knows neither nationality nor race'.[2] But the time was not yet ripe for views of that kind.

In the political arena, demands began to focus on the issue not of legislative but of administrative devolution. A campaign for the restoration of the Secretaryship for Scotland, led by the Earl of Rosebery, attracted large-scale politically bipartisan support. The climax of the campaign was a 'great national meeting' organised by the Convention of Royal Burghs for Scotland, held, appropriately, in the Free Church Assembly Hall on 16 January 1884. The fundamental message of the meeting was that Scotland deserved parity of esteem within the Empire: she had 'as much right as England to feel, that she. . . is sharing the danger and the glory on behalf of a common country and a united people'. The prominent Conservative, Lord Aberdeen, argued that 'by improving the inner circle of Scottish government, the grand system of the British empire would also be improved'.[3] Eventually, in 1885, the Government gave way and re-established the office of Secretary for Scotland. The first holder of the post, the Duke of Richmond, became a full cabinet member in 1892. The role of the new Scottish Secretary was at first focused on the supervision and co-ordination of other organisations, including various boards responsible for home affairs and the promotion of fisheries and industry, and the Scotch Education Department, now working on a system of secondary education. The result was the withdrawal of the Home Secretary from Scottish domestic affairs, and a major step forward in administrative devolution.

Although demands for parliamentary home rule continued until after World War I, and a bill for a Scottish parliament almost became law in 1913, only to be brought down by the outbreak of war, from that time the progress of home rule government was entirely within the administrative field. In 1887, the Scottish Secretary gained more powers of legislation; in 1894, Lord Rosebery set up a Scottish Grand Committee at Westminster to handle the committee stage of Scottish bills, and although this lapsed in 1900, it was revived in 1907 as a standing committee. In the wake of the crofting legislation of the 1880s, a bill of 1911–12 set up a Scottish Board of Agriculture, to pursue the Liberal Party's strategy of breaking up big country estates and settling the land. The system was underpinned by the reinforcement of local administration. In 1889, powerful county councils were set up, as were elected parish councils, in 1894; the county councils took over the functions of the County Road Trustees and the Commissioners of Supply. In 1897, the four cities were designated as 'Counties of Cities' with the same powers and autonomy as county councils. Increasingly, leading councillors played as important a role in national affairs as members of parliament.

These changes had no direct architectural repercussions. In Edinburgh, the new organisation (which soon began to be known as the 'Scottish Office') had a very modest provision, in the form of a temporary office at 6 Parliament Square, staffed by two people: the lettering, 'Secretary for Scotland's Office', is still visible above that door. In London, after successful lobbying by the Lord Advocate, the Prime Minister agreed to allow the Scottish Secretary the use of Dover House, a palatial classical mansion in Whitehall just acquired by the government. The original five-bay, three-storey house, set back from the street and built in 1755–8 to James Paine's designs, had been extended forwards from 1788 by Henry Holland, who added a colonnaded circular staircase hall fronted by an austere neo-classical screen wall in the style of a great Parisian *hôtel*. Although Dover House was shared with the Scotch Education Department (also under the Scottish Secretary's authority) and the Lord Advocate (who moved there from cramped quarters in the Home Office), it was at first

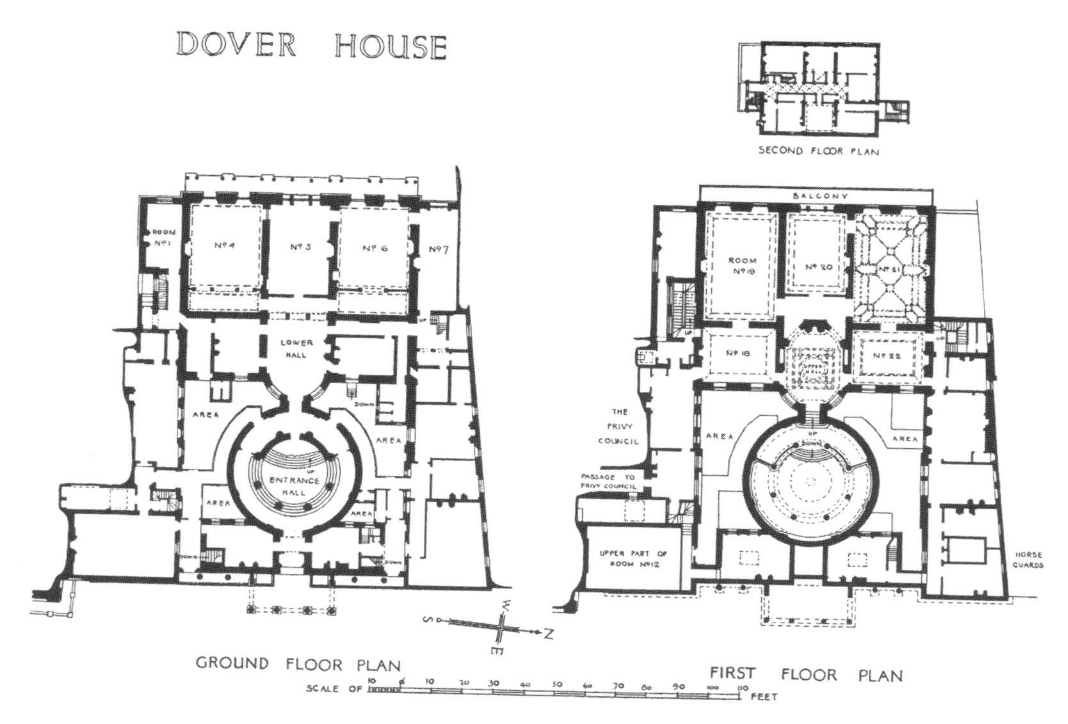

extremely under-occupied, with only seven staff supporting the two ministers.[4]

More generally, the concentration of devolution efforts on piecemeal administrative changes meant that there would be no grand new buildings of national government, no pre-1914 'imperial home rule architecture' to speak of. Scottish imperial commitment had a more diffuse effect on architecture, through the wealth it brought, and the variety of buildings that it made possible. Within local government, existing administrative complexes were extended, and authorities that had lagged behind tried energetically to catch up, all generally using variants of civic classicism. The Glasgow Municipal Buildings were extended to the rear (east) in 1914–23 with an austere Beaux-Arts classical office block by Watson, Salmond & Gray. The extension, which cost over £550,000, is linked across a road to Young's building by a pair of Ionic-columned triumphal arches.[5] In 1911, Dundee's new City Engineer and Architect, James Thomson, devised a Beaux-Arts scheme for redevelopment of the city centre, including a vast, domed Civic Centre; and eventually, in 1914, a great public hall, the Caird Hall, was begun to his designs. 'Church government' was

4.2. Dover House, Whitehall, London: ground- and first-floor plans. (RCHME)

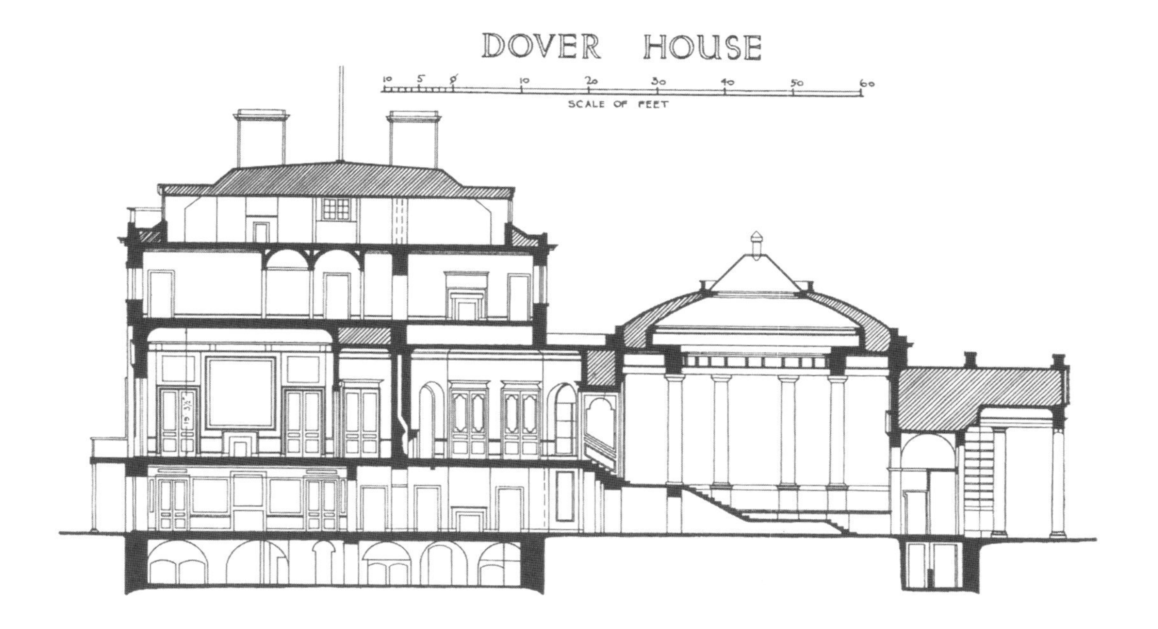

provided for, in the case of the United Free Church, by an ambitious, round-arched office palazzo, in George Street, Edinburgh (1911), designed by Sydney Mitchell with E.A.O. Auldjo-Jamieson. The work of the central government architects in Scotland came under the auspices of the London-based Office of Works, but their chief Scottish architect, W.T. Oldrieve, enjoyed considerable autonomy. In an attempt to evoke national associations, he avoided academic classicism, and designed countless small public-utility buildings in a Lorimer-like Traditionalist or Baronial style, with occasional large commissions such as the towered Aberdeen main post office (1907). An opportunity that would have crowned Oldrieve's career came in 1912, when the Liberal Scottish Secretary and crusading land reformer, Lord Pentland (John Sinclair), proposed a single government building on the site of the Calton Jail, to accommodate the rapidly growing functions of the Scottish Office. At that time, the symbolic role of national acropolis was beginning to shift back from Edinburgh Castle to Calton Hill, with a rash of proposals to complete the National Monument either as an imperial memorial or as a home-rule parliament. Oldrieve drew up plans for a cluster of massive towered

4.3. Dover House: section across the depth of the building. (RCHME)

blocks in a sixteenth-century royal palace style, closely resembling the Franco-Baronial 'Château' style used after 1913–15 for national institutions in home-rule Canada, especially under the 1920s government of W.L. Mackenzie King.[6]

In due course, the growth of 'home' government in Scotland would prompt the building of major monuments. For now, the architecture of government was mainly concerned with external and imperial matters, where it adopted a domineering rhetoric of grandeur, in implicit confrontation with France. But this architectural attitude was made more diffuse by the fact that architects, in all countries, were beginning to reject the use of ornament-loaded period styles, especially the explicit 'national' styles such as Scotch Baronial, as a way to denote different ideas or types of buildings. The demands for nationalistic buildings were growing, yet at the same time the way of expressing that nationalism was starting to become more indirect and subtle. Now, rather than trying to convey meaning through explicit historical style and historical narrative, architects began to emphasise the design of a building as a more abstract and integrated whole. One of the first stages of this trend was a general return to a more monumental classicism for great public buildings, especially those of national status.

The focus of efforts to express British power in stone was naturally not Edinburgh or Glasgow, but the imperial capital, London. Here, from the 1880s, pressure grew to re-order its cluttered squalor with public buildings of a stately classical kind, which could rival in grandeur the monuments of Paris. As classical architecture in England had been badly weakened by the Gothic Revival and Arts and Crafts movements, Scottish architects found themselves presented with an unparallelled opportunity. But – just as the Scottish competitors for the Westminster parliament had attempted – they had to package their designs in a way which would appeal to English national sentiment. Now this was to be done not through Gothic or Elizabethan but through English classicism, evoking the hallowed seventeenth-century work of Inigo Jones and Christopher Wren, as well as what Robert Adam had dubbed the 'rough jewels' of the eighteenth-century Baroque. To mark off this architecture from the unified Beaux-Arts ethos which prevailed in France, it was important that it should be more individualistic and 'Protestant' in character. The first steps were taken by the William Burn trained Richard

Norman Shaw, who pioneered the introduction of a more monumental classicism in designs such as the country house 'Bryanston' (1889–93), which clothed a palazzo-like block reminiscent of Kinross House with English seventeenth-century details.

The campaign of British/English architectural nationalism was stepped up to a much more explicit level by the architect John M. Brydon. Born in Dunfermline in 1840, Brydon trained with Bryce, Campbell Douglas and Shaw, and set up practice in London in 1880. In an important lecture of 1889, Brydon hailed the 'English Renaissance' of Jones and Wren for its 'stately picturequeness' and identified it as 'the national style – the vernacular of the country'. In 1898, this movement was given Government blessing when Scottish architects were awarded two commissions of high State symbolism. The first, designed by Brydon himself (but finished by government architect Sir Henry Tanner after Brydon's death in 1901), was the New Government Offices complex in Parliament Square, a setpiece of Baroque grandeur with its two-storey rusticated ground floor and cupola-towered roofline evoking St Paul's Cathedral; the courtyard plan of the adjacent Foreign Office was echoed here with a circular courtyard in the manner of Jones and Webb's Whitehall Palace scheme. In the same year, William Young, architect of the Glasgow Municipal Buildings, began a new complex for the War Office in Whitehall in a similar style. With its rusticated base and upper twin towers, it was designed so as to harmonise with Jones's adjacent Banqueting House and, with its corner turrets, to recall Wren's 1698 design for Whitehall Palace. Despite their external pomp, of course, these were only large office blocks; during World War II, Brydon's offices found a more utilitarian use, when their basement was reinforced to become the government's underground command bunker during German bombing raids.[7] The erection of these giant buildings coincided exactly with the height of Scottish imperialist fervour during the South African war. For example, after the relief of Mafekeng in 1900, traffic in Glasgow was brought to a standstill by a flag-waving procession of shipyard workers carrying an effigy of President Kruger marked 'To St Helena'. Those ideas continued in some quarters for several years. As late as 1906, former Prime Minister Lord Rosebery unveiled a mountainous rubble memorial to the Royal Scots Greys in Edinburgh's Princes Street, declaring that 'in the service of their Sovereign and their country they have undergone the

sharpness of death, and sleep the eternal sleep, thousands of miles away in the green solitudes of Africa'.[8] The mid-1900s brought a subtle shift in climate away from this blustering jingoism towards a subtler, but more menacing imperialism, with the construction of the Triple Entente against Germany in 1904–7. Almost overnight, francophobic individualism fell from fashion, and the monumental logic of French (and American) Beaux-Arts classicism was suddenly in demand. Here, yet again, the deficiencies of English classical training left the field open to the Scots. Now, what was relevant was not the old-style east-coast amateurism of Shaw and Brydon, but the new climate of Beaux-Arts logic that reigned in Glasgow, under J.J. Burnet. In 1905, the year that Lord (Richard) Haldane of Cloan took charge of the War Office and began his six-year transformation of the British army into a modern, logically organised force, Burnet was invited to London by the government to design the new King Edward VII Galleries of the British Museum, in a severely rationalist classicism reminiscent of the American east-coast work of McKim, Mead & White. Thereafter this Beaux-Arts classicism enjoyed the status of an official British imperial style.

Increasingly, the projection of government power was thought to demand coordinated interventions across the full range of the built environment. The ordinary 'home' came to be seen as a central pillar of social and racial cohesion, and the naval race with Germany was parallelled in the intense competition in town planning and the building of green, hygienic garden suburbs. The 1917 Ballantyne Report, which set out the agenda for state intervention in working-class housing, argued that it was 'the duty of the nation to undertake the great work of providing decent homes for the ctizens of a great Empire'.[9] And when the decision was taken to build a new strategic naval dockyard at Rosyth, in Fife, out of immediate range of German battleships, an extensive garden-suburb development of housing to service it soon followed (in 1914–23). 'Home' and 'empire' overlapped even more directly overseas, where there was a shift back to a classical and rationalist expression of British imperial government, both in the design of individual buildings and in layouts of towns. This was an area where Scottish engineers were in the forefront, in keeping with their leading colonial planning role since the Indian uprising of the 1850s. In 1910–12, for instance, Khartoum's chief municipal engineer, William McLean, designed a vast extension plan for the city on a

TOP.
4.4. Perspective of central court of J. M. Brydon's new Government Offices, Parliament Square, London (from 1898). (*Academy Architecture*, 1900/ii, 8)

BELOW.
4.5. Detail of the main south facade of Brydon's Government Offices, facing Parliament Square. (M. Glendinning)

Union Jack street pattern of rectangulars and diagonals (itself based on a previous plan of 1898 by Lord Kitchener), which he overlaid across numerous indigenous settlements. From 1914, McLean became engineer-in-chief to the British protectorate of Egypt, where he proposed monumental classical replanning projects for over fifty towns, their growing Beaux-Arts emphasis reflecting Franco-British joint interests in Egypt.[10]

THE ARCHITECTURE OF ADMINISTRATIVE POWER

Although Scotland experienced little direct damage from the twentieth-century European wars, and none of the chaos of territorial changes and population displacements, the climate of those years was still a threatening one: 'Britain' had changed from an offensive weapon to a defensive shield. The ideology of colonial mission was imperceptibly changing to one of world peace: John Buchan could argue that imperialism was similar to the League of Nations. This uncertainty was combined with internal instability: Scotland's military-industrial complex steeply declined, and with it the bombastic prosperity that had fuelled the prewar imperial home rule idea. Some responded by going further than home rule, and calling for Scottish independence, inside or outside the Empire. In 1928, the year that the Ottawa Conference charted the way to independence for the Dominions, the National Party of Scotland was inaugurated at Stirling on Bannockburn Day. But this movement was politically weak for its first few decades. Across society as a whole, the threatening overseas environment worked in the opposite direction, by restraining centripetal movement. And after 1945, the mobilisation of Europe into ideological blocs robbed this Scottish nationalism of force for over twenty years. Instead, the general concern of Scottish society for the time being was the building of 'democracy'. By contrast with the era of Walter Scott, this word was no longer seen as partisan or extremist. Everyone now accepted the legacy of the American and French revolutions and the 1832 reforms. These had reinvigorated the *res publica* ideal by the two great ideas of equality and freedom, and had bound it up with the representative democracy system. The main political controversy now lay in the balance *between* equality and freedom. In general, the twentieth century, in its hostility to laissez-faire capitalism, emphasised equality as the more urgent goal. Freedom was defined in relatively restrictive terms of collective emancipation, facilitated by technocratic efficiency.

In some countries, this restriction deepened into totalitarian tyranny. In Scotland, the new concept of the mass was channelled through the looser disciplines of representative democracy and the party political system. The great expansion of the franchise after the 1918 Reform Act, which doubled the electorate to include all working-class males, and women under the age of 31, gave a powerful boost to the social-democratic collectivism promoted by the Labour party. Socialism had assumed the social-reformist mantle once carried by nineteenth-century Presbyterianism. Correspondingly, the church began to look inwards rather than outwards, although that introversion was at first masked by the drama of reunification in October 1929, which finally brought the Disruption to an end, following years of negotiations and the government's acknowledgement of the Kirk's spiritual independence. The huge 'Union Assembly' of 2 and 3 October, at which the reunification was solemnised, was held not in either of the two General Assembly halls, which were far too small to accommodate the 12,500 congregation, but in the Annandale Street bus garage of Edinburgh Corporation. Converted for the purpose under the direction of artist D.Y. Cameron, this makeshift location poignantly echoed the utilitarian gasworks setting in which the Disruption had been formalised in 1843 (fig. 3.26). At the Union Assembly, the King's Commissioner, Albert, Duke of York, used as his throne the minister's chair of Kippen Parish Church, made by John Annand of Whytock & Reid to Cameron's design in 1925–6.[11] Ironically, this spiritual reunification was followed by a collapse in the Kirk's secular, social influence, as it diverted its energies into crusades against Catholicism and socialism: sectarian anti-Catholic rallies were held on the Mound in Edinburgh, beneath the towers of the Free Church College. The emotional and moral power once bound up with Presbyterianism and imperialism was now absorbed by secular government, with its new overarching claims of national community; the modern nation was in many ways quite like a religion. The aim was to heal the economic and social rifts that had opened up, and build a collective home for the whole nation. Most Scots saw social reform as far more urgent than constitutional change. Looming over all else was the problem of bad housing: it was above

OVERLEAF.
4.6. The last General Assembly of the United Free Church of Scotland, in the Free Church Assembly Hall: view taken on 24 May 1929, during the final debate on Union with the Church of Scotland. (RCAHMS)

THE LAST GENERAL ASSEMBLY OF T

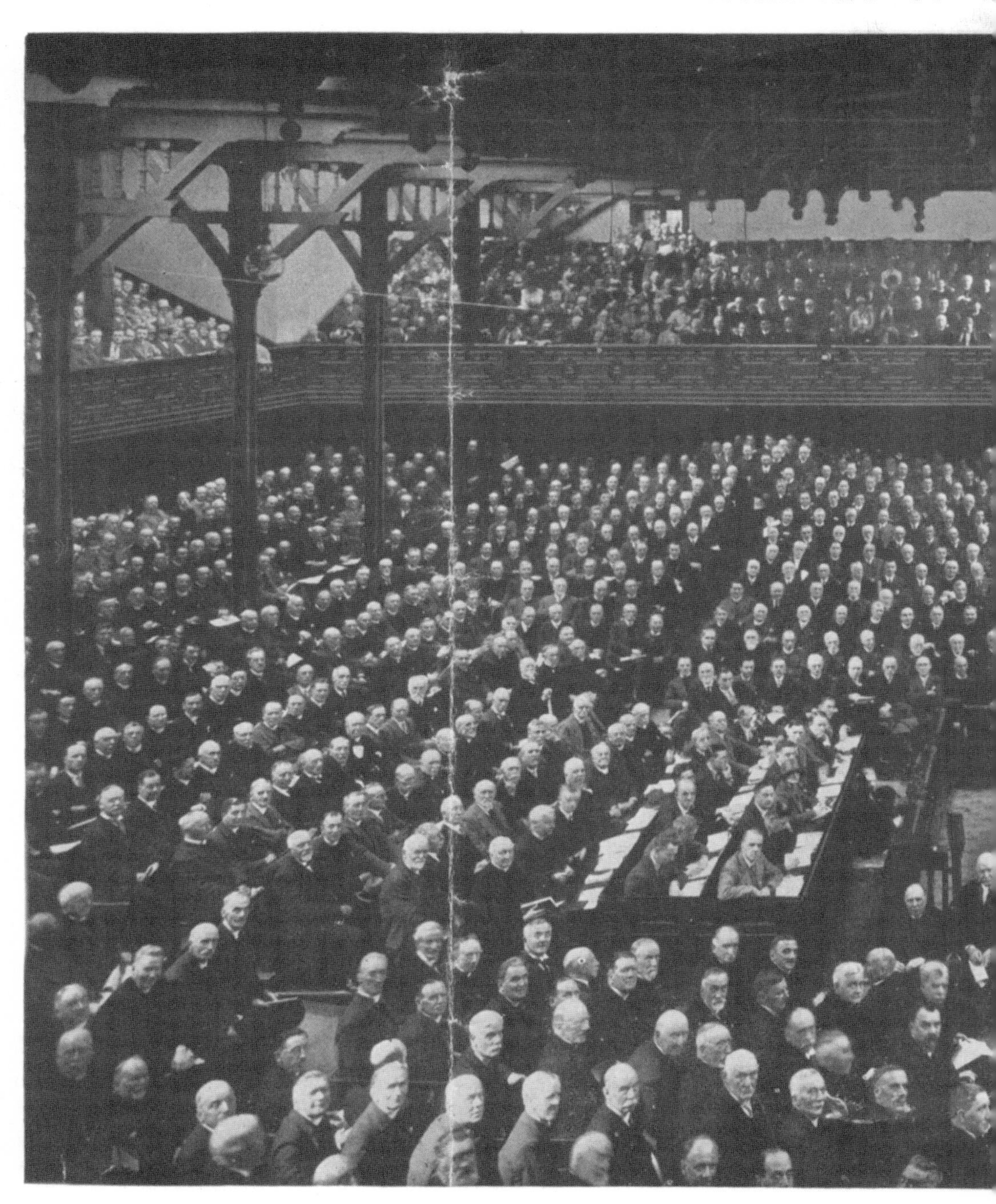

A Photograph taken during the final debate on Uni

ITED FREE CHURCH OF SCOTLAND.

[F. C. Inglis, Calton Hill, Edinburgh.

he Church of Scotland on Friday, 24th May 1929.

H

all through building homes for individual families that the national home would be made secure.

The government responded to this challenge not through any kind of legislative home rule – in fact, even the Scottish Grand Committee procedure fell into disuse. Instead, the response was a pragmatic but far-reaching process of administrative home rule, building on the existing nineteenth-century municipal and Scottish Office mechanisms with a rationally managed modernity. The key word of the new ethos was 'planning': for example, John Buchan called for 'planning ahead' in a debate on expansion of the powers of the Scottish Office in 1932.[12] Planning implied coordination and harmony. But in fact, one of the results of state intervention was to open up new arenas of conflict within the system, between local and national institutions.

The government system was reformed at both central and local levels. In 1926–8, the central boards responsible for health and housing, agriculture and prisons were reorganised into departments on the model of the Scottish Education Department (SED), and the Scottish Secretary became a Secretary of State. In 1937–9, on the recommendation of a report by Sir John Gilmour, there was an even more radical devolution of administration from London. All but liaison work was transferred, and the departments were consolidated under the headings of Agriculture and Fisheries, Education, Health and Home; the system of administrative devolution was established in all its essentials. At the same time, a new Edinburgh headquarters building, St Andrew's House, was built for these departments; we will return to its architectural design below. By 1939, when St Andrew's House opened, the Department of Health (DHS), with its growing housing and planning responsibilities, had become the largest, with 800 staff, whereas SED had only 150. Alongside these departments, there was a proliferation of semi-governmental boards and committees concerned with issues of the depression: a Commissioner for depressed areas was appointed in 1934, and new central government initiatives were begun from 1937 by the interventionist Tory Scots Secretary, Walter Elliot, including the building of industrial estates, subsidising of industries, and even the construction of public housing, under the aegis of the new Scottish Special Housing Association. During the same years, local government in both town and country saw a rapid process of consolidation into

PREVIOUS PAGE.
4.7. The 'Union Assembly' of the Church of Scotland and the United Presbyterian Church, held on 2 October 1929 in the Annandale Street bus garage of Edinburgh Corporation. (RCAHMS)

larger units. In 1929, as junior minister, Elliot introduced a Local Government Act which amalgamated nine different types of local authority and reduced 1,340 local government units to 226. As municipal spending in the cities and large burghs soared, especially in newly Labour-controlled Glasgow after 1933, power ebbed from the small burghs, the local bulwarks of the 1707 settlement, to the newly powerful county councils. Elliot wrote of 'the countification of the five great semi-national services – police, roads, health, education and poor law'.[13]

The parallel development of central and local administrative devolution carried within it the seeds of eventual conflict. But during World War II, that potential was obscured as the central state experienced another spectacular burst of growth, fuelled by the emergency climate of mass mobilisation. It was in these years that a new Scottish 'identity' to replace the old civic-based jingoism – namely, a welfare state autonomously administered by the Scottish Office – was constructed. In some ways the closest parallel to this was with the eighteenth-century age of 'managed' government, although the scale and the character of the institutions involved was radically different.

By coincidence, the new consolidated Scottish Office departments moved into St Andrew's House on the day following the outbreak of World War II. In London, bomb damage to Dover House in 1941 made it necessary to move to Fielden House, a brick-clad, steel-framed interwar building previously occupied by the railway companies. Two government agencies coordinated wartime civil administration: the Scottish regional commissioner (in charge of air-raid precautions, civilian rescue and emergency food supply) and the Secretary of State, who controlled the emergency hospital service, the national fire service, and food production. The potential for confusion was minimised by the fact that the Regional Commissioner prior to 1941 and the Secretary of State after 1941 were the same person: Tom Johnston. Johnston was a former socialist firebrand and home-ruler who exploited Cabinet fears of Scottish unrest to ensure that the machinery of postwar planning would be devolved rather than reserved in London. In 1943–4, he set up two regional planning projects covering the Central Belt, and a pioneering scheme to revive the economy of the Highlands through hydro-electric construction: the North of Scotland Hydro-Electric Board. Pushing the limits of symbolic sovereignty under administrative devolution, Johnston also established a 'Council of State' of former Scottish Secretaries, and what he called an 'industrial parliament', the Scottish Council (Development and Industry).

After 1945, the climate of military-style civil mobilisation continued for a while, in campaigns like the battle against the slums. By 1950, this boosted Scottish Office numbers above 5,000, less than half of them accommodated in St Andrew's House. The Secretary of State was like the head of an entirely administrative government with a miniature cabinet of civil servant under-secretaries, and a network of supporting non-departmental bodies. Of the main areas of domestic policy, only social security was lost to its control, when the Ministry of Pensions was created in 1949; to compensate, a 1953 Royal Commission on Scottish government administration gave the Scottish Office responsibility for roads and laid the ground for further administrative devolution.

But the affluence of the 1960s saw a change towards a new concept of planning, as a way of managing growth and prosperity: this philosophy was set out in the Toothill Report of 1961 on economic development. The Scottish Office was reorganised to give primacy to physical and economic planning, and underpinned by managerialist centralisation, reaching a maximum of 11,000 staff by 1976. In 1962 a new government department, the Scottish Development Department (SDD) was formed, uniting all functions concerned with planning and infrastructure; economic planning became a separate department in 1970. The whole country apart from Edinburgh was designated a 'development area' eligible for development grants, and a special initiative, the Highlands and Islands Development Board (HIDB), was started in the Highlands in 1965 to promote industry and integrated land use. Headed by the former government chief planner, Robert Grieve, the HIDB was attacked by Tories as an expression of 'undiluted Marxism'.[14]

Within this system of administrative devolution, the main clashes were not at central government level, between political parties, but between the central and local, or, more precisely, between central administrator-technocrats and local politicians.[15] While there seemed to have been a decisive shift in the nature of Scottish civil autonomy, from the confident masonic elite of the nineteenth-century cities to a centralised cadre of planner-technocrats, the situation on the ground was not so clear-cut. Owing to the lack of political expression at central government level, it was uncertain how much the general public could distinguish between retained and devolved activity, especially as many areas of policy were legitimised by pan-British labels, such as the National Health Service, the New Universities, the New Towns, comprehensive schools, and the National Plan (a 1965 project of George Brown's Department for Economic Affairs).

In fact, the most 'autonomous' governmental activity recognisable to voters, and politically accountable to them, was still at local level. The work of the local authorities, with their vigorous local issues and debates, not only carried on but was actively strengthened, through the councils' near-monopoly in working-class housing provision from the 1940s. But this activity was now carried on in constant tension with government technocrats, and was shaped by the agenda of central administration. There were incessant clashes, for example, between Glasgow Corporation and the planners over issues such as the location of new housing developments: should they be built within municipal boundaries under the control of housing committee councillors, or dispersed in new towns under the control of government-appointed management boards? These clashes were largely unrelated to the two-party system: both the planners and the councillors tended to be socialists, while the government ministers who arbitrated their quarrels could be Tory or Labour. It is not clear, in retrospect, whether these local-central clashes were a sign of the weakness of the system, or of its strength. In the 1970s, the Wheatley Report on local government tried to finally resolve the issue in the planners' favour, by creating a new tier of regional authorities to impose order on the cities, and finally abolishing the independent small burghs inherited from before 1707, with their separate tolbooths and administrations. But by then, with mounting economic crises, the viability of the entire welfare state was coming into question, tied as it was to assumptions of unlimited economic growth.

Architecturally, the response to these changes was not through simple changes in 'styles'. In fact, internationally speaking, one of the main developments in architecture was a further move away from the use of specific styles to signify meaning, including nationality. Instead, meaning and identity were denoted by more general architectural and urban qualities, with an emphasis on simple and massive forms, with results which looked very similar in different countries: national symbols were increasingly confined to sculptural and heraldic panels. Up to World War II, there was still a split between broadly classical public buildings and 'vernacular' domestic buildings, but after 1945 even that distinction disappeared. The focus of official government architecture was social provision for mass society. In western countries such as Scotland, great representational government buildings had become less important, and where they were built, ceremonial functions were dwarfed by bureaucratic office accommodation: the climax of this trend was the building of the Pentagon in Washington DC (completed 1943), which covered 27 acres, including a five-acre central court. In totalitarian countries, there was a return to building large open-air structures and covered halls for mass citizen assemblies, but now for demonstrations rather than debate and voting; the wider use of steel from the late nineteenth century had allowed vast spaces to be roofed or canopied, and the years around the First World War had seen the growing popularity of the fan-shaped or rectangular auditorium with numerous parallel rows of forward-facing seats, a strongly hierarchical arrangement that gave domination to the main stage. In Scotland, this type of auditorium was used mainly for entertainment buildings such as cinemas, alongside other variants such as the circular plan used at Edinburgh's Usher Hall of 1914 (by Stockdale Harrison) with its big cantilevered galleries. The same non-political, leisure-orientated character applied in the case of open-air stadia, where the 1920s saw the rebuilding of many large football grounds, including Celtic Park (expanded in 1929 with a new main stand by Duncan & Kerr) and Ibrox Park (with a new luxury main stand built in 1928–9 to Archibald Leitch's designs); April 1937 saw one of the largest football attendances recorded, with 149,000 spectators at a Scotland–England match at Hampden Park.[16]

In response to the new focus of a mass democracy of families, the physical focus of this state intervention shifted to the everyday environments of those households, and above all to housing, where municipal provision took over to an extent unparallelled in any other country. The overwhelming emphasis was on countering the muddle and density of the nineteenth-century legacy through cleaner and more spacious dwellings, especially through the greenery of garden suburbs. By the 1940s and '50s, under the influence of the vast aspirations of the Modern Movement, the emphasis had broadened to wider projects of replanning, including the dams and power stations of the Hydro Board, the emergency hospitals, the urban redevelopment of the Gorbals, and the new towns themselves. To support these programmes, there was a meteoric rise in the number of architects and planners directly employed by government organisations. The most important of these 'public authority architects' was Robert Matthew, who successively served as chief architect-planner of DHS and the London County Council (LCC), and then (in 1953) set up a private practice that specialised in design of large-scale government-sponsored social architecture complexes, and energetically promoted ideals of cross-disciplinary rationalism in planning.

Between the wars, the architecture of the most prestigious state institutions was dominated by a sober classicism. There were a number of variants. On the one hand, there was the possibility of a classical style with 'national' features, such as the 'Château' style of government buildings in the emergent Canadian state; the Scottish equivalent was a Traditionalist classicism with restrained Baronial features, exemplified in the Scottish National War Memorial built on the summit of Edinburgh Castle in 1924–7 by Robert Lorimer, an assembly-hall of the war dead, with its formal rolls of honour and steel casket of names. At Galashiels Municipal Buildings (1924), an extension took the form of a Lorimer war memorial tower of a massively Baronial character, evoking the sturdy tolbooth tradition. The other main type of classicism used for government buildings was a more cosmopolitan variant, generally identified in Scotland with the Beaux-Arts classicism of the Burnet dynasty. The international exemplar of this approach was the League of Nations headquarters in Geneva, built in 1927–38 after a competition whose jury included Burnet alongside Victor Horta, H.P. Berlage, Josef Hoffmann and Ivar Tengbom. The brief demanded a secretariat, a 2,600-seat assembly hall, and committee rooms. After an inconclusive judging process, the jury eventually delegated the project to Henri-Paul Nenot and J. Flegenheimer, with the help of Joseph Vago and two others; Burnet, an old friend of Nenot, was closely involved in the compromise design. Although many of the 377 entries were expressionistic, with tall towers, the eventually completed building at Ariana Park was dominated by a Versailles-like classical horizontality: there was a 400m-long façade, a U-shaped court of honour with a massive assembly block at the centre, and a long secretariat wing off to one side. To house the vast number of delegates envisaged in the assembly hall, the latter was arranged like a concert-hall auditorium, with forward-facing rows of seats; that arrangement was later to be influential in the planning of mass congress halls of mid-twentieth-century totalitarian regimes.[17]

In Scotland, the first and foremost government building project of the interwar years, St Andrew's House in Edinburgh (1934–9), stemmed not from any kind of legislative activity, but from the mushrooming growth of administrative devolution. The task was to build a new headquarters building for the consolidated Scottish Office departments, which by 1929 were spread over eighteen separate Edinburgh offices. The story is told in greater detail in David Walker's *St Andrew's House* (1989). The site chosen was Calton Prison, previously considered in Oldrieve's 1912 feasibility study for government offices. A new proposal was put forward in 1929, comprising three linked blocks: a central quadrangle block of offices flanked by an office and a sheriff-court block. The design, by the government Office of Works architects in London and their chief architect, Sir Richard Allison, was of a utilitarian classical character, pilastered evenly all around. Following protests by the Royal Fine Art Commission, a more heavily modelled alternative scheme on a colossal rusticated substructure was produced, but after the *Scotsman*'s publication in July 1930 of a sketch (by a student at Edinburgh College of Art) of the initial scheme, both were abandoned in the ensuing outcry against the 'huge barracks'. Outline schemes of 1933 by Sir George Washington Browne and the Office of Works architects established the principle of a U-shaped main block to give order to the huge mass, and in December of that year Burnet, Tait and Lorne were selected as architects. This premier Scottish architectural practice had since 1929 begun to modify their traditional Beaux-Arts *atelier* outlook with more American businesslike practices, in world-renowned projects such as the Sydney Harbour Bridge. The appointment of Burnet's firm to design St Andrew's House symbolised the changing orientation of both Scottish devolution and British imperialism, and their growing link to ideals of modernity and technical progress.[18]

TOP.
4.8. Site plan and ground plan of St Andrew's House, 1935, showing its location beside Calton Hill. (RCAHMS B7249)

BELOW LEFT.
4.9. St Andrew's House, centre of the devolved Scottish government administration, was built in 1936–9 to the designs of T. S. Tait. Here it is portrayed on the cover of J. A. Bowie's 1939 book, *The Future of Scotland* – a text advocating the modernisation and diversification of the Scottish economy.

BELOW RIGHT.
4.10. 1939 view of the main north entrance to St Andrew's House. (RCAHMS)

Burnet, Tait & Lorne had only eighteen weeks to plan the new Scottish government headquarters. From Tait's modern Beaux-Arts perspective, the clearly articulated classical blocks of the League of Nations final design now seemed old-fashioned, and something reflecting the more integral massing of American skyscrapers was

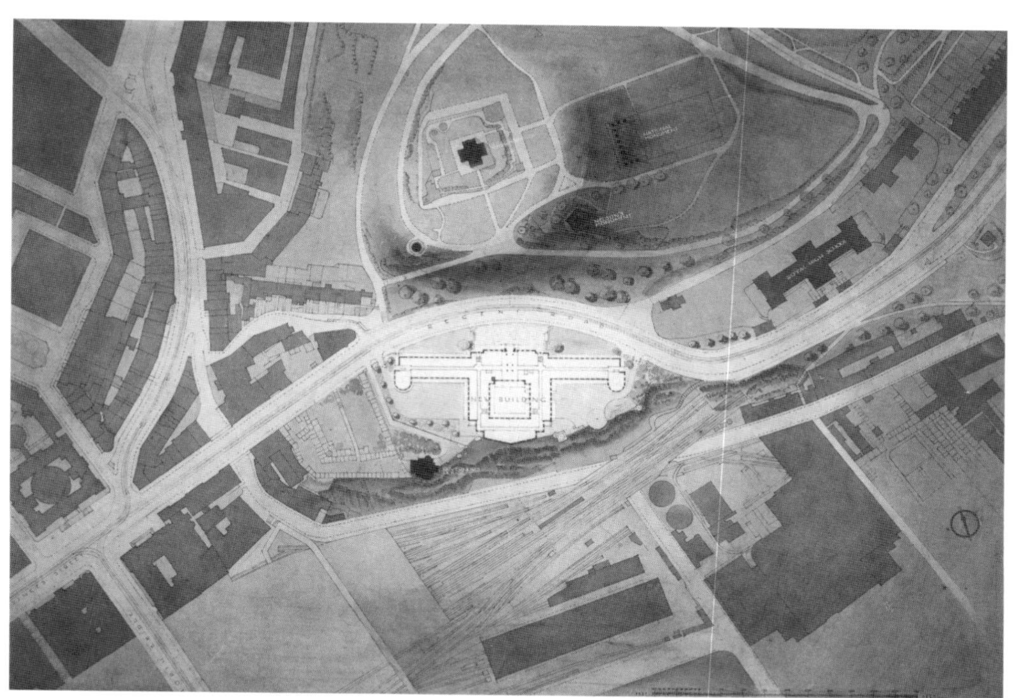
NEW BUILDING

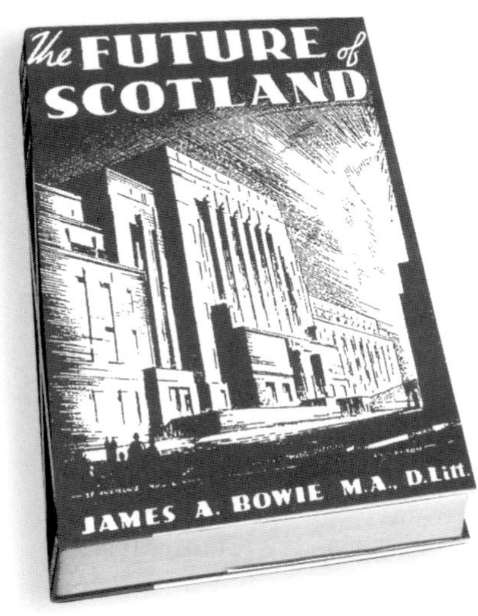
The FUTURE of
SCOTLAND
JAMES A. BOWIE M.A., D.Litt.

desirable. The finished design was a stepped, 'sculpturesque' group intended by Tait to 'grow out of the landscape and appear to be part of it', while harmonising with the classicism of the New Town. Tait described it as a 'Scottish "Acropolis"', which would provide 'proof that architecture in our country, so long trammelled with traditional ornament and lacking in original thought, is again vibrant with imagination and in step with the progression of a great (or transitional) age'.[19]

The building was dominated by a U-shaped central mass seven storeys in height, with lower wings on each side and a three-storey block bowed out in front. Construction comprised steel-framing by Redpath Brown, on a twelve-foot grid; it was faced with Northumberland sandstone, although Tait had originally wanted to use Portland stone because of its brilliant whiteness. Internally, almost the whole building was planned with utilitarian corridors flanked by small offices: larger rooms included the two-storey entrance hall, the restrainedly sumptuous, walnut-panelled Secretary of State's room on the fifth floor, and libraries and boilerhouses in the basement. The two main staircases, at the north-east and north-west angles of the central block, had Art Deco balustrades decorated with stylised thistles.

Although site work began in November 1934, the mounting staff numbers of the Scottish Office forced several changes of plan and enlargements during construction, including the construction of a bomb-shelter in the basement – still surviving in 1999, complete with air-raid precaution notices. The severe entrance (north) façade, approached by a grand carriage entrance adorned by modernistic flagpole and lighting pylons, was redesigned by Tait with a wider, seven-bay central block. The latter's vertical window bays were divided by piers surmounted by figures of the four main departments, and of Architecture and Statecraft, by Sir William Reid Dick. Above the central entrance was a royal arms by Alexander Carrick, along with a lion and unicorn by Phyllis Bone. The bronze entrance doors, by Walter Gilbert, depicted Scottish saints, with the intention of evoking 'the Soul of Scotland . . . the call of service from all men for the fellowmen'.[20] By comparison with the flamboyant and profuse sculptural groups of the Glasgow Municipal Buildings, this kind of low-relief heraldic sculpture pointed to a more restrained, but intense national symbolism.

During the early twentieth century, some of the representational

TOP.
4.11. The Secretary of State's room, St Andrew's House; 1950 photograph. (RCAHMS)

BELOW.
4.12. One of the open-well staircases in St Andrew's House, including Art Deco 'thistle' balusters. (RCAHMS 1998 survey; D39198)

4.13. The main facade of the British Government Pavilion (designed by Herbert J. Rowse) at the 1938 Glasgow Empire Exhibition. (RCAHMS)

functions of the great state building were taken over by a new building type, the national or international exposition. Originally conceived in the mid-nineteenth century as a kind of vast trade bazaar, the dominant character of the 'expo' had changed by the 1930s to a vehicle for nationalistic self-promotion, as exemplified by the German and Soviet pavilions at the 1937 Paris exhibition, and the vast, globe-like 'Democracity' which formed the centrepiece of the 1939 New York fair. The major Scottish contribution to the expo movement, the 1938 Glasgow Empire Exhibition at Bellahouston Park, showed the Scottish and British identities in transition from global imperialism to home reconstruction and the welfare state. In contrast to the triumphal Glasgow Municipal Buildings sculpture of the 1890s, the emancipatory character and 'peaceful aspirations' of the Empire were now stressed. The exhibition included a 'peace pavilion' paid for by housebuilder Sir John Mactaggart, and designed by Alister MacDonald (son of Ramsay). Sponsored by the state and local industrialists, the Empire Exhibition was closely bound up with the expansion of Scottish administrative devolution, not least by the fact that its

4.14. Entrance courtyard of the British Government Pavilion at the Glasgow Empire Exhibition, with statue 'typifying man's questing spirit'. (RCAHMS)

coordinating architect was Thomas Tait, who used the same steel-framing constructional method (here clad with prefabricated sheeting) as at the exactly contemporary St Andrew's House; we should also remember Burnet's key role in the League of Nations project, nearing completion in the same years.

Laid out on formal Beaux-Arts lines, and crowned by the 91m-high Tower of Empire, the Glasgow Empire Exhibition had three major axes, representing the affiliations of the Scottish nation: the Scottish Avenue; Kingsway (Britain); and the Dominions and Colonial Avenues (the Empire). The central state was represented by the United Kingdom Government Pavilion on Kingsway, designed by the English architect Herbert J. Rowse. This 131m-long building was planned around a 'long gallery' giving access to exhibitions on industrial and social progress, such as 'The Fitter Britain Exhibition', prepared jointly by DHS and the English Ministry of Health. The main entrance was located at one end of the building: a lion-flanked staircase led into a 24m-high, austerely classical toplit entrance court, dominated by a 15m-high throne-like canopied recess containing 'a figure typifying man's questing spirit'. This statue is 'seen to ride a great silver wave. He bears symbols of energy which science has placed within his grasp'. The pavilion was hailed by Glasgow industrialist Sir Cecil Weir, chairman of the exhibition council of management, as 'a stately building, worthy of the Mother Country'. Writing in the *Daily Record*, Lord Kemsley, Chairman of Associated Scottish Newspapers Ltd, praised its 'quiet magnificence' as a symbol of 'the spirit of calm greatness that is characteristic of Britain'. By contrast with the social-democratic reformism emphasised in the government pavilion, the Church of Scotland's pavilion, a courtyard cloister and church with crowstepped tower designed by J. Taylor Thomson, seemed a little old-fashioned, intended as it was to showcase the Kirk's efforts 'for the moral and social well-being of young and old in its own land, for the upbuilding of the Empire, and for the enlightenment of backward peoples and the peace of the world'.[21]

After 1945, the tensions between the growing administrative apparatus of central government and the revitalised local-government world were reflected indirectly within architecture. Internationally speaking, the period was dominated by the rapid and complete victory of Modern architecture in Western countries, helped by the stigmatisation of monumental classical architecture by association with totalitarian regimes. In the architecture of government, even the modern Beaux Arts classicism represented by St Andrew's House now seemed impossibly authoritarian; 'freedom' meant the flowing, open-ended space and abstract, asymmetrical, contrasting shapes of the Modern Movement. The emblem of the future was the United Nations headquarters designed in New York by Wallace K. Harrison and others and built in 1947–53, its 544-ft-high, 39-storey secretariat tower soaring above a domed General Assembly Hall laid out in the unidirectional congress-hall manner.[22] It was followed in the 1950s by entire planned new cities with Modernist government complexes at their centres: Chandigarh, planned in 1950-7 by Le Corbusier, and Brasilia, 1958–60, by Lucio Costa and Oscar Niemeyer. Both of them

continued the formula of the tall secretariat slab juxtaposed in free space with lower and more sculptural legislative and ceremonial buildings: at Brasilia the forms were cleanly geometrical, at Chandigarh more sculpturally individualistic in concrete. After 1956 even communist countries also embraced Modernism, with some residual elements of classical formality: for example, the Palace of Congresses in the Moscow Kremlin (1961, by M. Posokhin and A. Mndoiants and others) combined a large hall with seats for 6,000 with a regularly columned, almost 'pilastered' front façade.

4.15. Senate chamber, Congresso Nacional, Brasilia (1959, by Lucio Costa and Oscar Niemeyer). (M. Glendinning; 1984 view)

The reaction in Scotland to these architectural developments was at first cautious. Within central government, much early postwar work remained faithful to the prewar classical ideas – where new projects could be afforded at all, rather than simply using the existing, mainly nineteenth-century administrative buildings. The Scottish Ministry of Works chief architect, Stewart Sim, designed a succession of monumental office blocks, including Montrose House in Glasgow (a prewar design built in modified form in 1951–3, with tall finned corner), and Greyfriars House in Aberdeen (1953), a U-shaped three-storey block, its main north façade articulated by an elemental colonnade of piers. The same applied in local government, where the construction of Carr and Howard's Kirkcaldy Town House to a prewar classical design continued until its completion in 1956. And it applied in non-departmental organisations, such as the North of Scotland Hydro-Electric Board, stronghold of a more assertively 'national' classicism. In 1946, the Traditionalist architect Leslie Grahame Thomson proposed a vast towered Hydro headquarters at Pitlochry, in a style resembling the 1920s work of Lorimer; but what actually happened was that the Board's offices stayed in a late nineteenth-century Edinburgh classical street (Rothesay Terrace, built from 1872 to Peddie & Kinnear's designs) until its privatisation several decades later.

Initially, there was a sharp contrast with this conservatism at home and the more adventurous external projection of government architecture by Scottish designers from the 1950s onwards. Now, that projection emphasised not the assertiveness of the old Imperial Scotland but the agenda of international cooperation and decolonisation, the latter symbolised by the Commonwealth as an egalitarian replacement for the Empire. This was a task of diplomacy as much as one of design. In the forefront of this work was Robert Matthew, who helped mediate in the architectural issues of the Cold War (as president of the Union Internationale des Architectes during the Cuban crisis) and contributed to the professional underpinning of the Commonwealth, as the co-founder of the Commonwealth Association of Architects in 1963–5.

In a number of key government and state representational buildings, Matthew and his friend and contemporary, Basil Spence, set out to express this new collaborative approach through abstract Modern forms. The first of these buildings, appropriately, was for the government of New Zealand, a country once closely bound up with Scottish colonialism, but which after World War II had set about energetically reforming its century-old parliamentary constitution. In

1947, New Zealand assumed full legislative sovereignty under the provisions of the 1931 Statute of Westminster, and in 1950 the parliament, or 'General Assembly', was reformed by the abolition of the upper house, leaving the lower house (the House of Representatives) as a unicameral body. In 1955, to signify this new and equal relationship, Matthew was commissioned to build an arrestingly modern representational complex in central London, a 'modern project in the heart of the Empire' which would combine the administrative accommodation of a high commission with trade and cultural promotion offices: high commissioner T. Clifton Webb demanded 'a building which looks to the future and thus symbolises the approach of New Zealand'. These functions were presented through a formula of unprecedented openness: a flowing atrium entrance hall, spanned by a second-floor bridge, gave access to offices on the upper floors, and the high commissioner's apartment at the top. The building comprised a four-floor podium with a slender, 14-storey tower on top – the first tower block built in Central London. Protests from amenity groups blocked original plans of 1956 for a 275-ft-high building, and forced its reduction by 68 ft; the revised design was built in 1959–61. An even more dramatic architectural expression of decolonisation was under construction by Matthew's firm in London at the same time: the Commonwealth Institute, a complex dominated by a 93-ft-square

4.16. 1955 sketch by Robert Matthew for New Zealand House, London (Lady Matthew)

concrete paraboloid-roofed exhibition hall, interpenetrated diagonally by a rectangular block containing art gallery and offices, and set in landscaping designed by Sylvia Crowe.[23]

Basil Spence used Modernist forms to symbolise post-colonial state power in a different, and more flamboyantly monumental manner, related to the pictorial expressionism of architects such as Eero Saarinen. In 1964, the New Zealand Government commissioned him to advise on the proposed extension of Parliament House in Wellington, a classical legislature building, by government architect John Campbell, that had been left half-completed in 1922; the unbuilt section had included ministerial, members' and committee rooms. Spence's concept design, dubbed the 'Beehive', was executed by others over several years from 1969 onwards, at a cost of over NZ$9 million. It comprised a 56m-high, 11-storey circular tower on a double basement, tapering sharply from a wide ring of ceremonial rooms at the bottom, to narrower suites of members' offices above, and ministerial and prime-ministerial suites at the top. In his design for the chancery at the British Embassy in Rome (commissioned in 1959 and built in 1968–71, to replace a previous embassy blown up by Zionist guerrillas in 1946), Spence elaborated this design philosophy, packaging an office block as a monumental pavilion in a formal

4.17. Sir Basil Spence's design for the 'Beehive' Parliament House extension at Wellington, New Zealand, built from 1969. (National Publicity Studios)

landscaped garden. The aim was to respect the historic location by Michelangelo's Porta Pia, while reasserting British prestige in relation to the ambitious contemporary embassy designs of the United States. Standing on columns over pools and fountains, the travertine-faced building disguises its prosaic function behind a stepped-out, highly modelled façade; inside, the first-floor plan features offices on one side of a corridor, including the ambassador's room at one corner, while the second floor has a central corridor with offices on either side.[24]

From the end of the 1950s, under the influence of Matthew's prolific work after his return from London in 1953 and the formation three years later of his joint practice with Stirrat Johnson-Marshall (RMJM), the Modernist approach to the architecture of government rapidly gained ascendancy within Scotland itself. The United Nations and Brasilia formula of integrated legislature and secretariat could only be fully applied in local government, with its strong political traditions; and the following decade duly saw the building or rebuilding of a large number of council headquarters. On the whole, the complexes built by the county councils, greatly augmented in their power by Elliot's 1929 legislation, tended to be more spacious and untrammelled in their newness than those of the older burghs and cities, many of which continued to make good use of their pre-1914 buildings. For instance, the massed building of 1960s tower blocks in Glasgow was planned from the neo-Renaissance splendour of Committee Room 1 in Young's municipal buildings.

4.18. The Glasgow Corporation Housing Committee discussing proposals for multi-storey blocks of flats in 1962, in the classical splendour of Committee Room 1 – one of five rooms lining the south side of the second-floor Committee Corridor in the City Chambers. The Convener and Sub-Convener, David Gibson and Edward Clark, are third and fourth from right. (Glasgow District Council; cf. 3.44)

Appropriately, the grandest of all new postwar council headquarters was built by the most powerful and assertive of the counties, Lanarkshire, which had embarked after 1945 on a crusade to regenerate a vast area of country left despoiled and derelict after the collapse of the local coal industry; that crusade included one of the largest council housing programmes in the country, directed by housing convener and council leader Hugh Brannan. The authority was finally broken up by the 1975 reorganisation, after it had vainly argued that it should become one of nine all-purpose authorities. The new Lanark County Buildings complex was constructed in 1960–64 in the county town of Hamilton, on an elevated plateau site somewhat outside the historic core of the burgh, replacing overcrowded buildings in central Glasgow. It was conceived as a modern acropolis, majestically surveying the vast landward expanses commanded by the County Council. Seen from the beginning as a showpiece of public architecture, it was designed by the County Council's own architectural staff, led by D.G. Bannerman, with engineering advice from W.V. Zinn and contractor Laing Construction; it was built in two phases at a total cost of £1.65m.

The Lanark County headquarters comprises two linked buildings set on a landscaped civic podium, adjoining interwar offices. On the east is the administrative block, a 17-storey, 60m-tall office tower aligned east-west, measuring 57m by 16m on plan. It is built of reinforced concrete frame with white ceramic mosaic-clad gable walls, and anodised aluminium curtain walling with vitreous enamelled steel infill panels on the main north and south façades. From the second floor upwards, the tower contains general office space with flexible partitioning, with restaurant and kitchen at the top. The building is completely air-conditioned, allowing the external profile to be extremely sheer. At the south-west is the council block, made up of a two-storey wing aligned north-south, giving access to a row of five committee and members' rooms; at the north end of the axis is a large county hall to accommodate 350. Attached to the south end of the council axis is a prominent circular council chamber cantilevered out at the base. The chamber is ringed by an access lobby with staircases; inside, the floor slopes down from the press gallery at the back (south), with the members' desks arranged in slightly concave tiers and the officials' and convener's tables facing in the other direction from the south end. Externally faced with precast concrete units and green slate

TOP.
4.19. Lanark County Buildings, Hamilton, 1960–4, designed by County Architect D G Bannerman. (RCAHMS C50524)

BELOW.
4.20. Lanark County Buildings, 1998 view of council chamber. (RCAHMS C42297)

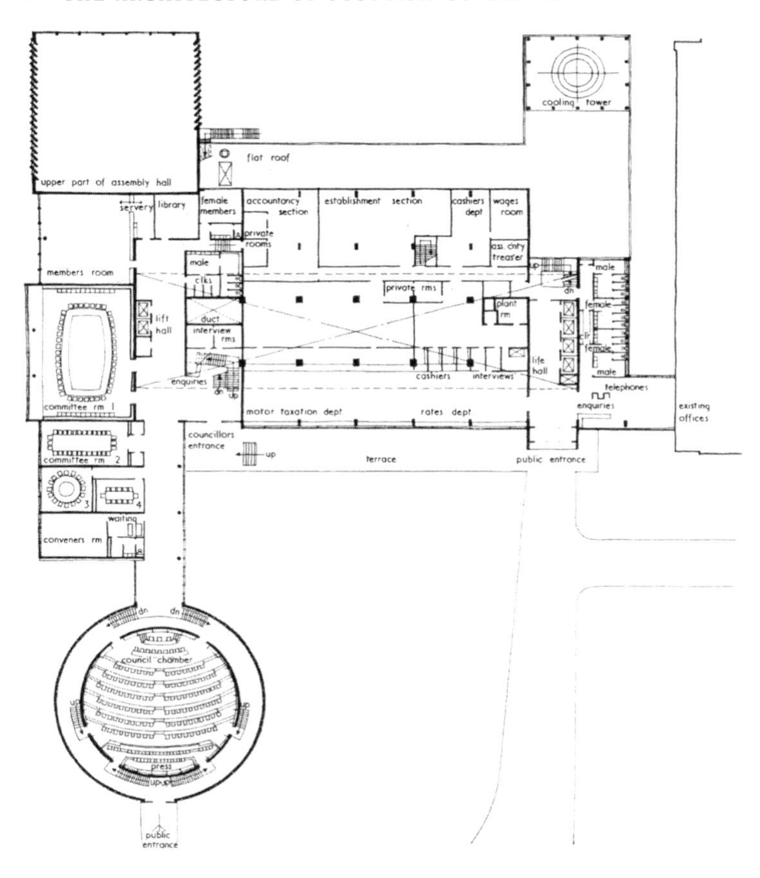

4.21. Lanark County Buildings, ground-floor plan. (*The Builder*, 4 September 1964, 472). The tower block occupies the area marked by a diagonally-crossed rectangle.

base, the chamber is publicly accessible by a concrete-canopied entrance at the south end. The surrounding area is laid out as a monumental entrance plaza, with paving, flagpoles, lawns, pools, and a ramp and bridge, electrically heated in winter. The entire Lanark County group, juxtaposing in flowing space a tall secretariat and lower, more sculptural legislature, is an explicit echo of the United Nations and Brasilia complexes: its designers described the asymmetrical group as a 'three-element composition', whose 'strictly formal' forecourt would 'lead the eye' from the council chamber to the 'severe angularity' of the tower's 'gigantic backcloth'. The break from the old concepts of the urban municipal palazzo, and the grand hierarchical symmetry of the League of Nations or St Andrew's House, is clear. But the concepts of monumental formality are not completely banished, given the building's emphatic 'front' entrance. Since 1996, this great building is once again the headquarters of an all-purpose authority,

South Lanarkshire; and in 1993 it was one of Scotland's first postwar Modernist monuments to be listed by Historic Scotland (at the highest category, A).[25]

Within the cities and large burghs, the problem was how to integrate new or extended headquarters buildings into a dense urban fabric. The most ambitious of the resulting programmes was in Aberdeen, where the Town House was now bulging at the seams with the demands of the town council and law-enforcement agencies. The county council had already vacated its section of the building for self-contained offices in Union Terrace between 1937 (when it last met in the Town and County Hall) and 1946. In the early 1960s, as part of a plan of comprehensive redevelopment for the whole city centre, a programme of functionally segregated new developments was begun, colonising the area to the rear of the Town House in separate but coordinated movements, the town council extending to the north-west and the justice authorities to the north-east. The demolition of old houses along Broad Street in the early 1970s made it possible to complete a stately zone of public and university buildings.

The first stage of this Aberdeen redevelopment, west of Broad Street, was intended to meet the city's crying need for more office space. Named St Nicholas House, it was designed by the office of City Architect George McI. Keith, and built from 1965. Like Hamilton County Buildings, this was a typically International Modern self-contained abstract landscape of blocks, but reflected its urban location with a more enclosed layout. The site was defined to the east, north and south by a three-storey block with a plan like a letter 'F'. This block mediated between modernity and tradition in its mixture of curtain wall bands and concrete-granite slabs, and in its slanting alignment to Broad Street, terminating in a peaked-roof collection office. In its sheltered western courtyard, sitting on a podium like a piece of rubble sculpture, is a preserved seventeenth-century building, Provost Skene's House. Perched above the southern wing of the three-storey group is an eleven-storey slab block of an unambiguously Modernist character, with alternating bands of windows and white mosaic cladding.

The next phases of Aberdeen's civic-administrative development took place in the 1970s. Two major new groups were built behind the Town House and to the east of Broad Street. They were linked visually to St Nicholas House in their use of Modern glass and mosaic in

4.22. Aberdeen Town House Extension (1975–7, by City Architect Tom Watson): the east frontage with bowed projection to the members' dining room. The St Nicholas House office tower of 1965 is in the background. (RCAHMS D41747)

combination with 'traditional' granite aggregate. In reaction to the growth of conservationism, the ambition to create a completely new environment, or new space, had been scaled down: the new buildings faithfully continued the centuries-old division of the complex into an eastern tolbooth/prison and a western townhouse. Behind the tolbooth was built a new police headquarters, forming a civic square, with a public hall and gymnasium on a podium with car park below, linked to a seven-storey police headquarters slab block, with mosaic-clad gable walls, and lower east wing; a separate cell block êwas constructed between these buildings and the tolbooth. The north-west wing of the Town House was extended by a four-storey block, and linked to it by a glazed bridge. This extension, designed by City Architect Tom Watson in 1974, contains sumptuous members' accommodation and committee rooms; its purpose was to cope with the new responsibilities and greater number of councillors after the 1975 reorganisation. Its façades are clad in two-tone mosaic and fronted by set-forward columns. The building is in two clearly differentiated sections, a north end containing a members' dining room

(externally expressed by a bow window to the east) with two-storey council chamber above; and a south end with a lofty stair-hall, offices and committee rooms. The stair-hall, three storeys high, has a complex cantilevered staircase and mosaic-clad walls. The council êchamber is a rectangular room with concrete panel side walls between slit windows. Intended to accommodate 52 members, it contains a double row of desks (each with electric voting console) arranged on a chamfered U-plan and set on a slightly tiered floor, facing a top table at the west end; an officials' table is set in the centre. A large public gallery is set into the back (east) wall, with a councillors' lounge below; a smaller recessed press gallery is set into the south wall. The flat ceiling is decorated with clustered globe lights. Construction of the Town House extension, by contractor Taylor Woodrow, started in May 1975, and the foundation stone was laid in November of that year by the Lord Provost, veteran Labour councillor Robert S. Lennox; the first District Council meeting in the newly completed chamber was held in June 1977.

4.23. The first meeting of the City of Aberdeen District Council to use the new chamber in the Town House Extension, October 1977. (*Press and Journal*)

The regional authorities created by the 1975 local government reorganisation did not, as a general rule, commission ambitious quarters for themselves. The largest and most powerful, Strathclyde Region, operated from a group of standard early 1970s office blocks, largely speculatively built, in Glasgow's India Street, alongside the inner ring-road motorway; the blocks had open-plan interiors and exteriors with window-bands or curtain walls. Most other authorities re-used existing county council buildings, some recently built. For example, the headquarters inherited by Grampian Regional Council – Woodhill House, a compact Modernist complex set in landscaped grounds in outer Aberdeen – had only just been built by Aberdeen County Council as a replacement for its city-centre Union Terrace offices. The building, constructed in several stages in 1970–5, was designed by the staff of County Architect John C. Arnott. Faced in mullioned precast concrete slabs and rubble, it comprised a four-storey office block and a concave-fronted, two-storey block of council rooms and halls.

While these diverse groups of buildings gave ample scope for postwar Scottish local government to express its power and pride, the central government, including both the devolved Scottish administration and the Scottish agencies of London ministries, had a more difficult architectural task. The only significant way in which they could express their aspirations for modern government was through permutations of the office block. By the mid-1960s, the Scottish Office was once again bursting out of its accommodation into a miscellany of buildings across central Edinburgh, including a number of standard speculative office blocks leased by the government. This seemed increasingly incompatible with the growing managerialist centralisation of the Scottish Office, in functions such as personnel, computers and finance. The result was a decision to build a new headquarters complex, New St Andrew's House, a short distance from its predecessor. Intended to house the most senior staff of all departments other than Agriculture, New St Andrew's House formed the most important part of the St James Centre, a massive, multi-level and multi-use redevelopment of the decayed St James Square area of the New Town, planned from the mid-1960s and built in 1969–75. Sited on steeply sloping ground, it comprised a podium of multi-storey car parking and shopping precinct, on which were perched a hotel and a department store as well as the government offices. Initial proposals showing a bulky townscape silhouette prompted fierce

TOP.
4.24. 1969 layout plan by Ian Burke Martin & Partners for the St James Square redevelopment in Edinburgh, topped by a ring of government offices for the Scottish Office (on completion, named New St Andrew's House). (Hugh Martin Partnership)

BELOW.
4.25. 1971 view from north-east of the St James Square redevelopment under construction, showing the reinforced concrete frame of the commercial substructure and the panel construction of the offices. (RCAHMS)

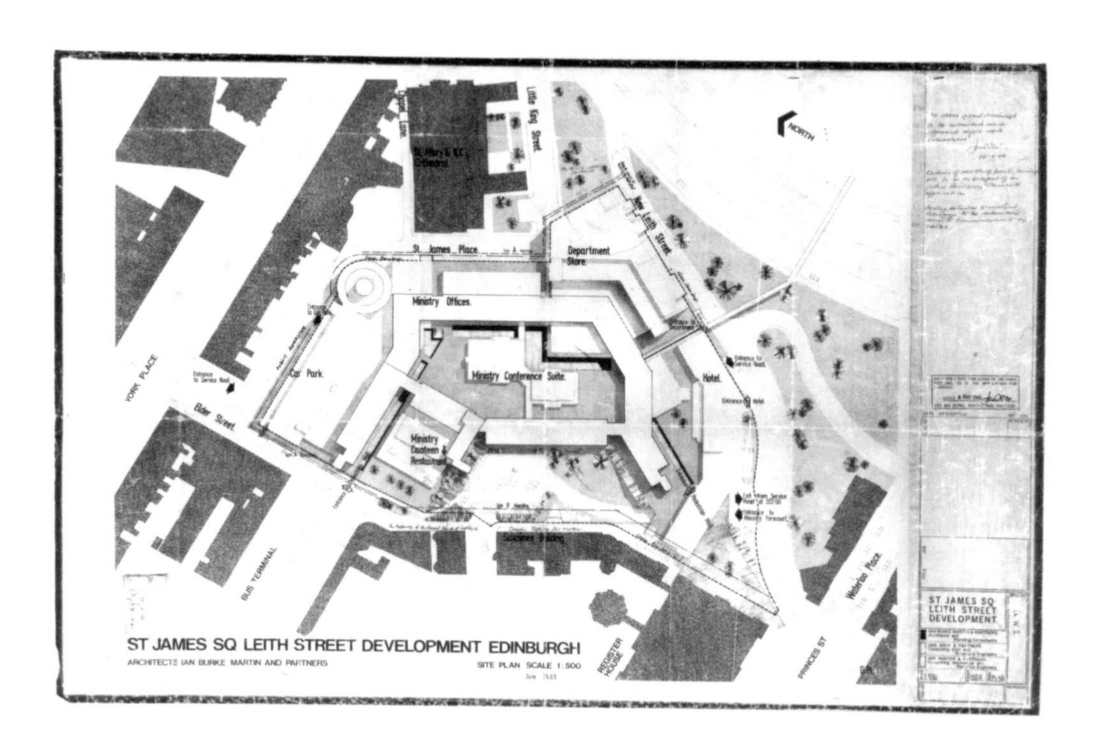
ST JAMES SQ LEITH STREET DEVELOPMENT EDINBURGH
ARCHITECTS IAN BURKE MARTIN AND PARTNERS
SITE PLAN SCALE 1:500
NORTH
Little King Street
St. James Place
Department Store
New Leith Street
Ministry Offices.
Ministry Conference Suite.
Car Park.
Hotel.
Ministry Canteen & Restaurant
Sasines Building
YORK PLACE
Elder Street
BUS TERMINAL
REGISTER HOUSE
PRINCES ST
Waterloo Place
ST JAMES SQ LEITH STREET DEVELOPMENT

opposition from the growing conservation movement and the Royal Fine Art Commission. In response to these criticisms, attempts were made to model the massive exterior in an asymmetrical, almost picturesque way. Working in collaboration with the city council and the Ministry of Public Building and Works, the developers were the Murrayfield Real Estate Co. and Ravenseft Ltd, both part of Sir Harold Samuel's Land Securities property empire; the architects were the experienced commercial firm Ian Burke Martin & Partners (later Hugh Martin & Partners), with Ove Arup as civil engineers.[26]

The New St Andrew's House government offices were laid out in an irregular oval with two wings and a lift tower to the west. Most of the offices are of seven storeys on a two-storey base, but the north-west wing is two storeys higher. In contrast to the integrated 1930s monumentality of St Andrew's House, this new building was rather more utilitarian and low-key in its planning. In the middle of the courtyard is a two-level conference suite. The offices all had a central spine corridor with freely planned spaces on either side. They were naturally ventilated, except for the fully air-conditioned ministerial and support suite on the top floor of the west central wing (Areas 24 and 25 of Level 300.5); the suite contained rooms for the Secretary of State and junior ministers, along with the most senior Scottish Office civil servants. The offices are constructed of load-bearing concrete, including precast units on the upper floors, and Dalbeattie exposed aggregate precast concrete wall panels with aluminium sliding sash windows.

In only one area did the Scottish Office administration begin to put down local roots: in the building of the five new towns, East Kilbride (designated in 1947), Glenrothes (1948), Cumbernauld (1956), Livingston (1962) and Irvine (1966). The development corporations charged with building these towns, under the powers of the 1946 New Towns Act, were managed by boards appointed by the Secretary of State, and were accountable politically as well as administratively to him: there were no elected councillors, and indeed relations with the 'host' county councils were often hostile, with the development corporations perceived as colonial-style interlopers, usually headquartered in a local country house. However, that picture is an over-simplification. Some of the new towns began to develop their own municipal traditions, in parallel with the development corporation administrations: East Kilbride was elevated to the status

4.26. 1989 aerial view from south of New St Andrew's House and the St James Centre; Robert Adam's General Register House, with its dome and centralised plan, is in the foreground. (RCAHMS B21803)

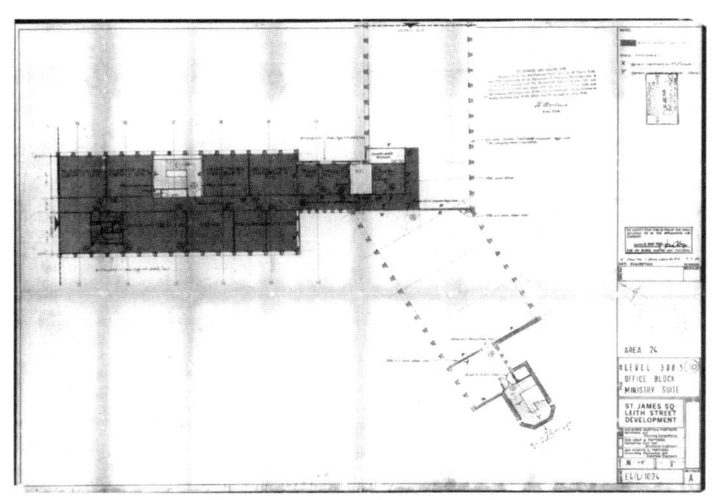
AREA 24
LEVEL 300.5
OFFICE BLOCK
MINISTRY SUITE
ST JAMES SQ
LEITH STREET
DEVELOPMENT
E4/L/1024
A

of a small burgh in 1963 and a large burgh in 1967, with control over health and social services, and built its own civic centre, complete with office tower and council chamber projecting at the north-east corner, as well as a boldly arched municipal swimming pool, the Dollan Baths, nearby (1965–8); and Irvine was from the start developed in close collaboration with the town council, which was anxious to reverse industrial decline.[27]

At Cumbernauld New Town there was an interesting dichotomy in the town's architecture of administration. The Development Corporation chose as its own headquarters the William Adam-designed Cumbernauld House (*c*.1742), which it set about extending with prefabricated office wings to the north and east. These were built in five phases in 1958–67 in informal groups around landscaped rear courtyards, using the Vic Hallam 'Derwent' system. Originally developed in England for school construction, this system comprised timber columns and plywood box beams with infill panels, all on a 1.93m square grid. These prefabricated offices were concerned above all else with the process of building the town, and were dominated by architects and planners. The civic administration provisions for the town itself were designed by the same architects, but in a very different form. The planning conception of Cumbernauld was a highly avant-garde one, which tried to break away from the low-density garden-suburb formula towards more densely clustered patterns. The focus of these clusters was the town centre, designed in 1958–63 by a brilliant young architect in the development corporation, Geoffrey Copcutt, as a single, complex structure, or 'megastructure', which would incorporate all the central functions of the town in an animatedly chaotic fashion. It included such civic functions as council offices, social security offices, and a community hall. Its concept was influenced by radical architectural movements of the late 1950s such as the 'Situationists', who argued that the making of architecture should be seen as an open-ended process, rather than as the creation of finite monuments. Cumbernauld Town Centre, with its huge scale but total lack of formality, was to symbolise the freedom of the car-owning consumer society in opposition to all the hierarchies and disciplines that had preceded it, including those of social-democratic collectivism; Copcutt even speculated that, should shopping patterns change in the distant future, the building could be converted into a gigantic automatic vending machine![28] Cumbernauld's megastructure,

TOP.
4.27. 1968 plan by Ian Burke Martin & Partners for part of the top floor of New St Andrew's House, containing the rooms of Scottish Office ministers and senior civil servants. This section was the only air-conditioned part of the building; it was fitted out within the standard dimensions and open-plan shell common to the whole building. (Hugh Martin Partnership)

MIDDLE.
4.28. Sir William Fraser, Permanent Under-Secretary of State (the head civil servant in the Scottish Office) in his New St Andrew's House office in 1986; the room was part of the ministerial suite, on the south-west side of the block. (Sir William Fraser)

BELOW.
4.29. Sir William Fraser in his London office at Dover House, also in 1986. (Sir William Fraser)

RIGHT.
4.30. 1991 view of the entrance board to Cumbernauld New Town Development Corporation's headquarters at Cumbernauld House, showing the prefabricated 'Derwent' system annexes (built in 1958–67 in five phases, and designed on a 1.93m square grid) in the background. (RCAHMS B57336)

OPPOSITE TOP.
4.31. G. Kenneth Davie, the third and last Chief Architect and Planning Officer of Cumbernauld New Town, seen in 1991 in his office in the south-east block of the prefabricated extensions to Cumbernauld House. (RCAHMS B57348)

OPPOSITE BELOW.
4.32. Cumbernauld Town Centre Phase One under construction in 1965. The civic/administration elements in this 'mega-structure' were located under the row of penthouses at the top. (RCAHMS)

like any town centre, contained a wide range of public and civic accommodation, including registry, social security and local authority offices. But none of these took the form of 'municipal buildings', or a 'civic centre' standing proudly on its own. From the Cumbernauld perspective of individualistic mobility, the self-contained Modernist elegance of Lanark County Buildings seemed as remote and obsolete as the pillared rhetoric of Glasgow Municipal Buildings. Within a decade of the Town Centre's completion, the collapse of confidence in unlimited economic growth and revulsion against the Modern Movement banished its brash optimism. But as we will see, its emphasis on open-ended flexibility was destined to re-emerge eventually in Scottish architecture, in a very different context: the design debates concerning the country's new parliament project at Holyrood.

By contrast with Cumbernauld Town Centre's exaggerated architectural individuality, the administration buildings built or leased by the London-based government ministries with pan-UK responsibilities were, as a rule, starkly straightforward in their conception. Planning of those built directly by the Government was carried out by the architects and other staff of the Ministry of Public Building and Works. The two most important projects of these years were both located on Clydeside, in accordance with the government drive to decentralise administration to economically depressed areas. The Post Office Savings Bank headquarters complex at Cowglen was a relatively utilitarian complex, designed by the Scottish office of the Ministry of Public Building and Works (superintending architect, G.A. Pearce).

H.M. INSPECTOR OF TAXES
CENTRE 1
OPEN FOR ENQUIRES
MONDAY-FRIDAY 8AM-4PM

Its development began with a group of prefabricated office buildings built in 1965–7 by Terrapin Ltd, followed by timber offices by Medway Buildings in 1968–9. The permanent complex, comprising a five-storey office block with gridded façades and square plan, and lower annexes, was commissioned in 1967 in a £3.5 million contract with Sir Robert McAlpine & Sons Ltd, and completed in 1970. More complex in its rationalistic governing concept was 'Centre 1' at East Kilbride, the prototype for an (in the event) unbuilt series of computerised tax centres. Completed in 1968 to the designs of R. Stevenson of the Ministry of Public Building and Works, Centre 1 comprised a 19-storey tower containing allocation units, and lower wings for processing of data; the juxtaposition of low and high blocks echoed the United Nations secretariat/assembly combination in a curious way. The heart of Centre 1 was not an assembly auditorium, however, but a huge ICT 1904 computer, fed by punched card and magnetic tape, which contained records of all two million employees and employers in Scotland. The Centre was seen by its designers as not just a soulless machine for producing data, but as a community of 1,600 people; its integrated social and sports facilities would pioneer 'new ideas on how people may work together'. It was replaced in 1992–4 by a four-storey brick building at the Peel Park Campus, designed by BDP Scotland, and the old building was demolished.[29]

The most innovative government complexes of those years were the least visible: the proliferation of command and monitoring centres built or adapted during the Cold War. Paradoxically, the most elaborate examples seem to date from the later years of the confrontation, at a time when the climate of wartime discipline across society as a whole had dissipated. In this account, we are not concerned with administration bunkers for exclusively military use, such as the naval command centre adjoining Pitreavie House in Fife, but with specialised postwar centres for civil purposes. However, many of the latter were originally constructed for military purposes in the 1940s and '50s and later converted. All these centres, whether for military or civil use, were generally similar in consisting of underground concrete structures with air-filtration, communications and other support systems.

Postwar civil defence bunkers fell into two main categories: firstly, emergency national and local government complexes controlling such services as rescue, food distribution and agricultural

TOP.
4.33. The 'Centre 1' Inland Revenue tower block at East Kilbride (designed by the Ministry of Public Building and Works architects), under construction in December 1966. (RCAHMS)

BELOW LEFT.
4.34. 1994 view of main entrance board at Centre 1, prior to its closure and relocation. (RCAHMS)

BELOW RIGHT.
4.35. 1994 view of 'SOVEX' paper lift system in operation in Centre 1: the system comprised swivelling buckets on a paternoster-lift principle. (RCAHMS C37395)

TOP.
4.36. Regional Government North Zone Headquarters, Troywood, Anstruther (originally built 1952 as early warning station): 1992 view of entrance pavilion. (RCAHMS C3308)

BELOW.
4.37. North Zone Headquarters, 1992 view of main underground conference room. (RCAHMS)

regeneration; and secondly, attack warning and monitoring centres. In the first category, that of emergency administration, after a number of interim arrangements immediately after the war, Scotland was from the late 1950s designated as a single 'home defence region', and was subdivided into north and south zones, either of which could serve as the national command centre. The North Zone headquarters was located at Troywood, near Anstruther. It was housed in a bunker originally built in 1952 by the RAF as part of 'ROTOR', a chain of early warning radar stations. Located in a concrete shell excavated 150 ft underground, the RAF bunker comprised a two-level operations room, reached by a 150m sloping access tunnel from a surface guardhouse, built in the style of a stone cottage. Redundant by 1958, the bunker was then taken over for civil defence purposes, and in 1968 was reconstructed as the North Zone HQ; it was subdivided by the Ministry of Works on behalf of the Scottish Office into two levels containing 23,000 sq ft of accommodation, subdivided into 51 rooms, with full nuclear, chemical and biological protection. These were to house some 300 personnel, including offices and dormitories for the Secretary of State, Minister of State, regional commissioner and senior civil servants, and broadcasting and communications facilities. The South Zone headquarters, at Camps, Kirknewton (near Edinburgh), was different in that much of its 42-room accommodation was above ground. Its original section, on the ground and basement floors, was built in the 1950s, while a two-storey block on the ground and first floors, containing extensive dormitories behind three-feet-thick

OPPOSITE TOP.
4.40. Official sign outside the Craigiebarns bunker: the facility was shared by the ROC and the UKWMO. (RCAHMS B74236)

OPPOSITE BELOW.
4.41. The main entrance to the UKWMO 30 Group regional headquarters at King Duncan's Road, Inverness (a refurbished RAF sector operations bunker), recorded in 1992 following closure. (RCAHMS B76008)

LEFT.
4.42. UKWMO HQ 30 Group, 1992 view of the upper level of the operations room. The small cabinet standing on the table in the centre of the photograph is an 'AWDREY' (Atomic Weapon Detection, Recognition and Estimation of Yield) electronic monitoring set. (UKWMO)

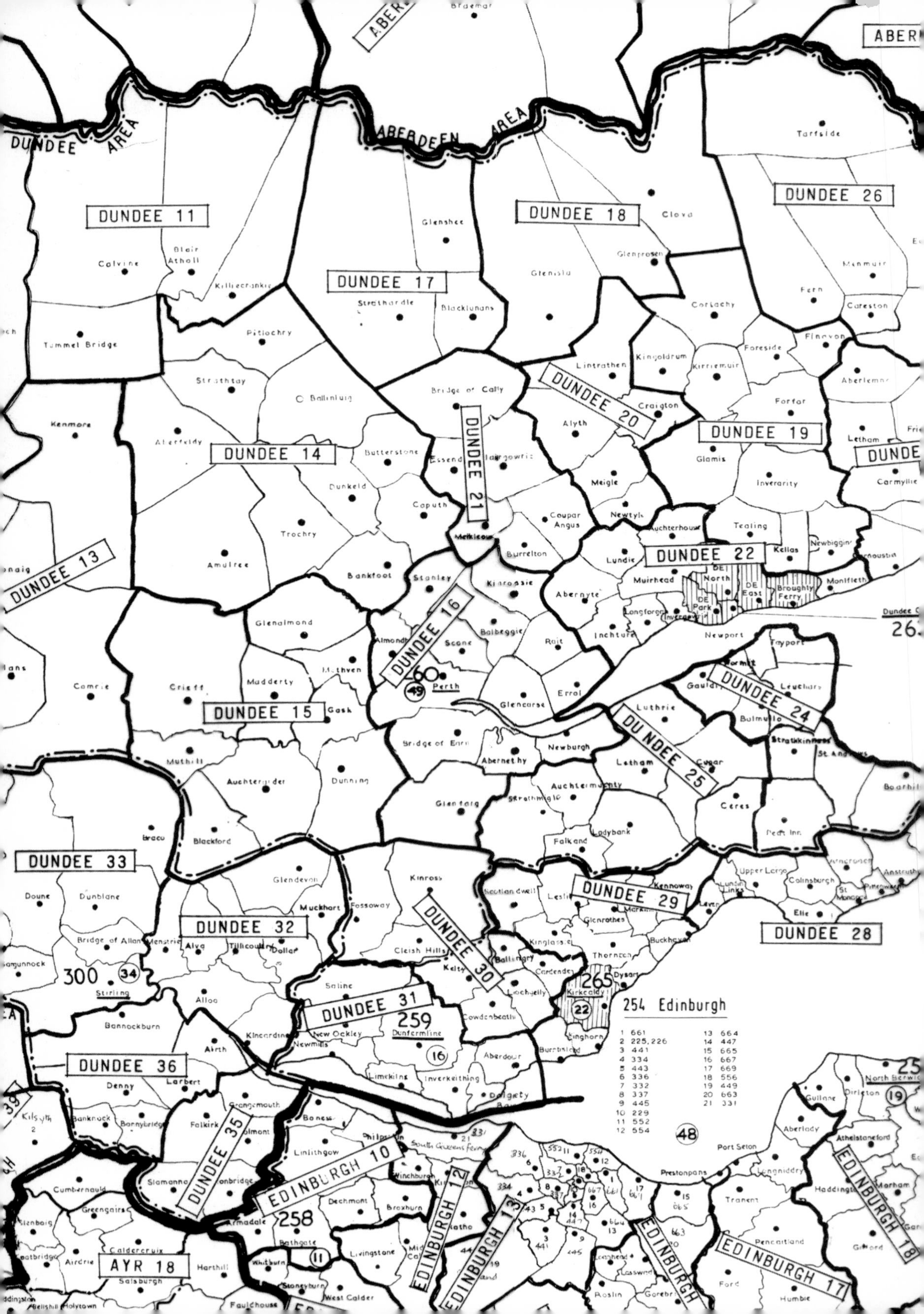
DUNDEE AREA
ABERDEEN AREA
DUNDEE 11
DUNDEE 13
DUNDEE 14
DUNDEE 15
DUNDEE 16
DUNDEE 17
DUNDEE 18
DUNDEE 19
DUNDEE 20
DUNDEE 21
DUNDEE 22
DUNDEE 24
DUNDEE 25
DUNDEE 26
DUNDEE 28
DUNDEE 29
DUNDEE 30
DUNDEE 31
DUNDEE 32
DUNDEE 33
DUNDEE 35
DUNDEE 36
EDINBURGH 10
EDINBURGH 12
EDINBURGH 13
EDINBURGH 17
EDINBURGH 18
AYR 18
Tarfside
Clova
Glenshee
Glenprosen
Glenisla
Calvine
Blair Atholl
Killiecrankie
Strathardle
Blacklunans
Cortachy
Menmuir
Fern
Careston
Tummel Bridge
Pitlochry
Kingoldrum
Kirriemuir
Foreside
Finavon
Lintrathen
Strathtay
Ballinluig
Bridge of Cally
Craigton
Forfar
Aberlemno
Kenmore
Aberfeldy
Alyth
Butterstone
Essendy
Blairgowrie
Glamis
Letham
Carmyllie
Dunkeld
Meigle
Inverarity
Caputh
Coupar Angus
Newtyle
Auchterhouse
Tealing
Newbigging
Trochry
Meikleour
Burrelton
Lundie
Kellas
Carnoustie
Amulree
Bankfoot
Stanley
Kinrossie
Muirhead
DE North
DE East
Broughty Ferry
Monifieth
Abernyte
Longforgan
DE Park
Invergowrie
Glenalmond
Almondbank
Balbeggie
Scone
Rait
Inchture
Newport
Tayport
Methven
Madderty
Crieff
Comrie
Gask
60
49
Perth
Glencarse
Errol
Gauldry
Forgan
Leuchars
Luthrie
Balmullo
Strathkinness
St Andrews
Muthill
Auchterarder
Dunning
Bridge of Earn
Abernethy
Newburgh
Letham
Cupar
Auchtermuchty
Strathmiglo
Glenfarg
Ceres
Peat Inn
Boarhills
Braco
Blackford
Falkland
Ladybank
Glendevon
Kinross
Upper Largo
Colinsburgh
Lundin Links
Kennoway
Leslie
Markinch
Scotlandwell
Doune
Dunblane
Muckhart
Fossoway
Glenrothes
Leven
Elie
St Monans
Pittenweem
Anstruther
Bridge of Allan
Menstrie
Alva
Tillicoultry
Dollar
Cleish Hills
Kinglassie
Buckhaven
Thornton
Ballingry
Kelty
Cardenden
Dysart
300
34
Stirling
Saline
Lochgelly
265
Kirkcaldy
22
Alloa
Cowdenbeath
259
Dunfermline
16
New Oakley
Newmills
Kincardine
Bannockburn
Airth
Kinghorn
Burntisland
Aberdour
Limekilns
Inverkeithing
Dalgety Bay
254 Edinburgh
1 661
2 225,226
3 441
4 334
5 443
6 336
7 332
8 337
9 445
10 229
11 552
12 554
13 664
14 447
15 665
16 667
17 669
18 556
19 449
20 663
21 331
48
Denny
Larbert
Grangemouth
Banknock
Bonnybridge
Falkirk
Polmont
Bo'ness
Kilsyth
Linlithgow
South Queensferry
Port Seton
Prestonpans
Longniddry
Gullane
Dirleton
North Berwick
19
Aberlady
Athelstaneford
Cumbernauld
Slamannan
Avonbridge
Winchburgh
Kirkliston
Tranent
Haddington
Morham
Greengairs
Dechmont
Broxburn
Glenboig
Armadale
258
Bathgate
11
Livingstone
Mid Calder
Ratho
Pencaitland
Gifford
Coatbridge
Airdrie
Caldercruix
Harthill
Salsburgh
Whitburn
Stoneyburn
West Calder
Fauldhouse
Loanhead
Lasswade
Roslin
Gorebridge
Ford
Humbie
Bellshill
Holytown

windowless concrete walls, was added in 1965. Following a 1980 review of civil defence, it was decided to replace these two bunkers by a new North Zone HQ at Cultybraggan, Perthshire, and a South Zone HQ at Peel Hospital. The former was constructed in 1989–91 by the Property Services Agency on a standard Home Office plan, but the latter was never built, owing to the end of the Cold War, which also prompted the closure and disposal of Cultybraggan, Kirknewton and Troywood; the latter was converted into a Cold War heritage centre, 'Scotland's Secret Bunker'. Operating in parallel with the central government command bunkers was a system of local-authority emergency centres under the control of county (after 1975, regional) councils; these were linked to each other and to the national centres by thier own private telephone network. The only fully hardened bunker was that of Inverness County Council at Raigmore, Inverness. Originally built in 1941–2 as a secret RAF 'radar filter' centre for the analysis and dissemination of radar data for Scotland and northern England, the two-level reinforced concrete complex was taken over in the 1950s by the county council; as recently as 1990–1 it was extensively reconstructed, including the insertion of an additional floor and NBC filters. Typical of non-hardened centres is Inverclyde Council's Emergency Planning Room, which simply occupies one of the large offices on the first floor of Greenock Municipal Buildings.[30]

The second category was that of the centres dedicated to the monitoring of, and direct response to, nuclear attack. This system was operated by two linked organisations, the United Kingdom Warning and Monitoring Organisation (UKWMO) and the Royal Observer Corps (ROC); the ROC was reformed in 1947 and the UKWMO was formed slightly later, and both organisations were eventually stood down in 1991–2. The UK monitoring network, controlled centrally by the Home Office, comprised 870 ROC monitoring posts, which reported to 25 'Group' centres (responsible for liaison with regional government and local authority bunkers); the latter in turn were grouped into five 'Sectors', charged with liaison with neighbouring countries. Scotland was covered by a single Sector Control, at Craigiebarns, Dundee, and four other regional centres at Ayr, Inverness, Aberdeen, and Turnhouse (Edinburgh). Indirectly linked to this system was the civil nuclear attack warning network of sirens, which was controlled by the UK Regional Air Operations Centre through some 250 'Carrier Control Posts' throughout Scotland,

4.43. Map of East Central Scotland, showing ROC warning posts. (UKWMO)

England and Wales; these posts would activate some 7,000 power-operated sirens (under police control) and some 11,000 hand-operated sirens, many located above ROC warning posts. The ROC underground posts, situated in clusters for triangulation purposes, were concrete chambers measuring 7ft by 16ft, and were mass-produced until the early 1970s on the model of a prototype built in 1956 in Surrey. The larger UKWMO centres, visible from the outside only by their concrete entrance and brick ventilators, were provided with measuring, meteorological and communications equipment, and a variety of illuminated charts for recording reports of fall-out and blast devastation; some were latterly also equipped with an 'AWDREY' (Atomic Weapon Detection, Recognition and Estimation of Yield) electronic monitoring cabinet. The UKWMO Caledonian Sector Control at Craigiebarns occupied an imposing two-level bunker immediately to the south of Craigiebarns House, and included the Tayside local authority emergency centre; the Inverness regional UKWMO centre was located in a refurbished RAF sector operations bunker at Raigmore, almost adjacent to the local-authority command centre.

FROM ASSEMBLY TO PARLIAMENT

The economic crises of the late 1960s and early '70s culminated in the 1976 calls by the International Monetary Fund for state spending cuts. These progressively undermined the cohesion of the social state that had replaced the Empire as a British focus for the affections of Scots. And the same years saw a growing scepticism across the West about the mass mobilisation model of representative democracy, with its oligarchic reliance on the rule of experts. The system had succeeded in delivering the things it had promised – new homes, social provisions and material goods – but that success had exposed it as obsolete. The reaction in Scotland was not rioting, but a sudden upsurge in constitutional nationalism. Gradually, 'democracy' was redefined so as to play down the aim of equality, as defined by class politics, and to emphasise that of freedom, in terms both of individuals in relation to the state, and of Scotland in relation to the UK. In response to the rise of the Scottish National Party, the Conservative and Labour parties set about an immediate revival of the dormant idea of legislative home rule, to complement the vast array of administrative powers already devolved. In 1968, Edward Heath's 'Declaration of Perth' committed the Tories to legislative devolution, and in 1974, following the 1973 report of the Kilbrandon Committee, Labour endorsed the idea of a new assembly. After an abortive first bill was talked out at Westminster in 1977, a second and more comprehensive bill was passed in July 1978, and only failed at a referendum in March 1979 when the voting hurdle was raised from 50% of votes cast to 40% of the total electorate. Under these proposals, the assembly would have assumed oversight of the existing administrative departments of the Scottish Office, while the latter, along with the Secretary of State, would have been detached and reduced in scope to become an arbitration and liaison agency with Whitehall and Westminster.

During the period from 1977, architecture was suddenly pitched into the midst of these debates, when it was realised that a home for the new assembly would quickly have to be found. That call came at a time, in the wake of the crisis of the Modern Movement, when the reputation of new architecture was at an all-time low, and the victory of conservation seemed complete. Nor was there enough time to build a new building; and thus it was a foregone conclusion that the assembly would be housed in a redundant historic building. The use of historic monuments for government purposes had already been presaged when, in 1966, the National Trust for Scotland was bequeathed 5-7 Charlotte Square, Edinburgh, part of Robert Adam's north-side terrace, on the death of the 5th Marquess of Bute, and no. 6 was passed to the government to become the official residence of the Secretary of State. And over the following decades, the colonisation of Edinburgh New Town by government agencies continued apace.

Rapidly, the choice for the assembly site fell on Thomas Hamilton's Royal High School building on the flank of Calton Hill, a complex, tiered Grecian composition dominated by a porticoed hall, and recently vacated when the school moved out to a modern building in the suburbs of Edinburgh. The Royal High School was ideally situated opposite St Andrew's House, which would become the executive office of the assembly. New St Andrew's House would remain the administrative nerve centre, but the rump Scottish Office and the Secretary of State would leave it for offices elsewhere in town. Inside the Royal High School assembly hall, the essentials of the neoclassical decoration were left intact: the shallow coffered ceiling,

RIGHT.
4.44. Royal High School, Edinburgh (Thomas Hamilton, 1825–9): 1895 view of assembly hall from south. (RCAHMS B64276)

OPPOSITE TOP.
4.45. Royal High School, the assembly hall seen from south in October 1979, following conversion work for use by the abortive devolved assembly. (RCAHMS)

OPPOSITE BELOW.
4.46. Royal High School, 1979 detail of presiding officer's chair. (RCAHMS)

tiered seats, galleries on iron columns with branched capitals, and the gilded anthemion railing. The side galleries were extended on a curved plan across the south end, but the general arrangement of the seating below, with high-backed continuous benches, was retained, as was the railed enclosure in the centre. Modern seating was substituted for the original seats, in an exaggeratedly geometrical style with slightly Pop-Art overtones, seen at its most marked in the speaker's chair; the resulting seating-plan was not dissimilar to the elongated 'U' layout of the Victoria Hall. The woodwork in the hall was renewed and left unpainted, with the pitch-pine exposed. This modest conversion project should be seen in the context of other contemporary debating chambers formed out of historic buildings: for instance, the conversion of the Swedish parliament from a bicameral to a unicameral system in 1971 was accommodated by building a new chamber above the roof of part of the existing complex (in 1974–83, designed by Ahlgren, Olsson and Silow).

The failure of the devolution referendum would defer home rule for nearly two decades, during which time the Conservative government of 1979–97 effectively dismantled the social-democratic state. As part of this retrenchment process, the Scottish Office was cut

back and reorientated from direct service provision to coordination; its staff numbers fell within a decade by 20% from their maximum of 11,000 in 1976. The collapse of the grand regional planning policies, however, was offset by an expansion of attempts to attract inward investment through the Scottish Development Agency. The policy which most directly undermined the old social-nation identity was the new confrontation between government and local authorities, and the curbs on the latter's activities and autonomy.

For the first decade of Conservative administration, the home rule cause remained despondent and relatively quiescent; efforts were largely channelled through the Campaign for a Scottish Assembly, founded in 1980 by Labour activist Jim Boyack and others. With the precipitate decline in the Conservative vote in the 1987 election, separating Scotland in effect from the Westminster two-party system, the Campaign began to gather momentum, and it appointed a constitutional steering committee chaired by the former chief government planner, Sir Robert Grieve. At the instigation of that committee, a document entitled *A Claim of Right for Scotland* was prepared in 1988, and a Scottish Constitutional Convention, representing a wide cross-section of political, social and civic groups, was called on 30 March 1989 to ratify it. Significantly, this first meeting of the Convention was held in the General Assembly Hall on the Mound, built originally by the Free Church as part of their own struggle to defend the doctrine of the 'two kingdoms'. The three Claims of Right, spaced out with coincidental evenness – 1689, 1842, 1989 – all presented themselves as protests against unjust rule, in the tradition of Greek and Roman constitutionalism. The 1689 Claim had opposed the tyranny of absolute monarchy, and the 1842 Claim had opposed the tyranny of the temporal over the spiritual. Now the 1989 Claim argued that the doctrine of absolute British parliamentary sovereignty was unjust, both in general and in relation to the Scottish nation in particular. It violated 'the sovereign right of the Scottish people to determine the form of government best suited to their needs'. In contrast to the entire Reform and representative democracy movement, and the class politics of socialism, this was not an argument about social inequality, to be answered by widening the franchise; indeed, it resembled more than anything else the charges made by opponents of fifth-century Athenian democracy, that the *demos* had become a collective tyrant. 'Democracy', as an overriding aim, had now been redefined to mean

TOP.
4.47. The Scottish Constitutional Convention's 30 March 1989 ratification meeting in the Church of Scotland (former Free Church) Assembly Hall, Edinburgh. (*Scotsman*)

BELOW.
4.48. At the March 1989 SCC meeting, the joint chairmen, Harry Ewing and David Steel, add their signatures to the 1988 Claim of Right. (*Scotsman*)

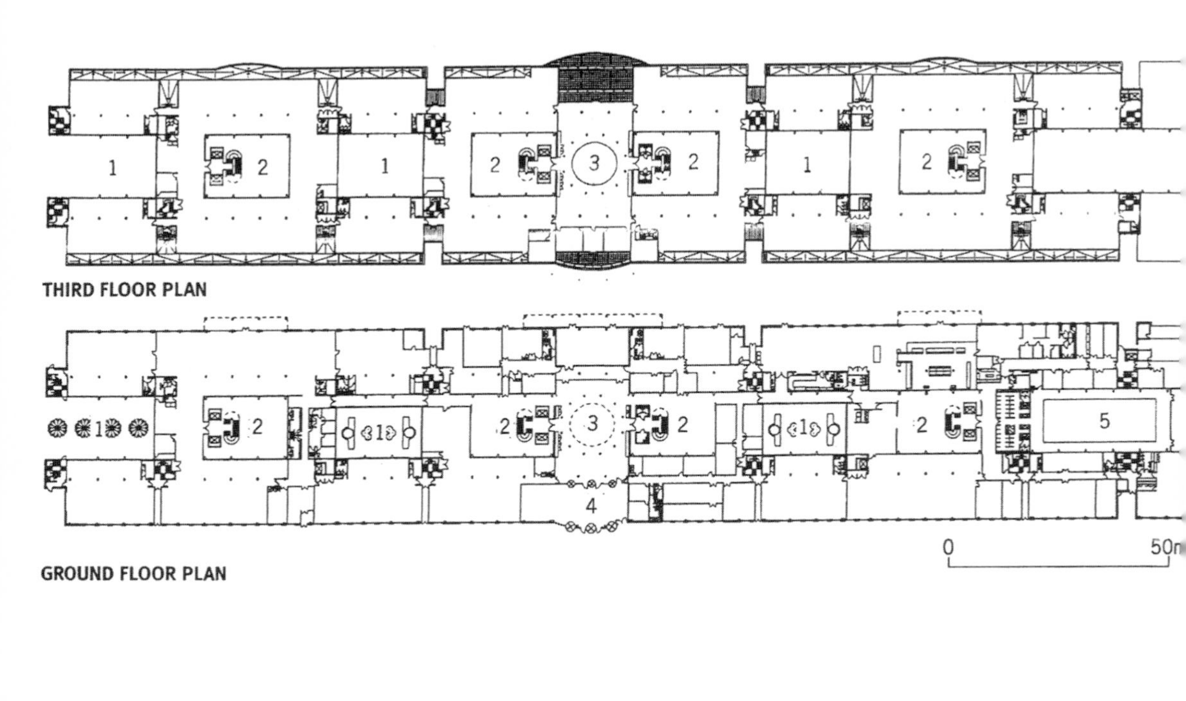

THIRD FLOOR PLAN

GROUND FLOOR PLAN

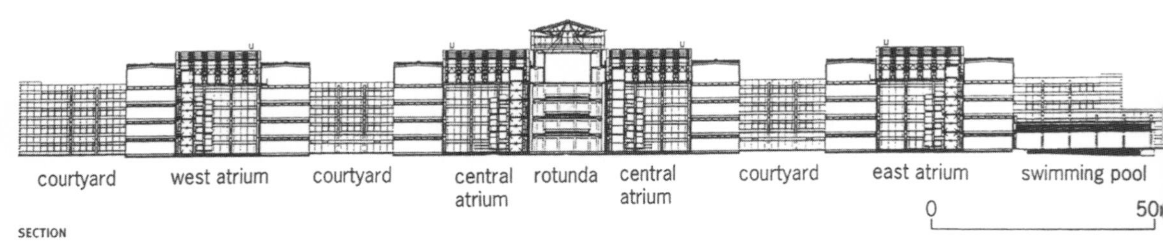

SECTION

freedom rather than equality. With this heritage in mind, Canon Kenyon Wright, executive chair of the Constitutional Convention, recalled with emotion that day in the General Assembly Hall, as the Convention members lined up to sign the Claim of Right: 'I had a strange sense that I was surrounded, not just by the many hundreds present in the Assembly Hall, but by a "cloud of witnesses" from the past'.[31]

From that point onwards, protest changed quickly to action, the aim now being defined no longer as an 'Assembly' but as a 'Parliament'. Although confidence was again dented by the result of the 1992 Westminster elections, work continued and, by the end of 1995, a detailed blueprint for legislative devolution in 29 areas of government had been drawn up, entitled *Scotland's Parliament: Scotland's Right. A Report to the People of Scotland by the Scottish Constitutional Convention.* On St Andrew's Day 1995, the report was received with acclamation and signed at a meeting in the General Assembly Hall, the first since March 1989. It was hailed by Rev. Andrew McLellan, Convener of the Church and Nation Committee of the Kirk, as a product of 'the best kind of nationalism, that knows how to love our own nation more without loving other nations less'.[32]

During all this time of nervous debate and energetic preparation, the architecture of Scottish government maintained a somewhat schizophrenic character. In the practical sphere, radical changes were underway, to sustain the apparatus of administrative devolution in good working order. Exasperated by the growing problems of New St Andrew's House, especially the need to strip out large quantities of asbestos, the Scottish Office decided to evacuate it, and, in 1993, began building a new and much larger building at Victoria Quay, overlooking Leith docks – a step which maintained the momentum of urban regeneration in Leith at a time of market recession. This project was a pioneer in the use of private-sector mechanisms in government building. The site was selected through a competition between developers, and the winning consortium (Victoria Quay Ltd) appointed the architects, RMJM (Robert Matthew's old firm) and the management contractor, Trafalgar House Construction Management Edinburgh; the building took only 21 months to construct and cost a total of £47m. It has an essentially Modernist linear or 'ladder' plan organised around a continuous internal 'street', along which are disposed semi-autonomous blocks of offices, each comprising

TOP.
4.49. Ground-floor plan and third-floor plan of Victoria Quay government complex, by RMJM (1993–4). Key: (1) courtyard; (2) atrium; (3) rotunda; (4) entrance hall; (5) swimming pool. (Scottish Executive)

BELOW.
4.50. Victoria Quay, sectional view along the length of the building. (Scottish Executive)

shallow-plan office accommodation grouped around a covered atrium, to promote departmental cohesion. As built, there are three of these blocks, containing a total of 36,000 sq.m of floor-space, but the site has space for another to be added at the western end; the central block is wider than the others, with two atria flanking a rotunda-topped hall stretching the full depth of the building. The building is organised so that the northern (quayside) façade is private to its staff, while the public entrance faces south, with 650 car parking spaces. Common user space serving all departments is at ground level; the first and second floors contain office space, and the third floor is designed as a mixture of glazed pavilions and terraces.

One of the central themes of the Victoria Quay project was a concern for energy efficiency and use of natural lighting and ventilation, exploiting the thermal mass for insulation and free cooling. The main structure of the Victoria Quay building, which is planned on a 1.5m grid, is reinforced concrete frame and precast floor units. Externally, it is clad with precast concrete by Trent Concrete Ltd; this is expressed in a pilaster-like pattern on the north façade and fronted by spindly two-storey columns on the south. The architectural effect is one of a repetitive and monumental Postmodern classicism, cloaking the modern plan and interior, and echoing St Andrew's House in its stepped-back profile. Chief project architect Michael Duncan described it as 'classically ordered both in plan and section'.[33]

On its completion in 1995, around 1400 Scottish Office staff moved to Victoria Quay from New St Andrew's House and other scattered offices, leaving around 450 staff of the Home Department at Saughton House, and 600 of the Agriculture and Fisheries Department at Pentland House, both on the western outskirts of Edinburgh. At almost the same time, the Industry Department moved out of its quarters in a dilapidated 1971 office block in central Glasgow, Alhambra House, to a newly built Postmodern complex nearby, Meridian House. These changes left St Andrew's House substantially under-occupied, with only about 500 resident staff, active occupation being concentrated in the central block, with its third-floor conference suite and fifth-floor ministerial corridor. New St Andrew's House, once emptied, was refurbished, renamed St James House, and then, in September 1999, bought by the Royal Bank of Scotland.[34] Dover House, by contrast, was unaffected, its role as a liaison post with Whitehall and Westminster remaining as important

as ever. By now, it was far more crowded than it had been in the late nineteenth century; the main Paine block was occupied by five ministerial rooms and computer-crammed private offices, along with the Permanent Secretary's room, while the flanking wings stretching south to Whitehall, and running behind the screen wall, contained support functions, including press office, post room, computer room, conference room and gymnasium.

Alongside all this building work for day-to-day government, the architectural symbolism of the constitutional debate existed in a strange state of suspended animation. The Royal High School remained the focus of the home-rule cause, and its classical architecture began to assume a symbolic role: for example, the logo of the Campaign for a Scottish Parliament was a seven-columned Grecian portico. In 1994, Edinburgh City Council bought the building at a cost of £1.8m and renamed it 'New Parliament House', and the eleventh meeting of the Constitutional Convention was held there. Increasingly Calton Hill, whose monuments once symbolised Scottish devotion to the Empire, began to be viewed as a beacon of constitutional Scottish nationalism. Following the 1992 general election, the protest group 'Democracy for Scotland' began a vigil

4.51. 1997 view of the 'Democracy Hut', a portakabin erected in April 1992 in Regent Road, Edinburgh, opposite St Andrew's House, to house a vigil in protest against the deferral of home rule. The hut (provided with the aid of funding from Scottish Trades Union Congress secretary Bill Speirs) was staffed continuously from then until the 1997 referendum which approved the Constitutional Convention's home-rule scheme; the vigil ended on 12 September 1997. (The People's Story Museum) opposite St Andrew's House, with a Portakabin hut, posters and signs, a vigil that was continuously maintained for five years until the 1997 election. In 1991, historian Michael Lynch had inconclusively compared the role of St Andrew's House to the seventeenth-century confrontations of Lauderdale with Parliament: 'Two impressions are possible: that this was another Dublin Castle, or that it allowed a unique measure of autonomy to the conduct of Scottish government – although the same could have been said of Dublin Castle before 1922'.

By summer 1997, all those issues seemed to have been settled. The May general election had brought to power a Westminster administration pledged to deliver home rule, and on September 11th the overwhelming 74% vote in the referendum made it certain that this aspiration would at last become a reality.[35] As it turned out, however, those decisions ushered in not an era of predictability and monotony, but one of the the most turbulent periods in the architectural history of Scottish government.

NOTES

1. *Hansard* (House of Commons), 24 November 1932, 272, column 267.
2. D.S. Forsyth, *Scottish Geographical Magazine*, January 1997; R.J. Findlay, *Partnership for Good. Municipal Glasgow*, 7. *The Evergreen*, Spring/Autumn 1895.
3. *Scotsman*, 17 January 1884; Gibson, *Thistle and the Crown*, 24; Forsyth, *Scottish Geographical Magazine*.
4. Gibson, *Thistle and the Crown*, 24–5, 43; N. Pevsner, B. Cherry, *London*, i, London, 1985 edition, 543; London County Council, *Survey of London*, volume 24, London, 1931, 56–7.
5. Corporation of Glasgow, *Glasgow*, Glasgow, 1938, 21.
6. D.M. Walker, *St Andrew's House*, Edinburgh, 1989, 7.
7. Pevsner and Cherry, *London*, i, 548–9.
8. C.W. Hill, *Edwardian Scotland*, Totowa (New Jersey), 1976, 158.
9. Report of the Royal Commission on the Housing of the Industrial Population of Scotland (Ballantyne Report), Edinburgh, 1917, Cd 8731, 6.
10. R. Home, *Of Planting and Planning*, London, 1997.
11. S.W. Carruthers, *The Scottish Church Union*, Edinburgh, 1929; R.W.A. Begg, *The Renovation of Kippen Parish Church*, Kippen, 1991 edition, 9.
12. *Hansard*, 272, columns 235–360.
13. Gibson, *Thistle and the Crown*, 72.
14. M. Lynch, *Scotland, a New History*, Edinburgh, 1991, 442.
15. See also Ian Levitt, 'New Towns, New Scotland, New Ideology', *Scottish Historical Review*, October 1997 (interpretation of Cumbernauld as expression of Tory anti-municipal market reformism).
16. S. Inglis, *The Football Grounds of Great Britain*, London, 1987, 297, 293, 301.

17. *Country Life*, 5 February 1938; J. Ritter, *Architectural Review*, July 1964.
18. Walker, *St Andrew's House.*
19. Walker, *St Andrew's House*, 39, 51; D. Caswell, 'The Economy of Style', *Architectural Heritage*, x, 1999, 74–89.
20. Walker, *St Andrew's House*, 61.
21. P. Kinchin and J. Kinchin, *Glasgow's Great Exhibitions*, Wendlebury, 1988, 150–2; G.F. Maine (ed.), *Scotland's Welcome*, Glasgow, 1938; *Daily Record*, 29 August 1938; Home Board of the Church of Scotland, *The Church of Scotland, Empire Exhibition 1938*, Edinburgh, 1938.
22. A. Bartos and C. Hitchens, *International Territory*, London, 1994, 14.
23. *The Builder*, 7 December 1956, 966–8; Professor B. Ward, *Cambridge Daily News*, 17 June 1954; M. Webb, *Architecture in Britain Today*, London, 1969, 206–8.
24. H.N. Dollimore, *The Parliament of New Zealand and Parliament House*, Wellington, 1973 edition; B. Bowden, *Parliament and the People*, Wellington, 1984; K. Jackson, *The Dilemma of Parliament*, Wellington, 1987. *Architectural Review*, September 1971; J.C. Loeffler, *The Architecture of Diplomacy*, Princeton, 1998.
25. *The Builder*, 28 March 1963, 1322; *The Builder*, 4 September 1964, 471–4; County Council of Lanark, *Lanarkshire Official Handbook*, 1964, 3, 9–10. *Prospect*, 19, 1960.
26. Edinburgh City Council, City Archives, Dean of Guild records, 6 May 1969; O. Marriott, *The Property Boom*, London, 1967, 75–81, 149–57, 303.
27. D. Cowling, *An Essay For Today*, Edinburgh, 1997; R. Smith, *East Kilbride*, London, 1979.
28. M. Glendinning (ed.), *Rebuilding Scotland*, East Linton, 1997, 87–92.
29. *Building*, 14 July 1967; Inland Revenue, *An Introduction to Centre 1*, London, 1968; *Architect's Journal*, 27 April 1995.
30. *Glasgow Herald*, 26 February 1993; *Evening News* (Edinburgh), 6 March 1993; information from Maurice Wilson, Scottish Executive Justice Department; *Scotland's Secret Bunker*, 1994; information from Grant Horsley, Highland Council Emergency Planning Officer, and Brian Purdie, Inverclyde Council.
31. K. Wright, *The People Say Yes*, Glendaruel, 1997, 54; O.D. Edwards, *A Claim of Right for Scotland*, Edinburgh, 1989; Wright, *The People say Yes*, 14.
32. Wright, *The People Say Yes*, 224.
33. *Architect's Journal*, 7 December 1995; *Building Design*, 29 March 1996; *Prospect*, Autumn 1995.
34. *Scotsman*, 10 January 1998.
35. Lynch, *Scotland, A New History*, 435; L. Paterson, *A Diverse Assembly*, Edinburgh, 1998; *Scottish Affairs*, Winter 1998, 1–15.

CHAPTER FIVE

Towards a New Parliament

Miles Glendinning

Scotland is a land . . . it is not a series of cities . . .
The people, the parliament sit in the land.
Enric Miralles Benedetta Tagliabue Architects, June 1998[1]

Scotland's new Parliament is a chamber of wonders on a scale not seen since the death of Antoni Gaudí almost a century ago.
Marcus Binney, 2004[1]

INTRODUCTION

Following the decisive change of government in May 1997, there began rapid preparations to draw up a scheme of Scottish parliamentary home rule. In its White Paper, *Scotland's Parliament*, published in July, the incoming government outlined a scheme of legislative devolution based substantially on the 1995 conclusions of the Scottish Constitutional Convention. The new Parliament would comprise 129 members, elected for a four-year fixed term, and made up of 73 territorial constituency representatives and 56 additional members selected from party lists. Its powers would take in all areas of government other than the strategic areas reserved for Westminster, such as foreign policy, defence, macro-economic affairs, employment, and social security. The new legislature would assume responsibility for the areas now controlled by the Scottish Office (law and home affairs, health, education, local government, housing, economic development, environment, transport, agriculture and fisheries), including some 12,000 staff in these departments and other public bodies.

In contrast to the 1978 devolution package, with its vice-regal status for the Secretary of State, administrative devolution was now to be transformed into legislative devolution in a neater way. The scope of the Parliament would correspond with that of the new Scottish Executive and its departments; in most respects this government would simply be the Scottish Office renamed, and preserving the subordination of the constituent departments within a corporate whole. This constitutional position of domestic autonomy alongside external Westminster powers was in some respects novel, but it also had some features in common with the seventeenth-century constitution, with the doctrine of absolute parliamentary sovereignty replacing the claimed authority of the absolute monarchy. In international terms, the complexity of this system fitted in well with the growing rejection of the nineteenth- and twentieth-century concept of the unitary state and the single, symbolic national parliament, with its dramatic conflicts of class politics. In this account, we cannot describe in any detail the workings of the new governmental and parliamentary system of home rule; readers are referred to the numerous recent publications on the subject.[2]

CALTON HILL TO HOLYROOD: SELECTING THE SITE

Within days of their accession to office, the new government realised that the generally accepted identification of the Royal High School as the future home of the Scottish Parliament would not be easy to translate into reality, and at the same time began the process of trying to turn that difficulty to advantage, by beginning to investigate the possibility of a completely new building. The practical problem lay in the small size of the High School building and the unsuitability of the converted debating chamber, especially for disabled access; what had been tailor-made for the limited assembly of the 1978 proposals seemed inadequate now. As early as 1992, Edinburgh architect Roger Emmerson had highlighted that problem, in a project commissioned by the National Union of Civil and Public Servants as a memorial to

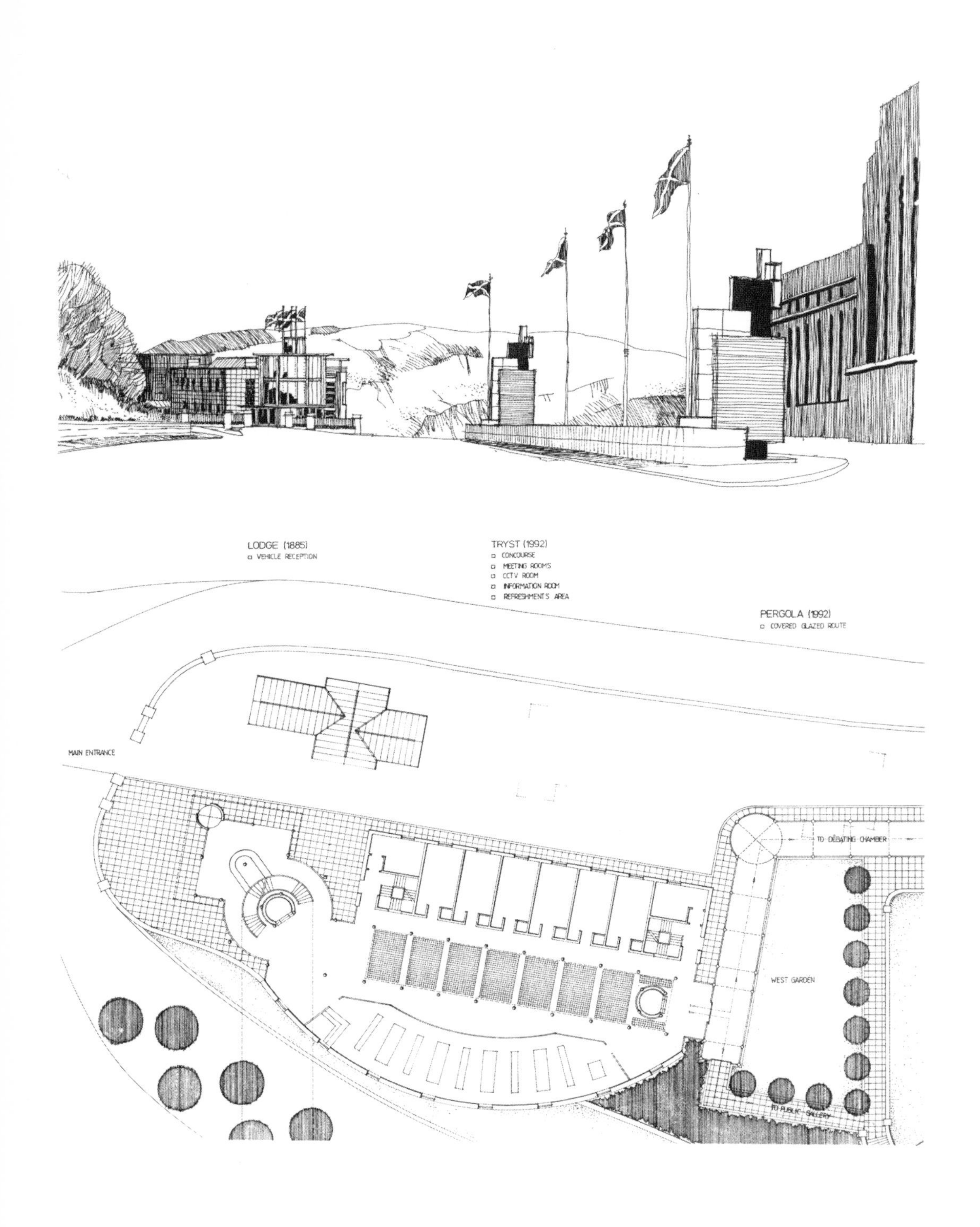

LODGE (1885)
VEHICLE RECEPTION
TRYST (1992)
CONCOURSE
MEETING ROOMS
CCTV ROOM
INFORMATION ROOM
REFRESHMENTS AREA
PERGOLA (1992)
COVERED GLAZED ROUTE
MAIN ENTRANCE
TO DEBATING CHAMBER
WEST GARDEN
TO PUBLIC GALLERY

home-rule activist Jim Boyack. Emmerson had suggested extending Hamilton's building with a new three-storey public reception block, linked at the east end to the High School and at the south-west, by tunnel under Regent Road, to the office accommodation of St Andrew's House. The 'symbolic, urban, and actual' focus of the new building, and the crossroads of public and members' access routes, would have been a glazed circular pavilion, 'The Tryst'. Emmerson's project raised the general issues of parliament architecture that would preoccupy so many people in due course, including the tension between monumentality and accessibility, and the relationships between public and parliamentarians, and between new buildings and old.[3] At the same time, the Scottish Office architects team was maintaining a watching brief on possible future sites for a devolved parliament (a task first set, surprisingly, in 1984), and Forth Ports had commissioned two proposals for parliament complexes on land reserved in Leith (including one scheme of 1994-5 by Holmes Partnership).

In May 1997, the government responded to the High School problem by raising the possibility of housing the Parliament on another site, and the Secretary of State within weeks took the key decision that any new building would have to be in Edinburgh. This made the option appraisal process simpler, and, in collaboration with the City Council, the Scottish Office architects began evaluating over thirty alternative locations, including Edinburgh historic buildings

OPPOSITE TOP.
5.1. 1992 proposal for a Parliament public-reception extension to the Royal High School. (R Emmerson)

OPPOSITE BELOW.
5.2. Plan of the proposed public-reception pavilion proposed by Emmerson. (R Emmerson)

ABOVE.
5.3. 1997 feasibility study for 'Parliament quarter' at Victoria Quay, Leith, prepared for Forth Ports PLC by architects CD Partnership: the Parliament building is the circular structure at centre. (RCAHMS/ Scottish Executive)

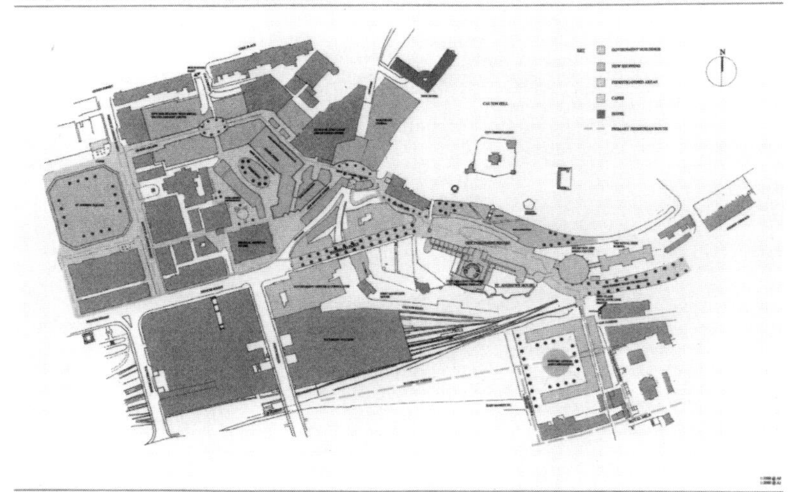

ABOVE. 5.4. 1997 feasibility plan by EDI for Calton Hill Parliament quarter, including chamber in the south courtyard of St Andrew's House. (RCAHMS/ Scottish Executive)

OPPOSITE TOP. 5.5. The December 1997 Parliament site studies: Benson & Forsyth's layout for the Leith site. (RCAHMS/ Scottish Executive)

OPPOSITE BELOW. 5.6. Section of Benson & Forsyth's proposal, with conical parliament chamber at the right. (RCAHMS/ Scottish Executive)

such as Donaldson's Hospital and the City Chambers. At first, it was generally assumed that the solution must necessarily be a refurbished or extended old building, but a number of commentators, led by Edinburgh architect Richard Murphy, began to suggest that a completely new building would provide a clearer symbol of the aspirations of the new Scottish democracy. From June onwards, three strands were actively pursued by the Scottish Office project team: development of the building brief; selection of the site; and development of a strategy for an architectural competition. Over the following month, the already-established concept of building a completely new parliament on a Leith site adjacent to Victoria Quay, possibly under a private finance arrangement similar to the Scottish Office complex, was revived and publicised by the Forth Ports harbour company, as an option which would combine administrative convenience with urban regeneration benefits. The architects CD Partnership prepared an initial proposal for the company, envisaging a 'parliament quarter' or 'compound' which would embrace the Victoria Quay offices and a drum-shaped parliament building to its north-west, adjoined by two new squares, an ocean terminal building and the royal yacht *Britannia*, and a miscellany of other structures of a mixed commercial/residential character.

Immediately, however, this proposal for a new parliament in Leith attracted strong opposition. This came from two by no means identical groupings: the home rule activists, who were wedded to

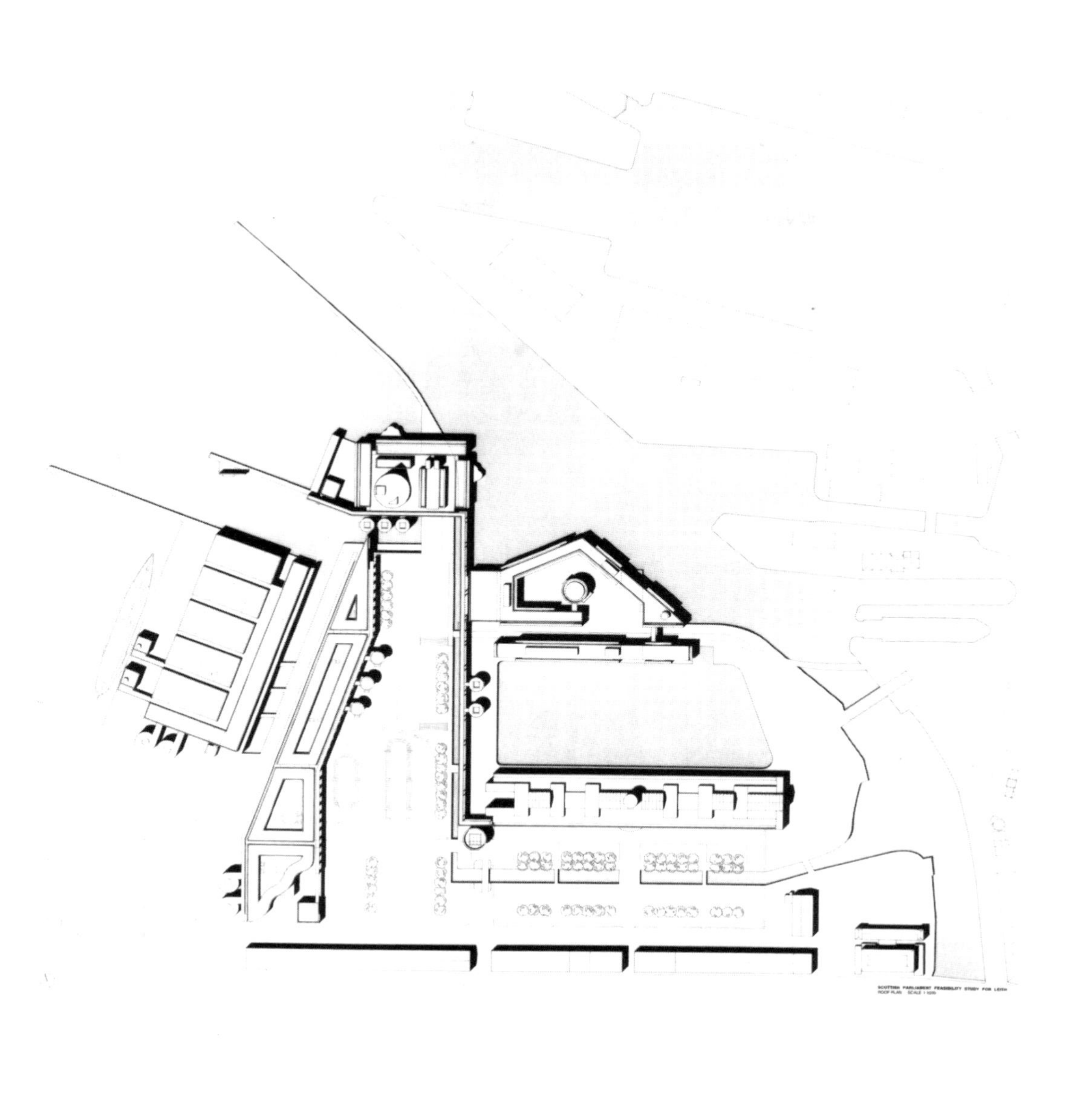
SCOTTISH PARLIAMENT FEASIBILITY STUDY FOR LEITH
ROOF PLAN SCALE

Calton Hill as a symbol of post-1979 radicalism, and the Edinburgh cultural establishment, who were opposed to the devolution of any cultural assets from the city centre. In their opposition to the Leith site, the two groups argued that Calton Hill was a unique microcosm of Scottish Enlightenment values, including the 'democratic intellect' tradition and European cosmopolitanism. The debate also began to take on economic overtones of competition between regeneration locations, when the municipal development company EDI put forward a counter-plan focusing on Calton Hill, and including extensive upgrading of the somewhat decayed areas immediately to the west and south. The focus of the pro-Calton Hill campaign subtly shifted from the High School building itself to the site. Under this plan, which developed and enlarged the 1992 Emmerson concept, the parliament would now be located within St Andrew's House; a debating chamber would be inserted in the central courtyard, taking the form of a massive drum (like that of the Leith proposal). The High School would be converted into committee rooms, with a circular media centre attached, while associated government offices would be located in the redundant Post Office complex above Waverley Station. In early November 1997, to test the outline building brief it had developed, the Scottish Office postponed the decision on the parliament site and commissioned three contrasting architectural practices to carry out feasibility studies; each was to study a particular location and produce a costed outline proposal. Benson & Forsyth, architects of the Museum of Scotland project then under construction in the Old Town, were asked to examine the Leith site. RMJM Scotland, architects of Victoria Quay, were assigned a cleared site in Morrison Street, conveniently close to Haymarket Station (a site originally suggested by developer Kantel and architect MacDonald Orr). Glasgow architects Page & Park, designers of the Lighthouse architecture centre and masterplanners of the Glasgow 1999 Homes for the Future area, were asked to evaluate the St Andrew's House proposal adumbrated by EDI. At the same time, in the background, a fourth site was being looked at closely: the Scottish and Newcastle brewery headquarters at Holyrood Road, opposite the front of Holyrood Palace. It had been one of the large batch of sites initially considered, but had been rejected at that stage because it seemed unlikely to be available before 2004. During September, however, the Scottish Office became aware (partly through a chance encounter on an Edinburgh-Glasgow train between a commercial chartered surveyor, John Clement, and civil servants) that the site was now available with a far earlier entry. In early December, therefore, the Holyrood site – which was privately favoured by Donald Dewar – was also made public and assigned as a study option to RMJM, alongside the less favoured Haymarket option.[4]

How was the architectural world prepared for this emerging opportunity? Back in the 1970s, at the time of the assembly referendum, the ascendancy of conservation had almost eclipsed the prestige of new architecture, and the most ambitious new Scottish public building, the Burrell Collection in Glasgow (1971-83, by B. Gasson, B. Andreson and J. Meunier) had actively effaced itself in a wood. But after the 1980s, the world of architecture recovered its optimism, and a new, overtly capitalistic, 'image-conscious' approach emerged. At first, this took the decorative form of 'Postmodernism', but later, from the late 1990s, there was a growing revival of the forms of 'Modern architecture'. This new Modernism drew only selectively on the many aspects of its mid-century predecessor. Where the original Modern Movement emphasised social egalitarianism alongside the poetic genius of individual master designers, the new Modernism was only concerned with the latter. This approach was combined with other ideas previously associated with opposition to Modernism, such as the reverence for historic or landscape 'context', the stress on environmental sustainability, and the insistence on user participation. The 'deconstructivism' of the early 1990s, a branch of a cultural and literary movement opposed to the idea of objective values and certainties, revived the exploded forms of the early twentieth-century Expressionist avant-garde. Yet paradoxically, alongside this emphasis on intense creativity, the overall social and economic context of architecture was dominated ever more strongly by market capitalism, with its tendency to reduce everything to a commodity. Architecture always, by definition, reflects to some extent the interests of the ruling power; but now architectural choices could be defined more precisely by their positioning on a scale of commodification and commercialism. This new relationship swallowed up some of the older defining polarities of architecture, such as the artistic and the pragmatic, the new and the old, the national and the cosmopolitan.[5]

In this disorientating context, the dilemma of the government architecture of modern representative democracy, always torn between

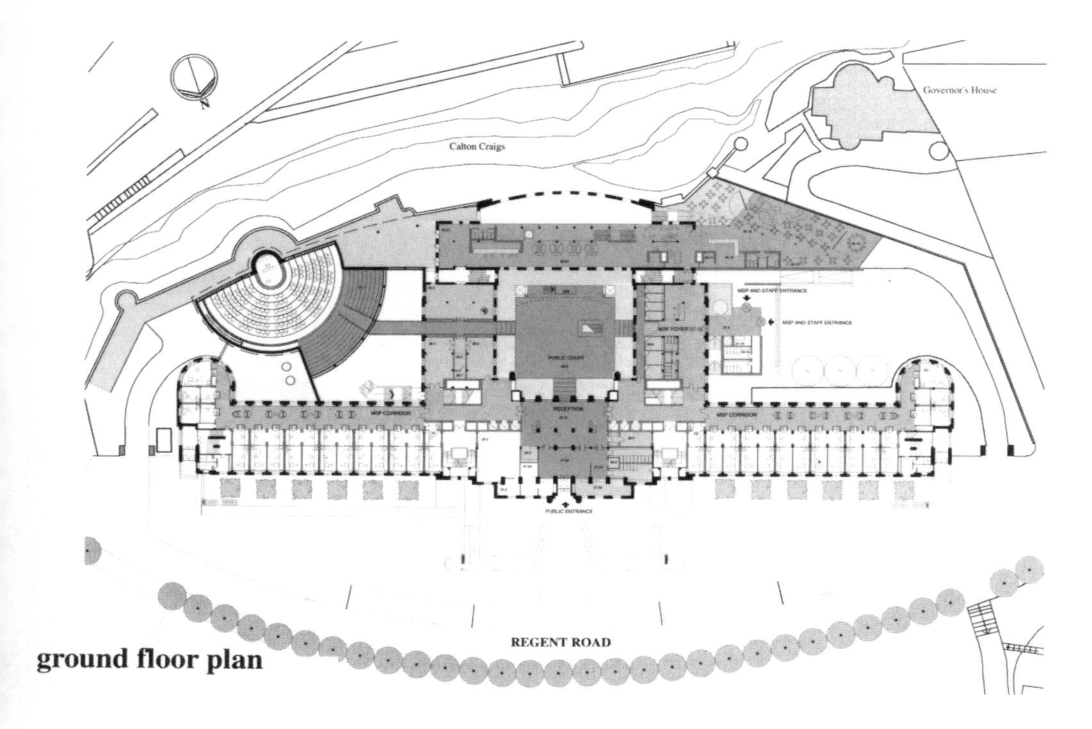

5.7. The December 1997 site studies: ground floor plan of Page & Park's study for St Andrew's House. (RCAHMS/ Scottish Executive)

celebrating and concealing state authority, became more acute than ever. On the one hand, all styles associated with open dominance or 'authentic' ideals were now discredited. This applied to soaring Modernist towers as much as to 'fascist' grand classicism. And it also applied to buildings' internal organisation, where all strongly hierarchical or ordered plans now seemed highly suspect. Yet post-structuralist theory and commodification had also destroyed the credibility of *anti*-authoritarian and avant-garde alternatives. A modern parliament building now faced the task of celebrating 'empowerment' and identity, the task of chipping away at the old-style monolith of the representative-democratic national legislature, without any generally accepted symbols or architectural means of doing so. Within the historic capitals of Europe, the most common response to this quandary was a formula which combined transparency of a literal kind, through the use of glass and the juxtaposition of public and politicians, with a respectful re-use of old buildings. Yet the old structures re-used in this way had themselves originally been bound up with systems of power, whether Baroque absolutism or nineteenth-century imperialism. The dilemma was seen

at its most acute in Germany, in two successive projects for the federal parliament, which set out to repudiate the country's authoritarian past: a completely new building by Behnisch & Partner for Bonn (1973-92), which set out to dissolve monumentality by enclosing its circular chamber on all sides by glazed walls; and the competition-winning design for Berlin by Sir Norman Foster (1994-9), which set a massive glazed cupola in the shell of the old Wilhelmine Reichstag building. Some new parliament complexes continued to be built, especially outside Europe, but here the heroic Brasilia approach had been replaced by a greater modesty, and an emphasis on organic or vernacular forms. The dilemma was between populist symbolism, with its danger of a conflation with tourist or theme-park art, and a more abstracted 'critical regionalism'. The 1950s, outside Europe, had provided the most important precedents in devising monumentally 'organic' Modernist forms which could serve as internationally recognisable images: we should especially note the clusters of sculptural shell shapes pioneered in the Sydney Opera House competition design of Jørn Utzon in 1956.

5.8. Night-time perspective of the Page & Park proposal. (RCAHMS/ Scottish Executive: painting by Alexander Stoddart)

The four completed studies for the Scottish Parliament site

selection, submitted to the government and exhibited publicly at the end of December 1997, all envisaged an overall building cost between £50m and £65m. The building brief was now quite complex. Key planning features included a debating chamber and offices for 129 members, six committee rooms, an underground car park and a security zone. All of the studies acknowledged the governing ideals set out in the White Paper, of public accessibility combined with modern efficiency; and some of them, especially Benson & Forsyth, went beyond the site selection task to produce an almost fully designed building. What distinguished the studies from one another, more than anything else, was one general variable, which would also dominate the eventual process of selecting a designer for the building: a tension between the image of the monumental, isolated, formal parliament standing proudly on its own, and the informal, less assertive building integrated with its setting, and envisaged merely as a 'piece of city'. Because these were feasibility studies, and the architects were not competing directly with one another, the element of commodification and branding was subsidiary, but it pointed the way to what was to follow.[6]

Benson & Forsyth's study of the Leith location represented an extreme of noble isolation, pushing the freestanding potential of the 10-acre Victoria Quay site to its limits by locating the parliament on a promontory jutting right out into the water. An underground car park would be constructed by emptying out a rubble-filled dry-dock, and a grand expanse of tree-lined public space would be created to the south. Benson & Forsyth's concept of a four-storey legislature building developed the confident handling of monumental form and space already evident in the architects' design for the Museum of Scotland (1995-8), and other competition-winning projects for public buildings in Edinburgh and Dublin. Here, in contrast to those city-centre interventions, the building was conceived as an all-round, almost freestanding design: almost, but not quite freestanding, as it was to be linked to the existing Victoria Quay office complex by a colonnade-like elevated walkway and tree-lined boulevard. In other words, this was an urban regeneration masterplan as well as a study of an individual public building.

The Page & Park study of the St Andrew's House site stood at an opposite extreme from Benson & Forsyth in its calculated modesty and avoidance of external gestures; the project was developed in close consultation with the government heritage agency, Historic Scotland. In contrast to the extrovert modernity of 1890s Glasgow architecture, this 1990s proposal could hardly be seen from the outside; even more than the same architects' Lighthouse architecture centre in Glasgow (1997-9), almost all its drama was internal. It exploited the steel-framed flexibility of Tait's building by proposing its complete internal reconstruction to provide both secretariat and ministerial accommodation. The new public and legislative spaces were to be accommodated in the open courtyards of Tait's south facade: the chamber was set diagonally in the south-east courtyard, and the central courtyard was assigned for use as a covered public space, or 'People's Forum', creating a right-angled approach to the parliament chamber from the entrance hall. All these rooms and spaces would enjoy dramatic views southwards to Holyrood Park, while all that would be visible from the outside would be discreet canopies and glazing. Page & Park's report argued that the reconstructed St Andrew's House would symbolise, in one building, the progression from administrative to parliamentary devolution, while rooting the new home-rule arrangements in the historical landscape of Edinburgh. The rebuilt complex would serve as a 'monumental symbol of the patient consistency of purpose of the Scottish nation in its pursuit of home rule throughout the 20th century'.[7] However, the proposal's combination of parliament and executive in one building, with the ministerial suites proudly occupying the summit, arguably diminished the relative importance of the legislature, and conflicted with the *res publica* ideal of constitutional separation of powers.

The RMJM studies of the Haymarket and Holyrood sites struck a mean between the extremes of assertion and discretion. Both envisaged a freestanding building set in open space, but, in keeping with the practice's heritage of restrained, rationalistic Modernism, set out to show that a self-contained dignity could be expressed without monumental rhetoric. The Haymarket site was a sloping area perched above railway tunnels (with accompanying security problems), without a single dominant townscape context. The architects worked out four alternative ways of developing the site with between 6,880 and 16,100 sq m of accomodation, depending on whether or not the tunnels could be overbuilt, and whether an exclusion zone was needed around the building; in all cases, stairs or escalators would have linked directly to Haymarket station. RMJM's site proposal for Holyrood

5.9. Perspective of St Andrew's House south courtyard, as converted to a central circulation space in the Page & Park study. (RCAHMS/Scottish Executive: drawing by Alexander Stoddart)

was of a subtly different kind. Located at the foot of the Canongate, the site was an elongated rectangle, aligned north-east/south-west, with two very different aspects. To the north and west, it abutted the dense urban fabric of the Old Town: to the west stretched an area of demolished brewery buildings under redevelopment as a housing regeneration area to a masterplan by John C. Hope, while immediately to the north lay the preserved seventeenth-century tenements of Robertson's Court (5-15 Canongate), and the courtyard-plan hostelry of Lady Stair's Close, reconstructed and refaced with a street arcade in 1961-4 by Sir Frank Mears. To the south and east, it faced an open setting which combined the hills of Holyrood Park and disparate freestanding buildings, including the nineteenth-century Baronial service courtyard of Holyrood Palace, the fifteenth/seventeenth century tenements of Abbey Strand, and a domed,

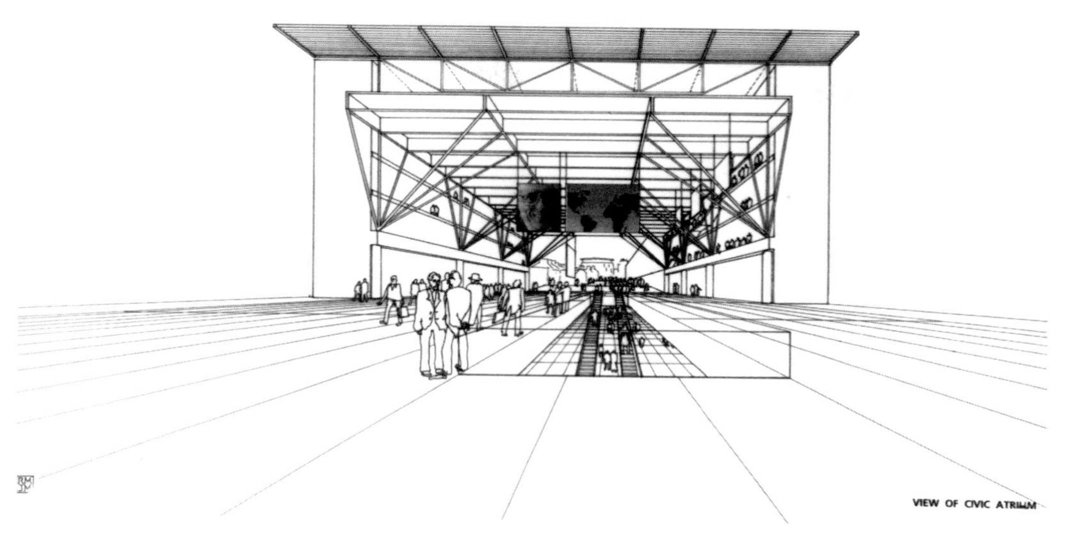

Postmodern theme park and a stepped-back newspaper headquarters under construction on a former brewery site, directly to the south.

The opportunity, but also the difficulty, of the Holyrood site lay in its intense ambiguity between landscape and old city. It could be developed in sharply contrasting ways, by pointing to one or the other extreme, or by attempting to reconcile the two through a mixture of freestanding and urban-grain building, as in the Haymarket options. RMJM's site study, costed at £50m, chose to contrast the parliament with the urban fabric, and to relate it to the pattern to the south and east, a pattern of large 'stand-alone buildings' set in their own green spaces. A single-storey plinth would support an austerely rectangular, four-storey pavilion, marked out as a great public building by a deep canopy and slender supporting colonnade. The pavilion would have a hollow square plan with a circular legislative area sitting in the central courtyard. This 'European-style horseshoe chamber' would be ringed by a public concourse and press centre at the lower levels, and offices above; a transparent 'wall of light' would allow the light from the chamber to be seen from Holyrood Park, showing the parliament at work at night. To accentuate the open orientation of the site, RMJM advocated that it should be projected out into Holyrood Park through an arrow-like linear band of landscaping pointing southwards, and involving the closure of existing roads to the south and east of the building; a public square would be formed facing Canongate.[8]

5.10. The December 1997 site studies: Option 2 of the RMJM Haymarket study, showing the suspended 'civic atrium' (RCAHMS/ Scottish Executive)

During December 1997, there was intense public and political debate about the merits of these sites. At a public 'forum' at the Royal Scottish Museum, most speakers backed the Calton Hill site, while Richard Murphy argued for a completely new parliament building, even in defiance of the city's conservation elite, on the grounds that 'you cannot make an omelette without breaking eggs'. At the same time, a working group chaired by Donald Dewar was evaluating the studies, and eventually, on 9 January 1998, the Secretary of State announced that Holyrood had been selected as the site for a new legislative building. He argued that the site would make it possible to build a purpose-designed complex without sacrificing the heritage resonances of the city centre: 'a new building, combining history with modernity'. The site posed 'the challenge of creating, with empathy, a twenty-first-century building that would be a gift from our time to succeeding generations'. While some commentators argued that Calton Hill had been rejected largely as a 'nationalist shibboleth', others claimed that Holyrood enjoyed a 'far deeper, more compelling symbolism' than Calton Hill, associated as it was with the sovereignty of the old Scottish kingdom – although, as we have seen, that sovereignty had been bound up with Stuart royal absolutism rather than with any modern-style representative democracy. The Secretary of State claimed that the St Andrew's House option had been rejected because Page & Park's 'elegant' adaptation would have provided 'no visible symbol of the new parliament', and because of the lack of space for expansion. The Holyrood site would, it was argued, allow separation of the legislative and executive arms of the Scottish government, with ministers based in a refurbished St Andrew's House.[9]

That potential could only be realised, however, once the site had been cleared. For unlike Haymarket, Holyrood in 1998 was not an empty wasteland, but was full of large buildings, many in active use. The site fell into two clearly demarcated sections. The north-east half was the company headquarters of Scottish & Newcastle Breweries, whose buildings were arranged around all sides of an irregular internal courtyard, leaving a hard outer edge on their street facades. Listed anti-clockwise from the south-west corner, these buildings comprised a Baronial office and boardroom range of 1903, a restrained classical block of 1961 by Gordon & Dey on the curved south-east corner, an L-plan four-storey row of open-plan offices of 1971 at the north-east

TOP.
5.11. Townscape view of the RMJM Holyrood study, looking westward towards the Castle. (RCAHMS/Scottish Executive)

BELOW.
5.12. Landscape plan of the RMJM Holyrood study. (RCAHMS/Scottish Executive)

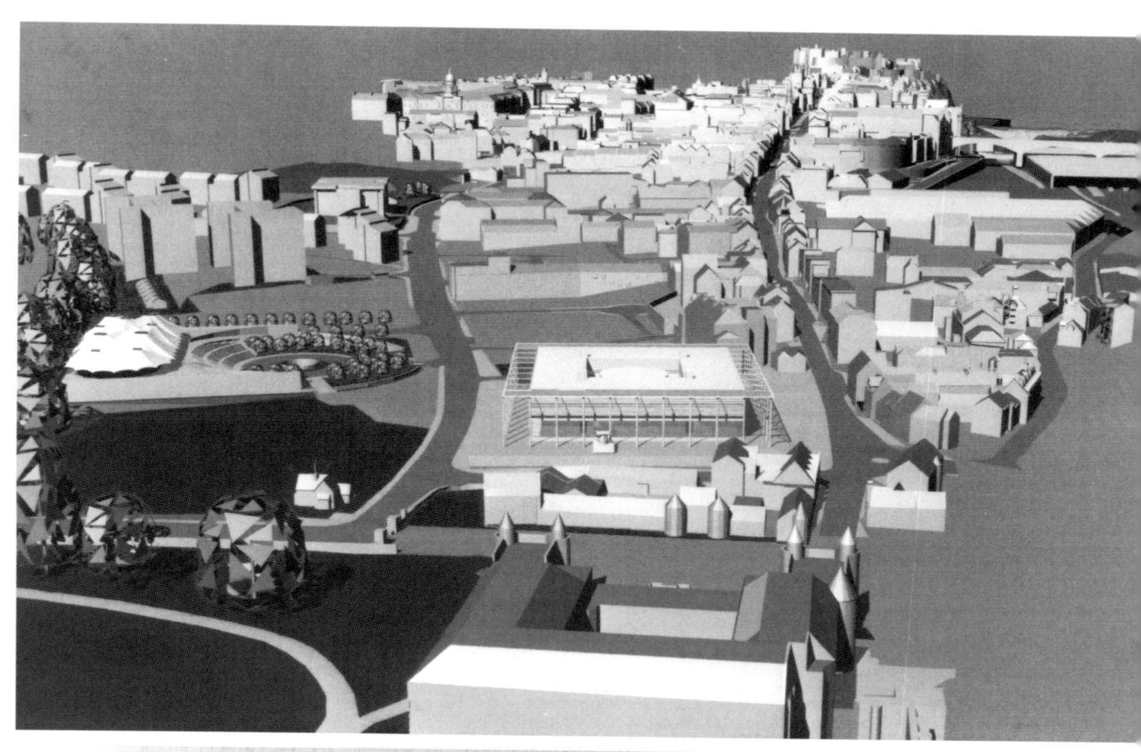

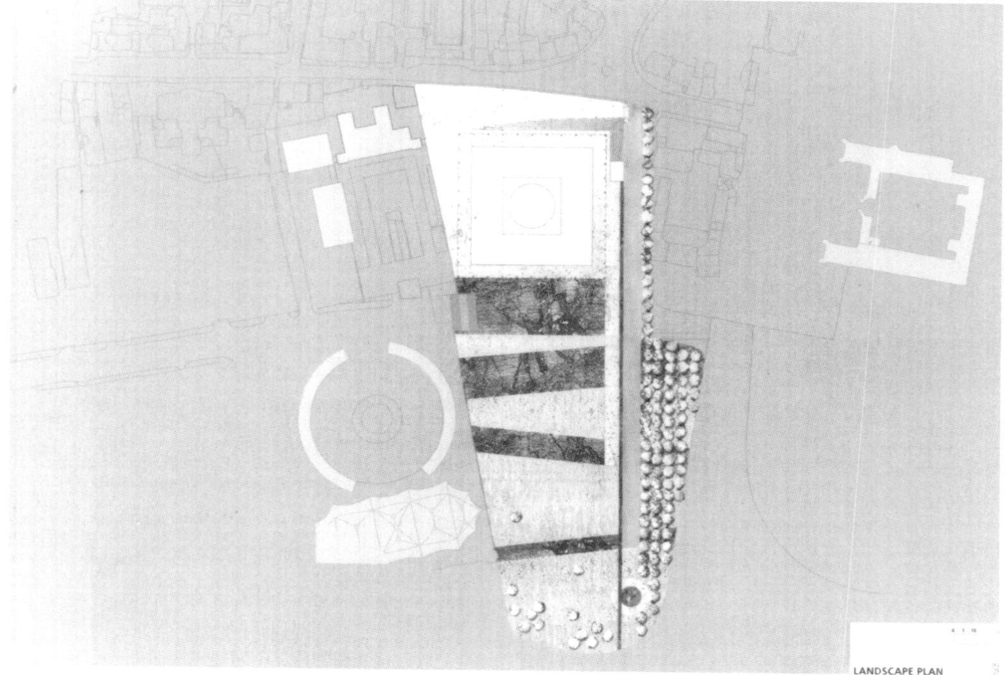

LANDSCAPE PLAN

corner, and a brick-clad, steel-framed brewery block, with clock tower, designed by J. A. McWilliam in 1936. The south-west half was largely occupied by a redundant hospital complex focused on Queensberry House, including nineteenth-century wings of former ward and barrack accommodation flanking an open courtyard to the south-east (originally part of the house's seventeenth-century formal garden), while the Canongate (north) side was occupied by groups of housing, including a late nineteenth-cenury tenement (58-62 Canongate) and two blocks of council flats in rubble and harl, in Canongate and Reid's Close (1960-1) by Ian Lindsay.[10]

At this stage, it was not clear how many of these buildings would be demolished for the new scheme (in the end, the reality was: almost all of them). What seemed certain was that Queensberry House, which had retained most of its 1690 layout, would be kept and used as parliamentary office accommodation. As a result of discussions, it was agreed with Historic Scotland that the house should be externally and internally remodelled to form an integral part of the working parliament complex.

'GATHERING FIELD': THE HOLYROOD PARLIAMENT PROJECT

How would the world of architecture respond to this opportunity, undreamt of only six months previously? The Government had given its first clue as early as July 1997, when it had announced there would be a competition for the parliament design, whether in a new or old building. The Secretary of State argued that a building of such significance would demand a designer of 'world class talent': 'I want to see a building that bears comparison with the best in Scottish architecture – and that sets a very high standard indeed'. At the end of January 1998, the site issue having been settled, the Scottish Office duly announced an international competition to select a design team. In this book, covering many centuries, the designer competition process for the new Parliament, and the initial designs by the selected architect, can only be described briefly.[11] Since June 1997, a dialogue had been underway within the government over the competition process. Eventually, in an announcement in late January 1998, the Scottish Office set out a process of three stages, spanning around six

5.13. Aerial view of Holyrood site from east, March 1998; the Scottish & Newcastle brewery buildings and Queensberry House are still intact, while the Dynamic Earth theme-park is under construction at left. (RCAHMS D28217)

months. The applicants would be vetted by a panel of judges, and a limited number would be picked for interview. From these, around three or four would be selected to draw up presentations of their overall design approach for public exhibition, as had been done in the site selection process, and finally a winner would be announced. Following consultation with RIAS and RIBA, it was emphasised that the competition was to select not a design but a design team, who would be expected to work in 'ongoing interface with the client': all applicants were asked to make a statement of design intentions. The initial tender invitation was issued at the beginning of February; it specified that the building would be of 17,000 sq m, and would cost around £50 million.[12]

Seventy pre-qualification questionnaires, from designers in 14 different countries, were returned by the deadline of 3 March 1998. On the same date, the judging panel for the competition was appointed. It comprised the Secretary of State for Scotland along with the Scottish Office Constitution Group head Robert Gordon, and three architects: John Gibbons (Director and Chief Architect of the Scottish Office Construction Group); Joan O'Connor (past President of the Royal Institute of Architects of Ireland); and Andrew McMillan (former head of the Mackintosh School of Architecture, Glasgow); the sixth member of the panel was television personality Kirsty Wark. The judges set about their initial task with energy, and by late March, after three long meetings, were able to announce an initial selection of twelve practices, to be called for interview. These were Glass Murray (Glasgow) in association with Denton Corker Marshall (Melbourne); Enric Miralles Benedetta Tagliabue, or EMBT (Barcelona); Groep Planning (Brugge); Peter Kulka (Köln); Allies & Morrison (London); Benson & Forsyth (London); Kohn Pedersen Fox Associates (London); Michael Wilford & Partners (London); Ahrends Burton & Koralek (London) with Behnisch & Partner (Stuttgart); Richard Meier & Partners (New York), assisted by Keppie Design (Glasgow); Rafael Viñoly Architects (New York); and Narud Stokke-Wiig (Oslo). During April, the first-stage interviews took place, focusing on issues such as the statement of design intentions. For the second stage, an unexpectedly large second selection was announced, comprising Glass Murray and Denton Corker Marshall; Wilford; Meier; Viñoly; and EMBT.[13] They were charged with preparing design concept presentations, for exhibition around the country during June. With the

growing recognition of the likely difficulties of non-Scottish practices working in Scotland, all the latter rapidly secured Scottish collaborators (if they had not already done so).

During this process, public and professional debate rapidly refocused from the question of which site should be chosen to that of the architectural design. The issues focused on by the mass media and non-architectural commentators were expressed differently from those which preoccupied the architectural community, but the underlying concerns were the same: the definition of identity and of democracy in a small country tightly integrated into the global capitalist economy. In the media and organised public opinion at large, these issues were packaged into a number of sharp polarities. Regarding national and communal identity: was the building to be 'traditional' or 'modern' in design, and would it express 'Scottishness' or not? Regarding democracy: would its design help or deter public participation, and would the layout encourage a 'confrontational' or 'consensual' style of politics?

In the case of democracy, the question was largely artificial. Late twentieth-century politics in all Western countries had already decisively downplayed class-based conflicts for a more participatory individualism, and almost everyone agreed that this ethos could directly be promoted in Scotland through use of a curved-plan chamber and greater use of committees, rather than the face-to-face layout popularly associated with Westminster; there was also

5.14. The Scottish & Newcastle directors' dining room in Gordon & Dey's classical corner block (1961) at the Holyrood brewery, photographed in 1998 before closure and demolition. (M Glendinning)

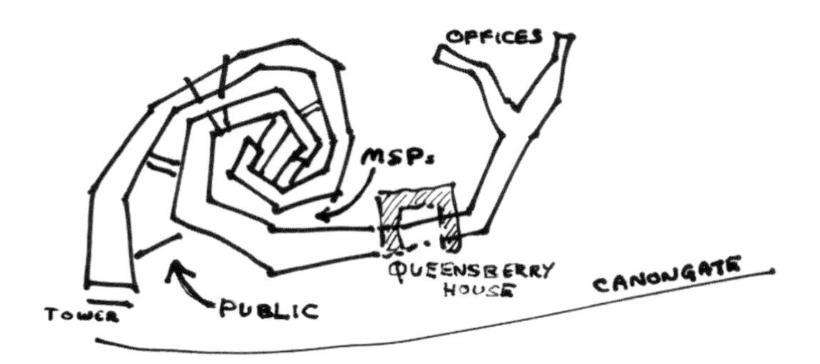

5.15. Holyrood designer selection competition (preliminary stage): concept drawing of February 1998 by Page & Park, with interlocking spiral plan of public and members' circulation; this was one of the practices eliminated at application stage. (Page & Park)

widespread talk of the democratising potential of advanced electronic media. In reality, however, there was no fundamental challenge to the late nineteenth-century concept of the parliament building as a self-contained community with its own institutional life, existing as distinct from the wider world. In the case of national and communal identity, there was greater controversy. The canvassed opinions of many members of the public, favouring 'tradition', however defined, seemed at variance with Andrew McMillan's warning that 'the conservation lobby should stay at home, and stay out of the game – this is a parliament for people with suits, not kilts'. In McMillan's view, what was required was nothing more complex than an international competition between artist-personalities, on the model of football: the aspiration was no more than a flamboyant modern image designed by 'an Italian superstar or a Spanish superstar, or a Dutch superstar'.[14]

However, among the competing designers, especially the five teams charged with preparing design concepts at the final competition stage, the issues of identity and democracy were addressed not through simplistic slogans such as these, but through more oblique combinations of ideas. That indirect approach was encouraged by the competition specifications, which made it clear that it was not 'designs' but overall conceptions that were needed. The main design dilemma posed by the site in general was its schizophrenic character, split between landscape and townscape. Just as in the case of the feasibility studies, the would-be design teams for Holyrood tried to reconcile the architectural extremes of the isolated monument in landscape and the complex piece of city. Their conceptions of the building itself bore more directly on the issues of democracy and identity. The concern was to resolve the potential conflict in

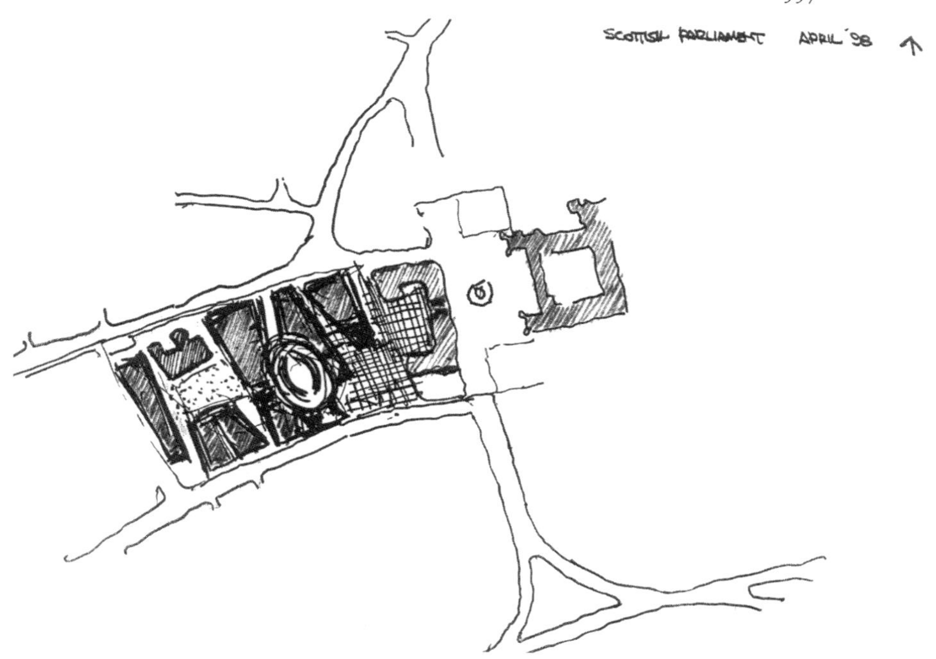

parliament architecture, between the demand for a self-effacing openness, and the continuing reliance on a degree of symbolism and assertion to support the ruling power.

The responses of the designers to this two-headed challenge again avoided extreme polarisations, and tried to sidestep its dilemmas with a variety of elements. Those concerned especially with the representation of democracy suggested that images of democratic transparency could be used in a monumental way, following the example of the large expanses of glass used in the parliament buildings designed in Germany by competitors Behnisch & Partner (Bundestag), and Peter Kulka (Saxony provincial assembly, Dresden); alternatively, modern participatory democracy could be symbolised through deliberately anti-monumental forms. A sharply contrasting approach was to divert attention away from visual monumentality towards images of social community, which could symbolise democratic participation and national solidarity at the same time; the importance of the debating chamber could be played down in favour of irregularly planned circulation spaces on the model of an agora or forum, perhaps linking directly to the wider civic space of the city centre. The process of design itself could also be envisaged as a contribution to communal life, through an open-ended readiness to develop the design in collab-

5.16. Holyrood competition (first stage): concept drawing of April 1998 by Peter Ahrends of Ahrends, Burton & Koralek – one of the twelve practices selected for interview, but not shortlisted. (Ahrends, Burton & Koralek) oration with the client. At a most general level, designers could either flow with the tide of globalism by producing memorable 'images', or they could wrestle with their dilemmas and produce more complex and variegated solutions. All solutions, however, had the same starting point in the general disposition pointed to by the RMJM study: the required retention of Queensberry House and elements of the garden to its south made it almost inevitable that the chamber should be located in the eastern half of the site.

Among the practices eliminated in the first and second rounds of the competition, several proposed approaches to the project which differed from the eventual finalists, by attempting to reconcile these conflicting demands in complex and relatively undemonstrative ways. The collaborating team of Ahrends, Burton & Koralek with Behnisch & Partner, for instance, sketched out a concept which contained a clearly articulated oval chamber 'held in place by fragments of urban form, whose adjacencies provide close-like passages to the north and south'. This combination of openness with wedge-shaped linear 'fragments' was designed to mediate subtly between the Old Town burgage-plot layout and the open landscape and palace to the south-east; there would be 'a new public place engaging the visible free face of the new chamber with the history and form of the palace forecourt. A duet of this parliament and that power'.[15] Ole Wiig was more concerned with the issue of national identity than with democratic transparency. The parliament, he believed, should aim to build, rather than represent, Scottish identity, through a quality of small-scale, intense monumentality: it should avoid overbearing scale, but should be invested with a timeless power. Page & Park's initial concepts for the site similarly tried to reconcile monumentality with intimacy, by proposing an irregular layout converging on the debating chamber at its core; this plan of twin spirals (for public and MSP circulation) was intended to 'unfurl the capital into the wider nation', and a slender tower of twin bronze slabs would signal the new democracy to the city.

The five design teams eventually shortlisted all proposed concepts of a bolder, more rhetorically accentuated character. Summarised briefly, the four runners-up emphasised solutions of a more or less monumental kind, closely bound up with the urban aspects of the site, while the eventual winner, EMBT, explicitly opposed those ideas and proposed a building dominated by organic or natural forms. However, there were significant contrasts among the four 'urban' proposals. In particular, that of Glass Murray/Denton Corker Marshall was expressed in an impressionistic form closer to that of EMBT than to any of the others. And the EMBT concept was also more complex than it seemed, as it combined a strong anti-monumentality and aversion to huge scale, with a highly explicit and almost autonomous form. The teams differed in their willingness to conform to the competition's call for a general conceptual approach: Viñoly, Meier and Wilford disregarded this instruction, and produced detailed designs.

The most extreme urban conception was that of Michael Wilford & Partners, heirs to the highly personal practice of James Stirling, who had in the 1980s accomplished the transition from an idiosyncratic Modernism to a monumental Postmodernism. The project team, led by Laurence Bain, argued that the entire site should be developed not with a 'setpiece building' but with a 'piece of city' on which the public could wander. There would be no separate blocks, but a single, highly integrated whole, with even Queensberry House relegated to a pavilion within an internal courtyard. The main part of the building would be a podium, reflecting the multi-level character of the Edinburgh Old Town, gradually rising from east to west, to reach its highest point in a massive, L-shaped block confronting Holyrood Palace: the architects' presentation declared that 'the city should shape the building and the building should shape the city'. The podium would be treated as a piazza leading directly off Canongate at the lower (west) end. Superimposed on this would be two further landmark structures – a transparent drum, clasped by slanting ramps, above the parliament chamber, intended to allow the public to look down on the debates, and a tapering stone-clad bell tower. This public podium principle would extend down into the building, which would be arranged with working circulation levels below, and public concourse levels above. In its crushing urban density, this proposal was like a 1960s megastructure clad in the stone rhetoric of national identity. Bain spoke of the 'tempietto'-like chamber lantern 'rising out of the rock of Scotland', and described the whole building as a 'castle without walls'.[16]

The proposal by Rafael Viñoly, a large New York firm specialising in commercial/cultural complexes, was in some ways similar in its massively monumental form, but was less intense in its exploitation of the site. And, again like Wilford, it benefited – here at the suggestion of Viñoly's Scottish collaborators, the Edinburgh firm Reiach & Hall – from a careful study of Edinburgh Old Town building typographies, especially the turn-of-century regeneration projects of Patrick Geddes. After analysing several possible approaches, all based around a circular chamber, Viñoly proposed a compromise solution, in which the site would be divided into a less dense version of the Wilford podium, at the palace end, and a more open area at the other end, to north and south of Queensberry House. The general circulation principle was to admit the public both at the top and at the bottom. The chamber would be ringed by a dramatic galleried concourse, surmounted by a completely glazed lantern with a balcony around, dominating the skyline of the building; around this, to the east, would have been set a U-shaped street wall of members' accommodation. The working heart of the building, the committee rooms, would have been directly below the chamber. As in the Wilford proposal, the roof would have been public space, and laid out as gardens. Public entry would have been from Holyrood Road, with entry either directly into the heart of the building or up a ramp rising around the outside of the encircling wall.

The other three proposals all treated the site in a more open fashion; where they differed was in their degree of monumentality. Richard Meier & Partners, working with Glasgow architects Keppie Design, proposed a solution uncompromisingly rooted in the mainstream Modernist tradition of clean, geometrical forms set in open space, the tradition exemplified by Lanark County Buildings. The entire accommodation was compressed into only two, clearly articulated buildings: a circular, slightly tapering debating chamber, and a seven-storey slab of administrative accommodation fronted by a wedge-shaped top-lit foyer; the ministers' offices would occupy a two-storey penthouse-loggia at the top of this slab. The extreme concentration of accommodation allowed the creation of a new, wide public space, or 'Parliament Square', on the east side of the building, a feature which was absent from the more crowded layouts envisaged by the other competing teams, and was intended for use by festivals and ceremonial events; the wedge plan of the office atrium made it possible for both this square and the garden facing Queensberry House to be rectangular in shape. There were only two concessions to explicit 'national identity': a suggestion that stone cladding would be used, rather than Meier's trademark white finish, and a claim that the

debating chamber pavilion was based on the building type of the broch.

The study by Glass Murray Architects of Glasgow, with Denton Corker Marshall of Melbourne – both large practices specialising in commercial and public projects – was similar in general layout to the Meier project, but was more complex and forcefully expressed, with some overtones of the 'crystalline' concepts of avant-garde Expressionism in the 1910s/20s; it set out to be both 'commanding' and 'accessible'. Helped by advisers including the author Candia McWilliam, this team, like Wilford and Viñoly, set out to analyse in depth the cultural and built context of the city. They concluded that the new complex must be highly urban in character, and rooted in what they described as the Old Town tradition of 'living' street-walls fronting 'gathering spaces'.[17] The building would be structured, formally, around an array of lofty, stone-clad walls slanting away south-eastwards from Canongate, and offset by the irregular elliptical form of the chamber, and a great transverse wall overlooking the main public entry from Canongate. The two western groups of walls would frame blocks of members' offices and other service rooms, on five floors, flanking the private garden south of Queensberry House. The semi-circular debating chamber would be contained in a vast, elliptical projection, a curving metal 'veil' perforated at its upper levels, and attached to one of these groups of walls. It would be adjoined by an agora-like, open public hall bounded, on the east edge of the site, by two further walls framing a ramp up to a public gallery and committee rooms. This grand hall would be entered from a new

5.17. Holyrood competition (second stage): Michael Wilford & Partners, layouts and perspectives. (RCAHMS/ Scottish Executive)

'Parliament Place' at the east end of Canongate through a sculptural glazed porch in the form of a 30m-high spire, intended to reconcile imagery of democratic openness and 'national pride', and a 'gestural sense of ceremony'. Thus, the building's dominant skyline presence, intended to evoke the density of the Old Town as well as the profile of Salisbury Crags, was combined with huge internal and open spaces. The main orientation of the proposal was towards the town, but the linear framework of the main groups of walls was not confined to the site, but was also projected out south-eastwards into Holyrood Park, in a landscaped wedge, to be called 'Parliament Fields': it was assumed that Holyrood Road would be blocked off and reclaimed into the park.

The remaining shortlisted team comprised EMBT, working now in collaboration with RMJM Scotland under an arrangement in which EMBT would lead the design stage, while RMJM would have the major responsibility for the planning and building process. On 6 July 1998, the Government announced that this team had won the designer competition, and would now be invited to begin developing a detailed design. This outcome had been predicted in the press since early June, although much of the public input into newspaper debates had remained trenchantly anti-modernist.[18] The experience and ideas brought by RMJM to the winning team were focused on a solidly rationalist approach to the design and delivery of public-sector architecture – a philosophy, rooted ultimately in the social or 'Functionalist' strand of Modernism, which had been consistently developed over the 45 years since the firm's foundation by Robert Matthew, and was exemplified in the Victoria Quay office project. The governing ethos of the EMBT practice stemmed from an almost diametrically opposite strand within the history of the Modern Movement, a strand of poetic or organic individualism expressed through an all-embracing artistic vision. In its modern form, this had emerged at the turn of the century, in the work of Mackintosh and others, as part of the reaction against mass-production capitalism; and in the 1950s and '60s, it had been rejuvenated with Modernist concepts of the poetry of everyday or utilitarian objects (ultimately an Arts and Crafts concept) and of flexible, open-ended design, as propagated by groups such as the Cumbernauld Town Centre designers. In their view, a total vision could be one of apparent chaos, whose underlying poetry would only be obvious to the discerning

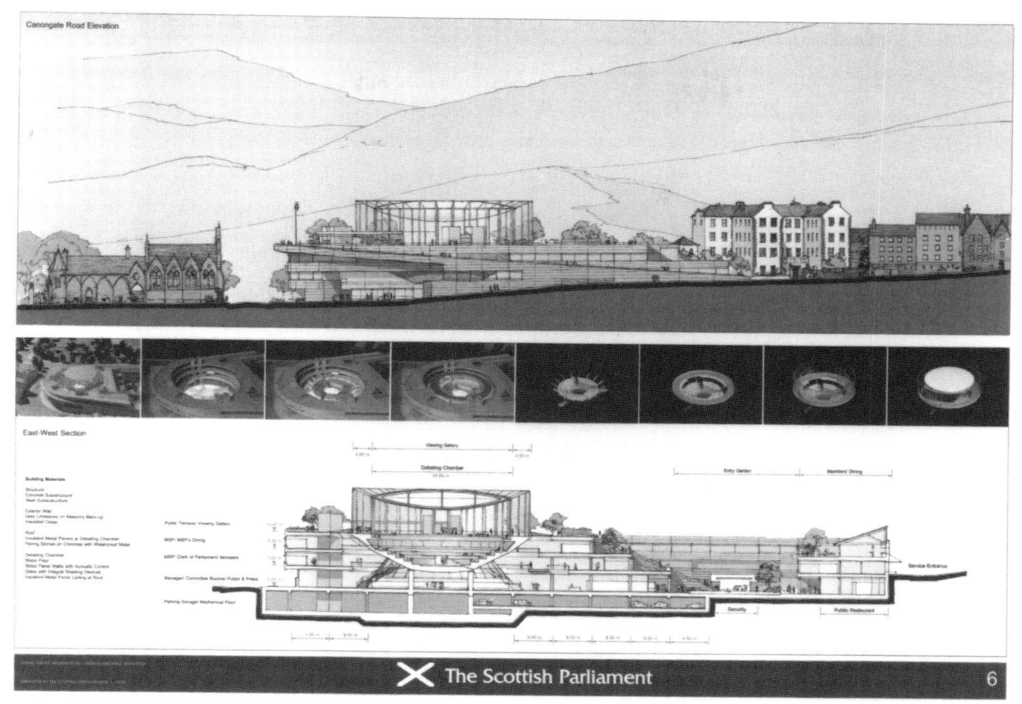

observer. In the 1990s, this strand of Modernism became shaped by, and integrated into, the global marketplace. The commissioning of highly individualistic works by a particular named designer, or assertively organic and place-specific designs, became one of a number of shortcut ways in which competing cities or countries could assert their identity and 'brand' themselves in competition with each other.

Working in Barcelona in the liberalising aftermath of the ending of Franco's dictatorship, EMBT partner Enric Miralles, and his former partner Carme Pinós, had developed their own personal permutation of these ideas, amounting to an architectural 'signature'. Buildings were planned in an organic or 'poetic' pattern composed of discontinuous elements, whose quality stemmed from a combination of intense integration into the natural terrain, a sensuous use of everyday or seemingly casual elements, and a metaphor-laden overall conception. Although the overall recipe was unique, there was also an obvious 'national' evocation of the turn-of-century Catalan *Modernismo* of Gaudí and others, as well as international links with the Deconstructivist movement of the late 1980s/early '90s. The most straightforward applications of this approach were landscape interven-

5.18. Holyrood competition (second stage): entry by Rafael Viñoly, elevation and section. (RCAHMS/ Scottish Executive)

The Scottish Parliament | Richard Meier & Partners/Keppie Design

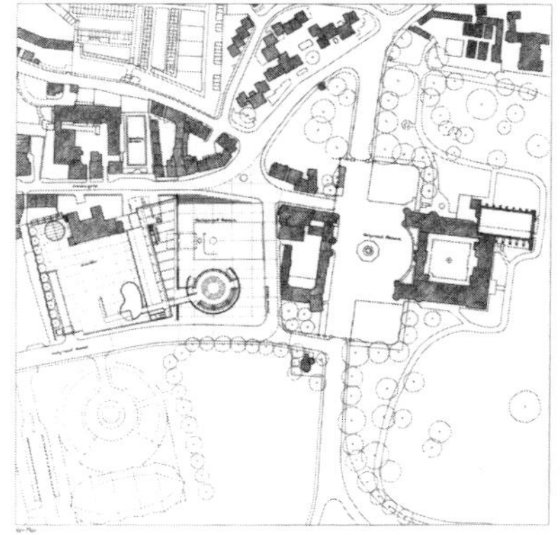

ABOVE. 5.19. Holyrood competition (second stage): Richard Meier & Partners/Keppie Design entry, layout plan and perspectives. (RCAHMS/ Scottish Executive)

OPPOSITE TOP. 5.20. Holyrood competition (second stage, June/July 1998): Glass Murray and Denton Corker Marshall, layout plan of 'parliamentary precinct'. (RCAHMS/ Scottish Executive)

OPPOSITE BELOW. 5.21. Holyrood competition (second stage): Glass Murray and Denton Corker Marshall, view of grand public hall from north. (RCAHMS/ Scottish Executive)

tions such as the Igualada Cemetery Park (competition win 1985, phase 1 constructed 1991-5), or the Olympic Archery Pavilions (1992), both in Barcelona: in these cases, the building and the site merged into one. To make sense of large freestanding buildings, different strategies were needed. For instance, at a national gymnastics centre built at Alicante in 1993, Miralles and Pinós developed a concept not unlike that of the 1950s/60s megastructure, with an outer framework of services, ramps and roofing, allowing the whole of the centre of the building to become one giant flowing 'balcony'.[19]

EMBT's winning conceptual scheme retained the existing split between the hospital and brewery sites. The courtyard south of Queensberry House would be flanked by new or preserved blocks, containing offices to the north-west and committee rooms to the north-east. The bulk of the brewery site would be filled by a debating chamber (with splayed U-plan seating) and ancillary and press accommodation, articulated not in consolidated blocks but in separate blocks with shell-like roofs: the debating chamber would deliberately avoid the stale idea of large-scale use of glass to symbolise 'openness'. Between these buildings and the committee block would run a curved concourse, laid out on an irregular and kinked plan, entered by the general public from Canongate (to the north) and by deputies from Holyrood Road (to the south). Construction would comprise a prefabricated structure clad in laminated timber and stone,

Glass Murray Architects
Denton Corker Marshall Group:
Architects in Association

3

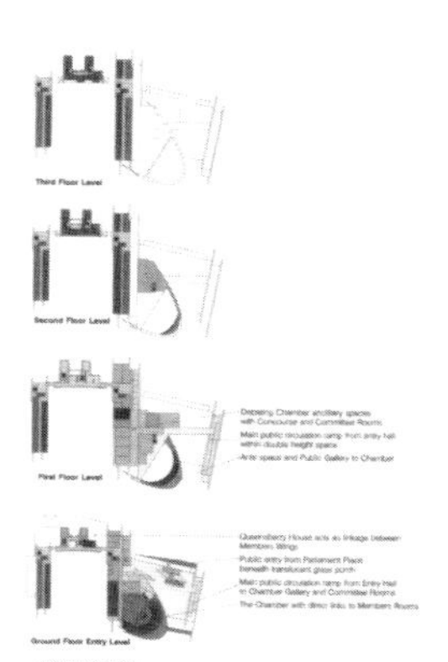

Lower Ground Floor

Basement

The Parliamentary Precinct

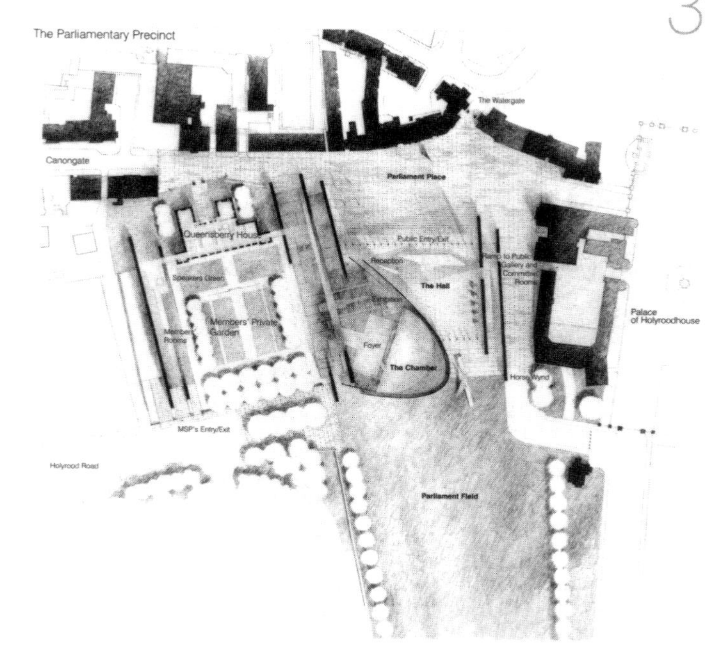

Glass Murray Architects
Denton Corker Marshall Group:
Architects in Association

6

The Principal Functional Elements

The Debating Chamber

In order to avoid the Debating Chamber being seen by the public as a 'precinct' and exclusive place, we propose an architectural expression which is neither an overt externally displayed sculptural object, nor a discrete internalised form apparent only from within. Nor is it seen as a fully glazed visually accessible volume either from the exterior (security considerations) or interior space (sense of privacy).

We propose that the Chamber be powerfully expressed both internally from the public foyers and externally from the Parliament Field, as a metal veil within which lies the Chamber. The veil itself forms a flowing line which notionally follows the stepped, semi-circular spatial form of the Chamber and gallery space and reflects the character of the hill slopes (Salisbury Crags, the Castle and Calton Hill).

This metal veil is solid at its base but becomes progressively more perforated as it reaches its upper level. Behind the perforations a glazed layer allows daylight into the Chamber and a ceiling void offering a degree of translucent natural lighting into the Chamber itself. Through the veil, the public gallery access and ante spaces would have views to both the foyer and exterior.

Thus, the reading of the Chamber is both internally and externally expressive of visual accessibility of Parliament without providing it in a literal sense.

Within the Chamber, a translucent glass ceiling plane in turn abstractly expressed at roof level is suffused with controlled natural light via a double layered void space. Within the Chamber, the ceiling, unequivocally the principal uninterrupted surface, can become a single etched canvas - the artistic centrepiece of the Parliament.

The significance of the Chamber is now reinforced and gradually revealed through the perforated veil as the visitor moves from the exterior into the foyer signalled on approach by the powerful curved form and ultimately on the final entry into the Chamber itself. From the interior, the veil and top lit ceiling offer an awareness of both exterior space and the commencement of the experience of entry.

The Entry Porch

The porch forms the first critical interface between the public and their Parliament. Security considerations must be accommodated yet the feeling of openness and sense of national pride should not be diminished.

The porch facilitates a spacious and sheltered transition between exterior and interior - a place to congregate, wait, and for contemplation before passing through security. It effectively 'extends' entry to the entire facade, giving a clear and appropriate gestural sense of ceremony.

The proposal is a simple sculptured form - a translucent glazed wedge approximately 30 metres tall and 6 metres deep at the base. The inner face extends to ground level and contains entry doors; the outer face is held some 4 metres above ground across its full width.

The light flooded volume thus contained is impressively scaled as a prelude to the foyer and becomes an entry experience of considerable significance.

The supporting structure and the glazing system itself, will allow complexity of detail and be a symbolic expression of the relevance and importance of the Parliament to the nation. At night, the porch would be lit from within, forming a glowing marker of location clearly visible from many parts of the city.

The porch as a symbol of entry, welcome and shelter, will become the immediately recognisable symbol of the Parliament as the forum for open and frank representation.

The Hall

with turf used for grading. Like the Glass Murray proposal and the RMJM site study, the parliament reached out into the landscape of Holyrood Park, but in the form of sinuously undulating traces rather than a neat wedge; and it was dissolved out at the eastern side into an open plaza facing Holyrood Palace.

The special, winning quality of EMBT's formula lay not in the practical aspects of its layout, which, like all the other competitors except Wilford, was conditioned generally by the RMJM site study. Nor did it lie in its architectural novelty, as its broadly deconstructivist approach had been widespread since the late 1980s, and the firm's earlier works had already shown how deconstructivism could be re-styled in a more organic manner, dissolving the building into the landscape rather than into jagged fragments. What was special was its ideological presentation, or, more precisely, the way in which the firm's 'house style' of landscape-orientated deconstruction was integrated with an ingenious formulation of the 'identity versus democracy' debate. EMBT's presentation was far more flamboyant than those of the other competing teams. Its artistic manifesto-like format, with collaged poetic slogans and freehand drawings in the style of the early Modern Movement avant-garde, contrasted with the others' more pedestrian and factual presentations, their conventional rhetoric of identity and democratic involvement, and their presentation of specific 'designs' rather than outline ideas. As Donald Dewar later recalled, 'When Mr Miralles first appeared before the judges, he produced splendid, large panels that were full of sweeping colour and vision and occasional pieces of script . . . great big boards, advertising hoardings for his talent'. Within the selection panel, concerns were expressed, especially by Joan O'Connor, about the potential effect of Miralles's poetic perfectionism on design costs and timekeeping, but in the end the promise of a bold architectural solution prevailed.[20]

EMBT's central idea, or slogan, was that 'the land' could be used as a metaphoric factor which could overcome the potential conflict of national identity and democracy, and weld the two into a more general community feeling, through 'the intuition that individual identification with land carries collective consciousness and sentiments'. Land symbolised national identity because it represented the country as a whole, as opposed to the urban image of Edinburgh: 'Scotland is a land . . . it is not a series of cities. The Parliament should be able to reflect the land which it represents'. This was almost the reverse of the centralist Calton Hill or Geddesian vision of an urban beacon or outlook tower of enlightenment. EMBT's Holyrood Parliament would come from outside, and 'should arrive in the city almost out of the rock'. Physically, therefore, the building would have to reflect the land, evoking the qualities of peat and water in its site: 'the building should be land . . . built out of land'. The formal novelty of the solution would also help the international interests of Scotland, in the competition between cities under global capitalism: EMBT asked, 'How is it going to be *fundamentally distinctive* from other European Parliaments?'[21]

The land could equally serve as a metaphor for the new democracy, a metaphor for participation and inclusiveness more subtle than any amount of glass walling. The focus of the metaphor was not traditional representative democracy, but the old Athenian image of the direct democracy, of the assembly of citizens in the open. EMBT argued that the open site by Salisbury Crags formed a Pnyx-like 'natural amphitheatre', 'a huge, long, low seat' for citizens to 'sit together'; 'the people, the parliament sit in the land'. The only possible architectural response was a modest intervention in the landscape, 'a fragment of a large gathering situation . . . to carve in the land the form of *gathering* people together. *Not* a building in a park nor a garden'. What were not needed were the 'rhetorical forms' of an 'overwhelming monument'. In their view even a roof, let alone a massive building, almost seemed an affront to the natural setting. This should be '*not* a single building . . . it is an orchestrated series of constructions. *Why one building?*' To underline this rejection of monumentality, EMBT proposed that the main halls should be covered in shell-like structures inspired not by any kind of building but by upturned boats or leaves, shifting and organic forms 'floating in the landscape'.

But EMBT's forceful contrast between their own anti-urban design philosophy and the 'rhetoric' of the traditional monumental urban legislature immediately begged the question of the relationship of image and reality in postmodern culture. Could EMBT's evocation of participatory ruralising community rooted in 'the land', with its trademark motifs of boats, bundles of leaves or castles, be any less 'rhetorical', any more critically detached from global capitalism, than a national pavilion in a world's fair or even an office complex in Hong Kong? Might the individualism of a 'signature-architect' not merely

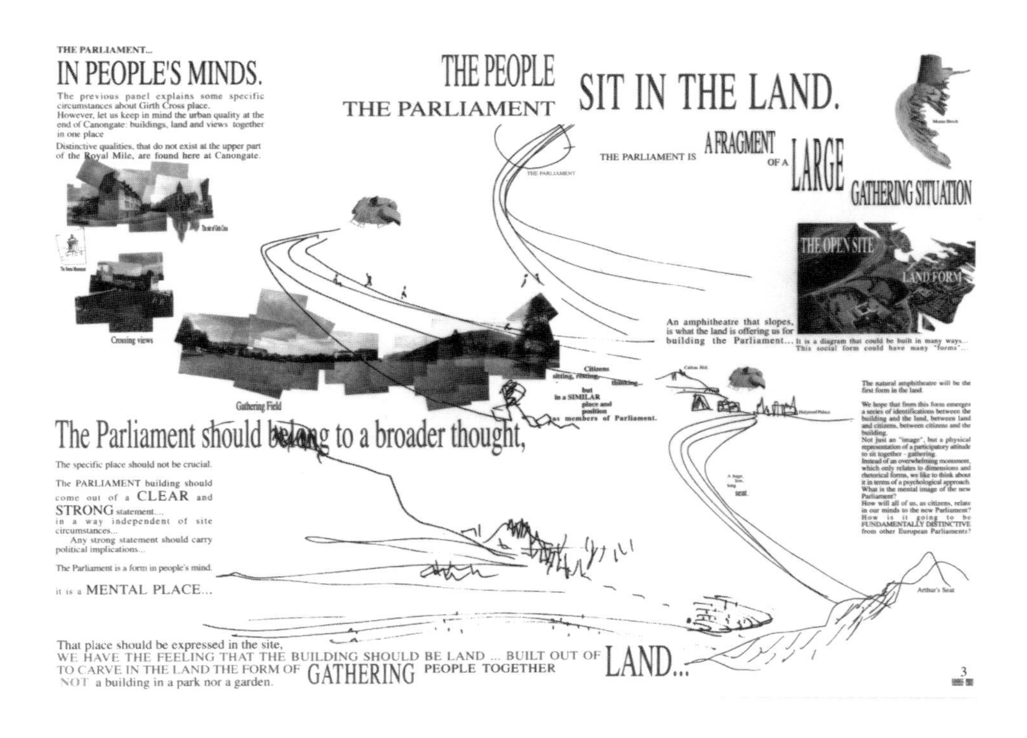
THE PARLIAMENT...
IN PEOPLE'S MINDS.
The previous panel explains some specific circumstances about Girth Cross place.
However, let us keep in mind the urban quality at the end of Canongate: buildings, land and views together in one place
Distinctive qualities, that do not exist at the upper part of the Royal Mile, are found here at Canongate.
Crossing views
Gathering Field
THE PEOPLE
THE PARLIAMENT
SIT IN THE LAND.
THE PARLIAMENT
THE PARLIAMENT IS A FRAGMENT OF A LARGE GATHERING SITUATION
THE OPEN SITE
LAND FORM
An amphitheatre that slopes, is what the land is offering us for building the Parliament...
It is a diagram that could be built in many ways... This social form could have many "forms"...
Citizens sitting, resting... thinking... but in a SIMILAR place and position as members of Parliament.
The natural amphitheatre will be the first form in the land.
We hope that from this form emerges a series of identifications between the building and the land, between land and citizens, between citizens and the building.
Not just an "image", but a physical representation of a participatory attitude to sit together - gathering.
Instead of an overwhelming monument, which only relates to dimensions and rhetorical forms, we like to think about it in terms of a psychological approach. What is the mental image of the new Parliament?
How will all of us, as citizens, relate in our minds to the new Parliament? How is it going to be FUNDAMENTALLY DISTINCTIVE from other European Parliaments?
The Parliament should belong to a broader thought,
The specific place should not be crucial.
The PARLIAMENT building should come out of a CLEAR and STRONG statement....
in a way independent of site circumstances...
Any strong statement should carry political implications...
The Parliament is a form in people's mind.
it is a MENTAL PLACE...
seat.
Arthur's Seat
That place should be expressed in the site,
WE HAVE THE FEELING THAT THE BUILDING SHOULD BE LAND ... BUILT OUT OF LAND...
TO CARVE IN THE LAND THE FORM OF GATHERING PEOPLE TOGETHER
NOT a building in a park nor a garden.
3

PERSPECTIVE VIEWS
SECTION
CANONGATE ELEVATION
5

amount to just another type of 'branding', which could actually help reinforce capitalist globalisation? Anticipating such a post-structuralist critique, EMBT used in defence the standard nineteenth- and twentieth-century architectural argument of the simple correspondence of aesthetic and social patterns: their design would be 'not just an "image", but a physical representation of a participatory attitude to sit together – gathering'. Certainly, while their concept represented a sharp break from the monumental, stone traditions of Scottish architecture over the centuries, those traditions had been ones that had openly celebrated the exercise of power and authority, and had indirectly championed the values of imperialism and militarism. The repudiation of that ambiguous heritage was arguably a step in the right direction.

During the four months that followed their competition win, EMBT and RMJM worked up their initial concept, presenting it officially at the end of October 1998, and refining it into a relatively detailed proposal in spring 1999. The overall theme – the supposed link between land, democracy and anti-monumental design – remained the same. As the Secretary of State put it, this would be 'not an authoritarian building but a democratic dynamo . . . the people's building', formed from 'a group of buildings that would grow out of the site', while retaining a 'more abstract and timeless' character. In keeping with the EMBT ethos of open-ended design, the continuing 'incompleteness' and 'working dialogue' was emphasised as a central part of the project's poetic character; all that was absolutely clear at this stage was what the building must not be. According to Miralles, it must be 'a parliament not a hospital, . . . a parliament not a headquarters'.[22] The detailed drawings of this stage of the design process retained the exploded character of deconstructivism, combined with the use of collaging: for example, small fragments of castle drawings from McGibbon and Ross were scattered across them.

The general layout concept remained the same, but there were a number of significant adjustments. The most important, in terms of practical planning, was that the public and members' entrances were changed round, so that the public now entered the entire complex and the central concourse from the southern, park end, requiring the creation of a new public route round the edge of the site, on the east side of the chamber. The formal and ceremonial members' entrance would be through a wall at the end of Canongate, while the working

TOP.
5.22. Holyrood competition (second stage): EMBT entry, display of explanatory slogans and sketches. (RCAHMS/ Scottish Executive)

BELOW.
5.23. Holyrood competition (second stage): EMBT entry, site layout plan. (RCAHMS/ Scottish Executive)

and staff entrance would be from the Canongate side of Queensberry House. The most significant presentational or ideological adjustment was a retreat from the anti-urban overtones of the original concept, towards the Calton Hill idea of an urban outlook tower over the country. Now the building was seen as a dividing-line between urban Edinburgh and rural Scotland, with a massive boundary wall on the Canongate frontage seen as the point of 'leaving Edinburgh and entering Scotland'; the complex would be rendered facing the Old Town and ashlar-clad on its open frontages.

In this detailed design, the accommodation on the eastern part of the site was dealt with in a more densely packed form than that of the outline project, and now resembled a single mass carved into segments by deep fissures, leaving almost no open space on the inside: it would be 'a campus of striking fragments'. Partly, this was for practical reasons: the staff accommodation envisaged in EMBT's original concept had now been expanded by 44%, to 23,000 square metres, and other practical elements such as additional fire staircases inserted. At the same time, the size of public circulation areas was also expanded, enhancing the building's ceremonial status. With such an enlargement, it would take all the architects' ingenuity to maintain the anti-monumental modesty of the original concept of fragments scattered in the landscape.[23] In its new, denser form, the design attempted to retain elements of the original concept of organic deconstruction and 'non-hierarchical communication': according to the architects, the openings in this more compressed built fabric were intended not as deconstructive gestures but as practical ways to admit light, while the decision to keep use of large windows to a minimum was justified by reference to the small windows of Scottish castle building.

The building now comprised a semi-polygonal debating chamber, committee rooms, ministers' offices and media centre in a scattering of leaf-shaped forms connected by a curved concourse. The separate leaf forms of the committee rooms, fanning out from the north-east, replaced a single block in the outline concept, while the debating chamber still retained its 'boat' roofs. The new public entrance at the south-east corner would be marked by fan-shaped glazed canopies, pointing out towards the park landscape. The western part of the site would be built on top of a basement car park, accessed by a ramp from Holyrood Road, and the gate-lodge retained as a crèche. In place of Queensberry Lodge, a slab block rising to a height of six storeys and 80ft, with an irregularly staggered plan, would house the members' offices. The rooms would be laid out on a double-depth arrangement similar to that of Page & Park's St Andrew's House study, with the First Minister's suite on the fifth floor. Constructed in precast concrete on a 3m grid, the block would be linked to Queensberry House by a low covered concourse.[24] By placing this tall block on the western edge of the site, its size could be merged into the general density of the Old Town. The blocking-off of roads was less complete than in the original sketches, but the landscape traces would still stretch to the south-east.

The external finishes of the complex, left unspecific on the earlier models, were now defined in more detail. At this stage, an influential role was played by RMJM's design staff, especially Michael Duncan (previously the project architect for Victoria Quay). The main cladding materials were to be timber screens and stone slabs, interspersed with concrete slabs and glazing in a deconstructive, collaged manner; the roofs would be of steel. The administrative slab block was to be of buff-coloured precast stone with steel and timber framed windows. The architect's 'signature' was stamped across the detailed treatment of the exterior through an approximately 'L'-shaped facade motif, used in a number of variants and orientations. This motif was inspired, according to Miralles, by the human iconography of Le Corbusier's Modulor, as well as by a more populist Scottish source: Sir Henry Raeburn's painting of Rev. Robert Walker skating on Duddingston Loch (*c*.1784). On the administrative block, the motif was used mainly on the windows, which formed part of a rectilinear Modernist pattern on the courtyard (east) facade, and a jaggedly expressionistic pattern on the outer (west) facade, facing the Old Town. On the assembly building, it was used in the form of cladding panels and marble facing panels.

What had also now been finalised was the more prosaic matter of how the Holyrood site was to be redeveloped, and in what stages. Except for the housing blocks on the Canongate frontage and Queensberry House itself, all buildings on the site were now to be demolished. Phase 1 of the demolition, from October 1998, took in the hospital and housing zone; Phase 2, from January 1999, removed the 1936-7 brewery block; and Phase 3 (from April 1999) the remainder. Some of the stonework from Queensberry Lodge and Murray Lodge was recovered for possible re-use in the new buildings.

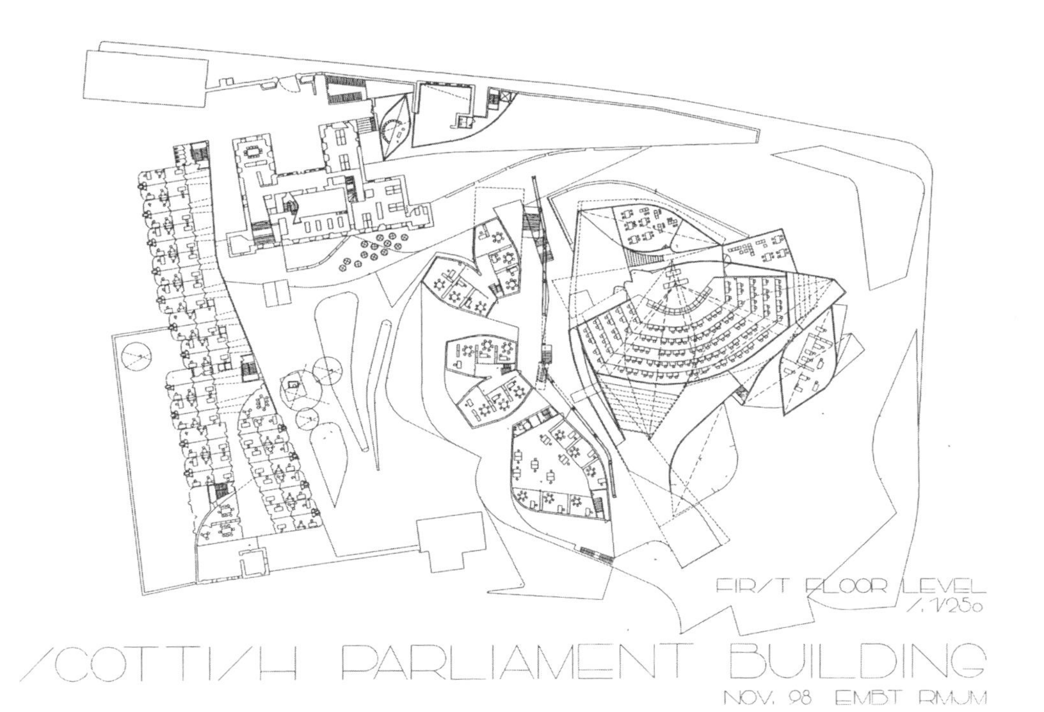
FIRST FLOOR LEVEL
S. 1/250
SCOTTISH PARLIAMENT BUILDING
NOV. 98 EMBT RMJM

PARLIAMENT ON THE MOUND: THE INTERIM COMPLEX

In advance of the lengthy construction of the permanent parliament, another, more modestly scaled 'parliament building' project was necessary: the preparation of an 'Interim Complex', to house the new legislature and its secretariat staff for (as it transpired) five years, from the day after the inaugural election, Friday 7 May 1999; the formal opening would be scheduled for the beginning of July in that year. That need for temporary accommodation was addressed through a similar two-stage process to that of the new building, with selection of the site, in March 1998, preceding the appointment of the architect by four months.

Prior to then, the Church of Scotland General Assembly Hall on the Mound (the former Free Church General Assembly Hall, in New College) had been the favoured candidate, but at the beginning of March, because of the lack of available office space nearby, the Scottish Office announced that it was closely examining the former headquarters of Strathclyde Regional Council in India Street, Glasgow: the legislative seat would have been the assembly hall of the former Glasgow High School, arranged with a U-shaped layout of tables and individual chairs, with a public gallery at the back and a stage proscenium overlooking the presiding officer's desk. Two of the adjacent 1970s blocks of offices, with accommodation for up to 1,000 staff, were immediately available. Possible sites were costed by the Scottish Office, at £5 million for the Royal High School, £4 million for New College and only £3 million for the Strathclyde option.[25] Stimulated into action, the Edinburgh City Council leadership proposed to decant the 370 staff currently working in the former Midlothian County Council office block on George IV Bridge (designed by Sir Robert Matthew in 1964 and built from 1967). The latter would be used for MSP offices, with overspill rooms and committee meetings in the City Chambers, and parliamentary administration offices in Baden-Powell House, Victoria Terrace and 302 Lawnmarket. At a cost of around £500,000, the General Assembly Hall would be vacated by the Kirk, and the right-angled arrangement of green benches would be ripped out and replaced by a curved layout of new seats; the Moderator's suite would be occupied by the First Minister, with other rooms occupied by the speaker and clerks. The

TOP.
5.24. Layout of EMBT/RMJM Holyrood scheme as at October/November 1998. (EMBT/RMJM Ltd)

BELOW.
5.25. Inspection of model of Holyrood project in its revised May 1999 form by First Minister Donald Dewar and EMBT partner Enric Miralles. (Roger Donovan; *Herald*, 10 May 1999)

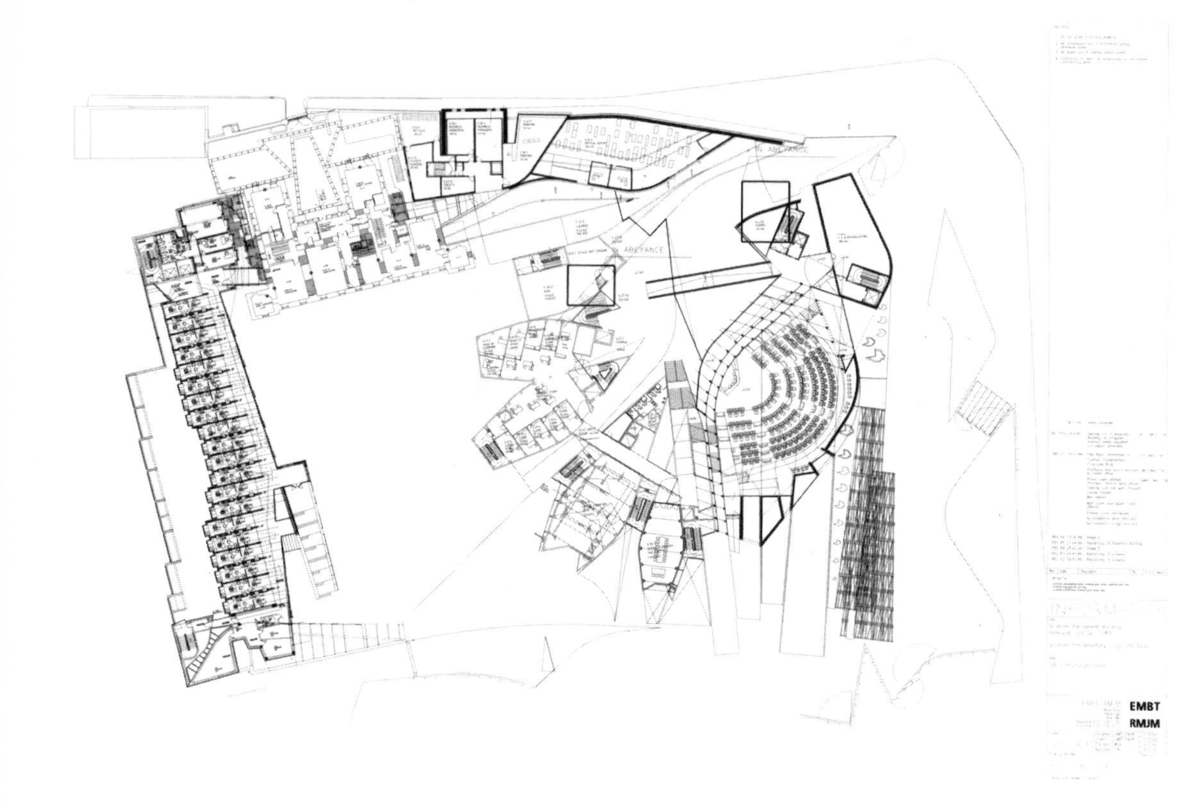

5.26. The May 1999 version of the EMBT/RMJM Holyrood scheme: concourse level. (EMBT/RMJM Ltd)

Church of Scotland General Assembly would be held elsewhere in May 1999, but would return temporarily in 2000 and 2001, requiring certain features to be demountable and replaceable.

The Edinburgh proposal was accepted by the Government, and in July 1998 it was announced that the design team for the Interim Complex would be led by Edinburgh architects Simpson & Brown. In their scheme, the three levels of the Assembly Hall were exploited to provide segregated accommodation for MSPs, on the lower floor, and for press and public, in the upper galleries and corridors. The new seating was arranged in rows of desks faced in Scottish sycamore, with electronic voting apparatus, on a bright blue-green carpet. Of the £7.5m cost of the scheme, £1m was spent on the chamber itself, £3.5m on office conversions nearby, and £3m on furniture and computers. To allow complete segregation of access to the public viewing gallery, a separate public entrance was provided from Milne's Court to the east, and a temporary timber entrance pavilion, with flat roof and overhanging canopy, was constructed. In parallel with the Interim Complex scheme, St Andrew's House was also refurbished as a ministerial centre at a cost of £20m, with the 500 resident staff moving around the building while the work proceeded, until 2001; open-plan office space was introduced where possible. By coincidence, the rival General Assembly hall, Gillespie Graham's next-door Victoria Hall, was undergoing conversion at the same time into the headquarters of the Edinburgh Festival Society ('The Hub'), in a £7.5m scheme designed by Benjamin Tindall: its staircase became a statue hall and the main hall a multi-purpose space.[26]

The Interim Complex, in the Free Church General Assembly Hall, made an almost complete contrast with EMBT's new building, both architecturally – standing as it did in a monumental position at the head of a grand classical axis – and in its original association with a militant Protestantism closely bound up with Scotland's old society of power and domination. But the very fact that the hall's old sectarian overtones had now been expunged, and that the 1989 Claim of Right was signed there on behalf of the whole nation rather than any religious or political faction, made it all the stronger a symbol of democratic renewal. As early as 1910, the hall had already been the scene of the momentous meeting of the World Missionary Conference, widely regarded as marking the beginning of the modern ecumenical movement. And in May 1982, the college courtyard, with its presiding statue of John Knox, had witnessed a historic meeting between Pope John Paul II and the Moderator of the General Assembly, Professor John McIntyre.[27] At the first meeting of the new parliament on 12 May 1999, the symbolism formally emphasised was that of the pre-union heritage – although the architectural background sprang from the sovereignty issues of the nineteenth rather than the seventeenth century. On 1 July, there followed the formal state opening. A grand ceremony at old Parliament House was followed by a procession on foot by MSPs, civic heads and young people to the General Assembly Hall, entering the chamber to the accompaniment of a fanfare composed by James MacMillan. The new era of home rule had begun in a setting which emphasised, above all, the continuity with Scotland's diverse architectural heritage of sovereignty.[28]

THE BUILDING AND RECEPTION OF HOLYROOD

The construction management contract for the permanent parliament building at Holyrood was let to Bovis in January 1999: in the interests of speed, building was to start before detailed designs were completed. But before the project could finally proceed, it first had to overcome the beginnings of disquiet and opposition among media and professional groups, and – most importantly – the newly elected MSPs themselves. Within the press, growing concern in the spring of 1999 began to focus on the mounting cost of the new project, while Edinburgh conservationists criticised the claim that the rebuilding of Queensberry House was a 'restoration' scheme, noting that the pantiled roofs envisaged by Miralles had no accurate basis in historical fact.[29] The most significant challenge, prompted especially by the revisions to the brief and the resulting rise in anticipated building costs from £50m to £62m, came from a cross-party group of MSPs, who put forward a motion to postpone the letting of construction contracts until a special committee had investigated both the costs question and the possibility of alternative sites, including the permanent use of the Interim Complex. In a parliamentary debate on 17 June 1999, First Minister Donald Dewar argued that most of the cost overrun was attributable to the 44% increase in the administrative accommodation, and appealed to members to 'stand by a radical vision'. In the vote that followed this debate, the project was approved. By this stage, the total anticipated cost was £109m (although another estimate by cost consultants Davis, Langdon & Everest put the figure at £136m). Subsequently, following consultations between the architects and the 'client' – the Scottish Parliament Corporate Body – some design alterations were agreed in response to members' criticisms. These affected, for instance, the chamber design, whose finally agreed form was based on the top section of a true ellipse. As part of a rearrangement of the eastern extremity of the site, the chamber was rotated to an almost north/south alignment, instead

ABOVE.
5.27. South elevation of the April 2000 Holyrood scheme, showing the denser useof the area in front of Queensberry House. (EMBT/RMJM Ltd)

OPPOSITE.
5.28. Aerial view of Holyrood site from south-east in February 2002. The MSP administrative block is almost complete, and the assembly block is under way. (RCAHMS)

of north-east/south-west, and was pushed closer to the eastern site boundary. As a result, two leaf-shaped buildings housing press and administrative facilities were displaced to the north and north-west of the chamber. In early July 1999, excavation work began on the foundations, and by September, piling on the Holyrood site was well under way.[30]

In early and mid-2000, the fortunes of the project underwent further vicissitudes. At a personal level, it was hit by the deaths of its two major figures, architect Enric Miralles (in July) and First Minister Donald Dewar (in October). Prior to that, a further and, it seemed, final adjustment had been made to the plans, chiefly in response to the need to provide an additional 2,275 square feet of accommodation. The site was now to be more densely exploited: the MSP entrance area was adjusted and a new, medium-height building was added on the Canongate frontage; and the main circulation route from the MSP administrative block to the assembly building was removed from Queensberry House to a new, two-storey foyer structure in the garden area. The external cladding of the parliament complex was changed in a striking way. The brownish, somewhat 'organic' appearance of the earlier plans was replaced by a range of shades of grey, including granite and slate facing to the walls, and steel roofing and sheet cladding; precast concrete blocks would be used for the garden-level base. This restrained colour scheme made an especially striking contrast with the cheerful 'fishing-village vernacular' restyling devised by Miralles for Queensberry House, complete with red pantiled roof. The £1.3m contract for the 1,000 tonnes of granite required for the cladding of the new building was eventually let to Scottish firm Fyfe Glenrock in December 2000.

By this stage, however, controversy about the delays and rising cost of the project was growing rapidly, and although a 'cap' level of £195 million was set by MSPs in September 2000, the likely cost soon escalated beyond that. The project's future had nevertheless been assured by a further vote by MSPs on 5 April 2000, and by the end of that year, the structure of the new MSP administrative building was virtually complete and substructure work had begun on the main debating chamber complex. Following the death of Miralles, and the parliamentary approval vote, the main outlines of the project seemed to be irrevocably fixed, with all further development of the design only a matter of detail – although the heightened concern with terrorism after 2001 led to the incorporation of substantial new security provisions. As construction proceeded, some architectural commentators continued to acclaim Miralles's design: for example, Duncan Macmillan argued in early 2003 that 'We seem unable to lift our eyes from the cost of the building itself to see what we are getting from our money. But sheathed in scaffolding and polythene sheeting, our parliament is a chrysalis. In a month or two a marvellous butterfly is going to emerge to astonish us all'. Among the wider public, however, the cost increases and building problems – the latter being tackled energetically by RMJM – by now overshadowed the architectural aspirations, and continued to do so for the rest of the construction period: by March 2002 the estimated final cost had reached £280m, by January 2003 £338m, and by February 2004 £431m. In spring 2003, First Minister Jack McConnell argued that 'the cost is currently far too high . . . the timetable slipping has damaged the reputation of the parliament', and promised an independent public investigation into the commissioning, design and building of the structure: accordingly, over an eight-month period between October 2003 and May 2004, Lord Fraser of Carmyllie chaired a formal inquiry into the project (held at the offices of the Scottish Land Court, Grosvenor Crescent, Edinburgh).[31]

The text of *The Architecture of Scottish Government* was finalised in spring 2004, several months before the publication of the Fraser Report, but much of the evidence presented to the inquiry suggested that the cost increases could largely have stemmed from a combination of the overriding emphasis on speed, and the specialised requirements of Miralles's complex design, both of which might have allowed contractors to charge higher prices – a similar situation to that which prevailed in the 1960s mass-housing 'systems boom', when the no-holds-barred push for speed and higher output through complex factory production fuelled sharp cost rises.[32] But by spring 2004, at any rate, the timescale for the final opening of the Holyrood complex was becoming firmer. Staff would begin moving in during late August, and parliamentary business would start in early September, with the official royal opening earmarked for 9 October, including a modestly scaled inaugural procession down the Royal Mile; external landscaping work would continue until November, and internal snagging (tidying up) work would continue into the next year. On 21 June, George Reid, Presiding Officer, commented that 'everyone in

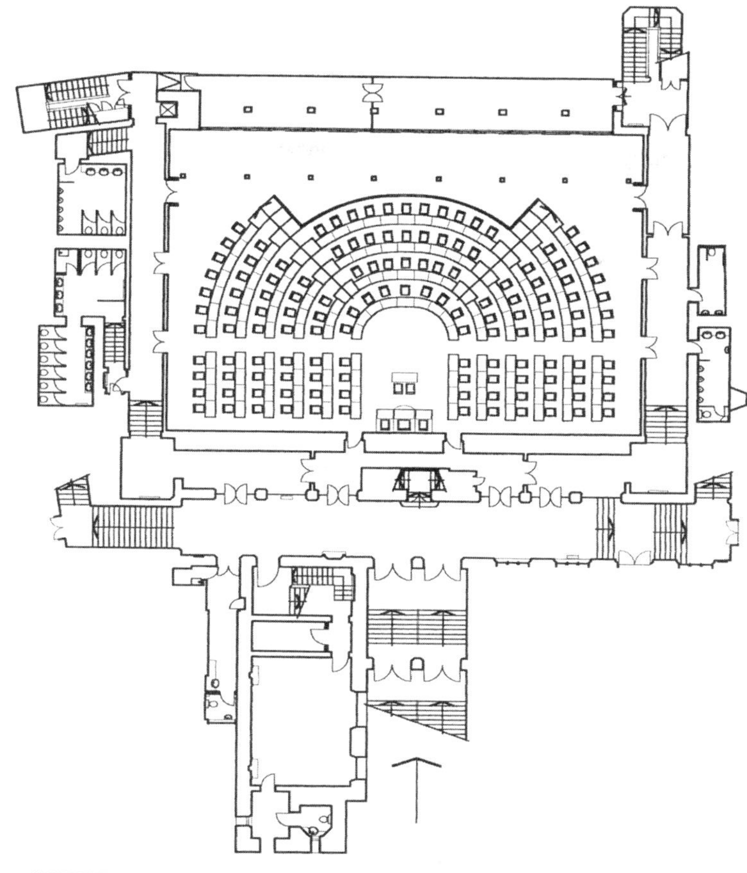

OPPOSITE.
5.29. The ceremonial approach to the interim Parliament chamber, in the Church of Scotland Assembly Hall, was through New College courtyard. It was this place, in 1982, that saw the formal meeting of Pope John Paul II and the Moderator of the General Assembly of the Church of Scotland – under the gaze of John Knox's statue. (Scottish Media Newspapers)

TOP.
5.30. 1998 layout plan by Simpson & Brown of the conversion of the Assembly Hall into the interim Parliament chamber. (Simpson & Brown)

BELOW.
5.31. The interim Parliament chamber in its newly-converted state, April 1999. (Simpson & Brown)

the parliament will no doubt share my happiness that this long and difficult process is coming to an end'.[33]

Now, increasingly, the tone of debate began to shift once again, with architectural evaluations of the nearly completed Holyrood building presenting a highly positive picture. These judgements were based not so much on the overall architectural conception – difficult to judge in the midst of what was still a building site – as on individual features and the detailing (aspects that have always been important in Britain, given the enduring power of Arts and Crafts values). The critic Hugh Pearman, for instance, argued that 'the quality of the finished work, the level of the detailing, is prodigious. It is remarkable to find such a level of individual craftsmanship in a building of this size'. Deyan Sudjic, former director of the Glasgow 1999 architecture festival, claimed more simply that 'Scotland's parliament is emerging as one of the finest modern British buildings of the last 50 years'. And finally Marcus Binney, writing in *The Times*, highlighted the building's wider international status, hailing it as 'a chamber of wonders on a scale not seen since the death of Antoni Gaudí almost a century ago. Enric Miralles has created a thrilling masterpiece full of suspense and invention. So heady and intoxicating is the experience that one wonders if there can be any bounds to the dreams and ambitions of MSPs'.[34]

NOTES

1. EMBT text, Royal Museum of Scotland exhibition, June 1998. M Binney, *The Times*, 22 May 2002, 11.
2. See for example G. Hassan (ed.), *A Guide to the Scottish Parliament*, Edinburgh, 1999; J. McFadden and M. Lazarowicz, *The Scottish Parliament – An Introduction*, 1999; Scottish Parliament Public Information Service, *The Scottish Parliament Factfile 3*, 1999; *Instant Portraits: the Handbook of MSPs*, Edinburgh, 1999.
3. *Herald*, 11 February 1992, 13; R. Emmerson, *Designs for the Scottish Parliament*, Dunfermline, 1992.
4. Kenneth Mailer, *Scotsman*, 20 January 1998; *Scotsman*, 17 September 1997; *Herald*, 20 October 1997; *Scotsman*, 17 October 1997; *Scotsman*, 6 November 2003, 21; *Scotsman*, 15 November 2003, 8.
5. *Scotsman*, 30 November 1998; Glendinning *et al*, *History of Scottish Architecture*, Chapter 9; M. Glendinning and D. Page, *Clone City*, 1999, Chapters 1 and 2.
6. *Daily Mail*, 24 December 1997.
7. Page & Park, *St Andrew's House: Scotland's Parliament on Calton Hill*, report issued 12 December 1997.
8. *Daily Mail*, 24 December 1997.

9. Royal Scottish Museum, 'Public Forum on Scotland's Parliament Building', debate on 4 December 1997; *Scotsman*, 10 January 1998; A. Massie, *Scotsman*, 14 January 1998; *Scottish Parliament Official Report*, 17 June 1999.
10. Edinburgh City Archive, Dean of Guild records, 27 May 1936 and 25 November 1960; RCAHMS, Threatened Buildings Survey, record notes by S. T. Green, 1998. See also forthcoming Historic Scotland/SUAT research report, edited by Gordon Barclay.
11. Scottish Office press release, 1 July 1997. For a fuller account of the competition process, see J. Gibbons, 'The Scottish Parliament Building Competition', in M. Fraser (ed.), *Essential Scotland*, London, 1998.
12. *Architect's Journal*, 5 February 1998; *Evening News*, 5 June 1998.
13. *Scotsman*, 28 March 1998, 4.
14. Royal Fine Art Commission for Scotland, Minds Meeting seminar, 21 August 1998 (M. Rawls); *Scottish Affairs*, special issue, 'Understanding Constitutional Change', March 1998; Andrew McMillan, 'One Foot in the Past', BBC television programme, 5 May 1998.
15. Information and notes from P. Ahrends, December 1998.
16. Text by Wilford, exhibition at Royal Museum of Scotland, June 1998; Minds Meeting, 21 August 1998 (L. Bain); *Scotsman*, 6 June 1998.
17. Minds Meeting, 21 August 1998 (Gordon Murray); *Herald*, 20 July 1998.
18. *Scotsman*, 6 June 1998; *Herald*, 26 June 1998 (anti-modern), *Scotsman*, 18 June 1998; *Scotsman*, 6 December 2003, 6.
19. P. Jodidio, *Contemporary European Architects*, iii, Köln, 1995, 113; H. van Dijk, 'Hejduk en Miralles, en dubbel verlies', *Archis*, September 2000.
20. First Minister: *Scottish Parliament Official Report*, 17 June 1999; lecture at opening of Miralles and Mackintosh exhibition, Hunterian Gallery, 1 November 1999; *Scotsman*, 26 November 2003, 11.
21. Quotes in this and following two paragraphs: EMBT presentation, exhibition, Royal Museum of Scotland, June 1998. See also F. Massad and E. Guerrero Yeste, *Enric Miralles: Metamorfosi del paesaggio*, Testo & Immagine, Roma, 2004, 42-4 and 81.
22. Secretary of State: *Scotsman* and *Herald*, 31 October 1998; *Scoop*, September 1998; *Sunday Times*, 25 October 1998, 10; exhibition panels, Royal Museum of Scotland, November 1998.
23. *Herald*, 31 October 1998. Enlargement: *Scottish Parliament Official Report*, 17 June 1999.
24. *Scotland on Sunday Magazine*, 14 November 1999, 20; *Scotland on Sunday*, 27 June 1999; *Evening News*, 8 June 1999, 2.
25. *Scotland on Sunday*, 1 March 1998; *Scotsman*, 2 March 1998, 21 March 1998.
26. *Scotsman*, 9 March 1999; *Prospect*, 69, 1999; *Scotsman*, 21 March 1998; *Scoop*, September 1998; *Herald*, 17 August 1998; *Scotsman*, 25 June 1999.
27. P. Jennings and E. McCabe, *The Pope in Britain*, London, 1982, 100-1.
28. *Scotsman*, 1 and 2 July 1999.
29. *Daily Mail*, 11 June 1999; *Sunday Times*, 16 May 1999; *Scotland on Sunday*, 14 March 1999 and 30 May 1999; *Scotsman*, 21 May 1999; *Evening News*, 25 May 1999. Bovis: *Scotsman*, 6 December 2003, 1.
30. *Scottish Parliament Official Report*, 17 June 1999; *Daily Record*, 18 June 1999; *Evening News*, 27 May 1999; *Scotsman*, 17 December 2003, 19.
31. See for instance *Evening News*, 17 November 1999, 11 December 1999, 12 January 2000, 14 March 2000; *Scotland on Sunday*, 5 March 2000; *Scottish Sun*, 24 February 2000; *Scotsman*, 26 February 2000; *Scottish Parliament Official Report*, 5 April 2000; EMBT/RMJM, Scottish Parliament Building, Holyrood, Edinburgh, Amendment to Planning Consent Report (unpublished report), Edinburgh, April 2000; R. W. Black

(Auditor-General for Scotland), *The New Scottish Parliament Building – An Examination of the Management of the Holyrood Project* (official report), Edinburgh, 19 September 2000; P. Wilson, 'No More Messiahs', *ARCA*, 4, 2000, 15-18; *Sunday Herald*, 9 July 2000; D. Black, *All the First Minister's Men*, Edinburgh, 2001; *Scotsman*, 20 June 2001, 8; *Scotland on Sunday*, 24 June 2001, 7 and 12; G. Stamp, *Country Life*, 23 August 2001; *Scotsman*, 14 November 2001, 6 and 11; P. Wilson, *Scotsman S2*, 15 November 2001, 23; D. Macmillan, *Scotsman S2*, 6 March 2003, 2; *Evening News*, 8 April 2003, 1; *Herald*, 11 April 2003, 13; *Sunday Times*, 20 April 2003, 2. Cost overruns: *Scotsman*, 7 June 2003, 5; *Scotsman*, 27 June 2003, 3; *Scotsman*, 25 February 2004, 1; *Scotsman*, 8 May 2004, 19.

32. *Sunday Herald*, 24 September 2003, 15 (quotation by Adrian Barrick, editor of *Building* magazine); *Scotsman*, 26 May 2004, 7. 1960s comparison: M. Glendinning and S. Muthesius, *Tower Block*, 1994, Chapters 22, 24, 31.
33. *Herald*, 22 June 2004, 6.
34. *Sunday Herald*, 23 May 2004, 1; *The Times*, 22 May 2004, 11; see also J. Merrick, *The Independent Review*, 9 June 2004, 12.

CONCLUSION

In its report on the 1883 foundation-laying of its new Municipal Buildings, Glasgow Town Council boasted of the four successive headquarters buildings it had occupied during the course of the nineteenth century. The council represented this progression as a simple, linear narrative of ever-increasing size and grandeur, concerned with only one focal building at any one time. The national story set out in this book has been in many ways the opposite to that neat, well-defined pattern. In this account, we have witnessed a complicated, even at times chaotic, mosaic of cultural contexts, building programmes and formal architectural responses.

As was clear at the outset, this volume has not been concerned solely or even largely with the conventional grand legislature or government ministry buildings of recent centuries, standing in proud isolation. Such an approach would have left little to tell between the union of 1707, on the one hand, and, on the other, the commissioning of St Andrew's House in 1934 (or even the decision to build a new parliament in 1997). In some respects, the nineteenth- and twentieth-century concept of the grand national institution – including even, perhaps, the new Scottish parliament building – now seems an aberration from more enduring and complex patterns. To us, it appears obvious that any history of the buildings of state power must necessarily address a vast variety of types and variants. Today, we can appreciate that the lack of a formal 'parliament building' in Scotland during the eighteenth, nineteenth and twentieth centuries did not prevent, and may even have assisted, the commissioning of a wide variety of other buildings of government and assembly, all of which contributed to the shaping of the country's collective cultural identity.

But despite this diversity, all the buildings and building types covered in this book, even those for local or specialised purposes,

LEFT.
5.32. Royal Bank of Scotland chief executive Sir George Mathewson launches a commemorative £1 note, featuring the interim Parliament/Free Church College building, on 11 May 1999. (*Herald*, 12 May 1999; Scottish Media Newspapers)

BELOW.
5.33. Group photograph of the newly-elected MSPs in the interim chamber on the day of the first meeting of Parliament, 12 May 1999. (National Galleries of Scotland; photograph by Robin Gillanders)

OPPOSITE TOP.
5.34. State inauguration of the Parliament, 1 July 1999: part of the public procession seen on the Mound. (RCAHMS D65712)

OPPOSITE BELOW.
5.35. The west facade of the members' office block, Holyrood parliament, seen in May 2004. (M. Glendinning)

LINLITHGOW

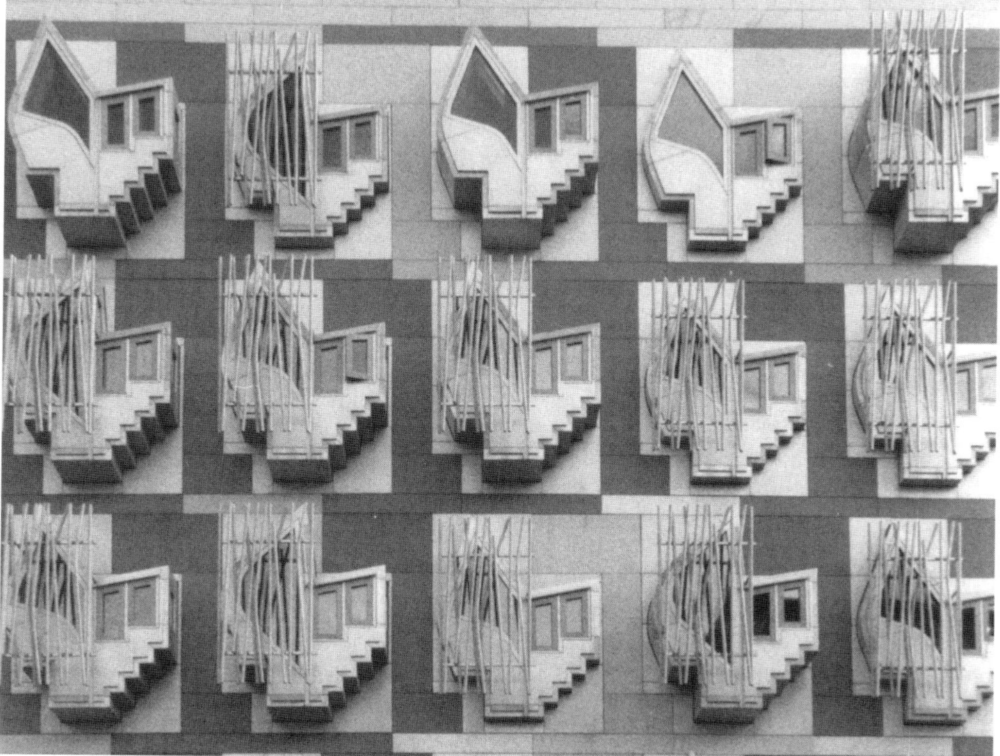

had one thing in common. They were concerned to a greater or lesser extent with the problems of 'government' and 'political life', problems first identified and defined by the Greeks and Romans. Their task was the adaptation of the *res publica* ideal to very different circumstances during the medieval and modern ages.

During the era of monarchy and estates, the enduring ideal was a 'community of the realm' which would balance the interests of the king, the nobility and the church, meeting in a mixture of royal, noble, civic and religious buildings; whereas after the Reformation that balance was replaced by confrontation and even civil war. Parliamentary and governmental institutions, and building projects such as the Parliament House legislature and the enlarged Holyrood royal palace in Edinburgh, reflected that shift from consensus to conflict. There was a polarisation between an absolutist monarchy and an oligarchic government by committee or assembly; but the small-scale, elite, face-to-face processes inherited from antiquity remained undisturbed.

In the modern age of 'Improvement' and urbanisation, a wider but more stable formula of government was adopted. This formula was rooted in the greater breadth of the new mass society, but was also more institutionally autonomous and self-absorbed than the face-to-face mechanisms of earlier ages, in some ways existing largely for its own sake. Political activity was controlled through the system of representative democracy and mass citizen elections, while administration was supported by an ever-growing bureaucracy. With the departure of the royal court and the legislature to London, the emphasis of this activity, especially following Reform in 1832, moved to a local municipal level, where a multiplicity of civic administration and council-chamber buildings was built, and to the church, where the emerging conflict between presbyterians and the state was highlighted in the rival general assembly projects of the main Protestant sects.

And after 1885, with the establishment and growth of the Scottish Office as an administration-only system of devolution, the importance of legislative or assembly-based activities relative to bureaucracy declined steeply within central government, but was preserved within local government; an increasing number of issues of 'democratic government' saw elected councillors lined up on one side, and Scottish Office civil servants on the other. Although in

5.36. The debating chamber in the new Scottish Parliament complex at Holyrood, Edinburgh. (Adam Elder © Scottish Parliamentary Corporate Body 2004)

other countries, monumental parliaments and representative national capitols continued to be constructed, in Scotland the architecture of government in this age was dominated by office buildings, including central and local government centres as well as the fortified emergency complexes built in defence against mass warfare. The post-1968 undermining of the social-administration formula of government opened up the field of 'national politics' once again, with the national question replacing class conflict and social provision as the focal issue. Accordingly, the national legislature building-type began to re-emerge as a key issue within the architecture of Scottish government, whether through the re-use of old buildings (at Calton Hill and the Mound) or through the commissioning of a brand-new design. How long that position will be maintained, in the new century, can only be a matter of conjecture.

What has emerged above all, however, from this millennium-long story of Scottish government and assembly buildings is the fact that while their overall political task has remained the same as that handed down by antiquity – to try to capture in built form the ever-shifting balance between the monarchical, oligarchic and democratic concepts of sovereignty – the building types and architectural responses to this task have varied constantly and radically. It seems inevitable that they will continue to do so for the foreseeable future.

APPENDIX

Nicholas de Gueudeville, *Chart giving a general idea of the government of Scotland, the order of the procession or riding of its parliament and of the sitting of that illustrious body.* Published in Chatelaine, *Atlas Historique*, Amsterdam, 1708.

TRANSLATION AND COMMENTARY BY ATHOL MURRAY

TRANSLATED ANNOTATIONS TO VIEW OF PARLIAMENT HALL

Text by de Gueudeville

Parliament in session.

1. The king's throne
2. Lord High Commissioner
3. Lord High Chancellor
4. Great Officers of State
5. Table for the king's crown and sword
6. Lord High Constable
7. Great [Earl] Marischal
8. Lord Clerk Register
9. Secretary of State
10. Lyon King of Arms
11. Gentleman Usher
12. Heralds and pursuivants
13. Tellers of votes
14. Archbishops
15. Earls
16. Bishops and viscounts
17. Barons
18. Commissioners of shires and burghs
19. Pallas representing Scotland, holding a sword in one hand, the arms of Scotland in the other, treading trophies beneath her feet, and on her breast the cap of liberty

TRANSLATED ANNOTATIONS TO VIEW OF PROCESSION OR RIDING OF PARLIAMENT

Order of the procession of the Scottish Parliament members, to and from the Parliament on the first day of a session [reading from the top].

Door of parliament
(first row, left to right)
Trumpeters; pursuivants; commissioners of shires, burghs and towns
(second row, right to left)
Commissioners of shires, etc; Lord Advocate [and Lord Justice Clerk]; lords barons; bishops; archbishops; earls and viscounts
(third row, left to right)
Earls; viscounts; king's trumpeters; pursuivants; heralds; Lyon King of Arms; Gentleman Usher; macer; marquess bearing the king's crown; macer
(fourth row, right to left)
Earl bearing the king's sword; earl bearing the king's sceptre; bearer of the king's commission; High Constable; High Commissioner; Earl Marischal; Master of Horse; captain of the king's guards; king's guards
Abbey of Holyrood, or Holyrood house.

GENERAL REMARKS IN MARGIN OF PICTURE

Translation of text by de Gueudeville

Scotland is governed by much the same laws as England, consisting of civil law, royal ordinances and acts of parliament, which are called municipal laws. Royal authority over Scotland has the same prerogatives as in England to adjourn, prorogue or dissolve parliament, and increase or decrease the number of members composing it. He [the king] is the embodiment of justice and of the laws. The power of making war and peace is solely in his hands. All naval and military officers belong to him, and all the armed forces of the kingdom. He can erect bishoprics, and impose duties and customs on all kinds of merchandise entering or leaving the kingdom. He can also require his subjects to furnish him with 20,000 foot soldiers and 2,000 horse.

Parliament, as represented here, is composed of four estates, namely the higher nobility, the clergy, the members for the shires and the members for the towns and burghs. The clergy are represented by the Archbishops of St Andrews and Glasgow and the bishops of the kingdom. The Archbishop of St Andrews is primate of the kingdom; the bishops are peers of the realm and have, like those of England, courts in which they judge without colleagues, and all acts of court proceed in their name, not the king's. They preside over the provincial synods of their dioceses, held twice a year in April and October, for reformation of morals. The nobility is divided into two orders; those of the first rank are the lords, or the peers of the realm, who are dukes, marquesses, earls, viscounts and barons. Their number is almost as great as in England. The second nobility comprises the lower barons, who are nobles sent by the shires to attend parliament in their name. Formerly they had the right to appear there, or to send such number of deputies as they wished, but the great costs which they were obliged to lay out led them to petition James I to exempt them. This was done by an act of 1430, by which the king left them free to come in person or to send deputies, without fixing the number. They lost this privilege by negligence or the mischance of civil wars, so that, to re-establish the ancient form of government, James VI ordained that each shire should choose two nobles by a plurality of votes, that the deputies they had elected should have the rank and quality of lesser barons, and that they should be called commissioners for the shires. The people were represented in parliament by the commissioners for the towns and burghs.

When it pleased the king to call his parliament, and the members had come to Edinburgh, capital of Scotland, they assembled at the Abbey of Holyrood, or Holyroodhouse, to go in procession on foot or horseback, as shown here. In this ceremony, having arrived at the Parliament House, the High Commissioner takes his seat on the throne, beside him the Great Officers of State, and on either side the prelates and secular peers, the commissioners for the shires to the right and those for the burghs to the left. The regalia are placed on a table by the High Constable and the Earl Marischal. After prayer by the Bishop of Edinburgh, the roll of members is read. Thereafter the Lord Chancellor approaches the throne, kneels down, and receives from the High Commissioner's hands the king's commission, which he gives to the Secretary to read. Next there is read the form of words, which is the manner and order of [constituting] the meeting, after which Lyon

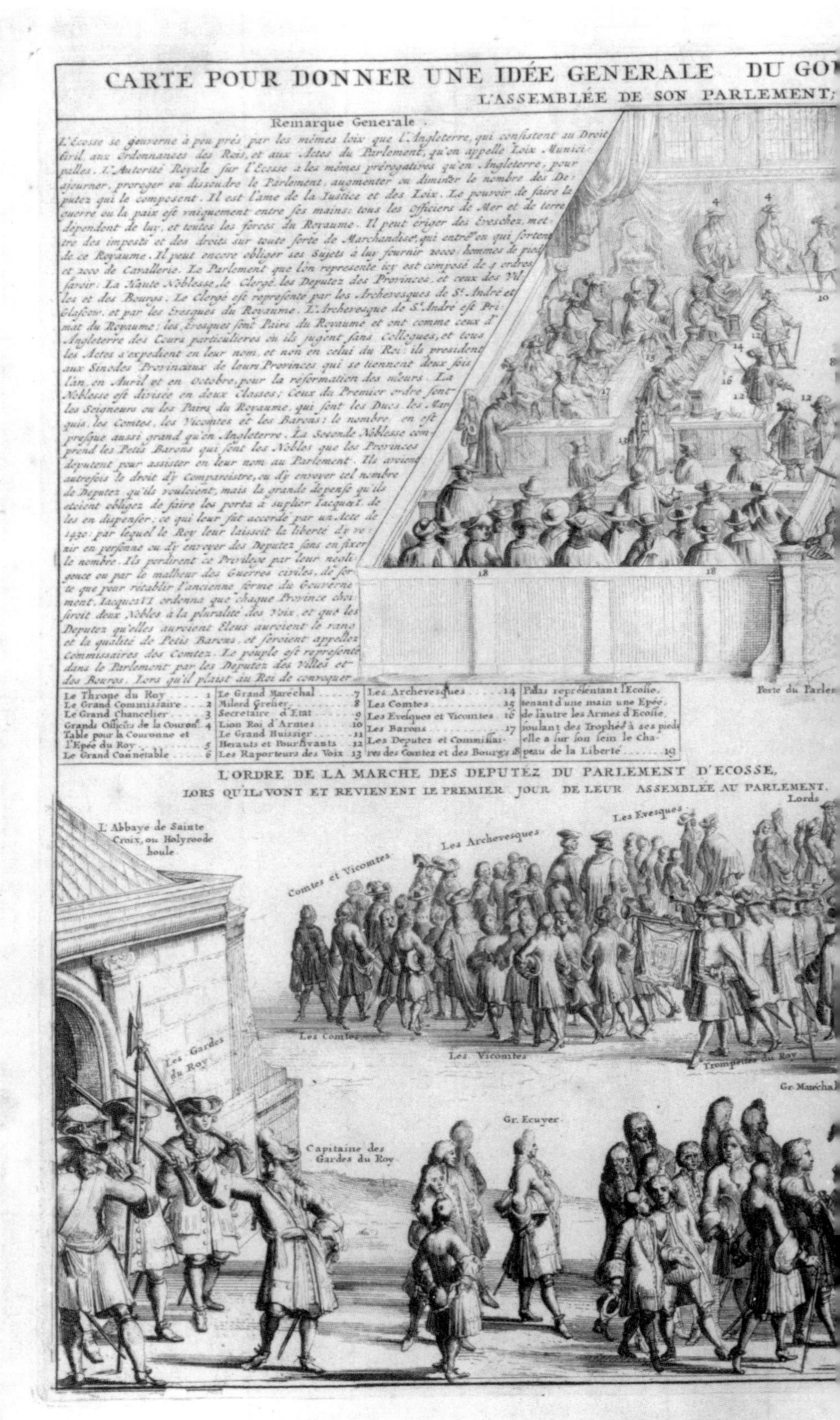

CARTE POUR DONNER UNE IDÉE GENERALE DU GO
L'ASSEMBLÉE DE SON PARLEMENT;
Remarque Generale.
L'Ecosse se gouverne à peu prés par les mémes loix que l'Angleterre, qui consistent au Droit
tivil, aux Ordonnances des Rois, et aux Actes du Parlement, qu'on appelle Loix Munici-
palles. L'Autorité Royale sur l'Ecosse a les mémes prérogatives qu'en Angleterre, pour
ajourner, proroger ou dissoudre le Parlement, augmenter ou diminuer le nombre des Deputez qui le composent. Il est l'ame de la Iustice et des Loix. Le pouvoir de faire la
guerre ou la paix est vniquement entre ses mains: tous les Officiers de Mer et de terre
dépendent de luy, et toutes les forces du Royaume. Il peut ériger des Eveschez, met-
tre des impests et des droits sur toute sorte de Marchandise, qui entre en qui sorten
de ce Royaume. Il peut encore obliger ses Sujets à luy fournir 20000. hommes de pied
et 2000 de Cavallerie. Le Parlement que lon represente icy est composé de 4 ordres
savoir: La Haute Noblesse, le Clergé, les Deputez des Provinces, et ceux des Villes et des Bourgs. Le Clergé est represente par les Archevesques de St. André et
Glascow, et par les Evesques du Royaume. L'Archevesque de St. André est Pri-
mat du Royaume; les Evesques sont Pairs du Royaume et ont comme ceux d'
Angleterre des Cours particulieres où ils jugent sans Collegues, et tous
les Actes s'expedient en leur nom, et non en celui du Roi: ils president
aux Sinodes Provinciaux de leurs Provinces qui se tiennent deux fois
l'an, en Avril et en Octobre, pour la réformation des mœurs. La
Noblesse est divisée en deux Classes; Ceux du Premier ordre sont
les Seigneurs ou les Pairs du Royaume, qui sont les Ducs, les Marquis, les Comtes, les Vicomtes et les Barons; le nombre en est
presque aussi grand qu'en Angleterre. La Seconde Noblesse com-
prend les Petis Barons qui sont les Nobles que les Provinces
deputent pour assister en leur nom au Parlement. Ils avoient
autrefois le droit d'y Compareistre, ou d'y envoyer tel nombre
de Deputez qu'ils vouloient; mais la grande depense qu'ils
etoient obligez de faire les porta à suplier Iacques I. de
les en dispenser; ce qui leur fut accordé par un Acte de
1430: par lequel le Roy leur laissoit la liberté d'y ve-
nir en personne ou d'y envoyer des Deputez sans en fixer
le nombre. Ils perdirent ce Privilege par leur negligence ou par le malheur des Guerres civiles, de sorte que pour rétablir l'ancienne forme du Gouverne-
ment, Iacques VI ordonna que chaque Province choi-
siroit deux Nobles à la pluralité des Voix, et que les
Deputez qu'elles auroient Eleus auroient le rang
et la qualité de Petis Barons, et seroient appellez
Commissaires des Comtez. Le peuple est represente
dans le Parlement par les Deputez des Villes et
des Bourgs. Lors qu'il plaist au Roi de convoquer
Le Throne du Roy ... 1
Le Grand Commissaire ... 2
Le Grand Chancelier ... 3
Grands Officiers de la Couronne ... 4
Table pour la Couronne et l'Epée du Roy ... 5
Le Grand Connétable ... 6
Le Grand Maréchal ... 7
Milord Grefier ... 8
Secretaire d'Etat ... 9
Lion Roi d'Armes ... 10
Le Grand Huissier ... 11
Herauts et Poursuivants ... 12
Les Raporteurs des Voix ... 13
Les Archevesques ... 14
Les Comtes ... 15
Les Evesques et Vicomtes ... 16
Les Barons ... 17
Les Deputez et Commissaires des Comtez et des Bourgs ... 18
Palas representant l'Ecosse, tenant d'une main une Epée, de l'autre les Armes d'Ecosse, foulant des Trophée à ses pieds elle a sur son sein le Chapeau de la Liberté ... 19
Porte du Parle
L'ORDRE DE LA MARCHE DES DEPUTÉZ DU PARLEMENT D'ECOSSE,
LORS QU'ILS VONT ET REVIENENT LE PREMIER JOUR DE LEUR ASSEMBLÉE AU PARLEMENT.
L'Abbaye de Sainte Croix, ou Holyroode house
Comtes et Vicomtes
Les Archevesques
Les Evesques
Lords
Les Comtes
Les Vicomtes
Trompettes du Roy
Les Gardes du Roy
Capitaine des Gardes du Roy
Gr. Ecuyer
Gr. Maréchal

NT D'ECOSSE; L'ORDRE DE LA MARCHE OU CAVALCADE DE
SÉANCE DE CET ILLUSTRE CORPS.

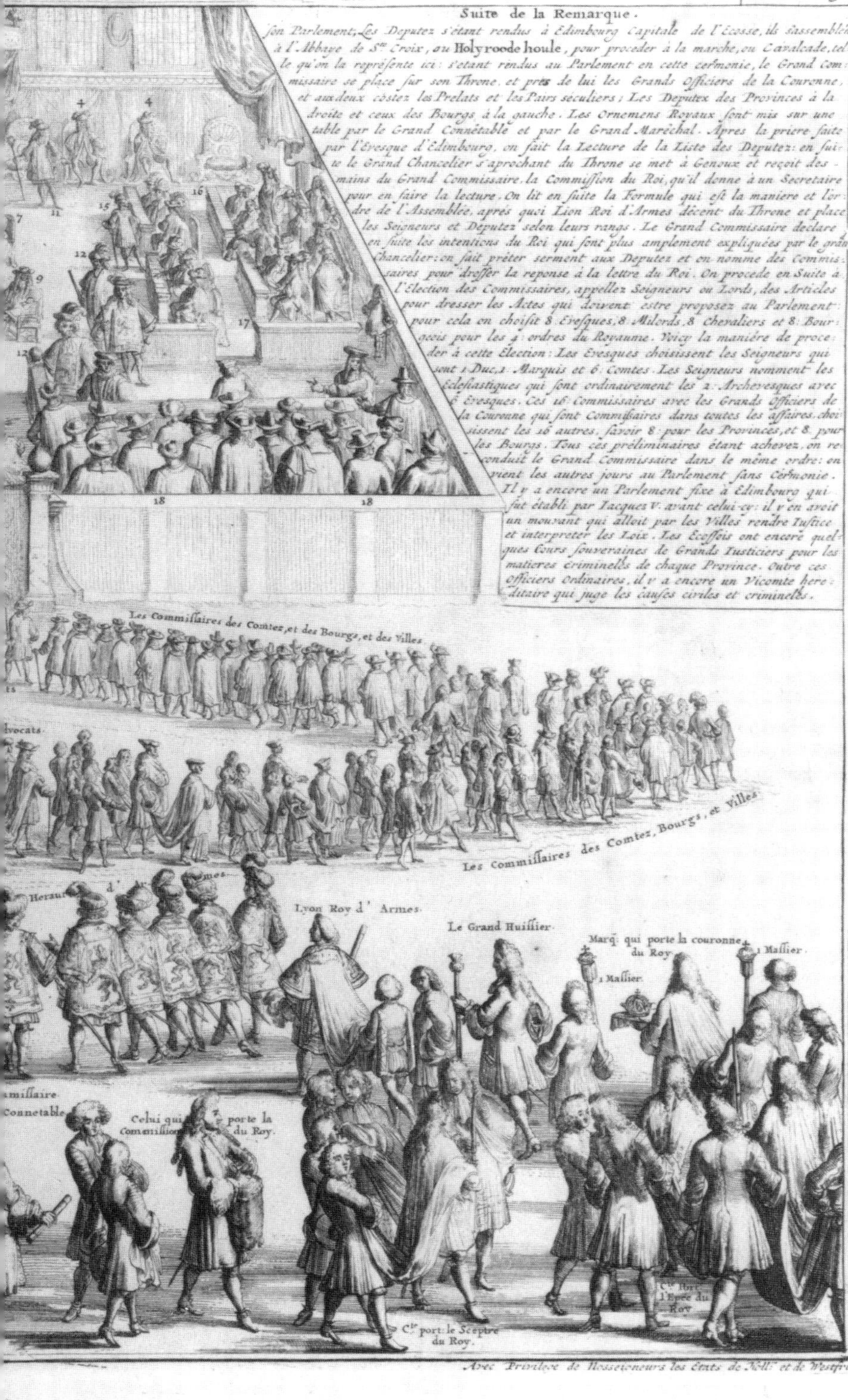

Suite de la Remarque.

son Parlement, Les Deputez s'étant rendus à Edimbourg Capitale de l'Ecosse, ils s'assemblen à l'Abbaye de S.te Croix, ou Holyroode houle, *pour proceder à la marche, ou Cavalcade, telle qu'on la représente ici: s'etant rendus au Parlement en cette cermonie, le Grand Commissaire se place sur son Throne. et près de lui les Grands Officiers de la Couronne, et aux deux côstez les Prelats et les Pairs seculiers; Les Deputez des Provinces à la droite et ceux des Bourgs à la gauche. Les Ornemens Royaux sont mis sur une table par le Grand Connêtable et par le Grand Marêchal. Apres la priere faite par l'Evesque d'Edimbourg, on fait la Lecture de la Liste des Deputez: en suite le Grand Chancelier s'aprochant du Throne se met à Genoux et reçoit des mains du Grand Commissaire la Commission du Roi, qu'il donne à un Secretaire pour en faire la lecture. On lit en suite la Formule qui est la maniere et l'ordre de l'Assemblée, aprés quoi Lion Roi d'Armes décent du Throne et place les Seigneurs et Deputez selon leurs rangs. Le Grand Commissaire declare en suite les intentions du Roi qui sont plus amplement expliquées par le gran Chancelier: on fait prêter serment aux Deputez et on nomme des Commissaires pour dresser la reponse à la lettre du Roi. On procede en Suite à l'Election des Commissaires, appellez Seigneurs ou Lords, des Articles pour dresser les Actes qui doivent estre proposez au Parlement: pour cela on choisit 8. Evesques, 8. Milords, 8. Chevaliers et 8. Bourgeois pour les 4. ordres du Royaume. Voicy la manière de proceder à cette Election: Les Evesques choisissent les Seigneurs qui sont 1. Duc, 1. Marquis et 6. Comtes. Les Seigneurs nomment les Ecclesiastiques qui sont ordinairement les 2. Archevesques avec 6 Evesques. Ces 16. Commissaires avec les Grands Officiers de la Couronne qui sont Commissaires dans toutes les affaires, choisissent les 16 autres, savoir 8. pour les Provinces, et 8. pour les Bourgs. Tous ces préliminaires étant achevez, on reconduit le Grand Commissaire dans le même ordre: on vient les autres jours au Parlement sans Cérmonie. Il y a encore un Parlement fixe à Elimbourg qui fut établi par Jacques V. avant celui-cy: il y en avoit un mouvant qui alloit par les Villes rendre Justice et interpreter les Loix. Les Ecossois ont encore quelques Cours souveraines de Grands Justiciers pour les matieres criminelles de chaque Province. Outre ces Officiers Ordinaires, il y a encore un Vicomte hereditaire qui juge les causes civiles et criminelles.*

Les Commissaires des Comtez, et des Bourgs, et des Villes

vocats

Les Commissaires des Comtez, Bourgs, et Villes

Herauts d'Armes

Lyon Roy d'Armes

Le Grand Huissier

Marq. qui porte la couronne du Roy

1 Massier

1 Massier

missaire

Connetable

Celui qui porte la Commission du Roy

C.er port: le Sceptre du Roy

C.te port. l'Epée du Roy

King of Arms comes down from the throne and seats the lords and members according to their rank. Then the High Commissioner makes known the king's proposals, which are explained more fully by the Lord Chancellor. The oath is tendered to the members, and commissioners are nominated to draft the reply to the king's letter. After that they proceed to the election of commissioners, called Lords of the Articles, for drawing up the acts that are to be put forward to parliament. For this there are chosen eight bishops, eight lords, eight knights, eight burgesses, for the four estates of the realm. The election proceeds in this way: the bishops choose the lords, who are a duke, a marquess and six earls; the lords name the bishops, normally the two archbishops and six bishops. These commissioners, with the Great Officers of State, who are commissioners for all business, choose the other sixteen, namely, eight for the shires and eight for the burghs. Once all this preliminary business is completed, the High Commissioner is brought back [to Holyroodhouse] in the same manner as before. On other days they come to parliament without ceremony. There is another parliament [the College of Justice] sitting at Edinburgh, which was established by James V, before which there was an itinerant one which went from town to town, to deliver justice and interpret the laws. The Scots have other supreme courts of High Justices [Lords of Justiciary] for criminal matters in each shire. Besides these ordinary officials there is a hereditary sheriff [in the shire], who judges civil and criminal cases.

HISTORICAL NOTE

Athol Murray

This engraving, showing the procession from Holyroodhouse to Parliament House and the scene inside the chamber, is the only known representation of the pre-union Scottish parliament in session. It appeared in Chatelaine's *Atlas Historique*, published in Amsterdam in 1708, along with similar pictures of the parliaments of Ireland, England and other countries. The Scottish parliament is shown, not as it was in 1707, but as it was more than twenty years earlier. From internal evidence and the accompanying text (by Nicholas de Gueudeville) it seems likely that the scene is of the opening of James VII's parliament on 23 April 1685, with the Lord Chancellor kneeling to receive the royal commission from the High Commissioner. This was the last parliament in which bishops sat as one of the Estates and Lords of the Articles were elected to manage parliamentary business. Though perhaps working from a contemporary drawing, the engraver has used artistic licence. The Parliament Hall was longer and narrower than the chamber depicted in the plate. The space nearest the door, shown as occupied by the commissioners of shires and burghs, must have been at least double the size to accommodate more than sixty of each, besides the 'strangers' having business with the parliament, who were allowed to occupy the rear form. The door itself was at the north-east of the east wall, not at the centre of the north wall, and was crowned by the royal arms, flanked by statues of Justice and Mercy, not by a symbolic figure of Pallas.

Considerations of space may have suggested showing a foot procession to the Parliament, rather than the actual mounted Riding of Parliament. This is described in contemporary records and depicted in drawings by Roderick Chalmers (Ross Herald 1724–46), from which sets of engravings were made by Thomas Sommers and Alexander Kincaid. There are other errors: for instance the commissioners for the burghs preceded those for the shires, and viscounts preceded earls; the 'Lords Advocats' are those Officers of State who were not peers (in 1685 the Advocate and Justice Clerk); the 'Honours' (crown, sword and sceptre) are shown in the wrong order; and the rear of the procession was brought up by the Horse Guards.

Gueudeville's text may derive, in part at least, from an English (or Scots) original, in places imperfectly understood by the translator, notably in dealing with the ceremony of 'fencing the parliament' which followed the reading of the royal commission. The text seems to equate the College of Justice (Court of Session) with a French *parlement*, and gives a very brief and garbled account of the High Court of Justiciary and the office of sheriff. The present English translation has tried to restore the proper terminology and to give the persons depicted their correct Scottish titles.

Further reading: see Bibliography (Chapter 2 section).

BIBLIOGRAPHY

GENERAL

D. Dean and C. Jones (eds.), *Parliament and Locality, 1660–1939*, Edinburgh, 1998

J. Durm, H. Ende and E. Schmitt (general eds.), *Handbuch der Architektur, Band iv (7:2): Parlamentshäuser und Standehäuser*, 2nd edition, Stuttgart, 1900

M. Glendinning, R. MacInnes, A. MacKechnie, *A History of Scottish Architecture*, Edinburgh, 1996

J.S. Hearn, 'The social contract', *Scottish Affairs*, Spring 1998

H.R. Hitchcock and W. Seale, *Temples of Democracy*, New York, 1976

V. Herman and F. Mendel, *Parliaments of the World*, London, 1976

D. Hooson, *Democracy and National Identity*, Oxford, 1994

H. Kalman, A *History of Canadian Architecture*, Oxford, 1994, 720–1

P. Laundy, *Parliaments in the Modern World*, Aldershot, 1989

S. Muthesius, 'Parliamentarism, Giganticism, Style and Criticism', in Museum of Fine Arts (Budapest), *The House of the Nation: Parliament Plans for Budapest*, Budapest, 2000, 289–96

N. Pevsner, *A History of Building Types*, London, 1976

M. Pittock, *The Invention of Scotland*, London, 1991

Scottish Parliament Public Information Service, Factfile 2: *The Scottish Parliamentary Tradition*, Edinburgh, 1999

L.J. Vale, *Architecture, Power and National Identity*, New Haven, 1992

INTRODUCTION

M.I. Finley, *Democracy Ancient and Modern*, London, 1985

W.G. Forrest, *The Emergence of Greek Democracy*, London, 1966

E. Guhl and W. Koner, *Everyday Life of the Greeks and Romans*, London, 1989

P. Jones and K. Sidwell, *The World of Rome*, Cambridge, 1997

A.W. Lawrence, *Greek Architecture*, London, 1983

R.P. McBrien (ed.), *The Harper-Collins Encyclopedia of Catholicism*, New York City, 1995

O.F. Robinson, *Ancient Rome, City Planning and Administration*, London, 1994

F. Sear, *Roman Architecture*, London, 1989

Vitruvius, *The Ten Books on Architecture*, New York, 1960 edition (trans. by M.H. Morgan)

CHAPTER I

Acts of the Lordship of the Isles, 1336–1493, Scottish History Society, Edinburgh, 1986

S. Airlie, 'The view from Maastricht', in B. E. Crawford (ed.), *Scotland in Dark Age Europe*, St Andrews, 1994, 33–46

L. Alcock and E. A. Alcock, 'Reconnaissance excavations on early historic fortifications and other royal sites in Scotland, 1974–84: excavations and other fieldwork at Forteviot, Perthshire, 1981', *Proceedings of the Society of Antiquaries of Scotland*, 122, 1992, 215–93

W. Bower, *Scotichronicon*, edited by D.E.R. Watt and others, 9 volumes, Aberdeen, 1987–98

I. Campbell, 'Linlithgow's "Princely Palace" and its influence in Europe', *Architectural Heritage*, 5, 1995, 1–20

J. Cunningham, *The Church History of Scotland*, 2, Edinburgh, 1859

A Diurnal of Remarkable Occurrents that have passed within the country of Scotland from the death of King James the Fourth till the year 1575 (Bannatyne and Maitland Clubs), Edinburgh, 1833

J.G. Dunbar, 'The palace of Holyroodhouse during the first half of the sixteenth century', *The Archaeological Journal*, 120, 1964

J.G. Dunbar, *Scottish Royal Palaces*, East Linton, 1999

A.A.M. Duncan, 'The early parliaments of Scotland', *Scottish Historical Review*, 45, 1966, 36–58

R. Fawcett, *Scottish Abbeys and Priories*, London, 1994

R. Fawcett, *Scottish Cathedrals*, London, 1997

S. Foster, I. Macinnes, and R. MacInnes (eds.), *Scottish Power*

Centres, Glasgow, 1998
The Historie and Life of King James the Sext (Bannatyne Club), Edinburgh, 1825
A.C. Lawrie (ed.), *Early Scottish Charters prior to 1153*, Glasgow, 1905
J. Cameron Lees, *St Giles'*, Edinburgh, 1889
D. MacGibbon and T. Ross, *The Ecclesiastical Architecture of Scotland*, Edinburgh, 1896–7
P.G.B. McNeill and H.L. MacQueen (eds.), *Atlas of Scottish History to 1707*, Edinburgh, 1996
R. Myers, *Parliaments and Estates in Europe to 1789*, London, 1975
R. Oram and G.P. Stell (eds.), *Lordship and Architecture in Medieval and Renaissance Scotland*, East Linton, forthcoming
R.S. Rait, *The Parliaments of Scotland*, Glasgow, 1924
RCAHMS, *City of Edinburgh*, Edinburgh, 1951
RCAHMS, *Tolbooths and Town Houses*, Edinburgh, 1996
G.P. Stell, 'The Earliest Tolbooths', *Proceedings of the Society of Antiquaries of Scotland*, 1981
J. Stuart and others (eds.), *The Exchequer Rolls of Scotland*, Edinburgh, 1878–1908
R. Tanner, *The Late Medieval Scottish Parliament*, East Linton, 2001
T. Thomson and C. Innes (eds.), *The Acts of the Parliaments of Scotland*, Edinburgh, 1814–75
D.E.R. Watt, 'The Provincial Council of the Scottish Church, 1215–1472', in A. Grant and K.J. Stringer (eds.), *Medieval Scotland: Crown, Lordship and Community*, Edinburgh, 1993, 140–55

CHAPTER 2

D. Allan, *Philosophy and Politics in Later Stuart Scotland*, East Linton, 2000
H. Armet, 'All the statelie buildings of Thomas Robertson' and 'Notes on Rebuilding in Edinburgh in the last Quarter of the Seventeenth Century', *Book of the Old Edinburgh Club*, 29, 1956
H. Arnot, *The History of Edinburgh*, London, 1779
R. Baillie, *Letters and Journals* (Bannatyne Club), Edinburgh, 1830
E.W.M. Balfour-Melville (ed.), *An Account of the Proceedings of the Estates in Scotland, 1689–90*, Scottish History Society third series, 47, Edinburgh, 1955
I.G.Brown, *Building for Books: the Architectural Evolution of the*

Advocates' Library, 1689–1925, Aberdeen, 1989
R. Cant, *The University of St Andrews*, Edinburgh, 1970
Lord Cullen, *Parliament House, A Short History and Guide*, Edinburgh, 1992
G.M. Ditchfield, D. Hayton and C. Jones (eds.), *British Parliamentary Lists, 1660–1800: a Register*, London, 1995
J.G. Fyfe, *Scottish Diaries and Memoirs: 1550–1746*, Stirling, 1928
J. Goodare, 'The Scottish Parliament of 1621', *Historical Journal*, 38:1, 1995, 29–51
J. Goodare, 'Scottish Parliamentary Records, 1560–1603', *Historical Research*, October 1999
J. Goodare, *State and Society in Early Modern Scotland*, Oxford, 1999
J. Grant, *Old and New Edinburgh*, London, n.d.
R.K. Hannay and G.P.H. Watson, 'The Building of the Parliament House', *Book of the Old Edinburgh Club*, 13, 1924
J. Imrie and J. Dunbar (eds.), *Accounts of the Masters of Works for building and repairing Royal Palaces and Castles*, 2, Edinburgh, 1982
T. Innes of Learney, 'The Scottish Parliament: its symbolism and its ceremonial', *Juridical Review*, 1932
C. Jones (ed.), *The Scots and Parliament*, Edinburgh, 1996
M. Lee, *The Road to Revolution: Scotland under Charles I, 1625–37*, Urbana and Chicago, 1985
A. MacKechnie, Scots Court Architrcture of the early 17th Century (unpublished PhD thesis, University of Edinburgh), 1993
Mackie, J.D., 'The order of the holding of the court of parliament of Scotland', *Scottish Historical Review*, 1948
R. Miller, *The Municipal Buildings of Edinburgh*, Edinburgh, 1895
A.S. Myers, *Parliaments and Estates in Europe, to 1789*, London, 1975
J. Nicoll, *A Diary of Public Transactions and other Occurrences chiefly in Scotland from January 1650 to June 1657* (Bannatyne Club), Edinburgh, 1836
H. Ouston, 'York in Edinburgh: James VII and the Patronage of Learning in Scotland, 1679–1688', in J.Dwyer *et al* (eds.), *New Perspectives on the Politics and Culture of Early Modern Scotland*, Edinburgh, n.d.
R.S. Rait, *The Parliaments of Scotland*, Glasgow, 1924
RCAHMS, *City of Edinburgh*, Edinburgh, 1951
Register of the Privy Council

Rev. C. Rogers (ed.), *The Earl of Stirling's Register of Royal Letters Relative to the Affairs of Scotland and Nova Scotia*, Edinburgh, 1885
Scottish Parliament Public Information Service, Factfile 2: *The Scottish Parliamentary Tradition*, Edinburgh, 1999
D. Shaw, *The General Assemblies of the Church of Scotland, 1560–1600*, Edinburgh, 1964
J. St Clair and R. Craik, *The Advocates' Library*, Edinburgh, 1989
J.H. Shennan, *The Parlement of Paris*, London, 1968
D. Stevenson (ed.), *The Government of Scotland under the Covenanters, 1637–1651* (Scottish History Society, 4th Series, 18), Edinburgh, 1982
M. Swain, *Tapestries and Textiles at the Palace of Holyroodhouse*, Edinburgh, 1988
T. Thomson and C. Innes (eds.), *The Acts of the Parliaments of Scotland*, Edinburgh, 1814–75
J. Wormald, 'James VI and I: two kings or one?', *History*, 223, June 1983
J. Young, *The Scottish Parliament, 1639–1661*, Edinburgh, 1996
M.D. Young (ed.), *The Parliaments of Scotland: Burgh and Shire Commissioners*, Edinburgh, 1992–3

CHAPTER 3

J. Anderson, *Sir Walter Scott and History*, 1981
W. Bagehot, *The English Constitution*, 1867
H.J. Brandt, *Das Hamburger Rathaus*, Hamburg, 1957
G. Brown, *History of the US Capitol*, Washington DC, 1900
L. Colley, *Britons*, New Haven, 1992
M.S. Cullen, *Der Reichstag*, Berlin, 1995
R.J. Finlay, 'Caledonia or North Britain?', in D. Brown (ed.), *Image and Identity*, 1998
R.J. Finlay, 'The rise and fall of popular imperialism in Scotland', *Scottish Geographical Magazine*, 113, 1997
T. Friedman, 'A palace worthy of the grandeur of the king', *Architectural History*, 29, 1986
Glasgow Town Council, *Description of Ceremonial on the occasion of Laying the Foundation-stone of the Municipal Buildings*, Glasgow, 1885

J. Grant, *Cassell's Old and New Edinburgh*, Edinburgh, 1882
H.-R. Hitchcock and W. Scale, *Temples of Democracy: The State Capitols of the USA*, New York City, 1976
J. Innes, 'The local acts of a national parliament', in Dean and Jones (eds.), *Parliament and Locality*, 23–47
J. Cameron Lees, *St Giles'*, Edinburgh, 1889
J. Macaulay, 'The architectural collaboration between J Gillespie Graham and A W Pugin', *Architectural History*, 27, 1984
G. Morton, *Unionist Nationalism*, East Linton, 1999
G. Morton, 'Scottish rights and centralisation in the mid 19th century', *Nations and Nationalism*, 2:2, 1996
G. Morton, 'What If?', in D. Brown (ed.), *Image and Identity*, 1998
M.H. Port, *The Houses of Parliament*, London, 1976
M.C.H. Stewart, 'An Exiled Jacobite's Architectural Activities', *Journal of the Architectural Heritage Society of Scotland*, 1987
M.C.H Stewart, Lord Mar's Plans, 1700–32 (M.Litt. thesis, University of Glasgow), 1988
I. Sweeney, The Municipal Administration of Glasgow (Ph.D. thesis, Strathclyde University), 1990
W. Young, *The Municipal Buildings, Glasgow*, Glasgow, 1890

CHAPTERS 4 & 5

D. Caswell, 'The Economy of Style: Thomas S Tait and the interiors of St Andrew's House', *Architectural Heritage*, 1999
J. Convery, *The Governance of Scotland – a Saltire Guide*, Edinburgh, 2000
Country Life, 5 February 1938 (Empire Exhibition)
O.D. Edwards (ed.), *A Claim of Right for Scotland*, Edinburgh, 1989
Empire Exhibition, 1938
R. Galbraith, *Without Quarter*, Edinburgh, 1994
J. Gibbons, 'The Scottish Parliament Building Competition', in M. Fraser (ed.), *Essential Scotland*, London, 1998
J.S. Gibson, *The Thistle and the Crown*, Edinburgh, 1985
Glasgow Corporation, *Municipal Glasgow*, 1914
Guide to the Pavilion of His Majesty's Government in the United Kingdom, Glasgow, 1938
C. Harvie and P. Jones, *The Road to Home Rule*, Edinburgh, 2001
G. Hassan (ed.), *A Guide to the Scottish Parliament*, Edinburgh, 1999

G. Hassan and C. Warhurst (eds.), *The New Scottish Politics*, Edinburgh, 2000

C.W. Hill, *Edwardian Scotland*, Totowa, New Jersey, 1976

C.M.G. Himsworth and C.R. Munro, *The Scotland Act 1998*, Edinburgh, 1999

Inquiry into the Scottish Economy, Edinburgh, 1961 (Toothill Report)

P. and J. Kinchin, *Glasgow's Great Exhibitions*, Wendlebury, 1988

J. McFadden and M. Lazarowicz, *The Scottish Parliament – an Introduction*, 1999

B. Miller Lane, 'Government Buildings in European Capitals, 1870–1914', in H. Teuteberg (ed.), *Urbanisierung im 19. und 20. Jahrhundert*, Wien, 1983

Memorandum on the Secretaryship for Scotland, 1920 (National Archives of Scotland, reference HH 1/888)

Sir D. Milne, *The Scottish Office*, London, 1957

W.G. Pottinger, *The Secretaries of State for Scotland*, Edinburgh, 1979

Report of the Royal Commission on Housing, Edinburgh, 1917 (Cd 8731: Ballantyne Report)

J. Ritter, *Architects' Journal*, July 1964 (League of Nations)

A. Service, *Edwardian Architecture*, London, 1977

Simpson & Brown, *Queensberry House, A Study for the Scottish Office*, Edinburgh, 1998

L.J. Vale, *Architecture, Power and National Identity*, New Haven, 1992.

D.M. Walker, *St Andrew's House*, Edinburgh, 1989

H. Wefing, *Parlamentsarchitektur*, Berlin, 1995

INDEX

Note: the index covers names of persons, buildings, places, organisations, etc. Page numbers in italics refer to illustrations.